T0355447

Nasty Politics

The Logic of Insults, Threats, and Incitement

THOMAS ZEITZOFF
Associate Professor, School of Public Affairs, American University

OXFORD
UNIVERSITY PRESS

OXFORD
UNIVERSITY PRESS

Oxford University Press is a department of the University of Oxford.
It furthers the University's objective of excellence in research, scholarship,
and education by publishing worldwide. Oxford is a registered trade mark of
Oxford University Press in the UK and in certain other countries.

Published in the United States of America by Oxford University Press
198 Madison Avenue, New York, NY 10016, United States of America.

© Oxford University Press 2023

All rights reserved. No part of this publication may be reproduced, stored in a retrieval system,
or transmitted, in any form or by any means, without the prior permission in writing of Oxford
University Press, or as expressly permitted by law, by license or under terms agreed with the
appropriate reprographics rights organization. Inquiries concerning reproduction outside the scope
of the above should be sent to the Rights Department, Oxford University Press, at the address above.

You must not circulate this work in any other form and you must impose this same condition on any acquirer

Library of Congress Cataloging-in-Publication Data

Names: Zeitzoff, Thomas, author.
Title: Nasty politics : the logic of insults, threats, and incitement /
Thomas Zeitzoff, Associate Professor, School of Public Affairs, American
University.
Description: New York : Oxford University Press, [2023]
Identifiers: LCCN 2023007157 (print) | LCCN 2023007158 (ebook) |
ISBN 9780197679487 (hardback) | ISBN 9780197679494 (paperback) |
ISBN 9780197679500 (epub)
Subjects: LCSH: Political violence–Case studies. | Communication in
politics–Case studies. | Press and politics–Case studies.
Classification: LCC JC328.6 .Z45 2023 (print) | LCC JC328.6 (ebook) |
DDC 320.9001/4–dc23/eng/20230302
LC record available at https://lccn.loc.gov/2023007157
LC ebook record available at https://lccn.loc.gov/2023007158

DOI: 10.1093/oso/9780197679487.001.0001
DOI: 10.1093/oso/9780197679494.001.0001

Printed by Marquis, Canada

Nasty Politics

This book is dedicated to my wife, Jocelyn, and our little guys.

CONTENTS

PREFACE

When I started my PhD at New York University (NYU), I originally planned to study the politics of the American bureaucracy. As I progressed in the program my research interests changed, and I became interested in conflict and political violence. Yet across my five years at NYU, I ended up serving as a TA several times for an undergraduate introductory class on American politics. Maybe this was because I had originally said I wanted to be an Americanist, or, more likely, we had so many PhD students studying Comparative Politics and International Relations that we needed graduate students to cover undergrad classes in American politics. I was taking classes and conducting research on political violence, becoming a comparativist in the process, all while teaching undergraduates about pivotal politics in the U.S. Congress (Krehbiel 1998).

The contrast between the seemingly stable nature of U.S. politics—with its campaign rules, organized parties, and strong institutions—and places where armed groups were the de facto political parties was jarring. American institutionalists had their models of legislative bargaining. If you could figure out what the president, the median member of Congress, and the veto override all wanted, you could predict what policy was likely to be enacted in the U.S. I took it for granted that American politics was different, more orderly, and more structured. Part of this stems from the fact that NYU was one of the foremost places to study positive political economy and rational choice.

I ended up doing my dissertation research in Acre, Israel, on the 2008 Yom Kippur Riots (Zeitzoff 2019). Acre is a mixed city in northern Israel on the coast that is two-thirds Jewish and one-third Palestinian citizens of Israel (Palestinian Israelis). It's known as much for the Old City that is buttressed by Ottoman and Crusader-era walls—a UNESCO World Heritage site—as for the quality of its hummus. The Yom Kippur Riots began when a Palestinian resident of Acre, Tawfik Jamal, drove into a predominately Jewish neighborhood on Yom Kippur, the holiest day of the year for Jews. Jewish youths in the neighborhood stoned his car, and chanted anti-Arab slogans. Palestinians from the predominately Palestinian Old City section of Acre mistakenly believed Jamal had been killed, and went to the ethnically mixed city center armed with stones and knives. They vandalized Jewish cars and shops. Jewish youths responded by torching Palestinian Israeli businesses. Police were eventually called, but the riots lasted for four more nights with more than 60 people arrested and several million dollars in damage (Ratzlav-Katz 2008).

I lived in Acre for four months in the spring and summer of 2011. Acre was and remains a geographically segregated city. Jews are concentrated in the eastern neighborhoods known as the "Shikun," and Palestinians live mostly in the Old City, with the city center (HaMerkaz) ethnically mixed. My research focused on how anger about past violence like the Yom Kippur Riots shapes present-day attitudes. Does it make individuals more discriminatory towards an outgroup? Does it make them more trustworthy towards their ingroup? To answer these questions, I conducted interviews, surveys and behavioral economic experiments. My main finding was that priming anger over the riots reduced altruism to all groups, and that blame for the riots fell on both ingroup and outgroup members.

What my dissertation didn't answer, but was hinted at when talking to people in Acre, was that many politicians exploited and amplified grievances from the Yom Kippur Riots. For instance Yuval Steinitz, a right-wing Likud Member of the Knesset (MK), called the riot a "pogrom" against Acre's Jews. Palestinian Israeli MK (Ta'al Party), Ahmed Tibi said it was a "pogrom" against Palestinian Israelis (Cook 2008). I wanted to understand how politicians exploited violence and contention. How do politicians used insults, accusations, intimidating statements, incitement, and actual violence against their political opponent? I also wanted to understand the logic behind this nasty style of politics. My initial view was that nasty politics was a phenomenon that largely happened outside of American politics. It was something that was a regular feature in places with political violence like Israel, or in less mature democracies (like Turkey or Ukraine)—but not in the U.S. As an assistant professor, I ended up conducting most of my field research outside of the U.S., including Israel, Turkey, Georgia, Mexico, and Ukraine.

But as the 2016 U.S. presidential election approached, I realized a lot of things that I took for granted about the uniqueness of modern U.S. politics—in particular the lack of contention and nastiness—were wrong. In other countries in which I've done research, nasty politics is not some political sideshow, but a prominent rhetorical strategy. For instance, in 2015 Israel's right-wing foreign minister and head of Yisrael Beitanu, Avigdor Lieberman, spoke about Israel's Palestinian minority, "Those who are against us, there's nothing to be done—we need to pick up an axe and cut off his (their) head. Otherwise we won't survive here" (Tharoor 2015).

Trump's presidential campaign began with his speech that Mexico "was sending rapists" across the border. And his presidency ended in January 2021 following a failed coup attempt that culminated in his armed supporters storming the U.S. Capitol in an attempted insurrection.[1] Trump's presidency showed that the factors that made America exceptional—a stable two-party system and strong presidential system—also masked some important facts about American politics that were less exceptional (Zeitz 2018). Scholars of racial politics have long recognized this more violent and contentious nature of U.S. politics. (Davenport 2009; Enos, Kaufman, and Sands 2019; McAdam 2010; Mickey 2015). Politicians in the U.S. play the "race card" and prime threat from minorities and immigrants to try to build coalitions and win elections (Jardina 2019; Mendelberg 2001; Valentino, Hutchings, and White 2002). The U.S. was thought to be the exception to Juan Linz's argument that strong presidential systems tend to polarize society, are inflexible, and can lead to political instability and coups (Linz 1990). But the U.S. is no longer the exception to the rule (Carey 2021).

Traditionally, Comparative Politics—the study of places and politics outside the U.S.—and American Politics have been separate subfields in political science. The contention and nastiness of politics in places like Acre, Israel are distinct from the well-defined rules of the U.S. Congressional committee system. Yet, American politics has a lot more in common with the contentious contexts (Israel, Ukraine, etc.) than the subfield boundaries in political science would have us believe.[2] All politics involves comparisons: " 'why did candidate X do this, but Y did that?" We are all comparativists trying to make sense of why things happened in one place or context and not in another. Name-calling and intimidating statements that happen in Ukraine, Israel, or the U.S. come in different flavors. But there are similar strategies employed.

In this book I take a comparative approach rooted in political violence to study nasty politics. Why do politicians insult, accuse, intimidate, incite violence, and even engage in actual violence against their political opponents? This question is puzzling because there's strong evidence that the public doesn't like nasty politics (Frimer and Skitka 2018; Herbst 2010; Sydnor 2019). Across Ukraine, the U.S.,

[1] There is a debate about whether the events that proceeded and included the storming of the U.S. Capitol on January 6, 2021, by Trump supporters at the encouragement of President Trump qualifies as an insurrection or coup. For the purposes of this book, the storming of the U.S. Capitol on January 6 will be referred to as an "insurrection"—a violent attempt to overthrow the sitting government. The multi-pronged campaign and attempt to subvert the peaceful transition of power is an attempted coup, or technically an autogolpe—an illegal attempt by President Trump to stay in power. See Ingraham (2021) and Call (2021) for more discussion.

[2] Levitsky and Ziblatt (2018) make a similar argument when discussing democratic breakdown urging those interested in preserving U.S. democracy to learn from other countries' experiences with democratic breakdowns.

and Israel, I show that there's a strategic logic to the nasty style of politics: certain personality types are more open to it, it grabs attention, and signals toughness in the face of threats. Finally, the threat of actual violence lurks behind nasty politics. This has important implications for democracy—nasty politics influences who runs for office and who drops out, citizens' willingness to participate in politics, and actual violence and political stability.

Supplementary Appendix

Additional results and information on the data collection can be found in the Online Data Appendix available on my website www.zeitzoff.com.

ACKNOWLEDGMENTS

This book was a journey of over six years, and I am thankful to all those people who have helped me along the way.

I am incredibly thankful to the feedback and comments I received at seminars and conferences where I presented preliminary versions of the research that would form the core of this work. This includes seminars and seminar participants at American University, UCLA, Washington University in St. Louis, and Columbia.

Feedback, suggestions, and help from other scholars was also incredibly valuable. I wish to thank Anna Getmansky, Tolga Sinmazdemir, Candice Nelson, Sam Hirsch, Yuri Zhukov, Rose McDermott, Jim Goldgeier, Dave Marcotte, Tricia Bacon, Cynthia Miller-Idriss, Shana Gadarian, Omar García-Ponce, Hannah Baron, Zachary Steinert-Threlkeld, Brendan Nyhan, Jake Shapiro, Nilouffer Sidiqqui, Mashail Malik, Irina Soboleva, Tamar Mitts, Sam Hirsch, Bruce Bueno de Mesquita, Daniel Dreisbach, Christopher Miller, Michael Bang Petersen, Molly Roberts, Mathew Nanes, Yonotan Lupu, Nick Davis, Joshua Kertzer, Nathan Kalmoe, Dan Silverman, Joshua Gubler, Steve Webster, Paul Staniland, Rich Nielsen, Livio Di Lonardo, Chagai Weiss, Lotem Bassan-Nygate, Joe Young, and Lauren Young.

I want to give a special thanks to the participants in my book conference in January of 2021 including Erica Chenoweth, Shana Gadarian, Anna Grzymala-Busse, Josh Kertzer, and Joshua Tucker. This book is much better because of their close reading and excellent suggestions. They urged me to take a broader view of all the different tactics involved in nasty politics, and I thank them for this suggestion.

I could not have completed the book or done the research without immense help along the way. I want to thank my incredible research assistants: Divya Ramjee, Alexandria Samson, Kat Parsons, Sasha Jason, Bogdan Belei, Moshe Kwiat, Molly Parris, Oleh Ivanov, Polina Lypova, and Liana Novikova. The Kyiv

International Institute of Sociology was an academic home away from home for me and I want to give a special thanks to Anton Grushetsky and Oleksandr Shcherbatiuk.

The support of my home institution American University, and Nicole Gordon and Nik Walker at the Charles Koch Foundation were instrumental in providing the resources to carry out this project.

Thanks to David McBride and Oxford University Press for believing in this project, and to Emily Benitez for helping bring this project across the finish line. Thanks to Guillem Casasus for the amazing cover illustration.

I also want to send my support to the Ukrainian people. They've suffered tremendously for their freedom and dignity since 2014. Ukrainians want what everybody wants and deserves: freedom, prosperity, security, and sovereignty.

A special thanks and lots of love lots of love goes to my family—Maggie, Peter, and David—for supporting me as a scholar, and during my many trips to Ukraine for this research. I love all of you. Finally, I want to acknowledge my wife, Jocelyn, for her willingness to read earlier drafts of this, let me bounce ideas off of her while watching bad reality television, and tolerance for late-night coding and writing. I love you.

LIST OF FIGURES

LIST OF TABLES

1

The Nasty Style of Politics

On Monday, January 17, 2022, former Ukrainian President Petro Poroshenko flew back to Ukraine from Warsaw, Poland. Poroshenko's arrival in Kyiv was no ordinary homecoming. He was there to face charges of high treason brought by allies of current President Volodymyr Zelensky. Poroshenko was alleged to have directed and profited from a scheme where Ukrainian state companies bought coal from Russian-backed separatists in Donbas in 2014–2015, and thus financed Ukraine's enemies.[1] Ukraine had been at war with Russia and Russian-backed separatists—or as Ukraine designates them, "terrorists"—in the east in Donbas since 2014, so the charges against Poroshenko were quite serious (Harding 2022). Poroshenko and his allies accused the prosecutors of acting "shamefully" and claimed that the case was a "fabricated farce" concocted by Zelensky to sideline one of his major rivals (Poroshenko) (Al Jazeera 2022).

This was not the first time that Zelensky and Poroshenko had tussled. Back in April of 2019, and ahead of the second-round presidential voting election that featured Poroshenko versus Zelensky, then President Poroshenko claimed that: "he (Zelensky) is a Kremlin candidate, a puppet of Kolomoisky" (Maheshwari 2019). The "Kremlin candidate" charge was a serious one given the ongoing War in Donbas. The "puppet" claim was designed to sting too. Zelensky had parlayed the success of his popular TV show "Servant of the People"—about an ordinary history teacher who becomes president of Ukraine—to a meteoric political rise. The show appeared on the *1 + 1* channel which was controlled by the fugitive oligarch, Ihor Kolomoisky.[2] Zelensky's popularity stemmed from the perception that he was not part of the corrupt political status quo that included

[1] Donbas is a portmanteau of Donets Basin, and refers to the Donetsk and Luhansk oblasts in Eastern Ukraine. Oblasts are the primary geographical administrative unit in Ukraine, and there are 24 of them.

[2] Poroshenko's government accused Kolomoisky of engineering a massive fraud of billions of dollars of the largest Ukrainian bank, PrivatBank. See Troianovski (2019).

Nasty Politics: The Logic of Insults, Threats, and Incitement. Thomas Zeitzoff, Oxford University Press.
© Oxford University Press 2023. DOI: 10.1093/oso/9780197679494.003.0001

the incumbent Poroshenko. In May 2019 Zelensky handily defeated him in the second round of voting—73% to Poroshenko's 24%.

The treason charges brought against Poroshenko in 2021 were part of a broader anti-oligarch push by President Zelensky. He claimed that "Ukraine's unelected elite (the oligarchs) has (have) rigged the system" (Zelensky 2021). In November 2021 President Zelensky signed a new law that targeted Ukraine's oligarchs. It wasn't just Poroshenko. In May of 2021 Zelensky's prosecutors charged Ukrainian oligarch and pro-Russian lawmaker, Viktor Medvedchuk, with treason and placed him under house arrest (Rudenko 2021). Poroshenko and Medvedchuk were alleged to have colluded on corrupt fuel schemes with Russian separatists in Donbas. And at a press conference in November 2021 Zelensky accused Rinat Akhmetov, one of the richest men in Ukraine, of plotting a coup against him with Russian backing (Stern 2021). To many observers it looked like President Zelensky was weaponizing questionable accusations and using the pretext of Ukraine's very real problem of oligarchic meddling in politics to cripple his political rivals.

The accusations of coup plotting (against Akhmetov) and treason charges (against Medvedchuk and Poroshenko) were not happening in a vacuum. Throughout the fall and winter of 2021 and into February 2022 Russia had amassed more than 100,000 troops on the border with Ukraine (Reuters 2022*a*). While Ukrainians initially downplayed the threat publicly, U.S. and Western intelligence officials became increasingly certain that Russian President Vladimir Putin had decided to invade Ukraine (Pilkington 2022). On February 24, 2022, Russian forces launched missile strikes on targets across Ukraine as Russian poured into Ukraine on multiple fronts. This signaled the start of the large-scale Russian invasion of Ukraine. The 2022 Russian invasion of Ukraine is one of the most important geopolitical events of recent years. It triggered the largest refugee crisis in Europe since World War II. As of May 2022 nearly 30% of Ukraine's population (12.8 million people) were displaced from their homes, of which 6.8 million had become refugees and fled the country (UNHCR 2022). Ukrainian resistance to the invasion was much stronger than many anticipated. And evidence would emerge of atrocities committed by Russian forces including torture, rape, and indiscriminate killings of civilians (Al-Hlou et al. 2022).

With the Russian military pounding targets across Ukraine and threatening Kyiv itself, Zelensky's campaign against his domestic political rivals, and especially Poroshenko, would take a pause. During the early weeks of the war Poroshenko frequently appeared on Western media outlets wearing battle gear and brandishing an AK-47 saying Ukrainians were united against the Russians (Romaliiska 2022). But in April and May of 2022, as the war shifted to the east and Donbas, and it became clear that Kyiv would not fall, the detente between Poroshenko and Zelensky faded. Viktor Medvedchuk, the former oligarch and pro-Russian Ukrainian politician who was also accused of treason, testified in a

Ukrainian court in May of 2022 against Poroshenko. Medvedchuk had escaped house arrest in the early stages of the invasion, and was eventually recaptured by Ukrainian forces allegedly trying to flee the country in April 2022 (BBC 2022). The large-scale Russian invasion of Ukraine in 2022 could only temporarily stop the nasty style of Ukrainian politics.

***

With pepper spray, metal pipes, tactical vests and helmets, and even an American flag pole used as a weapon, supporters of President Donald Trump stormed the U.S. Capitol on January 6, 2021, at approximately 2:00 PM (Daly and Balsamo 2021; Magnan and Miao 2021). The crowd that stormed the Capitol was a diverse group. There were Trump supporters wearing MAGA hats; anti-government militias such as the Three Percenters and the Oathkeepers in tactical gear; the far-right, neo-fascist group the Proud Boys; and QAnon conspiracy theorists dressed up like shamans (Barry, McIntire, and Rosenberg 2021). The attackers were united in their belief that the 2020 presidential election had been stolen from President Trump, and they were there to stop the formal certification of Joe Biden as the winner. As the crowd entered the Capitol Building, many of the pro-Trump mob chanted "hang Mike Pence," viewing his certification of Biden's victory as a betrayal of Trump (Reeves, Mascaro, and Woodward 2021). With the building breached the U.S. Capitol Police declared a lockdown.

Congressional staff barricaded themselves in their offices, while members of Congress and Vice President Mike Pence were evacuated by the Capitol Police. The people who stormed the Capitol vandalized and looted offices, and some even tried to find members of Congress to hold as hostage. One insurrectionist, Ashli Babbitt, an Air Force veteran, was shot and killed by police as she tried to break into the House Chamber (Barry, Bogel-Burroughs, and Philipps 2021).

It was nearly four hours until the Metropolitan Police of D.C., U.S. Capitol Police, and the D.C. National Guard would have the building secure. Images of a masked man with zip ties ostensibly to take members of Congress hostage and of smoke billowing out of the Capitol were broadcast around the world (Hsu 2021). But it wasn't immediately apparent just how intense and violent the siege was. Members of the mob clashed with an undermanned U.S. Capitol Police using knives, pipes, fists, police shields they confiscated, and other improvised weapons (Cleveland 2021; Leatherby et al. 2021). Police injuries detailed the extent of the violence. Nearly 140 law enforcement officers were injured, including concussions, rib fractures, burns, a heart attack, and the death of an officer (Schmidt and Broadwater 2021). Four pro-Trump participants in the siege also died. By May 2022 nearly 850 people faced charges ranging from conspiracy to interfere in Congressional business, assault on federal officers, trespassing on federal property, disorderly conduct, theft, and destruction of federal property (Hall et al. 2022). Later in that same evening, after the attack ended, members of Congress returned to continue the process of certification. At 4:00 AM on January 7, more than 12 hours after the siege, and after objections to the certification from several Congressional Republicans, Joe Biden was certified the winner of the 2020 presidential election.

The January 6, 2021, attempted insurrection by pro-Trump dissidents and supporters was not a spontaneous event. It was the part of an organized campaign by President Trump. This campaign included pressuring state election officials and fellow Republican lawmakers and attempts to seize control of the U.S. Department of Justice all aimed at overturning the 2020 presidential election—in other words it was an attempted coup (Sheerin 2022).[3] Hours before the pro-Trump mob stormed the Capitol, several Republican lawmakers, President Trump's own family, and President Trump spoke to his supporters at the "Save America Rally," stoking the crowd with baseless conspiracy theories about the election being stolen and exhorting them to pressure the "weak Republican lawmakers." President Trump said:

> All of us here today do not want to see our election victory stolen by emboldened radical-left Democrats, which is what they're doing. And stolen by the fake news media. That's what they've done and what they're doing. We will never give up, we will never concede.

He then told his supporters to directly confront Congress:

> Now it is up to Congress to confront this egregious assault on our democracy. And after this, we're going to walk down, and I'll be there with you.... We are going to the Capitol, and we are going to try and give—the Democrats are hopeless, they are never voting for anything, not even one vote, but we are going to try—give our Republicans, the weak ones, because the strong ones don't need any of our help, we're try—going to try and give them the kind of pride and boldness that they need to take back our country.[4]

Adding to the ominous atmosphere and threat of violence, amidst a sea of Trump flags, his supporters had constructed makeshift gallows and noose while the crowd chanted "fight for Trump!" (Godfrey 2021).

[3] I follow the University of Illinois Cline Center, who label it as a coup—they refer to it as a "dissident coup" (Cline Center 2021). However, some criticize the coup label since elements of the U.S. military were not involved in the effort (Singh 2021).

[4] See a full transcript available via National Public Radio (Naylor 2021).

Trump and his allies sought to overturn the election results under the guise of the "Stop the Steal" campaign. As part of the campaign, President Trump and his supporters tried to coerce state Republican officials in Arizona and Georgia to overturn the results on baseless fraud allegations. And when the officials didn't, he and his supporters called them "weak" and "cowardly." Trump and his supporters circulated baseless conspiracy theories about election "horror stories" and accused, without any evidence, Democratic election officials in swing states of ballot stuffing and banning Republican observers (Romero 2020). Before the election even happened, Trump and his allies threatened to sue to stop the counting of ballots beyond election day, in order to disrupt the counting of absentee ballots that in 2020 skewed heavily Democratic (Sherman and Gresko 2021). President Trump's allies in Congress also promised not to certify the election results on January 6.

Trump's team was also operating behind the scenes to subvert the election. For example conservative lawyer John Eastman wrote a memo to Trump and his confidantes that circulated in the White House in the days leading up to January 6. It provided a blueprint for how Vice President Mike Pence could ignore the election results and keep President Trump in office—a self-coup (*autogolpe*) (Schmidt and Haberman 2021). Trump also pressured U.S. Department of Justice officials to declare without evidence widespread fraud and "irregularities" in the vote in key swing states to give a pretext to contest and potentially change the final vote tally and stay in office (Barrett 2021).

Finally, there's evidence that Trump himself helped incite the violence. He tweeted in mid-December 2020, after the state Electoral College voters had already met, "Statistically impossible to have lost the 2020 Election. Big protest in D.C. on January 6th. Be there, will be wild" (Carless 2021). The charge that Trump "incited an insurrection" would form the basis for Democrats to impeach him in the House on January 13, 2021. Trump would later be acquitted in the Senate on February 13, 2021.

This book focuses on two sets of questions. First, why do politicians like Trump and Zelensky engage in nasty politics against their domestic political opponents? Why do they insult them, accuse them of crimes and conspiracies, attempt to intimidate them, encourage violence against them, and in some rare cases actively attack them with physical violence? These are puzzling questions since there is good evidence that voters decrease support for politicians who use nasty rhetoric (Frimer and Skitka 2018, 2020; Gerstlé and Nai 2019; Nai and Maier 2021) and are seriously concerned about actual political violence (Kalmoe and Mason 2020).

Second, how do external threats (the Russian invasion of Ukraine in 2022) or internal threats (January 6 in the U.S.) influence nasty politics?

Third, what are the effects of nasty rhetoric on democracy? How do insults, conspiracies, accusations, threats, and violence shape the way voters feel about politicians and politics, and their willingness to participate in politics? How does it influence the kinds of politicians that run for office? Perhaps most important, when do insults and accusations bleed over into incitement and actual violence?

1.1 Why Politicians Engage in Nasty Politics

1.1.1 What Is Nasty Politics

What do we mean by nasty politics? Nasty politics is an umbrella term for a set of tactics that politicians can use to insult, accuse, denigrate, threaten, and in rare cases physically harm their domestic opponents. These occur at campaign rallies, speeches, via social media, or face-to-face in debates and actual violent confrontations. We can think about nasty politics as capturing a broad set of tactics that vary in their intensity. This is similar to studies in International Relations that use events data to measure conflict intensity (Goldstein 1992; Schrodt, Davis, and Weddle 1994; Ward et al. 2013; Zeitzoff 2011). Studies in international relations take reported events—such as demands for action, threats of state-backed violence, and actual violent events—and scale them to an underlying cooperation or conflict intensity within and between countries.

The model of nasty politics used here allows us to distinguish between different types of rhetoric based on how threatening and close they are to actual violence. Figure 1.1 presents the staircase model of nasty politics. The least threatening and lowest step on nasty politics is insults, and the highest step on the scale tactic is actual physical violence. Implicit in this coding scheme is that

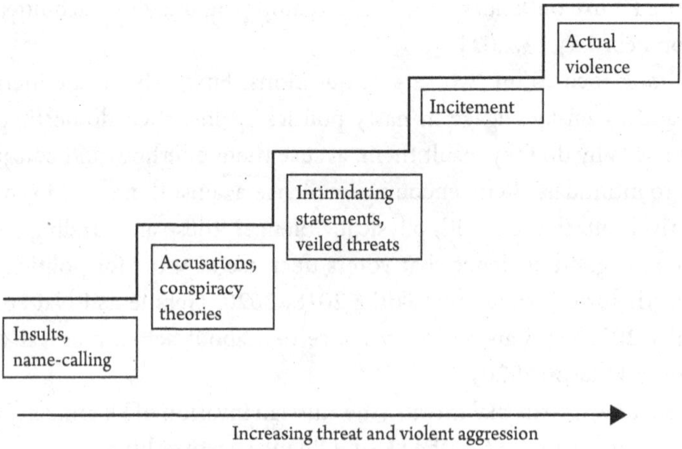

Figure 1.1 Escalating model of nasty politics and threats.

while all types of nasty rhetoric contain some aggression, certain types, such as incitement, are more threatening and more likely to provoke actual violence.

Different tactics of nasty politics may vary in their underlying aggression and threat, but they all are designed to hurt their target. They also share a common logic, so there is value to studying the more quotidian insults with rare and more threatening tactics like incitement. To psychologists yelling in somebody's face versus punching them in the face are behaviors with different levels of hostility, but both of are manifestations of aggression (Buss and Perry 1992). Likewise, while calling someone a "scumbag" (insult) is less threatening than telling them that they should be "put down like an animal" (incitement), they both are hostile and manifestations of nasty politics.

Name-calling and insults are at the lowest level of threat. Name-calling can be relatively mild such as when a politician refers to opponents as "liars" or "idiots," or it can be a much more serious charge, such as saying their opponent is guilty of "treasonous" crime. Or it could involve using foul language such as suggesting they are "assholes," "motherfuckers," "bastards," or "jerks." Many insults are implicit, with politicians using frames and extended metaphors to disparage or describe targeted groups or individuals. These nasty metaphors influence how people make judgments and interpret situations (Kalmoe 2014, 2017; Kalmoe, Gubler, and Wood 2018; Lakoff and Johnson 2008). Many of them are also dehumanizing. Dehumanizing rhetoric is where politicians describe certain individuals or groups as "animals," "cockroaches," or "a cancer" (Cassese 2019; Kteily et al. 2015). When you frame your opponents in terms of an infestation or a disease, you are saying that they need to be exterminated, eliminated, or cut out and removed to keep the country healthy. Even referring to other politicians as "enemies" sets up the logic that they are not to be bargained with, or accorded normal rights, but rather treated as a threat to be eliminated.

After name-calling and insults come accusations and conspiracy theories. These include accusing opponents of doing something illegal, corrupt, shady, or of engaging generally in bad behavior. It also includes accusing opponents of stoking partisan hatred or violence. Promulgating conspiracy theories about opponents, such as saying they are secretly engaged in voter fraud, controlling the economy, or committing serious treason fall into this category as well (Douglas et al. 2019; Radnitz 2021; Uscinski and Parent 2014). For something to be considered an accusation, it can't just be name-calling an opponent—e.g., "corrupt," "fraud," or "traitor"—there needs to be a specific allegation.

It's worth pointing out two implications that follow from the insults and accusations categories. First these two categories encompass much of the political incivility and negative campaigning literature in American politics (Ansolabehere and Iyengar 1997; Evans et al. 2017; Gervais 2015; Herbst 2010; Lau, Sigelman, and Rovner 2007; Stryker, Conway, and Danielson 2016; Sydnor

2019). Second, and perhaps just as important, a key assumption of this nasty politics typology is that accusations can be both true and false. So a baseless conspiracy theory of election fraud falls into the same category as a credible allegation of election malfeasance. Some might object to not weighing the veracity of accusations, viewing baseless lies as much nastier than evidence-based accusations. But there's a strong reason for this assumption. Voters don't perceive information objectively. Rather they process it subjectively, with their preconceived biases (Sigelman and Kugler 2003). Correcting misinformation about politics is also tough. Most voters have incentives to view their side as correct, they don't closely follow politics, and, in general, people have a low opinion of politicians ("they are all liars") (Nyhan 2020; Swire-Thompson et al. 2020; Walter and Murphy 2018). So when they see allegations or accusations many times it gets viewed through the lens of political mud-slinging. Second, the media is not unbiased in how they report on accusations. Media in both Ukraine and the U.S. regularly slant coverage and have interests in pushing certain accusations over others (Boxell, Gentzkow, and Shapiro 2017; Pleines 2016). Thus for the purposes of classifying nasty politics, we only care about the fact that an accusation or conspiracy was leveled, rather than whether it was true or not.[5]

Intimidating statements and veiled threats are a step higher on the nasty politics staircase. They are more threatening than insults and accusations because they are advocating taking action against opponents. Intimidating statements including those that are designed to threaten some kind of non-violent action that will be taken against an opponent. This includes threatening to throw someone in jail, saying "they should be investigated," arguing that they need to be thrown off social media, or "cancelled." It also includes veiled threats that are ambiguous in how menacing they are, such as saying an opponent "should watch out," or they "better be careful."

Incitement is the most threatening rhetorical category before actual physical violence. Following others, I define incitement as instances where politicians actively threaten or encourage violence against their political opponents and, if the statement were followed, it would result in physical harm to opponents (Wilson 2017). This threat of violence is the key difference between incitement and intimidating statements, such as veiled threats. Incitement includes explicit threats of violence which are very rare, such as saying an opponent "should be beaten up" or "shot," or that supporters "should come armed and ready to throw down." More common are forms of implicit incitement, such as saying opponents should be "roughed up," "eliminated," "be made to feel scared." Incitement also includes campaign ads or social media posts with politicians posting pictures or images of guns, weapons, or crosshairs toward likenesses of their opponents.

[5] It also prevents the tricky prospect of evaluating which pieces of claims or accusations are true, partially true, partially false, false, or unknown.

The highest level in the staircase model of nasty politics scale is actual physical violence. It's also the rarest. Violence can include a politician directly orchestrating violent protests, having their bodyguards or supporters beat or kill someone, or throwing punches or engaging in violence themselves.

Different types of nasty politics don't happen in isolation. They tend to happen together, with higher, more threatening and aggressive tactics alongside lower levels of tactics. Many times accusations also include insults. For instance if a politician says to her supporters: "My opponents are traitors, and they are trying to sell out our country. They need to be eliminated." This statement contains three kinds of nasty rhetoric: (1) insult ("traitors"), (2) an accusation ("trying to sell out our country"), and (3) incitement ("need to be eliminated").

There's one final point that needs to be clarified—what do we mean by "domestic political opponents"? Politicians don't only engage in nasty politics against their political rivals. They also use it against various other domestic actors. These include: political parties, partisans, ethnic groups, police and security services, immigrants, judges, businessmen, companies, journalists, members of the press, NGOs, government officials, military, business groups, or other domestic political opponents broadly construed. The majority of non-political opponent attacks are part of broader political attacks. For example in July of 2018 President Trump tweeted out: "The FAKE NEWS media (failing nytimes, CNN, NBC-News and many more) is not my enemy, it is the enemy of the American people. SICK."[6] President Trump's tweet plays into beliefs among Republicans that the mainstream media are biased towards Democrats (Brennan and Stubbs 2020). Or in September of 2018, the right-wing Israeli Minister of Justice Ayelet Shaked promoted her successful appointment of more right-wing judges to the Supreme Court of Israel, saying it no longer operates as a "branch of Meretz" the left-wing dovish Israeli political party (Winer and Staff 2018). Shaked was echoing beliefs among the Israeli right that the Israeli Supreme Court is biased against them. In practice attacks against many of these non-political affiliated domestic groups are still partisan attacks. Finally, while the use of threats against foreign political opponents and rival leaders is a core part of international relations, it is beyond the scope of this book.

1.1.2 Preview of the Theory

Why do politicians use the nasty style of politics against their domestic political opponents, when the public on average dislikes it? Insults, accusations, veiled threats, incitement, and actual violence are distinct tactics. But like other scholars of aggression and violence, I see different types of nasty politics sharing a core logic (Collins 2009; DeWall, Anderson, and Bushman 2011).

[6] He later added ABC and CBS to this list. See Davis (2018).

It's helpful to think about nasty politics in terms of supply and demand. The demand side of nasty politics focuses on individual-level factors and personality traits, as well as macro factors (e.g., level of polarization and political conflict) that shapes the public receptivity to the nasty style of politics. The supply side focuses on factors that influence when and why particular politicians choose to go nasty. This supply and demand framework provides a logic to (1) how the public will respond to nasty politics, (2) which politicians will use it and when, and (3) the effects of nasty politics on democracy.

The Demand Side: What the Public Wants

On average voters don't like nasty politics, and they aren't lying when they say they don't like it. The more violent and threatening the tactic the less likely voters are to approve of it. But not all voters are equally nasty-averse. People who are aggressive or support tough leaders may not punish a politician for using this kind of language and in fact might support it (Kalmoe 2014; Westwood et al. 2022).

Some of these personality traits are clustered among those who support right-wing nationalist parties (Hetherington and Weiler 2009; Stenner 2005). But this is not simply a story that right-wing supporters like nasty politics and left-wing supporters don't. Both voters on the left and right are willing to embrace nasty politics when they feel their side is threatened or under attack. During times of heightened threat, or social polarization, voters will find it more acceptable and may take comfort in their side protecting them with harsher rhetoric and tactics (Braley et al. 2021).

The Supply Side: Why Politicians Go Nasty

There are several factors that influence whether a politician will choose to go nasty or not, and how threatening they want to be.

While the public may find it distasteful, insults, accusations, threats, and actual violence receive out-sized attention from the media. For instance, if a politician says, "I respectfully disagree with my honorable political opponent" that's not going to receive much attention. In contrast, if that same politician calls their opponent, "a traitorous bastard" it will get covered by the media. The nastier and more threatening the language the less acceptable the public will find it, but the more attention the politician will receive for using it. The key audience for violent rhetoric is voters, and the media as well, who can amplify a politician's message towards voters.

Insulting, threatening, and attacking opponents are all ways to signal to voters that a politician is willing to fight for the ingroup, and that they will protect their supporters from the outgroup. During times of threat or heightened uncertainty, politicians have even more leeway to use more threatening tactics. Citizens may take comfort in such rhetoric, thinking, "hey, this politician might be a jerk, but they're the kind of tough leader we need now, and won't sell us out." This dynamic provides incentives for political outsiders and politicians losing support to stoke perceived threats, or engage in actual violence to win support.

Finally nasty politics is a strategic tool that politicians can use when other options are not available. Politicians have several, less charged strategies including credit-claiming, constituency services, or endorsement from popular politicians or figures—all to try to increase their support or get policy passed. Yet just as some social movements use contentious tactics such as protests, sit-ins, or even violence when conventional political avenues are closed, so too will some politicians use nasty politics if they believe that it is the only way they can win.

Nasty Politics and Democracy

What does nasty politics mean for democracy? The effects are mixed. Voters dislike the nasty style and many find it disgusting. Yet they also are captivated by it. This means that nasty politics can be a way for outsider politicians to grab attention, or for mainstream politicians losing support to change the conversation.

Another key point is that there is an asymmetric response to nasty politics. When outgroup politicians use nasty politics it's more likely to be viewed as threatening, or as a cheap tactic to grab attention, and stir up violence. In contrast, ingroup politicians that use it are thought to be just responding to attacks, and protecting the ingroup. There is the potential for nasty politics to spiral from threats to incitement to actual violence, when the ingroup feels it needs to protect against outgroup provocations.

Second, nasty politics and incivility are legitimate weapons for opposition politicians representing marginalized groups to fight for what they believe in, and sound the alarm about injustice. But cynical politicians can play on the public's response to nasty politics, to garner attention and build up a base of support within the ingroup.

Nasty politics also imposes costs on democracy. It reduces political participation, and changes who is willing to run for office. The public becomes more cynical about politicians who are always attacking each other, and this makes people less likely to vote and participate. And in turn honest politicians become turned off from the political process and are unwilling to run. They are replaced by more aggressive, nastier politicians. Thus the intensity of nasty politics is both a symptom of underlying threat and political violence, and also a cause of it.

1.2 Previous Scholarship on Nasty Politics

Nasty politics encompasses insults that are quite common in staid political campaigns, but also includes threats, incitement, and violence seen in some of the most contentious elections. So it makes sense to draw on research from several different subfields. This includes research from research from Comparative Politics on political violence and democratic backsliding, American Politics on negative campaigning and polarization, and from the Political Psychology literature on campaign communication and incivility.

1.2.1 Insights from Comparative Politics and Political Violence

Following the end of the Cold War, security scholars turned their focus to the outbreak of civil wars where ethnic identities were salient. There were two conflicts that became a focus of much of this research: the Rwandan Genocide and conflicts in the former Yugoslavia (Fearon and Laitin 2003; Kaufman 2001; Petersen 2002). The common thread from research on ethnic violence in the post-Cold War world is the important interaction of threat and opportunity (Gagnon 2006; Lake and Rothchild 1996; Mueller 2000; Posen 1993). Ethnic groups across different contexts were concerned that other rival groups would take advantage of the prevailing political uncertainty to attack them. During this period, new political entrepreneurs used ethnically charged rhetoric and preyed on people's fears of being victimized and grievances to build and solidify their coalition (De Figueiredo et al. 1999; Glaeser 2005; Petersen 2002).

Clever political leaders are skilled at deploying historical grievances and emotion-laden symbols (Kaufman 2001). Former Serbian president Slobodan Milosevic's rise to power was fueled by his ability to tap into historical Serbian grievances against the backdrop of increasing tensions in Yugoslavia. In 1987 he gave a speech in Kosovo in which he played on the historical Serbian and Christian victimization by the Muslim Ottomans and by extension Muslim Kosovar Albanians.[7]

Violent language also serves as a signal to the ingroup to mobilize, and can reduce the taboo of violence against targeted groups (Yanagizawa-Drott 2014). The 1994 Rwandan Genocide killed an estimated one million people, mostly the Tutsi minority. Following the genocide, many pointed the finger at the Hutu-hate radio station, Radio Television Libre des Mille Collines (RTLM), which broadcast messages calling Tutsis "cockroaches" and urging them to be killed

[7] Named after the monument to the battle where Milosevic gave his speech, the Gazimestan speech would help transform Milosevic into one of the leading voices of Serbian nationalism. See Traynor and Traynor (1999).

in the lead-up to and during the Hutu-led genocide. Yet, Straus (2007) doesn't find that Hutu-hate radio caused the outbreak of the Rwandan Genocide by persuading Hutus to kill their Tutsi neighbors. Rather he argues that the radio broadcasts were a signal to mobilize hard-line Hutus and reinforce Hutu power messages that were being delivered face to face as well (Straus 2007, p. 611).

Nasty politics doesn't just happen in the context of civil war. Politicians use ethnic and nationalist appeals for both ideological purposes and to consolidate their power even in less violent contexts. Politicians regularly try to manufacture lower-level violence, fights, or even riots during elections. A consistent finding is that aggression and violence of all types—from low-level discrimination, to riots, to terrorist attacks—clusters around elections (Dunning 2011; Michelitch 2015; Newman 2013; Rosenzweig 2017; Wilkinson 2006). Wilkinson (2006) looks at the causes of Hindu-Muslim violence in India. He argued that Hindu nationalist politicians sought to stoke communal violence, which in turn would polarize the population, and consolidate Hindu support between upper and lower castes. He describes how Hindu nationalist politicians would arrange for provocative Hindu religious processions to go into religious minority and Muslim neighborhoods in hopes of sparking violence (Wilkinson 2006, pp. 23–24). All of these findings show how during elections, or periods of instability and conflict, political entrepreneurs may seek to exploit ethnic or religious grievances to bolster their own support via emotional appeals (McDermott 2010), conspiracy theories against the outgroup (Glaeser 2005; Radnitz 2021), or outright calls for violence (Kaufman 2001; Wilkinson 2006).

Concerns about incendiary rhetoric aren't only about outright violence that can accompany it, but also about what nasty politics does to democracy. When politicians consider their domestic opponents traitors and illegitimate, or advocate violence against them, they violate a core tenet of democracy. You may not like your opponent, but you need to tolerate their right to contest elections (Gibson 1989; Habermas 1996; Sullivan, Piereson, and Marcus 1993). Uncivil disagreement between political opponents breeds mistrust in politics generally (Mutz and Reeves 2005). Yet this incivility is not just for marginal members of legislatures. Recent victories of populist nationalist leaders—Modi in India, Bolsonaro in Brazil, Orban in Hungary, and Trump in the U.S.—have raised a specter about a global wave of democratic backsliding (Diamond 2015*b*; Foa and Mounk 2016; Hafner-Burton, Narang, and Rathbun 2019; Levitsky and Ziblatt 2018).

Why do some leaders make these kinds of nasty appeals? First they are more likely to grab the attention of the media and their targeted audience (Ballard et al. 2022; Gerstlé and Nai 2019; Macdonald and Hua 2020). And second nasty rhetoric can be persuasive by striking an emotional chord with ingroup members (Blassnig et al. 2019; Schulz, Wirth, and Müller 2020; Wirz 2018).

Previous research from Comparative Politics and political violence suggests that politicians' use of nasty politics polarizes the populace by exacerbating existing ethnic and partisan tensions, solidifying ingroup supporters, and can pave the way for future violence and democratic breakdown (Glaeser 2005; Kaufman 2001; Levitsky and Ziblatt 2018).

1.2.2 Insight from American Politics

American Politics has approached the study of nasty politics in two distinct ways: (1) through the lens of negative campaigning and attack ads, and (2) the rise of partisan polarization and partisan media.

Why do politicians engage in nasty politics if the public dislikes it so much? Many U.S. campaign strategists I interviewed argued that the answer can be found in the effects of negative advertising. They argued that negative ads, and nasty politics in general, work. People may say they don't like attack ads, or the nasty side of politics, but that's because of "social pressure" to not appear to like things you shouldn't.[8] The conventional wisdom among U.S. campaign strategists is that negative ads are sticky and memorable. Nobody remembers the ad where a politician gives the standard montage of shaking hands with ordinary voters at a local diner while nodding in a calm and reassuring manner. But everybody remembers the ad where say your opponent is an ally of Republican Senate Majority Leader "Cocaine Mitch" McConnell of Kentucky and his (McConnell's) "China family." Don Blankenship actually ran this in a political ad in the West Virginia Republican primary for the 2018 U.S. Senate election. Blankenship is the former CEO of Massey Energy. He was convicted and spent a year in prison for lax safety standards that led to the Upper Branch Mine Disaster which killed 29 miners in West Virginia in 2010. Blankenship's campaign strategy in the primary was to pit himself against the establishment, and he did so by singling out Republican Senate Majority Leader "Cocaine Mitch" McConnell (Kentucky) and his wife, Transportation Secretary, Elaine Chao. Chao and her family own a large shipping business, and one of their ships was detained by police in 2014 in Colombia and found with cocaine on board. But no charges were ever filed, and neither Chao nor McConnell were ever credibly accused of anything to do with it. Blankenship's bizarre attacks on McConnell were unsuccessful and he lost the primary, coming in third (Rizzo 2018).

Leveling charges that an opponent is "shady," a "threat," or a "traitor" can be effective at controlling the narrative. It demands a response. Because if it's not

[8] Interview #US-R-B0619.

rebutted or denied, people will simply assume it's true.[9] It opens the politician up to the critique, "well, you never denied that you were into Bigfoot erotica." This line of attack actually happened in a U.S. Congressional election in Virginia in 2018. Democratic candidate Leslie Cockburn in July 2018 posted the following tweet: "My (Republican) opponent Denver Riggleman, running mate of Corey Stewart, was caught on camera campaigning with a White supremacist. Now he has been exposed as a devotee of Bigfoot erotica. This is not what we need on Capitol Hill." The tweet also contained a screenshot and Instagram post of Riggleman's that showed a picture of an erotic drawing of Bigfoot for a self-published book Riggleman was working on called "The Mating Habits of Bigfoot and Why Women Want Him." Cockburn's tweet was picked up in major U.S. media outlets including *CNN, New York Times, Los Angeles Times* and *Vox* which also had to explain to readers about the corner of the web devoted to Bigfoot erotica. Riggleman responded and said, "I thought it (the book) was funny. There is no way that anybody's dumb enough to think this is real . . . it's satire. . . . I do not believe that Bigfoot is real. . . . But I don't want to alienate any Bigfoot voters" (Charles 2018). Riggleman would go on to win the general election by more than 6 percentage points.

What's interesting about the near-universal belief in the power of negative attack ads by campaign strategists, and by extension many types of nasty rhetoric, is research in American Politics is mixed about their effectiveness. For example Ansolabehere and Iyengar (1997) found that negative advertising polarized the electorate, led to decreased voter turnout, and that politicians were forced to respond with counterattacks of their own. Jamieson (1993) further argues that these ads are used to distract from the real issues voters care about. All of this has concerning implications for democracy—(1) increased apathy and lower turnout, (2) greater polarization, (3) less focus on important issues, and more on sensationalism, and (4) an escalating cycle of attack ads.

More recent research takes a more nuanced view on negative advertising. Geer (2008) argues that attack ads, as opposed to positive ads, are more likely to provide voters with new information on salient issues. Thus they can in fact improve voters' ability to pick candidates. A meta-analysis of studies on negative advertising finds that while negative ads are more memorable than positive ads, they don't persuade voters, nor do they reduce turnout (Lau, Sigelman, and Rovner 2007). Dowling and Krupnikov (2016) argues that there may be times where negative ads play a pivotal role in campaigns—particularly if the attacks are viewed not as mud-slinging, but rather core to the campaign issues (Fridkin and Kenney 2019). Yet most of the time the effects of these attack

[9] Interview #US-D-M0319.

ads will be minimal, and are dwarfed by incumbency effects or other campaign fundamentals like the economy and candidate quality. This more muted take on campaign ads is in line with recent research that shows that persuasion in politics is hard, and most types of political campaigns have small effects that decay rather quickly (Broockman and Kalla 2020; Kalla and Broockman 2018).

What about polarization and the media? Scholars of U.S. politics view the nasty turn in U.S. politics as connected to two phenomena. First is the growth in partisan political polarization. Increasingly Americans don't simply view being a Democrat or Republican as belonging to a political party, but rather a part of voters' core social identity that overlaps with their other key identities (religion, education, race, etc.) (Abramowitz and Webster 2016; Iyengar et al. 2019; Jardina 2019; Kinder and Kalmoe 2017; Mason 2018). These identities even extend to some people not wanting to date or have their children marry outpartisans, or even a willingness to sell college football tickets at a discounted price to a copartisan (Engelhardt and Utych 2018; Iyengar et al. 2019). The second key factor is the rise of cable news and partisan media. The media has always had an incentive to frame politics as a blood sport, and overemphasize conflict (Groeling 2010). Cable news and the rise of partisan media has increased this trend, and is a direct contributor to growing partisan incivility (Atkinson 2017; Berry and Sobieraj 2013; Finkel et al. 2020; Gervais 2014, 2015; Herbst 2010; Prior 2007; Sydnor 2019; Young 2019). The growing partisan polarization is even more apparent on racial issues, where partisan cable news networks offer starkly contrasting views of the plight of Black Americans, particularly surrounding protests against police violence and brutality (Engelhardt 2019). The mix of increased partisan polarization, partisan media, and nasty rhetoric makes some citizens more likely to follow politics, and believe the stakes are higher for elections. But it also decreases the perception that the other side is a legitimate opposition.

In the 2016 U.S. presidential election Sides, Tesler, and Vavreck (2019) documents how candidate Trump used vitriolic campaign rhetoric to mobilize Republican voters on key identity issues, such as negative attitudes towards Black Americans, Muslims, and immigrants. The nastier Trump's rhetoric, and the more he stoked grievances, the more media coverage he received and was able to distract from his other scandals (Lewandowsky, Jetter, and Ecker 2020). Trump's rhetoric also tapped into the growing racial polarization among White Democrats and White Republicans (Engelhardt et al. 2019). Trump was able to send out provocative tweets to drum up news coverage and dominate the news cycle during the primary (Wells et al. 2016).

Recent research has called into question how much American partisans really want their representatives to go after the other side. For instance, Skytte (2020) shows that voters respond differently to polarizing rhetoric that is based on the issues versus incivility. While both increase affective polarization, only incivility decreases political trust. And Costa (2020) shows fighting for the issues rather than engaging in political mud-slinging. Finally, Westwood et al. (2022) find that few Americans support actual political violence against the other side.

In sum, the effectiveness and downstream effects of negative campaigning are decidedly mixed. The rise of partisan polarization and partisan media and social media provide new incentives for politicians to go nasty, but there are still limits to what partisans will tolerate and support.

1.2.3 Insight from Political Psychology and Political Communication

Research from political psychology and political communication shows the important role emotions and threat perceptions play in nasty politics, and in particular how leaders manage them. It also shows how certain personality types are more tolerant of the nasty style. In this section we will explore research related to both of these points.

In July of 2011 I interviewed several young Jewish men who had participated in the 2008 Yom Kippur Riots in Acre, Israel. The clashes between Palestinian-Israelis and Jewish Israelis lasted for four nights, and began on Yom Kippur, hence the moniker (Zeitzoff 2018). Several of the participants I interviewed expressed their admiration for former ultra-nationalist Rabbi Meir Kahane. Kahane was an ultra-nationalist, Zionist political leader who founded the Jewish Defense League (JDL) in New York City. He briefly served in the Israeli Knesset before being barred for inciting racism. The Anti-Defamation League (ADL), labeled Kahane a supporter of "a radical form of Jewish nationalism which reflected racism, violence and political extremism" (Anti-Defamation League 2017).

A telling moment during one of my interviews was when one of the Jewish riot participants I was interviewing grabbed my map of the city of Acre, and pointed to a particular part of the map while speaking animatedly, "the HaMerkaz (mixed Jewish-Palestinians area of the city center) is now controlled by the Arabs . . . there is no hope for coexistence with them. The Arabs are gangsters . . . we have to send them (Palestinian Israelis) away." His friend then jumped in and said, "we (Jewish residents of Acre) don't have security, we can't be secure because of the Arabs. . . . I can't go into the (mostly Palestinian) Old City without something bad happening to me. We need to ship the Arabs away from Akko (Acre)!"[10] These right-wing Jewish riot participants were adamant that Palestinian Israelis, and Arabs in general, represented a grave threat to Jewish Israelis. They supported politicians who argued for the expulsion or ethnic

[10] Author Interview #IS-RW-DSA0711.

cleansing, and were even willing to engage in outright violence to "protect" their family and friends.

People have to make sense of living in an uncertain world. Conflicts, pandemics, crime, and economic uncertainty all are threats that create underlying anxiety and even anger. When faced with anxiety and uncertainty, voters look for certainty and protection (Albertson and Gadarian 2015). Leaders can step in and provide this certainty, and one of the ways they do this is by providing an outlet for feelings of anger and anxiety (Merolla and Zechmeister 2009). By stoking outrage at outgroups, and framing them as an existential threat, leaders can potentially shore up support for both themselves and the ingroup (McDermott 2010; Webster 2020).

Which kind of personality types are more open to nasty rhetoric? The kinds of people that are more aggressive and who like to argue with others or get into bar fights are more tolerant of violent rhetoric (Kalmoe 2014; Sydnor 2019; Westwood et al. 2022; Zeitzoff 2014).

Research in political psychology shows that there are two constellations of traits that are associated with support for strong leaders and repressive policies. First people who have a preference for hierarchy are more willing to engage in aggression to maintain the existing hierarchy (social dominance orientation) and dehumanize the outgroup (Hodson and Costello 2007; Kteily et al. 2015; Petersen and Laustsen 2020). The second constellation of traits is known as authoritarianism, and includes those who (1) support obedience to authority, (2) favor traditional norms and conformity, and (3) are willing to engage in aggression to maintain order and security (Hetherington and Weiler 2009; Norris and Inglehart 2019). These authoritarian tendencies become activated during times of threats. Activated authoritarians are more likely to support strong leaders, tolerate nasty rhetoric, and favor laws that exclude and punish outgroups that are the perceived source of these threats (Petersen and Laustsen 2020; Stenner 2005). Providing supporters with an outgroup to fear and loathe also gives leaders a way to solidify the ingroup and mobilize supporters (McDermott 2010).

How do politicians actually employ nasty rhetoric? Rarely do they openly say, "this group should be thrown in prison" or "my opponent should be shot"—though sometimes their supporters say these things.[11] Politicians talk in extended metaphors to construct a frame for their supporters (Lakoff and Johnson 2008). Popular frames include politicians describing politics as a war, where they are willing to "go to battle" or "protect" the ingroup from the outgroup "enemy." These fighting metaphors are particularly effective for

[11] See the *New York Times* article: "Macabre Video of Fake Trump Shooting Media and Critics Is Shown at His Resort" (Schmidt and Haberman 2019).

mobilizing hardcore partisans or aggressive personality types (Bauer, Kalmoe, and Russell 2021; Kalmoe 2014, 2017; Kalmoe, Gubler, and Wood 2018). Another common tactic is to dehumanize political opponents or targeted groups (Kteily et al. 2015; Smith 2011). Calling them "rats," "dogs," "vermin," or "scum" sets up a dynamic where the targets don't need to be afforded the same empathy or rights afforded to ingroup members.

In addition to insults and violent threats, politicians can make unfounded allegations or circulate conspiracy theories about their opponents (Fenster 1999; Flynn, Nyhan, and Reifler 2017). Certain personality traits are more likely to believe in conspiracy theories, and certain political contexts are more likely to give rise to them. Those who believe in supernatural forces, or believe there's an ongoing struggle between good and evil, are more likely to engage in conspiratorial thinking. These conspiracy theories are more likely to gain traction during shifts in power or periods of uncertainty (Oliver and Wood 2014; Uscinski and Parent 2014). Political elites can choose to fan the flames with conspiracies and baseless allegations to increase negative feelings towards outgroups (Iyengar and Westwood 2015; Nyhan 2020). Or, as Radnitz (2016) argues, elites can use conspiracies and shared narratives to cement ingroup coalitions following contentious events.

1.2.4 What's Missing?

So what's missing from this story of nasty politics? A lot. We'll focus in this section and in the broader book on two unanswered questions: (1) why do politicians go nasty if voters don't like it? And (2) what are the effects of nasty politics, given the mixed evidence on persuasion and voters' general disdain for it?

First, most of the studies of nasty rhetoric in the U.S. focus on incivility at the lower end, which is seen as a side effect of America's calcified partisanship. But there is more to nasty politics than just partisanship. In places like Ukraine, where partisanship has historically been weak, there's still much if not more violent rhetoric and actual violence between politicians (D'Anieri 2015).

Second, what is the strategy behind nasty politics? Which politicians are likely to turn nasty, and when? Is going nasty a calculated move? For example, in 2016 during the Republican presidential primary Florida Republican Senator Marco Rubio went after his rival candidate, Donald Trump. He compared Trump to a con artist trying to take over the GOP and that Trump was "prey(ing) upon people's (worst) fears to get them to vote" for him (Siddiqui 2016). Four years later and Rubio's opinion on Trump had changed. In early November 2020, just two days before the U.S. presidential general election, Rubio spoke at a Trump rally. He echoed President Trump's smear that Joe Biden was "sleepy." Rubio also showed his support for Trump supporters who had recently attempted to run a Biden campaign bus off the road in Texas saying: "We love what they (the Trump supporters) did, but here's the thing they don't know: We do that in Florida every day. I love seeing the boat parades.... We thank all the great patriots" (Cillizza 2020).

Or is nasty politics a style that some politicians use from the start? In Ukraine, far-right nationalist politician Andriy Biletsky came to prominence as leader of the Azov Battalion, a militia with links to neo-Nazis that was formed to fight Russian separatists in Donbas in 2014 (Miller 2018*a*). The Azov Battalion has been credibly connected to torture and human rights abuses during the War in Donbas.[12] Biletsky previously was a leader in the neo-Nazi Patriots of Ukraine paramilitary organization. The Patriots of Ukraine were known for their Nazi-like torch-lit marches, messages filled with racism and antisemitism, and violent attacks on migrants and other political opponents (Kharkiv Human Rights Protection Group 2008). Following the Euromaidan protests in 2014, Biletsky was elected as an independent candidate into the Ukrainian parliament, the Verkhovna Rada.[13] He later became the leader of the far-right National Corps party in 2016, a political wing of Azov. Once in the Rada Biletsky continued his thuggish approach to politics. In the lead up to the presidential elections in March 2019 his National Corps supporters, backed by their newly formed paramilitary National Militia, heckled President Poroshenko and violently clashed with Ukrainian police. Afterwards, at a press conference, Biletsky accused President Poroshenko and his allies of trying to "physically eliminate (assassinate)" him and others in the National Corps leadership. Biletsky went on to elaborate:

> There are only two criminal organizations in Ukraine: (1) the DNR/LNR (Russian separatists), and (2) the fifth column, led by their henchmen Medvedchuk (an oligarch, and pro-Russian deputy in the Rada) and his cadre, all of which operate with full consent and the blessings of Petro Poroshenko and his presidential administration.[14]

Biletsky was loud and vocal out in the streets, but rarely present in the Rada to do his job. During his first three years as a deputy he participated in less than 3% of votes, one of the worst voting records in the Rada (Ukrainskaya Pravda 2017*a*).

[12] See Office of the United Nations High Commissioner for Human Rights (OHCHR): "Report on the human rights situation in Ukraine 16 November 2015 to 15 February 2016" at https://www.ohchr.org/en/countries/enacaregion/pages/uareports.aspx.

[13] Rada for short.

[14] See Milanova (2019).

So why do some politicians avoid nasty politics all together, while others use it sparingly, and still others employ it as their signature style? This is a tricky question to answer without longitudinal data. We know discrimination, calls for violence, and actual violence all tend to increase during periods of instability and intense polarization, especially around elections (Chaturvedi 2005; Collier and Vicente 2012; Harish and Little 2017; Michelitch 2015; Rauschenbach and Paula 2019; Straus 2007; Wilkinson 2006). But this doesn't tell us is which politicians were engaging in nasty politics before the onset of instability, which started using it after, and which eschewed it altogether?

Another gap in prior work is that it either focuses on the less threatening tactics such as insults and incivility, or at the highest end, incitement. Or, it combines all the nasty rhetorical tactics together under the banner of "violent rhetoric." While insults and violent threats may both be designed to intimidate the outgroup, the level of underlying threat is far different.

Finally, much of the previous research assumes that nasty politics is persuasive. But polling tends to find the opposite—voters abhor it.[15] This is not just confined to the U.S. A 2015 survey in Ukraine carried out by Kyiv International Institute of Sociology (KIIS) found that only 5% of Ukrainians had trust in the Rada, compared to 77% who mistrusted it. This loathing of the Rada stemmed from two factors. First, Ukrainians believed that most politicians were only in office get personally rich and didn't care about the struggles of ordinary Ukrainians (i.e., gas prices or the cost of healthcare).[16] Second, they routinely viewed the boorish behavior of deputies in the Rada—insults, fights, and generally vulgar behavior on TV, political chat shows, and in the Rada itself—as inauthentic and only "for show" (Whitmore 2019). The Israeli Democracy Institute (IDI) in a 2016 survey found that only 17% of the Israeli public believed the Knesset was functioning well, and the most-often cited reason was the "(poor) behavior" of Members of the Knesset (30%).[17] And a September 2020 IDI public opinion survey, found that 71% of Israelis believe that incitement and incendiary discourse is widespread in Israeli politics, and nearly half (45%) fear a major political assassination.[18]

[15] See a Quinnipiac July 2018 poll where 91% of U.S. voters view incivility and harsh rhetoric in politics as a "serious problem" https://poll.qu.edu/national/release-detail?ReleaseID=2554. And 85% of the American public in a July 2019 Pew Research Poll think rhetoric has gotten worse, and 78% say it makes violence more likely https://pewrsr.ch/2GiQUup.

[16] See "KIIS survey report: Corruption in Ukraine" http://kiis.com.ua/?lang=eng&cat=reports&id=595&page=1.

[17] See report: "The public's view of the Knesset continues to fall" https://www.idi.org.il/articles/2156.

[18] See report "25 Years after the Assassination of PM Yitzhak Rabin—Survey on Incitement" https://en.idi.org.il/articles/32615.

1.2.5 Resolving the Paradox of Nasty Politics

The standard view of nasty politics is that it's a distasteful part of politics, but it works. The nasty style appeals to the lowest common denominator of society, and reflects the corrupt motivations of the politicians themselves. As one Ukrainian military veteran and member of the center-Right *Samopomich* party said, "The majority of politicians in the Rada have low-levels of self control, that's why they can easily go from violent words to actual violence with their fists and kicking.... They (members of the Rada) use this kind of rhetoric because they won't face any consequences. Their popularity won't decrease, it can sometimes increase."[19]

This argument assumes that nasty rhetoric is popular and effective. Yet polling consistently finds the opposite. For example, an October 2018 NPR/PBS NewsHour/Marist Poll found that nearly 80% of Americans were concerned "the negative tone and lack of civility in Washington will lead to violence or acts of terror" (Montanaro 2018). In September of 2020 an omnibus survey conducted by Kyiv International Institute of Sociology (KIIS) found that nearly 70% of Ukrainians believe that politicians use tough or nasty language mostly to get attention for themselves, rather than fight for what they believe in.[20] Israeli voters are also turned off by the nasty turn in Israeli politics, with 58% of voters in a 2019 survey viewing their leaders as corrupt (Times of Israel 2020*a*).

Scholarly research confirms this view that nasty rhetoric is a turn-off for voters. Across several experiments and observational studies in the U.S. during the highly polarized Trump presidency, Frimer and Skitka (2018) and Frimer and Skitka (2020) found that supporters rewarded politicians who responded civilly to attacks, and punished incivility—even among President Trump's die-hard supporters. They also found that the public held political leaders to a higher standard of civility than the rank-and-file politicians.

Nasty politics is troubling because of its association with violence, but it is also puzzling. If the public doesn't like politicians who go nasty, why do politicians do it? If it only disgusted voters, then why aren't all the nasty politicians voted out of office instead of winning elections?

Using data from Ukraine, the U.S., and Israel I show that the public is sincere in that they generally don't like politicians who insult, accuse, and threaten violence against their opponents. But, voters who like tough and strong leaders, are more aggressive, or feel that their group is under threat are more willing to support a nasty politician who they feel can protect their group. For politicians, going nasty can be a way to grab attention. This is particularly helpful for outsider politicians

[19] Interview #Ukr-S-S0219.
[20] Survey question included at the author's request.

who are looking to disrupt the status quo, opposition politicians trying to make their voice heard, or incumbents losing power. Nasty politics is the weapon of outsiders and losers. Its effects on democracy are mixed. It can be a legitimate tool for the powerless to grab attention. Or it can be a cynical ploy for incumbents to hold onto power. Nasty politics influences the kinds of politicians who run for office, and its repeated use can turn voters off from politics, and make them less likely to participate. Finally, the potential for actual violence from nasty rhetoric is always lurking in the background.

1.3 Case Selection

Why Ukraine and the U.S.?

Why choose the U.S. and Ukraine when they are such different cases (Seawright and Gerring 2008)? The U.S. is a highly polarized democracy with closely contested elections between two entrenched parties. Many observers and expert indices—including Freedom House, Varieties of Democracy, Polity, and the Economist Intelligence Unit have argued that the U.S. democracy has eroded considerably since 2016 under the Trump presidency (Levitsky and Ziblatt 2020; Osnos 2020). The refusal of Trump to concede the 2020 election, along with his supporters' attempts to violently overturn it by attacking the U.S. Capitol underscore this erosion. Yet it still has a stronger democratic tradition than Ukraine. Ukraine is a flawed democracy, with oligarchs controlling politics. It also has experienced two popular protests that ousted incumbent interests—the Orange Revolution (2004–2005) and Euromaidan Protests (2013–2014) (Verlanov 2020)—and the massive Russian invasion in February 2022 triggered the heaviest fighting in Europe and largest refugee flow since World War II (Cheng 2022). The fact that the U.S. and Ukraine are so different is precisely the point. If there are universal rules to the nasty style of politics in these very different countries, then it shows that my theory can be applied more generally to places where there are contested elections.[21] And that the underlying logic that drives nasty politics in both countries is not purely due to the sensationalist media in Ukraine, or partisan polarization in the U.S.

Ukrainian and U.S. politics are markedly different in terms of their political stability. Threats of violence, and actual violence carried out to further political ends all make nasty politics more likely (Stenner 2005). Ukraine is still emerging

[21] My theory covers places where there are contested and competitive elections—in other words, places where politicians have to be mindful of voters. Nasty politics, and propaganda in particular, serves a very different purpose in authoritarian settings. See Wedeen (2015) and Roberts (2018) for examples.

from a political revolution and reforms following the Euromaidan protests in 2013 and 2014 (Foxall and Pigman 2017). Since gaining its independence from the Soviet Union, Ukraine has faced political turmoil related to two issues: (1) its relationship with Russia, and (2) corruption and the influence of oligarchs on politics and the economy (Darden 2009). The Euromaidan protests of 2013–2014 against President Viktor Yanukovych were sparked by anger at Yanukovych's perceived corruption, and his decision to spurn closer economic relations with the European Union (E.U.), and instead move closer to Russia (Onuch 2015). The protests eventually led to Yanukovych's ouster.

Support for the Euromaidan protests has historically fallen along one of the main political cleavages in Ukraine: the social and political divide between Eastern (and Southern) Ukraine and Western Ukraine (Hale 2010; Hesli, Reisinger, and Miller 1998; Onuch and Hale 2018). A survey conducted by Kyiv International Institute of Sociology in February of 2014 showed that in the country as a whole 40% of the population supported Euromaidan, but this varied from a low of 8% in the Eastern Ukraine to 80% in Western Ukraine (Paniotto 2014). This divide lingered up until the 2022 Russian invasion. Pro-Western and Pro-European Ukrainians largely viewed the Euromaidan protests as a popular protest movement against the corrupt regime of President Yanukovych. In contrast, Ukrainians with more pro-Russian sentiment tended to take a dim view of the Euromaidan protests, and saw it as as a nationalist coup d'état against President Yanukovych, a view echoed by pro-Russian media (Onuch, Mateo, and Waller 2021).

The Russian annexation of Crimea in March of 2014 ratcheted up the East-West tensions in Ukraine. Beginning in April of 2014, the Ukrainian government waged war against Russian-backed rebels in Donetsk and Luhansk (Donbas region). This War in Donbas has led to over 13,000 deaths and more than 1 million displaced.[22] The February 2022 Russian Invasion was a massive escalation by Russia. In the first 100 days of the conflict Russian forces struck targets all over Ukraine, attempted to take the capitol Kyiv, and committed multiple atrocities—including rape and summary executions of Ukrainian civilians (Al-Hlou et al. 2022; Psaropoulos 2022). Approximately 1 in 3 Ukrainians were either internally displaced or had fled the country as refugees.[23] Viewed in the

[22] See Office of the United Nations High Commissioner for Human Rights (OHCHR): "Report on the human rights situation in Ukraine 16 May to 15 August 2019" at https://www.ohchr.org/en/countries/enacaregion/pages/uareports.aspx.

[23] See UNHCR "Where we are now: 100 days of crisis in Ukraine" from June 2022 https://www.unrefugees.org/news/where-we-are-now-100-days-of-crisis-in-ukraine/.

broader context the 2022 Russian invasion was part of efforts since 2014 to reassert Russia's influence over Ukraine's politics (Rumer and Weiss 2021).

The second key issue in Ukrainian politics is endemic corruption. Politicians and political parties in Ukraine have more closely resembled an organized criminal syndicate than a coherent ideological organization designed to implement policy (Way 2019). In October of 2021, investigations of a massive trove of leaked financial documents related to offshore companies involved in money laundering and tax evasion by the International Consortium of Investigative Journalists (ICIJ)—known as the Pandora Papers—document just how deep political corruption goes in Ukraine. Ukraine was the country with the highest number of politicians listed having offshore assets (38), twice as much as the next highest country Russia (19) (Chen 2021). Ukrainian President Volodymyr Zelensky's who came to office in 2019 pledging to root out corruption was himself mentioned in the Pandora Papers.

U.S. political history is quite different from Ukraine's. The U.S. is a developed democracy, with a strong two-party system and highly institutionalized legislative rules and norms (Krehbiel 1998). Yet partisan polarization in the U.S. has steadily grown since the 1980s, both at the elite and mass levels (Iyengar et al. 2019; McCarty, Poole, and Rosenthal 2016). Many consider the 2016 presidential election and the Trump presidency as both a cause and consequence of a sharp increase in partisanship and reduction in the quality of democracy (Graham and Svolik 2020). Researchers have documented how polarization in the U.S. has trickled down from the elite level, and even led to discrimination against outgroup partisans in everyday encounters (McConnell, Margalit, Malhotra, and Levendusky 2018).

Scholars and pundits connect President Trump's hyperbolic and nasty rhetoric towards Democrats and his political opponents to increased support for political violence (Kalmoe and Mason 2022). For instance over 45% of Republicans and 41% of Democrats think the other party "is so dangerous that it is a threat to the health of the nation" (Pew Research Center 2016).

The U.S. and Ukraine have strikingly different levels of partisanship and party stability. Before the 2022 Russian invasion, positive versus negative views towards the Euromaidan protests were a major political cleavage in Ukraine, but partisan attachments were weak.[24] Political parties in Ukraine have historically been driven by personalities, rather than political cleavages and strong

[24] One issue area where there has been partisan polarization in Ukraine involves attitudes toward the "Opposition parties"—Opposition Platform–For Life and the Opposition Bloc–Party of Peace that formed following the Euromaidan protests. These Opposition parties are largely made up of former members of Yanukovych's Party of Regions. Opponents of these parties regularly accused them of being Putin supporters. See Dreyfus (2020).

ideological party brands. Ukrainian political parties have been ephemeral, weak, and served as highly personalized vehicles for individual politicians (D'Anieri 2015). The names of parties and factions in Ukrainian politics underscore this point: e.g., Petro Poroshenko Bloc, Yulia Tymoshenko Bloc, and Radical Party of Oleh Lyashko. New parties regularly spring up around key personalities, and career politicians rotate among these new parties. Party switching is also common in the Rada. People's Deputies (members of the Rada) that get elected under one party often leave that party for another after assuming office (Krymeniuk 2019).

In contrast, partisanship and party identity are hardwired into American politics. Scholars of American Politics point to the rise in affective partisan polarization as a key culprit behind the rise of nasty politics: ordinary Democrats and Republicans increasingly distrust each other (Iyengar et al. 2019). In Ukraine, strong partisanship is absent, but there's still plenty of nasty language and actual violent behavior from politicians. This points to the shortcoming of U.S.-politics focused theories—it's not just partisan polarization that drives nasty politics.

Trust in institutions influences a politician's incentive to use nasty rhetoric. During the periods covered in this book, the public's trust in politics and institutions is quite low in both the U.S., and extremely low in Ukraine. Surveys conducted in the U.S. (68%) and Ukraine (87%) showed that a majority "somewhat" or "strongly agree" with the statement that most politicians are crooked. Only 11% of Americans have "great deal" and "quite a lot" of trust in Congress, and only 7% of Ukrainians approve of the Rada.[25]

Both the U.S. and Ukraine elected populist leaders in Donald Trump and Volodymyr Zelensky. Donald Trump's election as president in 2016 stemmed from his ability to galvanize his supporters with anger at elites, the Republican establishment, immigrants, trade partners, and others who were "ripping off" the U.S. He used nasty rhetoric to drive media coverage (Sides, Tesler, and Vavreck 2019). In a similar way, in May 2019 actor and political novice Volodymyr Zelensky merged widespread anger at political corruption with his affable, comedic charm to win the Ukrainian presidency (Ryabinska 2020). In the second-round run-off he beat incumbent Petro Poroshenko by nearly 50 percentage points. And in July 2019 Zelensky's newly formed "Servant of the People" party ran in legislative elections. The party's name was a particularly unique form of personalistic politics even for Ukraine. The party took its name from Zelensky's popular Ukrainian satirical television show *Servant of the People.* Zelensky's Servant of the People party swept the 2019 Rada elections winning

[25] October and November 2018 surveys conducted on the U.S. Amazon's MTurk platform ($N = 457$) and face to face in Ukraine with KIIS ($N = 1,030$). See Appendix for sample information.

more than half of the seats, as well as winning across both Eastern and Western Ukraine (Soltys and Motyl 2019).

Previous research finds that different electoral systems provide different electoral incentives and can lead to different types of political crises (Linz 1990). Electoral systems also influence politicians' incentives to cultivate a personal vote. Do politicians choose to build their own brand and pitch directly to the voters (i.e., voters directly electing candidates), or do they owe their loyalties to parties as in proportional representation systems (Carey and Shugart 1995)? The Rada in Ukraine is unicameral and follows a semi-presidential system. Half of the 450 seats in the Rada are allocated in a closed party list via proportional representation, and the other half elected in first-past-the-post in single-member districts. The U.S. is a fully presidential system with legislators chosen via open primaries, then general elections with first-past-the post voting, and contains an upper house, the U.S. Senate (100 members, 2 per state), and the lower U.S. House of Representatives (435 members) representing single-member districts.

Political parties in Ukraine compete in a flawed democracy, or hybrid regime, with the concentration of oligarchic wealth, widespread corruption, and biased media preventing truly free and fair elections (Knott 2018). Politicians in the Rada regularly trade insults which can descend into physical brawls. There is evidence that these legislative brawls relate to the weakness of institutional norms in the Rada, where various factions (pro-Europe/anti-Yanukovych vs. pro-Russia/pro-Yanukovych) suspect the other side of rigging the rules in their favor (Gandrud 2016). One of the key factors in Ukrainian democratic dysfunction is the fact that oligarchs control large swaths of the media. Estimates are that Ukrainian oligarchs control around 85% of publications and broadcast television (Gongadze 2020). Oligarchs thus can reward politicians with favorable coverage and punish those who cross them (Verstyuk 2013).

Name-calling, threats, and actual violence are one of the trademarks of Ukrainian politics. Right-wing nationalist and populist politician Oleh Lyashko is famous for using aggressive and crude language towards his political opponents. Lyashko personally led a vigilante militia to fight in Eastern Ukraine during the early parts of the War in Donbas in 2014. They filmed their exploits battling Russian separatists. In a notable video clip Lyashko confronted a local police chief and accused him of being a traitor and supporter of the Russian separatists. On camera and surrounded by his thugs, Lyashko asks the police chief, "should I shoot you now or later?" (Ostrovsky 2014). The video clip is hard to watch. There are moments where Lyashko preens and strains to act like some tough cop in a poorly scripted show. But other moments, such as when Lyashko's men are verbally abusing suspected separatists who they have detained, are disconcerting, especially given the credible accounts of Lyashko's militia executing suspected separatists (Miller and Webb. 2014).

Lyashko parlayed his tough-talk and actions into a third place finish in the 2014 Ukrainian presidential election, and guided his party into a coalition government with Poroshenko in the Rada. This juxtaposition of theatrical, over-the-top rhetoric backed by the threat of actual violence encapsulates Ukrainian politics.

In the U.S., scholars say three factors explain the rise of the nasty style politics: (1) heightened partisan media (Mutz 2016; Sydnor 2019), (2) the arrival of the Tea Party (Gervais and Morris 2018), and (3) the election of President Trump and his prolific use of Twitter to attack political opponents and the media. Growing partisan polarization is seen as the main culprit behind all of them (Abramowitz and Webster 2016; Kalmoe and Mason 2022).

In sum, Ukraine and the U.S. are very different cases. They have different levels of partisan attachment and polarization, party stability, and institutional design. It's worth emphasizing again the vast difference in partisan attachment and partisan polarization. This difference is important. Ukraine has weak parties and weak party attachments, yet nastier and more violent politics. This challenges the assumption that partisan polarization is the chief driver of nasty politics.

Israel: The Middle Case

The bulk of this book will focus on the cases of Ukraine and the U.S. How does the nasty style of politics play out in Ukraine, with weak partisan attachments, compared to the U.S. with its strong partisanship? Yet, a skeptical reader might question this comparison: "don't most countries fall somewhere in between these two cases—more meaningful political parties than Ukraine, but not the divisive partisanship and hardened identities of U.S politics?" That's precisely why Israel is included. It's a test of how the theory holds in a country whose partisan cleavages lie between the U.S. and Ukraine. Israel serves as a shadow case, not the main case of intensive study but rather an external validity check (Gerring 2016). Jewish Israeli voters self-identify with right, center, and left, which corresponds to how they view the security situation in Israel.[26] Right-wing supporters take a harder line towards Palestinians and support a more hawkish foreign policy compared to leftists and centrists. Yet, partisanship is not as hard-baked as in the U.S., as voters switch their allegiance between parties, and new parties emerge to challenge existing ones. For instance, the poor electoral prospects for traditional left-wing parties such as Labor and Meretz in 2019–2020, led many leftist Jews to switch their votes to the traditionally Arab Joint-List (Shezaf 2020). And former Netanyahu allies, Naftali Bennett

[26] The Arab-Palestinian public have traditionally participated at lower rates in Israeli elections than Jewish Israelis. Their chief voting concerns are public safety and discrimination within Israel. But given the tightness of elections they have become an increasingly important voting bloc. See Rudnitzky (2021).

and Avigdor Liberman, tried to peel off right-wing voters by forming their own parties and challenging Netanyahu (Mualem 2020). This is in part a function of Israel's political system. As a parliamentary democracy, voters don't vote for individual politicians or the prime minister, but rather parties.

Israel is a consolidated democracy like the U.S. But two factors have characterized Israeli politics since Netanyahu became prime minister in 2009. First, Israeli politics have increasingly drifted to the right, and the leftist parties, particularly the Israeli Labor Party, are weaker than they have been historically (Pedahzur 2012; Shindler 2015). Second, Israeli politics began to revolve around where voters and other politicians stand on Netanyahu himself. Netanyahu's primacy in Israeli politics, and hard-nosed governing strategy, led to a significant uptick in polarization between the right and the center-left in Israeli politics (Bassan-Nygate and Weiss 2020). Israel's democracy was increasingly under strain. In less than two years Israel underwent four elections to break a stalemate between pro- and anti-Netanyahu forces (April 2019–March 2021). The third election in March 2020 took place against the backdrop of the COVID-19 pandemic, and the indictment of Netanyahu on corruption charges (Knell 2020). With the stakes so high—Netanyahu's political and legal fortune in the balance—Israeli politics turned even nastier. During the closing days of the March 2020 election campaign Netanyahu's campaign advisor was heard saying on a recording "hatred is what unites" Netanyahu's supporters. Benny Gantz, a former general and Netanyahu's centrist opponent in the first three elections, accused Netanyahu of "lying, attacking, dividing, mud-slinging, spreading malicious rumors and inciting... Netanyahu, you're poisoning Israel" (Halbfinger and Balilty 2020). After a fourth close election in March 2021, Netanyahu was finally ousted from power in June 2021 by a broad coalition. In his fiery exit speech in front of the Knesset, Netanyahu accused his opponents on the left of claiming incitement while fanning flames: "As far as you're concerned, criticism from the right is always incitement, even when there isn't a hint of violence. Whereas incitement from the left, about sending people to the garbage dump, and the hangman's noose, and guillotines, oh, that's always freedom of speech" (*Times of Israel* 2021*a*).

1.4 Outline of the Book

To answer the puzzle of nasty politics, I collected a variety of novel datasets. These include:

1. Multiple surveys and survey experiments fielded in the U.S., Ukraine, and Israel.

2. Historical time series data of news coverage of nasty politics in the U.S., Ukraine, and Israel.
3. Nasty social media behavior of key politicians in the U.S., Ukraine, and Israel including more than 33,000 tweets and nearly 5,000 Facebook posts around recent contentious political events (2019–2022).
4. 301 disruptive events in the Ukrainian Rada from 2001–2019.
5. Databases of nasty political events from 2016–2019 in the U.S. (1,407 events) and Ukraine (347 events).
6. Surveys of political elites in the U.S. (N = 520) and Ukraine (N = 174).
7. A survey of political science experts (N = 180).
8. In-depth interviews with political elites, journalists, and campaign strategists in the U.S. and Ukraine (N = 59).

How these datasets are used, and the structure of the rest of the book are discussed below.

Chapter 2 presents the theory of nasty politics. It describes how nasty politics is a series of tactics from mundane insults to threats and outright violence. The public on average doesn't like it when politicians engage it, particularly the more extreme forms of incitement and violence. Yet certain personality types are more tolerant or even attracted to nasty politics. And during periods of heightened polarization or threat, voters may view nasty politicians as tougher and better able to protect the ingroup. Politicians can use nasty rhetoric to grab attention, or signal their toughness to the ingroup. This can be a particular effective strategy for opposition or outsider strategies to grab attention, or incumbents whose support is slipping. The effects on democracy are mixed. Insults and intimidating statements coming from the ingroup can be viewed as legitimate or protective, while from the outgroup they are threats. Nasty politics can also breed cynicism in politics and crowd out good politicians from running.

Chapter 3 provides a historical overview of violent rhetoric in the U.S., Ukraine, and Israel. It looks at the drivers of historical nastiness, and then examines particular dynamics of nasty politics. In Israel and the U.S., we'll look at how key politicians employ nasty rhetoric on social media during protests and contentious politics in the initial stages of the COVID pandemic in 2020. And in Ukraine we'll examine how key politicians use nasty rhetoric on social media during the lead up to the 2019 presidential and legislative elections. Finally, we'll conclude with case studies of how Donald Trump and Oleh Lyashko employed nasty politics. Social media data from different contexts and platforms will show that nasty social media posts get more engagement.

Chapter 4 examines how the public responds to violent rhetoric using a series of surveys and survey experiments in the U.S. and Ukraine. First, we'll see that the public distinguishes between insults, accusations, intimidating statements, and incitement, and views the latter two as more violent and less acceptable. Additional survey evidence will highlight how certain personality types—those that like tough leaders, are more aggressive, and believe violence can sometimes be justified—are more willing to tolerate violent rhetoric. Finally, a series of survey experiments will show that the public is more supportive of a politician who uses nasty rhetoric when it's directed against the outgroup as opposed to the ingroup, and believe it's more justified when the outgroup is framed as an existential threat.

Chapter 5 looks at how politicians use nasty politics. To examine this we'll explore databases in the U.S. and Ukraine from media sources on nasty politics from 2016–2019. The findings will show that in both countries a few key politicians—mainly from the opposition–are responsible for the majority of nasty politics, and low level insults are much more common than intimidating statements, incitement, or rarest of all—physical violence. We'll also examine a dataset of disruptions in the Rada including blockades, vandalism, and fights. Disruptions peak in key eras of polarization in Ukrainian politics, and are more likely to be used by the opposition. Finally, using a dataset of incivility in U.S. Congressional tweets we'll see that uncivil tweets get more engagement (likes and engagement), and are more likely to be posted by Democrats, a period in which they were in the opposition.

Chapter 6 provides survey data of U.S. and Ukrainian elites, political scientists, along with in-depth interviews with political operatives in both countries to better understand how elites and other political operatives see the strategy behind violent rhetoric. The findings from the elite surveys mirror those of the general public—insults and name-calling are less threatening than more serious veiled threats and incitement. The in-depth interviews with political operatives will highlight the importance of media attention, and appearing tough and strong for core supporters in driving nasty politics. The operatives also suggest how financial concerns and authenticity can influence the decisions for politicians to go nasty.

Chapter 7 presents case and survey evidence from Ukraine, the U.S., and Israel to trace the mixed effects of nasty politics on the quality of democracy. A series of surveys and experiments will show that on average voters don't like it when politicians use violent or harsh language, and think it has corrosive effects on democracy. However, there's variation in support for the positive aspects of violent appeals. The public is more likely to take a dim view of nasty rhetoric when the outgroup uses it compared to the ingroup. Ingroup politicians are more likely to be viewed as fighting for what's right and calling out bad characters when they use it. While nasty rhetoric boosts perceptions of threat from the outgroup, it doesn't translate to increased support for democratic subversion. Additional surveys in the U.S. and Ukraine will show that nasty politics depresses voters' willingness to participate. Through case studies in Israel, the U.S., and Ukraine, we will discuss how nasty politics plays an important role in who drops out of politics, and who decides to run.

In the conclusion in Chapter 8, we'll return to lead up to the 2022 Russian invasion of Ukraine and the insurrection at the U.S. Capitol on January 6, 2021. We'll examine the social media data of President Zelensky and other key Ukrainian politicians, as well as President Trump and his Congressional allies during these crucial time periods. We'll place these findings in the broader context of how internal and external threats influence nasty politics. Finally, we'll conclude by discussing the summary of findings about the logic behind nasty politics, and offer directions for future research.

2

A Theory of Nasty Politics

In December 2018, Oleh Barna, a mustached and muscled deputy from Ukrainian President Petro Poroshenko's party, attacked a fellow deputy on a political chat show on television. Barna and Yuriy Levchenko, the rival Deputy from the far-right Svoboda Party, had exchanged insults. Barna claimed Levchenko was sexually "impotent" just like the small faction of Svoboda in the Rada and "hiding behind slogans." Levchenko accused Barna of being an alcoholic, and reminded the audience of when Barna got into an accident with a tram in Kyiv (TSN UA 2018). After this last accusation Barna had heard enough, and sprang across the studio to punch Levchenko in the head, throwing him to the ground before the two were forcibly separated.

The incident with Barna contained insults, accusations, and even actual violence. And it points to our two key questions for the book. The first question lays out the puzzle of nasty politics, and the second its implications. This chapter provides answers to these key questions and describes the core logic of nasty politics.

Question 1: *Why do politicians go nasty—insult, accuse, threaten, encourage violence against, and occasionally engage in actual violence—against their opponents if the average voter doesn't like it?*[1]

There are seven factors that answer the puzzle of nasty politics. Four factors are related to the public's response to nasty politics (the demand side). And three factors are related to politicians' incentives to go nasty (the supply side). The four demand-side factors that explain why voters may excuse nasty politics or even embrace it:

[1] Note, this theory of nasty politics applies to places where there are contested elections, and where parties have a chance of losing (Przeworski 1991). In autocratic regimes, nasty politics may be a tool of intimidation and coercion, or a coordinating mechanism. This is outside the scope of this book.

Nasty Politics: The Logic of Insults, Threats, and Incitement. Thomas Zeitzoff, Oxford University Press.
© Oxford University Press 2023. DOI: 10.1093/oso/9780197679494.003.0002

Factor 1: *The public is more tolerant of low-levels of nastiness, so insults and accusations are more common than incitement.*

Factor 2: *The public perceives outgroup politicians to be nastier than ingroup politicians who say or do the same things.*

Factor 3: *Certain personality types—those who score higher on authoritarianism, aggression, and have preferences for strong leaders—are more tolerant and accepting of nasty politics.*

Factor 4: *While on average voters are indeed against nastiness, some value protection for their ingroup more than they do civility, particularly when they feel their group is under threat.*

There are certain incentives for politicians to go nasty. These three supply-side factors explain why:

Factor 5: *It allows politicians to get attention for themselves, and can shift the focus away from unfavorable topics.*

Factor 6: *Politicians use nasty politics to project strength in ways that show they will protect the ingroup.*

Factor 7: *It can be a strategy for outsiders to circumvent conventional party politics.*

The second key question relates to nasty politics and democracy:

Question 2: *What are the effects of the nasty style of politics on democracy?*

Four of the five effects of nasty politics on democracy are negative.

Effect 1: *It can destroy faith among citizens in the political system.*

Effect 2: *Those in power can use it to as pretext to silence their rivals and damage democracy.*

Effect 3: *Nasty politics can spiral into significant violence.*

Effect 4: *It shapes the type of politicians and political leaders that eventually lead a country (who runs and who retires), and over time can make the pool of politicians nastier.*

But, there is some positive utility to nasty politics for democracy:

Effect 5: *It can serve as a way for marginalized outsiders to make inroads into a political system.*

This chapters builds on these basic insights, and develops a theory of nasty politics to answer why politicians go nasty, and what are its effects on democracy. But before discussing the theory below, it's helpful to say what nasty politics isn't. Nasty politics isn't particular to one context. Each country and political era has its own flavor of nasty politics. But there is a logic to the nasty style that we'll explore in contemporary Israeli, Ukrainian, and U.S. politics. Nasty politics doesn't happen in one specific setting. It can occur via Twitter (U.S.), on political chat shows on TV (Ukraine), or in a fiery campaign rally (Israel). It can be impersonal, or face-to-face. Nasty politics isn't one type of rhetorical technique. It's an escalating set of rhetorical tactics and actions—including violence—that politicians use strategically. Nasty politics isn't just about attacking other politicians. It also includes attacks on the other side's supporters, minorities, bureaucrats, businesses people, and other domestic opponents who politicians feel make useful targets.

This brings us to the final and most important point. Nasty politics isn't only about partisan political polarization. Yes, partisan polarization matters, and can give politicians an easy outgroup to attack and try to make look bad to score political points. But as we will see, nasty politics can be a way for politicians to gain attention—a valuable currency in politics.

2.1 Are Voters Just Lying to Us and Themselves?

A central premise of our puzzle of nasty politics is that in general voters don't like it. Yet are voters being insincere when they say they don't like it? This goes to a deeper question in political science and public opinion—what are we measuring when we ask people their opinion on politics? Do people just respond to surveys with what's on the top of their mind (Zaller 1992)? Or are they parroting talking points of the ingroup or elites (Bullock 2011; Bullock et al. 2015; Campbell et al. 1960)? Or is public opinion about nasty politics, similar to what people used to say about foreign policy—it's too erratic and volatile to hold consistent views (Almond 1950)?

If the public's distaste for nasty rhetoric was a weakly held view, then we shouldn't see structured views on nasty politics. But evidence shows the opposite. An October 2019 Georgetown University poll of Americans found that most believe political divisions are getting worse, with 88% concerned and frustrated by incivility.[2] This is just one poll, but it's part of a larger story that voters care about the way politicians act and are worried when they engage in nasty behavior.

Its not only a U.S. phenomenon. As Whitmore (2020, p. 102) shows, Ukrainians see disruptive behavior and fights in the Rada as "*pokazukha*" (for show) or "*zakazukha*" (ordered window-dressing) and are disgusted by it. Ukrainians view the nasty style as part of the culture of corruption. This disgust with Ukrainian politics was arguably one of the chief reasons that Zelensky won in 2019 (Bateson 2019). And in Israel, one of the major gripes that Netanyahu's critics had with his stranglehold on Israel politics, besides the alleged corruption, is the way his embrace of combative, nasty politics coarsened Israeli political discourse (Rosner 2019). Nasty politics is not a low stakes issues for voters, but rather one of the key issues that they dislike about politics and politicians.

A key refrain from many campaign consultants is that people aren't being honest, or are not fully self-aware when they say they don't like nasty politics. As one article in *The Hill* stated, "The dirty secret about negative campaign ads they work" (Ricci 2016). So like bad soap operas, car crashes, and other bawdy spectacles, people don't want to admit they enjoy nasty politics. And when people respond to surveys with a socially desirable response, they're just going to say they dislike all the mud-slinging. But the reality is they love a "good show"—right?

The reality is more complicated. A popular theory of Trump's surprising victory in 2016 was that it was because of "shy Trump voters"—people didn't want to admit they liked Trump's brash style (Russonello 2019). Yet, research by Coppock (2017) finds a lack of support for the shy Trump voter thesis. Blair, Coppock, and Moor (2018) further shows that socially desirable responding on surveys is rarer than many people believe (closer to 10%), and for many sensitive questions social desirability bias is zero. So it's unlikely that voters are lying or being insincere when they say they don't like violent rhetoric.

We shouldn't shrug off voters as insincere dupes when they say they don't like nasty politics, and are willing to punish politicians who use it. This echoes a veteran Democratic campaign strategist who said, "I do think there is a genuine desire for civility and decency, but perhaps it's somewhat smaller than what you

[2] See Georgetown University October 2019 "Battleground Poll" (GU Institute of Politics and Public Service 2019*a*).

would find in a poll."[3] On average voters don't like the nasty style. But nasty politics serves other ends that conventional, civil politics doesn't.

2.2 Demand Side

What do people want from their political representatives? People want politicians that show integrity, are competent, strong, hard-working, warm, and authentic (Clarke et al. 2018). The public increasingly desires the last two (Laustsen and Bor 2017; Stiers et al. 2019). The public wants politicians who exude warmth, and are not simply parroting talking points, but being authentic with voters. For example New York Democratic Rep. Alexandra Ocasio-Cortez, a social media superstar who has more than 8 million followers on Instagram and 12 million on Twitter, held a social media training session for Democrats in early February 2021. The focus of the training session was on connecting with voters via social media by being more authentic (McCammond 2021).

Why would voters support politicians who say awful things about their opponents, make baseless allegations, and even risk actual violence (Nacos, Shapiro, and Bloch-Elkon 2020; Wilkinson 2006; Yanagizawa-Drott 2014)? Nasty politics doesn't seem to fit into this calculus. But in fact, it does. Certain voters are more predisposed to tolerate, and even like when politicians attack their opponents. Voters may in fact want a politician to protect the ingroup, especially in periods of heightened threat. They are willing to trade-off warmth, for toughness. This is similar to the idea that voters might be willing to bend the rules and norms of democracy, if it means their party wins (Graham and Svolik 2020). The nasty politics model also suggests something about the acceptability of this trade-off. Recall that the scale ranges from (1) insults and name-calling at the lowest end, (2) accusations, allegations, and conspiracy theories, (3) intimidating statements, (4) incitement, and (5) actual violence as the most threatening and aggressive. Voters may tolerate insults or name-calling, but only under high levels of perceived threat will they be willing to excuse to incitement and violence. Polling in late 2020 and early 20201 among Trump supporters in the lead up to and following the attempted coup and January 6 insurrection finds support for this idea. More than 90% of Trump supporters believed his baseless election fraud claims. And more than 75% believe that "real Americans are losing their freedom," and "the traditional way of American life is disappearing" (Sebastian Parker and Blum 2021). Nearly 40% of Republicans agreed with the

[3] Interview #US-D-D0719.

statement, "if elected leaders won't protect American then the people must act—even it means violence"—more than twice the percentage of Democrats (17%) (Beauchamp 2021*b*). If you believe that the threat is extreme, then extreme action is not only acceptable, it's needed.

2.2.1 Don't Go Too Nasty . . . Except if You're in My Ingroup

Voters don't like it when politicians go nasty. But they especially don't like it when politicians choose the upper end of the nasty politics spectrum (incitement and violence). This is perhaps the least controversial point of the theory. Voters punish politicians more when they use nastier and more threatening tactics. Evidence from protests and contentious politics support this argument. The public reduces support for groups and politicians who use, or seen as supporting, more violent or extreme tactics (Simpson, Willer, and Feinberg 2018; Wasow 2020). As Chenoweth and Stephan (2011) argues, movements that use non-violent resistance tactics are generally more successful at achieving their aims than violent resistance movements. Politicians may be able to get away with using low-level insults or accusations, but voters will tend to reduce their support for politicians who engage in more threatening tactics.

But there's a huge caveat. Nasty politics done by the outgroup will be perceived as more aggressive and threatening than the same tactics used by the ingroup. Evidence from contentious politics show that protesters that are affiliated with the outgroup are perceived to be more violent and threatening than the ingroup, even if they use the exact same tactics (Hsiao and Radnitz 2021; Muñoz and Anduiza 2019).

There are two key implications from this:

Implication 1: *More aggressive and threatening nasty tactics (such as incitement and violence) will be viewed as less acceptable than lower level insults and accusations. Insults and accusations will be more common than more aggressive and threatening tactics.*

Implication 2: *The same nasty tactics done by outgroup politicians will be viewed as more threatening and less acceptable compared to when ingroup politicians do it.*

2.2.2 Personality Driven Politics

Not everyone is equally turned off by the nasty style. Just like certain people love gangster movies like *Goodfellas* and *The Departed,* while others find Scorsese too decadent and violent, there's variation in receptivity to violent appeals. Political scientists and psychologists have consistently found that a few personality characteristics are correlated with receptivity to violent appeals. Those who are more combative and aggressive (Kalmoe 2014; 2017); favor obedience to authority and strong leaders (Hetherington and Weiler 2009; Stenner 2005); are more supportive of hierarchy (Laustsen and Petersen 2017); and are more conflict-prone (Sydnor 2019) all are less likely to punish a politician who uses aggressive and nasty rhetoric.

There are two important caveats to this personality story. First, voters are not randomly assigned to parties. Certain policies, like being tough on immigration, strong on national defense, or staunchly nationalist are more attractive to aggressive, authoritarian personalities. In the U.S., Republicans and Democrats have increasingly sorted along personality and ideological characteristics, with Republicans attracting more authoritarians (Hetherington and Weiler 2009; MacWilliams 2016; Mason 2018).[4] So in parties with more authoritarians, politicians may not pay the same penalty from voters for engaging in nasty politics. Second, these personality characteristics become activated during times of heightened threat—both real (wartime) or symbolic (a changing country) (Laustsen and Petersen 2017; MacWilliams 2016; Stenner 2005).

Ukrainian President Petro Poroshenko followed this playbook in his failed 2019 reelection bid. He warned that Zelensky was unprepared to handle Russian President Vladimir Putin and the War in Donbas. In his farewell speech in the Rada in May 2019, Poroshenko said, "The enemy (Russia) is openly trying to use this period of political turbulence to wreck our achievements on the path of reforms and European integration. To sow strife, hostility and chaos in our society, to set the people and the authorities against each other . . . and destroy Ukrainian statehood" (McLaughlin 2019). And in the lead up to elections in Israel in 2015, Netanyahu released a racist campaign video on his Facebook page saying that Arabs (Palestinian Israelis) were "flocking to the polls in droves" (Zonszein 2015). For Netanyahu, this wasn't a dog whistle to his right-wing supporters, it was a foghorn.

Parties and politicians that stress toughness, nationalism, and law and order policies are likely to have a higher concentration of voters who tolerate and may even enjoy the nasty style. At a rally in Montana President Trump called Montana Republican Rep. Greg Gianforte a "tough cookie" and then mimed a body-slam motion. His supporters responded with loud laughter and hoots. Trump was alluding to the fact that Gianforte had been convicted of assaulting and body-slamming a reporter from *The Guardian* in 2017 (Pilkington 2018).

[4] Other studies argue that this story about certain personalities sorting into parties is more nuanced. Bakker, Lelkes, and Malka (2021) finds that voters also adjust their self-reported personality traits to be more in line with their self-reported partisanship.

Implication 3: *Those that score higher on trait aggression, are more authoritarian, and favor tough leaders are less likely to reduce their support for politicians who use nasty politics.*

2.2.3 Looking for a Little Protection

Sometimes we need a bit of nasty on our side. Bill Laimbeer is considered one of the dirtiest NBA players of all time. He played 13 seasons in the NBA, 11 of which were with the Detroit Pistons (1982–1993). At a muscled 6 feet 11 inches, Laimbeer was known more for his cheap shots, elbows, and the fights he started than his rebounding and scoring prowess. Laimbeer was a four-time NBA All-Star, and won back-to-back NBA Championships in 1989 and 1990 as a key member of the so-called Pistons "Bad Boys."[5] His teammate and point guard Isaiah Thomas famously broke his hand punching Laimbeer during a practice after Laimbeer set a dirty screen on him (Concepcion 2017). Thomas later said of Laimbeer, "If I didn't know Bill Laimbeer, I wouldn't like him either." Laimbeer's antics made him one of the most hated players during his time in the NBA (Burke 2020). Yet Laimbeer's teammates and Pistons fans embraced and loved his badness because he was on their team. And most importantly they believed his toughness helped them win.

Political science research on leaders backs this up. During times of economic uncertainty or in the midst of social conflict, people have a preference for strong, tough leaders (Kakkar and Sivanathan 2017; Laustsen and Petersen 2017). Voters are more willing to tolerate, and may even embrace nasty rhetoric when it comes from a member of their own group, or party, especially during times of threat.

A preference for tough politicians is linked to the tension first pointed out by Fenno (1978) in how people think about politicians and their representatives. Why do Americans like their own representatives, but hate Congress? This paradox became known as Fenno's Paradox, and has been found to be true outside of the U.S. as well. People may not like it when politicians stoke anger in general, but respond with increased loyalty when their side does it (Webster 2020). Polling evidence backs up this idea that people disapprove of nasty politics in general, but also like it when their side stands up and fights. A poll from April 2019 found that 88% of U.S. voters were frustrated with rude and uncivil behavior of

[5] Other members included Isaiah Thomas, Laimbeer, Dennis Rodman, Rick Mahorn, James Edwards, John Salley, and Joe Dumars.

politicians. But 84% were also “tired of leaders compromising their values and ideals and want leaders who will stand up to the other side.”[6]

Nasty rhetoric is one way politicians can signal their toughness. By talking tough about their opponents, politicians can show they are willing to be a protector for the ingroup. And voters will tolerate and may even seek out politicians who talk nasty and tough when they feel threatened or anxious about the state of the world. The logic of this was laid out in a widely-shared tweet by prominent Christian conservative Jerry Falwell Jr. about his support for President Trump (Klein 2019):

> Conservatives & Christians need to stop electing “nice guys.” They might make great Christian leaders but the US needs street fighters like @realDonaldTrump at every level of government b/c the liberal fascists Dems are playing for keeps many Repub leaders are a bunch of wimps![7]

In Falwell’s tweet nasty politics is framed in terms of the defending the ingroup. Sometimes people want a politician who is going to fight for their side. Vaishnav (2017) lays out this logic in the context of why Indian voters support politicians with criminal background:

> Where the rule of law is weak and social divisions are highly salient, politicians can use their criminality as a badge of honor—a signal of their credibility to protect the interests of their community and its allies. (p. 20)

It’s worth reiterating that nasty politics isn’t aggressive for aggression’s sake. Politicians don’t implore their supporters to insult, threaten, or engage in violence with groups on a whim. Instead, as Falwell’s tweets shows, nasty politics is framed as an aggressive tool of defense. Humans have an innate need to protect and be vigilant about threats to them and their group (Albertson and Gadarian 2015; De Dreu and Gross 2019). We have a heightened need to defend ourselves and our group when there is increased threat and uncertainty. Clever politicians can use tough talk and action to allay these fears, or even stoke them for their own political advantage (De Figueiredo et al. 1999; Lake and Rothchild 1996; Posen 1993). Nasty politics provides a playbook for politicians to show the ingroup

[6] See Georgetown University April 2019 “Battleground Poll” (GU Institute of Politics and Public Service 2019*b*).

[7] Falwell Jr., Jerry. (@JerryFalwellJr). Twitter, September 28, 2018. https://twitter.com/JerryFalwellJr/status/1045853333007798272.

that they will not sell them out, will protect them in a scary, uncertain world, and punish those who deserve it.

Implication 4: *Voters will view politicians who use nasty rhetoric as tougher, and be more willing to excuse nasty politics during periods of heightened threat.*

2.3 Supply Side

In International Relations proponents of rational choice theory argue that leaders are largely driven by staying in office. This allows leaders to achieve their other goals, e.g., getting rich and maximizing their power (Bueno de Mesquita et al. 2005). Similarly Fenno (1978) famously argued that members of Congress are driven by three things (1) winning re-election, (2) maximizing power in Congress, and (3) achieving policy. To stay in office, politicians develop a representational style to communicate to their constituents about how they serve their interests (Grimmer 2013).

The choice to insult, accuse, intimidate, or incite violence against opponents is an extreme style of representation, but one that comes with its own logic.

2.3.1 Attention and Distraction

Shock jocks like Howard Stern have long recognized that stoking outrage in their audience can be a winning strategy. Stern used his battle with the Federal Communications Commission (F.C.C.) over obscenity and indecency charges in the 1980s and early 1990s to drive ratings and dub himself the "King of All Media" (Cox 2005). Conservative political talk radio hosts—like Rush Limbaugh, Sean Hannity, and Glenn Beck—all of whom made the jump to television—made a lucrative career out of stoking political outrage and pushing the boundaries of acceptable political discourse (Sobieraj and Berry 2011). It's no surprise then that politicians too crave attention. As Paul Begala, the Democratic strategist, said, "politics is show business for ugly people" (Roberts and Argetsinger 2010).

Nasty politics grabs attention. Mud-slinging may be distasteful to the public, but that doesn't mean the public isn't going to pay attention to when it happens. As one long-time Democratic consultant put it, "Who you want to be, who you think you are supposed to be, and who Jesus wants you to be are one category—and what you respond to emotionally is another."[8] Another U.S. campaign strategist further reinforced this point about the benefits of going nasty, "People decry

[8] Interview #US-D-D0719.

all sorts of things they actually reward. They reward gutter politics, outrageous promises, etc. . . . Ultimately we are all political animals that respond to stimuli."[9]

Yet none of this matters if the media doesn't cover it. Fights, scandals, and outrageous comments all generate more attention (Maurer 1999). Conflict frames provide an easy way for journalists to cover political news—"Politician A got into a war of words with rival Politician B" (Atkinson 2017). Finally, the rise of partisan cable news media and social media have accentuated this tendency to cover politics as conflict (Boxell, Gentzkow, and Shapiro 2017; DellaVigna and Kaplan 2007). These outlets regularly push clips and stories about the "other side" doing nasty stuff to gin up outrage and engage viewers (Klein 2020; Webster 2020). When politicians insult or say nasty things about their opponents, it gets picked up by the media and then circulated even more widely.

The media's obsession with nasty politics is not just a U.S. phenomenon. Ukrainian media is controlled by interlocking interests of oligarchs who back different politicians and political blocs (VoxUkraine 2019). Nasty politics in Ukraine grabs attention, and is used by the oligarchs to control the narrative and attack their political and business rivals.[10] As one Ukrainian political activist who participated in the Euromaidan protests said, "The main strategy or goal of such (violent rhetoric) is to get voters' attention and attract new supporters. Such name-calling is on purpose, and is pre-planned. The audience (public) like this—it's like a big show to them."[11] In Israel the introduction of the free newspaper *Israel Hayom* (Israel Today), a right-leaning free newspaper published by the casino mogul, and right-wing donor, Sheldon Adelson, aided the fortunes of Benjamin "Bibi" Netanyahu and his right-wing Likud Party (Grossman, Margalit, and Mitts 2020). The newspaper pushed stories that were favorable to Netanyahu, and circulated attacks against his opponents, earning it the moniker "Bibiton" (Bibi's newspaper) (Ronen 2015). In the abstract people don't like politicians who are rude, brash, or engage in name-calling. Yet, they also are attracted to the spectacle of the nasty style, and some may even enjoy it.

Studies of what goes viral on the Internet provide some clues as to why this rhetoric is so captivating. Certain high-arousal emotions—awe, outrage, anxiety—make us more likely to click on something and also more likely to share it (Wu 2017, p. 321). In fact whole websites and business models have been built around emotional virality and the need to share things. Buzzfeed, Upworthy, Mashable, and most notably Facebook have all monetized getting people to click and share their stories (Munger 2020). Research from psychology backs up these

[9] Interview #US-D-M0319.
[10] Interview #Ukr-J-C0120.
[11] Interview #Ukr-PE-A0219.

business models. Stories with high levels of emotional arousal lead people to be more likely to share information, and also also express happiness, sadness, or anger (Berger 2011; Kramer, Guillory, and Hancock 2014). It's not just arousal, but also perceptions of control. By sharing positive stories or condemning an outrageous story we give ourselves some sense of control (Jones, Libert, and Tynski 2016). Ryan (2012) in a field experiment using Facebook ads found that ads that induced anger were more likely to get clicks. Politicians calling attention to violations of norms or values by their opponents can be a strategy to both get attention and solidify support (Crockett 2017). We are drawn to stories of moral outrage—e.g., mistreatment of children or the elderly, or the burning of flags. Using actual tweets from U.S. national politicians (presidential candidates and House and Senate candidates) during the 2016 election, Brady et al. (2019) find that moral anger and disgust were more likely to be spread across social networks.

In particular moral outrage leads people to want to take action to shame or punish the actors responsible for the moral transgression (Jordan et al. 2016; Thomas, McGarty, and Mavor 2009). Politicians need to mobilize supporters, and divisive rhetoric that stokes outrage is one way to achieve this (Spring, Cameron, and Cikara 2018).

Social media has changed the way in which politicians and politics elites communicate with the public (Zeitzoff 2017). Twitter, Facebook, and Instagram allow world leaders and politicians to have direct access to their constituencies (Barberá et al. 2018; Barberá and Zeitzoff 2018). Now if you're a politician you don't have to rely solely on mainstream news coverage or access to journalists. The reverse is true. Many journalists use Twitter and other social media to track down leads and generate stories (Zeitzoff 2017). So now both the media and politicians' constituents are in the same place, increasing the incentives for nasty rhetoric.

One of the consequences of social media is that it's not just politicians who can use violent and uncivil rhetoric to abuse opponents, but their supporters and online mobs can do so as well (Theocharis et al. 2016). During the 2016 U.S. presidential election, Trump's White nationalist supporters engaged in online hate campaigns particularly targeting Jewish "never-Trump" conservatives and Jewish journalists, sending them Holocaust memes and saying they "deserved the oven." The far corners of the Internet have infected mainstream political discourse with trolling and outrage-inducing memes, all while allowing politicians some amount of deniability, "I can't control what they do online" (Gold 2016).

Social media allows for a more confrontational style of politics, that lets outsiders establish more intimacy with their audiences, and get attention by picking fights, or saying inflammatory things about their opponents. The *Cleveland Plain Dealer* called out Ohio Republican Senate candidate Josh Mandel in March 2021 for doing precisely this with his tweets in the run-up to the Republican primary.

> Mandel is pretty much a nobody right now, a nobody begging for people to notice his Tweets a year ahead of the Senate primary. Just because he makes outrageous, dangerous statements doesn't mean it is news.[12]

Another tactic of nasty politics is to make allegations or circulate conspiracy theories about their opponents. Thus politicians can tap into the need for ordinary voters to hear salacious gossip about an outgroup target (Bøggild, Aarøe, and Petersen 2021). These types of allegations can be tools to distract from unfavorable news to a politician. Lewandowsky, Jetter, and Ecker (2020) finds support for this with Trump's tweets. Trump tweeted salacious allegations about the various investigations in his administration to shift focus away from himself.[13] Hacker and Pierson (2020) further argues that the right-wing populist turn of the Republican Party under Trump was a strategic choice. Trump and his supporters push misinformation and stoke grievances as a strategy to distract voters from their policies that are heavily tilted toward the wealthy in an age of high inequality. Perhaps the most cynical version of this view was presented by far-right media personality and former chief strategist to President Trump, Steve Bannon: "The Democrats don't matter. The real opposition is the media. And the way to deal with them is to flood the zone with shit" (Illing 2020).

Finally, allegations and conspiracies about the outgroup are not just meant to distract. They also serve as an important tool for ingroup politics. Conspiracism can be a coping strategy for groups who are marginalized or out of power (Uscinski and Parent 2014). It also allows politicians to coordinate the ingroup on shared grievances and a common enemy (Petersen 2020; Radnitz 2016; Yablokov 2018).

Implication 5: *Nasty politics gets more engagement and attention for a politician. The nastier the politics, the more attention it grabs.*

[12] See Quinn (2021). Mandel would come in second to J. D. Vance in the 2022 GOP primary, losing by eight percentage points.

[13] The allegation was that the Trump campaign had improper contacts with Russia as it was engaged in a hacking of the DNC and misinformation campaign. Trump's "Obamagate" theory turns this theory on its head, and instead accuses the Obama administration of a sinister cover-up. It was Obama's team, rather than the Trump campaign, that really colluded with Russia during the 2016 campaign.

2.3.2 Sometimes It Pays to Be the Bully

Before the Euromaidan, Volodymyr Parasyuk was unknown to Ukrainians. But during the protests he became a household name as one of the "centurions"—forces designed to protect the Euromaidan protesters from Yanukovych's police and counter-protesters. At one of the pivotal moments of the protests on February 21, 2014, Parasyuk issued an ultimatum to President Yanukovych from the Euromaidan stage. He said if Yanukovych didn't step down Parasyuk and his comrades would storm the presidential office. Yanukovych fled Kyiv the next day. Parasyuk capitalized on his Euromaidan fame and won a seat in the Rada as an independent candidate from Lviv. His aggressive ways followed him to the parliament. Just three days after entering office, Parasyuk nearly caused a melee in the Rada when he turned towards former members of Yanukovych's party and told them "shut up or we will kick you out (deport you from Ukraine) and your millions (in wealth) won't help you" (Bateson 2014). Parasyuk's bullying ways would continue through his five years in the Rada. He physically fought with and threatened Ukrainian police officers, prosecutors, journalists, and his fellow deputies, accusing them of corruption and being in league with Russia (Ukrainskaya Pravda 2017*b*).

Parasyuk is an extreme example. But it's helpful to think about politicians at the extreme because they provide an intuition as to what politicians in general are trying to signal with aggressive, bullying behavior. The first important thing is toughness. Politicians seek to cultivate an aura that they are tough and equipped to handle threats for the ingroup. Signaling these kinds of threats is particularly important during periods of conflict (Stenner 2005). In uncertain times like post-Euromaidan Ukraine the public seeks out dominant leaders, so signaling toughness can be an effective strategy to garner support (Laustsen and Petersen 2017; Petersen and Laustsen 2020).

Sometimes the public doesn't just want tough, they want nasty. They support politician who are willing to dehumanize their opponents (Cassese 2019). And it's not just dehumanization. A sizeable fraction of partisans take pleasure in unfortunate events happening to outgroup partisans, including their deaths (Kalmoe and Mason 2022). This partisan schadenfreude is connected to a demand for candidate cruelty—politicians who support policies that actively harm the outgroup (Webster, Glynn, and Motta 2021). Politicians can use nasty politics to garner support by channeling ingroup supporters' resentment towards the outroup (Bonikowski 2017; Hart 2020). It's a strategy of "I'll echo how much my supporters hate the outgroup, so they will love me."

Being tough and nasty is one way to signal that a politician will fight for the ingroup. But it's also a proven bargaining strategy. There's a benefit to being perceived as nasty and tough in negotiations (Kahneman and Renshon 2007;

Little and Zeitzoff 2017; Steinel et al. 2009). Cultivating a sense of nasty can signal to your supporters that you're willing to engage in ruthless tactics to protect them.

Implication 6: *Politicians use nasty politicians to signal their toughness to their supporters. Nastiness will increase during periods of heightened threat and contention.*

2.3.3 The Outsiders and the Losers

Sometimes social movements that can't gain traction through traditional political avenues will take things to the street to disrupt the status quo via contentious politics (Chenoweth and Stephan 2011; McAdam et al. 2001; Tilly 2008). These contentious tactics include strikes, boycotts, protests, but also revolution and insurrection.

Like social movements, legislators also have a contentious toolkit. Gandrud (2016) shows that legislative brawls are more likely to arise in (1) new democracies, (2) disproportionate electoral systems where the proportion of votes a party receives doesn't match the proportion of seats in a legislature, and (3) places where winners restrict the ability of the opposition to compete in the future. Opposition politicians may turn to brawls and nasty rhetoric when they are locked out of formal legislative power. Ukraine leading up to Euromaidan fit this dynamic. Elites represented by Yulia Tymoshenko and Orange Revolution supporters squared off against Yanukovych and Kuchma supporters, with each side trying to consolidate their support and kneecap the opposition when they were in power (D'Anieri 2015). Similar disruptive tactics have been used within U.S. state legislatures. In Texas in 2003, Democrats fled to New Mexico to protest redistricting. And in Oregon Republicans fled the state (to prevent quorum) in June of 2019 rather than allow an environmental bill to pass (Vasilogambros 2020).

If being civil isn't working for politicians, then incivility, name-calling, and even threats can help them to break through. It's not just marginalized groups and peripheral politicians that campaign as nasty-talking outsiders. Those without access to mainstream political resources and power can use incivility to get noticed (Bonikowski 2016). Another example of this dynamic comes from Nielsen (2017) and his exploration of why certain Islamic clerics advocate radical and violent policies (Salafi-jihadism). Nielsen provides evidence that clerics that are blocked from cushy, funded clerical positions turn towards jihad both out of frustration for their scholarly dreams being thwarted, but also as an outsider strategy to attract attention, and hence supporters and funds. While Nielsen's study of Salafi-jihadi clerics is an extreme example, it captures this insider/outsider trade-off with respect to nasty politics.

There's also good evidence that social media allows for challengers outside of traditional channels to more easily garner support. The increasing prominence of social media in politics gives more tools for outsider politicians to disrupt and attract attention through saying controversial things (Enli 2017; Vaccari and Nielsen 2013). Recent research shows that more extreme parties elicit more emotional reactions on Facebook than conventional parties (Muraoka et al. 2021).

The literature on ethnic violence and terrorism also provides clues as to how outsider elites and political entrepreneurs use violence strategically to muscle their way into the mainstream. They can engage in nasty politics strategically to polarize the electorate (Brass 1997; Fearon and Laitin 2000; Wilkinson 2006). Extremist violence can also be a way to provoke a response, or spoil a peace deal, or even tip a society into revolution (Bueno de Mesquita and Dickson 2007; Bueno de Mesquita 2010; Kydd and Walter 2006). Escalating a conflict can also be a way for one faction to costly outbid rival factions, and sideline a more moderate faction (Gagnon 2006; Vogt, Gleditsch, and Cederman 2021). More radical factions can also use factionalism itself to divide a more moderate opposition and eventually take over the group. These effects are not just limited to political violence. Blum (2020) documents how the Tea Party behaved as an insurgent faction in the Republican Party. It used a variety of tactics including harsh rhetoric towards Democrats, as well as mainstream Republicans, who they viewed as too mainstream and insufficiently conservative. Tea Party Republicans were thus willing to kill the establishment Republican Party in order to take it over.

Nasty politics is generally the province of opposition and outsiders. But there is a prominent exception. When incumbent politicians and those in power are threatened they may turn to the nasty style. This is analogous to the finding from international conflict that leaders who are facing declining electoral prospects are more likely to "gamble for resurrection" by starting diversionary conflicts (Downs and Rocke 1994; Smith 1996). Politicians that feel their support is slipping have incentives to try to shift the conversation. For instance, in February of 2016 during the Republican presidential primaries Florida Senator Marco Rubio took aim at fellow Republican nominee Donald Trump in a rally. He said that Trump had "small hands" for his height. And then further told the crowd:

> And you know what they say about guys with small hands . . . (audience laughter) You can't trust 'em! (more applause). . . . (Trump) doesn't sweat because his pores are clogged from the spray tan . . . Donald Trump isn't gonna make America great, he's gonna make America orange. (Jaffe 2016)

Rubio's abrupt campaign shift to insulting one-liners make more sense when you realize that he had been one of the favorites going into the 2016 Republican presidential primary. But by February 2016 he was lagging behind Republican front-runner Donald Trump (Nelson 2015). Ukrainian President Petro Poroshenko found himself in a similar spot ahead of the second round of the 2019 presidential election. He was badly trailing Zelensky in early April of 2019 when he posted the following on his Facebook:

> Why are the Kremlin, its agents and fugitive oligarchs (Kolomoisky) operating in this year's (Ukrainian) election? And fate has brought me into the second round to face the puppet of Kolomoisky (Zelensky)?[14]

Poroshenko was accusing Zelensky of being under the control of the oligarch Kolomoisky, and of being the Kremlin's candidate. It was a stinging accusation designed to focus negative media attention on Zelensky. But it also had a whiff of desperation. Poroshenko was in a tough spot, and trying to make up ground.

Implication 7: *Nasty politics is more likely to be used by political outsiders, candidates in the opposition, and incumbents losing power.*

2.4 What Nasty Politics Means for Democracy

The final piece to understand the puzzle of violent rhetoric is that it's a signal to voters that things are not alright, and politics should not proceed as usual. In March 2019 Alabama Republican Rep. Mo Brooks read from *Mein Kampf* on the floor of the U.S. Congress. He claimed that the Democrats and the Robert Mueller's investigation into Russian interference in the 2016 presidential election, and whether President Trump and his allies played any part in it, were part of a "Big Lie."[15] When Brooks accused Democrats and the media of using Nazi propaganda techniques to smear the president he wasn't saying: "I respectfully disagree with the other side." Brooks was comparing them to Nazis. Likewise, when deputies in the Rada set off smoke bombs or throw eggs during debate on a bill it sends a strong signal to Ukrainians that whatever

[14] Poroshenko, Petro (petroporoshenko). Facebook, March 31, 2019. https://www.facebook.com/petroporoshenko/posts/1575810249220028.

[15] The Big Lie refers to a propaganda technique of the Nazi Party and Joseph Goebbels that pushed the baseless claim that Germany's defeat in World War I was because Jews had sold out the German nation to foreigners all while profiting off the war itself. The Big Lie now refers to a general coordinated propaganda campaign by the state, political parties, or politicians that contains repeated lies, mistruths, and distortions to slander enemies and rally the ingroup (Snyder 2021).

was being debated was poised to cross a bright red line. This is exactly what Ukrainian opposition lawmakers led by Yulia Tymoshenko were doing when they set off a full-scale riot in the Rada in April 2010. The trigger for the Rada riot was a bill sponsored by President Viktor Yanukovych and his allies to extend the Russian Black Sea Naval Base lease in Crimea until 2042 in exchange for cheaper Russian gas. Opposition lawmakers shouted "No to treason!" (Marson and Boudreaux 2010). Yulia Tymoshenko said that the law would "go down as a black page in the history of Ukraine and the Rada" (Stern 2010). Likewise when far-right Member of the Knesset Bezalel Smotrich compared the birthrate of Israel's Bedouin population to a "bomb that must be defused," he was signaling to his supporters that the issue both represented an urgent threat to the country and that extreme measures were necessary (Times of Israel 2020*b*).

The danger here is for escalating rhetoric to spiral into violence. Posen (1993) refers to the "spiral of insecurity" that can happen when rival groups distrust each other. These rival groups take defensive measures to protect their own group, but these are perceived as threatening to the other side.[16] This logic is particularly true when nasty politics takes hold, and rival politicians engage in escalating behavior under the guise of protecting their group (Kaufman 2001). This can then trickle down to supporters. There's good evidence from the Trump era for this phenomenon. The election of Trump increased the aggressive, nasty, and dehumanizing rhetoric towards minorities and other perceived pro-Democratic groups among Republican elites. This led to more Republican supporters to be more willing to express and excuse xenophobic rhetoric, and also corresponded with increases in actual hate crimes (Bursztyn, Egorov, and Fiorin 2020; Edwards and Rushin 2018; Nacos, Shapiro, and Bloch-Elkon 2020).

Nasty rhetoric and brawls worsen the public's view of democracy, but they also allow combative politicians to signal to supporters that they are literally willing to fight for them (Batto and Beaulieu 2020). These legislative disruptions are an important part of the messy democratic process, and allow lawmakers to symbolically fight for and represent their supporters (Spary 2013; Whitmore 2019). Yet Whitmore (2020) shows how in Ukraine frequent disruptions and nasty rhetoric bred cynicism and distrust from the public. Politics comes to resemble professional wrestling more than a deliberative body. This cynical brand of nasty politics distracts the public, lowers the discourse, and cheapens democracy (Jamieson 1993). It also can reduce political participation. Sydnor (2019) finds that certain personality types become turned off from politics and the democratic process due to incivility. In a more extreme example, Gagnon (2006) argues that nationalist politicians in the former Yugoslavia explicitly

[16] Fearon and Laitin (1996) provide a similar spiral logic about why inter-ethnic cooperation can break down.

stoked violence and used violent nationalist rhetoric to demobilize reform-minded citizens that would have voted them out of power.

Incivility is not always a cynical strategy that is bad for democracy. Disruptions and nasty politics serve as a way to communicate to supporters that everything is not copacetic. As one U.S. left-wing journalist and supporter of Bernie Sanders told me in an interview, "incivility is neither good nor bad, and it's neither bad nor counterproductive. Incivility can be a protest against treating things that are monstrous as normal."[17] Whether politicians choose to employ the nasty style is analogous to the choice social movements make: work through official channels or disrupt (Emerson et al. 2015; Freelon, McIlwain, and Clark 2016; Hirschman 1970; McAdam 1983). Many times calls for civility and criticisms of rude behavior are maneuvers by the powerful to block and censor groups with legitimate grievances (Bennett 2011). Social media provides more avenues for groups previously excluded from political channels to disrupt the system (Tucker et al. 2017). Yet, there's a tension here. When activists use more confrontational or violent tactics, the public views them as being more extreme and reduces support for them (Simpson, Willer, and Feinberg 2018).

All of this points to the competing uses of nasty politics. Nasty politics can be a cynical ploy for attention by elites in power, or it can be a legitimate weapon of the downtrodden. Cynical politicians can play on the public's response to attention-grabbing violent rhetoric and stoke division. Over time, and with enough politicians engaging in nasty politics, this degrades democracy—the public becomes more distrustful of politicians in general and less likely to participate. It also discourages honest politicians from running for office. Who wants to run for elected office if you are going to be routinely attacked and abused by your opponents and their supporters?

For example Hall (2019) argues that honest politicians that don't want to suffer the bruising reality of running for elected office is a major cause of polarization in the U.S. He shows that the costs to holding political office in the U.S. have risen dramatically. Politicians spend more time fundraising, while their pay has stagnated, and they face the increasingly harsh glare of cable news and social media trolls. As a result, why would anyone but the most die-hard Republicans or Democrats actually run? He shows that reduced willingness of moderate candidates to run is a big reason why polarization has increased in the U.S. The same dynamic is at work with nasty politics, but instead of moderates getting crowded out, it's honest, civil politicians.

The quality of politicians has historically been a major problem in Ukraine, where the majority of my in-depth interviews and the survey of elites all

[17] Interview #US-LW-D0120.

complained about the boorish behavior and "bad culture" of Ukrainian politicians. During one of my interviews in Ukraine with a campaign strategist for Zelensky, we were discussing the role of political chat shows. At one point he stopped and looked puzzled for a second and just asked himself this blunt question, "why are there so many dumb people in the Rada?"[18] Here again, the role of the oligarchs in Ukraine can't be understated. The oligarchs control between 40%–60% of the country's wealth, most of its media, and have a track record of violence against business rivals and dogged journalists who point out their criminal connections (Abrams and Fish 2016).

The tight interconnected network of oligarchs, politicians, and organized crime make it difficult for reform-minded candidates to run for office in Ukraine, let alone succeed. But there's a more sinister effect of nasty politics on democracy. Ruling politicians can use nasty politics as a pretext to kneecap their political rivals (Grzymala-Busse 2019; Levitsky and Ziblatt 2018). Nasty rhetoric serves as both a justification, and a cover under which ruling elites erode democracy. When the other side is painted as a "grave threat to the health of the country" it becomes natural that barriers should be erected keep these groups from holding office. Politicians can also use extreme and bombastic rhetoric to distract voters' attention to more subtle policy changes or shifts that are happening while they are distracted.

However, nasty politics and incivility can be a legitimate weapon of opposition politicians and less powerful groups to ring the alarm about injustice. For instance, American feminist writer and activist Jessica Valenti summed up her feeling on the cries for decorum in politics with a two-word Facebook post she shared in June 2018: "Fuck civility."[19]

In August 2014, Ukrainian politician Oleh Lyashko confronted Oleksandr Shevchenko—a deputy from President Petro Poroshenko's Bloc—in the Rada about the plight of Ukrainian soldiers fighting in the War in Donbas. Lyashko called Shevchenko a "pot-bellied fatty" and implied that he was a coward. Shevchenko responded by punching Lyashko in the face. All this happened in front of a crowd of lawmakers, media, and spectators at the Rada (Whittaker 2014). Was Lyashko's stunt a legitimate, if crude way to draw more attention to the sacrifices of the Ukrainian troops? Or was he simply goading Shevchenko for cheap thrills and media attention? This is one of the conundrums of nasty politics for voters and for democracy. How do we distinguish between those actually fighting injustice and the cynics?

[18] Interview #Ukr-Z-D0819.

[19] The post linked to an opinion piece she wrote for *The Guardian* entitled "Trump officials don't get to eat dinner in peace—not while kids are in cages" (Valenti 2018).

The following are the four negative implications of nasty politics on democracy:

Implication 1: *It makes people more cynical of democracy and less willing to vote and participate.*

Implication 2: *Politicians in power can use nasty politics as a tool to demonize their political rivals and stay in power, eroding democracy in the process.*

Implication 3: *An increase in nasty politics leads good politicians to choose not to run and to retire, and nastier politicians take their place.*

Implication 4: *Heightened nasty politics precedes actual political violence.*

One benefit of nasty politics for democracy is the following:

Implication 5: *It provides a tactic for marginalized groups and politicians to exercise power.*

2.5 Summing up the Theory of Nasty Politics

We now have a theory and intuition for why politicians engage in nasty politics and its effects in democracy. Table 2.1 shows the theory of nasty politics focusing on its implications for how voters respond to nasty politics (demand side), the incentives for politicians to use it, and its effects on democracy. The subsequent chapters will explore these implications.

There are two additional things worth noting that we haven't discussed. First, one criticism of this theory might be that we are ascribing logic and motives to behavior that is purely expressive. People who insult, threaten, incite violence against, and attack their opponents may simply be malignant narcissists behaving as they do, rather than the product of some deep, Machiavellian strategy (*The Daily Beast* 2020). Just because politicians are being expressive, or following their id, it doesn't change the fact that they can also be strategic. Expressive and instrumental politics are not an either/or proposition. And even if we accept this expressive story, it doesn't negate the downstream impact of nasty politics on who enters and exits politics when things get ugly.

The other point I haven't touched on is the possibility that perhaps politicians don't really understand voters. Some political scientists argue that politicians hold misperceptions about who their constituents are (Broockman and

Table 2.1 **Summary of theory of nasty politics.**

Effect	*Implications*
Demand side	Insults and accusations are perceived as less threatening than higher level incitement and actual violence. Insults will be common, actual violence will be rare.
Demand side	When ingroup politicians use it, it's perceived as less threatening than when outgroup politicians use it.
Demand side	Certain personality types are more tolerant of it.
Demand side	Politicians who use it, particularly in times of threat, will be viewed as tougher.
Supply side	Gets politicians attention.
Supply side	Lets politicians signal that they are going to fight for the ingroup, particularly in times of threat.
Supply side	Used more by outsiders, opposition groups, and incumbents losing power.
On democracy	Increases cynicism and decreases participation.
On democracy	Can be used by incumbents to justify anti-democratic actions against opponents.
On democracy	More nasty politics leads good politicians to retire, and nasty ones to take their place.
On democracy	Tool for marginalized and outsiders to get attention and fight.
On democracy	Increased nastiness can spiral into actual violence.

Skovron 2018) and how much voters will tolerate nasty politics (Rosenzweig 2017). Thus there isn't really a puzzle about violent rhetoric—it's just a story of politicians overestimating how much voters actually like it. Yet there are four reasons to be skeptical that misperceptions explain the bulk of nasty rhetoric. (1) Politicians and strategists may overestimate voters' appetite for it, but that still doesn't explain the systematic variation in politicians' use of violent rhetoric (i.e., who's using it and when), or the fact that violent rhetoric still grabs attention. (2) Most politicians want to maximize their chances of staying in office, and those that survive tend to figure out strategies to do so. So any strategy that uniformly reduces the likelihood of staying in office is likely to get weeded out. (3) Nasty politics tend to be used by those in the opposition, or those who have less access to traditional political resources. Consequently politicians who use the nasty style may lose more often than those who don't. But that doesn't mean it's the case that politicians lose *because* they used violent rhetoric. The nasty style may have allowed them to become more competitive, or at least be known to voters than if they hadn't used it. (4) Finally, in subsequent chapters I show that there's not a systematic misperception between how the public views nasty rhetoric and how elites perceive the public views it.

3

From Insults to Incitement in U.S., Ukrainian, and Israeli Politics

On May 18, 2011, Oleh Lyashko approached the speaker's podium in the Rada to give a speech. Lyashko was a deputy in the opposition at the time. Adam Martynyuk, a member of the Communist Party of Ukraine, and First Deputy Chairman in the Rada, controlled the list of those allowed to speak. Martynyuk objected to Lyashko trying to speak, and told Lyashko his name was not on the approved list of speakers (UNIAN 2011). Lyashko responded by insulting Martynyuk, calling him a "Pharisee" for being a sanctimonious stickler to the rules.[1] Martynyuk took umbrage at this insult and lunged at Lyashko. Martynyuk grabbed Lyashko by the throat and tossed him over the presidium railing. Deputies from several parties broke up the fight. Later when speaking from the rostrum of the Rada, Lyashko said, "Martynyuk better explain why he grabbed me and threw me over the presidium." Martynyuk cut Lyashko's microphone, and then retorted that next time, "I will not only grab your throat, but also your other parts," indicating Lyashko's testicles (Korrespondent 2011*c*). Martynyuk later apologized for his behavior, but said he had been forced to act because of Lyashko's "impudence" and that "you all are fortunate to not hear what this deputy (Lyashko) is saying... he crosses all sorts of boundaries (of good taste)" (Korrespondent 2011*a*).

Aggressive behavior in the legislature is not solely a Ukrainian phenomenon. Mid-nineteenth century U.S. politics were even more pugilistic. In the lead up to the Civil War, sectionalism and slavery divided U.S. politics. Taunts, slanders, fights, and the occasional duel were regular features of U.S. Congressional politics. Southern politicians were particularly sensitive to perceived slights, and Northern critiques of their "peculiar institution" (Freeman 2018).

[1] This is a reference to the first-century Jewish sect who were known for their strict observance of tradition and the written Jewish law, and in common parlance means being a sanctimonious stickler to the rules.

Nasty Politics: The Logic of Insults, Threats, and Incitement. Thomas Zeitzoff, Oxford University Press.
© Oxford University Press 2023. DOI: 10.1093/oso/9780197679494.003.0003

On February 6, 1858, at two o'clock in the morning the House of Representatives were debating the Kansas Territory's pro-slavery Lecompton Constitution. Democratic Rep. Laurence M. Keitt of South Carolina claimed that Republican Rep. Galusha Grow of Pennsylvania had stepped over the line into the Democratic side. Grow ignored Keitt. Keitt then insulted Grow, calling him a "black Republican puppy" (Danielson 2013, p. 37). Grow responded by saying that he would never take orders from a "slave driver." Following the exchange of insults a melee broke out in the floor of Congress between Republican supporters of Grow and Democratic supporters of Keitt (*Congressional Globe* 1858).

It's tempting to treat these insults and fights as sideshows to policy-making, or proof that some politicians are just jerks. In fact H. L. Mencken, the famous early twentieth-century American satirist and critic, was one such elitist critic of democracy. Mencken called "the average American"—who he called *boobus Americanus*—"ignorant, righteous, credulous, ready to follow any rabble-rouser who came along and yelled at him loud enough" (Acocella 2002). But that cursory treatment ignores the fact that many of these insults and fights are not random, and don't simply play to the lowest common denominator of society. Some politicians cultivate the nasty style, while others just dabble in it. Nasty politics tend to cluster around periods of heightened elite polarization and reflect deliberate strategies by certain politicians. This chapter provides evidence from the U.S., Ukraine, and Israel that: (1) nasty politics peaks in the lead up to political conflict; (2) gets politicians more attention, and (3) lets politicians signal that they are going to fight for the ingroup, which is particularly important during periods of heightened threat.

As if it to emphasize how similar nasty politics can be in different contexts, both Keitt in the U.S. Congress and Martynyuk in the Ukrainian Rada—even though separated by 150 years and an ocean—had the exact same response when provoked. They both lunged at their rivals' throats.

3.1 Factions and Nastiness in U.S. Politics

Many of the nastier aspects of U.S. politics are rooted in the U.S.'s legacy of racism and slavery. The American Civil War (1861–1865) was a culmination of years of ratcheting tension over slavery and what role it would have in an expanding United States. The newly established Republican party, along with many Northerners, saw slavery and its expansion to western territories and new states as an affront to the idea of "free soil, free labor, free speech, free men" (Foner 1995).[2]

[2] This is the slogan of the Free Soil Party that would later form an integral part of the Republican Party.

Elites on both sides of the slavery divide increasingly viewed the other side as not simply an adversary, but a direct threat to their way of life. This hardening of partisanship was reflected in increasing harsh rhetoric and actual violence. Insults and duels coincided with increasingly strong partisan attachments that mapped onto sectional divisions, making the situation even more combustible (Kalmoe 2020). The uptick in nasty tactics included threats, physical pushing, brandishing guns and knives, and fistfights—all on the floor of Congress (Freeman 2018).

Even after the Civil War, explicit racism from party leaders and politicians from both the North and South was common. For example, President Woodrow Wilson said of the Ku Klux Klan: "The white men of the South were aroused by the mere instinct of self-preservation to rid themselves, by fair means or foul, of the intolerable burden of governments sustained by the votes of ignorant negroes and conducted in the interest of adventurers" (Wilson 1901, p. 58). This view was common for much of the post-Civil War South and North for that matter. Following the U.S. Civil Rights Movement, many of these appeals became less explicit but no less racist. For instance in 1988 then Vice President George H. W. Bush ran the famed Willie Horton ad as part of his 1988 presidential campaign. The ad linked Democratic presidential hopeful and Massachusetts Governor Michael Dukakis to Horton, a Black man and a convicted felon, who during a scheduled weekend furlough had escaped and raped a White woman and assaulted her White fiance in Maryland. While the effectiveness of the ad has been called into question, the ad is part of a larger strategy of implicit racial appeals (Sides 2016). Politicians use these implicit appeals as dog whistles—referring to "thugs" or "welfare queens" (code for Blacks) or "illegal immigrants" (code for Latinos)—to activate latent racism among White U.S. voters (Haney-López 2015; Mendelberg 2001; Stephens-Dougan 2020).

The increase in nasty politics leading up to the U.S. Civil War is an example of how nasty politics serves as a leading indicator of actual violence. Competing partisans and polarization led to a tit-for-tat of escalating rhetoric and actual violent action between two opposed parties. It's largely a group-based explanation. But there are also individual incentives for politicians to engage in nasty politics to make a name for themselves. Conflict and nasty attacks attract media attention. Perhaps no American politician better understood this than former Wisconsin Republican Senator Joseph R. McCarthy. In 1946 he defeated long-time Republican incumbent, Robert La Follette Jr. in the primary, and then won the general election. He arrived in Washington at the perfect time to latch onto concerns about the threat of communism, and in particular concerns among right-leaning Americans about the infiltration of the American Communist Party in government positions (Fried 1991).

At a February 9, 1950, speech in front of the Women's Republican Club of Wheeling, West Virginia, McCarthy made his move. He claimed, "While

I cannot take the time to name all the men in the State Department who have been named as members of the Communist Party and members of a spy ring, I have here in my hand a list of 205" (Lindsay 2011). The speech led to the formation of a Senate subcommittee—the Subcommittee on the Investigation of Loyalty of State Department Employees (Tydings Committee) to look into McCarthy's charges. McCarthy used his perch on the Tydings Committee to launch more charges of communist influence at the State Department.

McCarthy's accusations were bombshells. Here was a sitting U.S. Senator saying that the U.S. diplomatic corps was riddled with enemy spies. McCarthy also understood that the press thrived on the conflict, so the more controversial his claims the more coverage he received. Willard Edwards, the former D.C. Bureau Chief for the *Chicago Tribune* reporter, "McCarthy was a dream story. I wasn't off page one for four years" (Schrecker 1999).

McCarthy had a keen understanding of how news coverage works. Newspapers would print McCarthy's accusations in headlines, and then rebut them in the body of the story. But most ordinary individuals would only take away the headline that "McCarthy claims communist infiltration," and wouldn't bother to read that these claims were at best shaky (Bayley 1981). President Trump followed in McCarthy's footsteps by weaponizing unfounded claims to drive headlines. It's not surprising, given that Roy Cohn, McCarthy's chief counsel during much of his time in the Senate, was also a mentor to and lawyer for Trump (Packer 2019).

McCarthy eventually fell out of favor with the public and the Republican Party. Key Republicans including President Eisenhower and Vice President Nixon turned on McCarthy. Once Edward Murrow and CBS aired their famously critical segment in 1954 entitled, "A Report on Senator Joseph. R McCarthy" popular sentiment turned against McCarthy and his antics (Protess 1992).

McCarthy's politics were just as much about the style—making unfounded allegations with which his name would come to be synonymous—as substance (anti-Communism). He also tapped a deep vein of suspicion and anxiety on the American right, and particularly among those who held disdain for elites (Rogin 1967). Those who were suspicious of Ivy League elites, leftists, and cultural institutions like Hollywood found a fighter in McCarthy. Finally, McCarthy and his disciples realized that a smear is even better if you can get the press to cover it and sell it for you.

Nasty politics is an integral part of U.S. politics. How does nasty politics in the U.S. vary across time? Is there more nasty politics in the lead up to periods of heightened political conflict? Or is it at a constant background level?

To examine the variation in nasty politics in the U.S. at the national level, I created a time series measure of the salience of nasty politics using historical

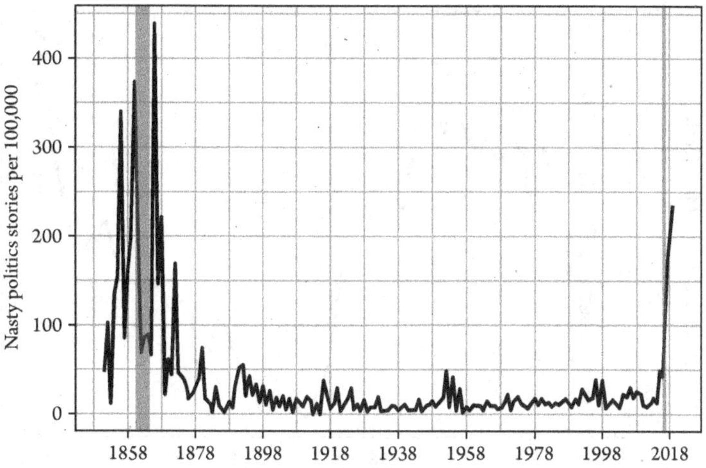

Figure 3.1 Nasty politics in the U.S. peaks around the Civil War and Trump's election (*New York Times* 1851–2019).

Note: Shaded vertical regions correspond to the U.S. Civil War (1861–1865) and the election of President Trump (2016).

newspaper coverage of stories about nasty politics.[3] While media coverage is an imperfect measure of the presence of nasty politics, there's good reason to think that media has an incentive to cover political conflict closely (Groeling 2008; Lewandowsky, Jetter, and Ecker 2020).

The findings in Figure 3.1 are stark, and correspond to the idea that nasty politics peaks in the build up to key times of intense elite polarization. The coverage of nasty politics peaked in the lead up to the Civil War. Additional mini-spikes occur during the McCarthy-era of the late 1940s–1950s, as well as stories about communist influence in the U.S. government and Democratic Party. There are also mini-spikes in stories about nasty politics in the lead up to the impeachment of President Bill Clinton in 1998–1999. Starting in 2011, and then accelerating following the election of President Trump in 2016, there is a sharp spike in the salience of nasty rhetoric.

This horseshoe pattern of high levels of nasty rhetoric leading up to and immediately following the Civil War, decreasing throughout much of the twentieth century, then increasing sharply in the twenty-first century, also corresponds

[3] I explored the *New York Times* archive for a list of political articles containing key words associated with nasty politics: "united states AND congress AND ('violent language, violent rhetoric, political insult, political smear, political duel, political brawl, OR political slander)." Others have used a similar technique of news coverage to measure salience Kiousis (2004); Mendelberg (2001); Webster (2020). The Online Appendix contains more details about how these and the other time series measures of salience of nasty politics were constructed.

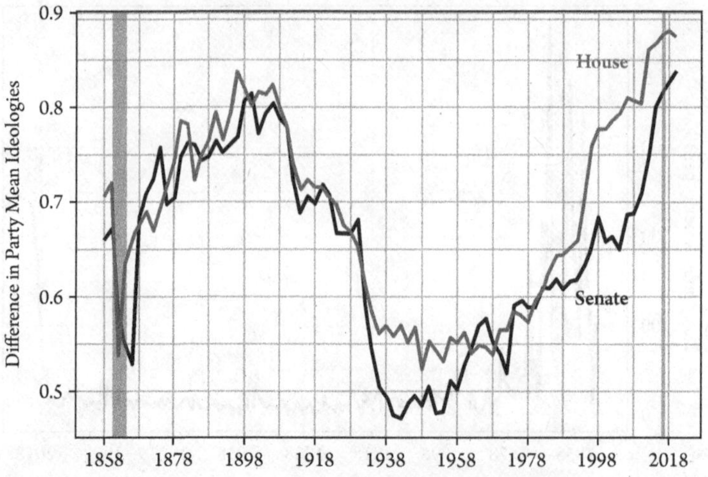

Figure 3.2 Partisan polarization in U.S. Congress reaches new heights.
Note: Difference in average ideology scores based on roll-call voting patterns (DW-Nominate) (1858–2020) between the two parties in the House (red) and Senate (blue). Shaded regions correspond to the American Civil War (1861–1865) and the election of President Trump (2016).

to shifts in elite ideological polarization in the U.S. based on roll-call voting behavior.[4] The principal left-right conflict and polarization is over economic issues (first dimension). The second dimension in DW-Nominate scores refers to relates to racial issues of equality (slavery and civil rights), and more recently cultural issues (such as abortion, immigration, and gun control). As Figure 3.2 shows, elite partisan polarization in the US, reached its nadir in the 1940s–1950s, and then over the past 30 years, reaching its post-Civil War height, and accelerating in the late 1990s–2000s. This also matches with the large increase in nasty politics picked up in the *New York Times* salience measures.

What happened to nasty politics during the Obama-Trump time period? To answer this question, I turned to a finer-grain measure of the salience of nasty politics in the media (compared to the yearly *New York Times* data in Figure 3.1). I used the same nasty politics keywords from the analysis in Figure 3.1 but searched the *Media Cloud* platform to get a monthly measure of the salience of nasty politics from January 1, 2011–October 1, 2019, across multiple newspapers.[5] The results are presented in Figure 3.3. The spike with the Trump presidency is not as abrupt as in Figure 3.1. But both time series show the same trend. Stories about nasty politics started to increase in 2014 and 2015, and then

[4] For discussion of DW-Nominate scores and data see (Lewis et al. 2020).
[5] Media Cloud is an open-source media aggregator and toolkit that tracks millions of online news stories. See https://mediacloud.org/.

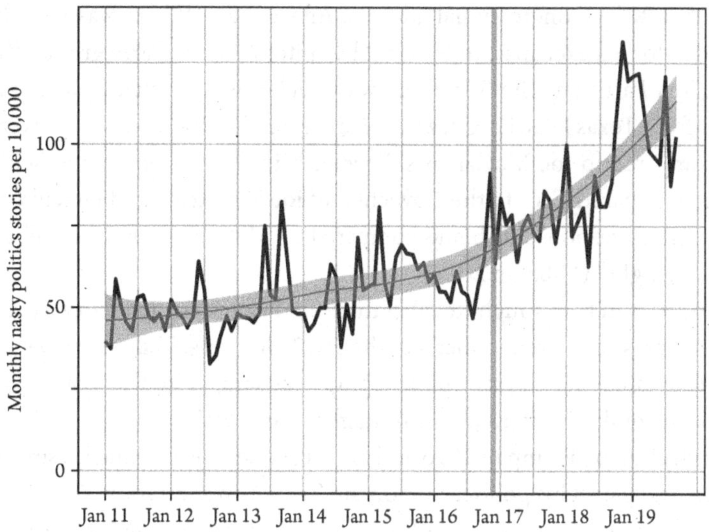

Figure 3.3 Salience of nasty politics accelerated during the Trump era. Monthly measures of salience of nasty politics (2011–October 1, 2019).

Note: Vertical shaded spike corresponds to the election of President Trump (2016). Media Cloud data. Sources include: *USA Today, Washington Post, New York Post, Wall Street Journal, Boston Globe, San Francisco Chronicle, Houston Chronicle,* and *Chicago Tribune.*

the trend accelerated following the election of Trump—more than doubling since 2011.

To make sense of this upward trend it's necessary to understand the politics of the Obama presidency and polarization—and in particular the Tea Party Movement. Bailouts of the banking industry, the Obama healthcare plan that would eventually become the Affordable Care Act, and high taxes were the stated reasons for the initial grassroots Tea Party protest that sprang up in cities across America in the spring and summer of 2009 (Madestam et al. 2013). The targets of the Tea Party were the Obama administration and their liberal policies. But Tea Party supporters also voiced their outrage at mainstream Republicans who they felt had sold out on true conservative principles—with 87% of Tea Party supporters reporting dissatisfaction with the Republican Party (Yourish et al. 2010). While ostensibly a movement about small government, researchers would show that the Tea Party was a reactionary movement steeped in socially conservative values (anti-abortion, pro-Gun, and anti-LGBT) and opposition to immigrants and other minorities (Parker and Barreto 2014).

Tea Party members in Congress showed a new willingness to engage in disruptive tactics and nasty rhetoric towards their opponents (Gervais and Morris 2018). For instance, South Carolina Republican Rep. Joe Wilson violated House decorum rules by shouting "You lie!" to President Obama during his

September 2009 Congressional address. Afterwards, Wilson was warmly congratulated for his exclamation by a local Capitol Hill Tea Party group (Kleefeld 2009). Tea Party favorite Ted Cruz was elected was elected as a Republican senator from Texas in 2012. Cruz's confrontational style and language were even been compared to Joe McCarthy's. Former Minnesota Democratic Senator Al Franken compared Cruz to the "lovechild of Joe McCarthy and Dracula" (Ehley 2016). Cruz's response to being compared to McCarthy, "maybe we're doing something right" (Gillman 2013).

Democrats in turn sought to label the Republicans as "Tea Party extremists." At a 2012 press conference ahead of the 2012 elections, Tennessee Democratic Rep. Steve Israel held a giant pink slip up that said, "Fire the Tea Party" after distributing pink slips to Republican staffers (Gray 2012).

The election of Trump in 2016 and his subsequent use of attacks, smears, and outright lies against his political opponents are not an aberration. As Gervais and Morris (2018, p. 231) argues with respect to the "coarsening of the American (political discourse)... he (Trump) is not the cause but a manifestation of it." Trump's style is not a break from the past. Rather it is a continuation of deeper polarizing trends, and the confrontational and reactionary style of the Tea Party. The use of the media to sell attacks, and make unfounded claims all have links to the McCarthy era and even the mud-slinging election of 1800 (Ferling 2004; Freeman 1999). Lest we think that duels have gone away, Texas Republican Rep. Blake Farenthold said in a radio interview in 2017 that there are several "female (Republican) senators from the Northeast"[6] who he criticized for not backing the repeal and replace of President Obama's signature healthcare bill, the Affordable Care Act. Farenthold went on to say, "if it was a guy from south Texas I might ask him to step outside and settle this Aaron Burr-style" (Schmidt 2017).

In sum, nasty politics has deep roots in American politics. It's a leading indicator of political conflict. Politicians like McCarthy, Trump, and the Tea Party members used it get attention, and signal that they are tough and willing to fight for the ingroup.

3.2 Oligarchs, Contention, and Nasty Politics in Ukraine

Since its independence in 1991 Ukrainian politics have revolved around three interrelated issues: regional divisions within Ukraine, external relations with Russia, and corruption and the influence of oligarchs (Snyder 2002). The most

[6] A loose allusion to Republican Senators Susan Collins (Maine), Shelley Moore Capito (West Virginia), and Lisa Murkowski (Alaska).

contentious periods in Ukrainian domestic politics: the Orange Revolution (2004–2005), trial and imprisonment of Yulia Tymoshenko (2010–2011), and Euromaidan (2013–2014) all have their roots in these issues. The divide between the Eastern and Southern regions and Western Ukraine captures distinct historical experience, languages spoken, and economic industries. Citizens residing in Western Ukraine are more likely to speak Ukrainian as a first language, and are also more pro-Europe in their outlook. In contrast, Eastern and Southern Ukraine has more ethnic Russians and Russian-speakers, and historically favored closer ties with Russia.[7] Eastern Ukraine is also more urban, has more factories and heavy machinery, and closer trade ties with Russia, while Western Ukraine has closer trade ties with Europe (Zhukov 2016).

Ukraine and Russia share an intertwined political and economic history. Yet this closeness has led to repeated tensions. One of the worst legislative brawls in the Ukrainian Rada occurred on May 24, 2012, over the status of Russian language in Ukraine. The bill was backed by then-President Viktor Yanukovych and his Pro-Russian Party of Regions (RFE/RL 2012).

Relations between Kyiv and Moscow are not symmetric. Russia, as the larger, stronger country, has not hesitated to flex its political muscle in Ukraine (Plokhy 2015). Russia could and did turn the gas off to Ukraine (and Europe) and damage Ukraine's economy (Balmaceda 2013). Before the 2022 invasion, and especially before the War in Donbas in 2014, Russia enjoyed cozy ties with many Ukrainian oligarchs (Carpenter 2019). Underscoring this point, President Viktor Yanukovych fled to Russia following the Euromaidan protests in 2014. Russia repeatedly used its military to threaten and coerce Ukraine. Since the Euromaidan, Russia has annexed Crimea, backed Russian separatists in Donbas, harassed and hijacked Ukrainian ships in the Sea of Azov, repeatedly massed troops on the Ukrainian border, all culminating in the 2022 invasion and war (RFE/RL 2021*a*).

Corruption and scandal play an outsized role in Ukrainian politics. In one of the most famous scandals to rock Ukraine, investigative journalist Georgiy Gongadze was kidnapped and later found decapitated outside of Kyiv in 2000. Gongadze had been investigating corruption in then President Leonid Kuchma's administration. Tapes later came out where Kuchma and his allies could be heard talking about the need to "silence" Gongadze (BBC 2019*b*). High-level corruption scandals have continued following the Orange Revolution in 2004–2005, and then the Euromaidan protests in 2013–2014. For instance, in February 2019 investigative journalists broke a story showing that members of President Petro Poroshenko's administration had fleeced the Ukrainian government out of

[7] Note this simplification, as there are many rural villages in Eastern Ukraine speak predominantly Ukrainian and identify as ethnically Ukrainian (Arel 2018). See also Pifer (2015).

close to 10 million U.S. dollars through kickbacks on defense contracts (Kossov 2019*b*). Corruption is not just an elite-level phenomenon. In a 2018 poll, more than a third of Ukrainians surveyed reported that they had been asked to a pay a bribe in the past year (Grytsenko 2018; Kupatadze 2012).

To understand the deep currents of corruption, you have to look into the role that oligarchs play in Ukraine. Oligarch is a catch-all term for the powerful business groups and individuals that control much of the Ukrainian media, economy, and provide financing for many of the political candidates and parties. Many are also politicians themselves (Pleines 2016). Like other post-Soviet states, many oligarchs in Ukraine gained their wealth during the dodgy privatization of state assets in the early 1990s (Kuzio 2008).

The corruption and influence of the oligarchs in media and politics all affect the quality of Ukrainian democracy (Levitsky and Way 2010; Way 2019). There are peaceful transitions of power and free elections, but access to power is limited to those with connections to powerful economic elites (Kuzio 2015). The real fights and competition occur outside the public view between jockeying oligarchic factions (Matuszak et al. 2012)—hence the name oligarchic democracy.

A key part of the oligarchs' power in Ukraine stems from their control over the media and their ability to use it to influence public opinion (Pleines 2016, p. 116). As one veteran political observer and pollster in Ukraine said, "Media in Ukraine is greatly affected by who owns it. More than 70% (of the Ukrainian population) receive their information from TV. And we have 5–6 main TV channels, and all are controlled by different oligarchic business interests... which they (oligarchs) use to shape the narrative favorably to them."[8] Ukraine has a rich tradition of political talk shows, informally known as "chat shows" on TV. In these chat shows, hosts and journalists bring on rival politicians to discuss policies and disagreements. Many times these shows descend into angry exchanges or even blows.

For example, in September of 2016, two rival deputies—Volodymyr Parasyuk, the ultra-nationalist prominent leader from the Euromaidan protests and a veteran who fought in the War in Donbas; and Oleksandr Vilkul, a member of the pro-Russian Opposition Bloc, and a former supporter of President Yanukovych—appeared on a chat show on the popular *112* channel. During the show Parasyuk said to Vilkul: "Choose your words very carefully. I regret that we have not deported you from here (Ukraine) and have not liquidated you." Vilkul responded to Parasyuk and said, 'It is difficult to argue with underdeveloped imbeciles (like you)." Parasyuk then called Vilkul a "Kremlin whore" (Bespalov 2016). After the on-air back-and-forth, Parasyuk confronted Vilkul in the

[8] Interview #Ukr-P-A0120.

hallway and punched him in the head, where a scuffle ensued until the two were separated. All of this happened on channel *112*, which is owned by Viktor Medvedchuk, a close friend of Vladimir Putin, and an opponent of Euromaidan (Carroll 2018).

Nasty politics plays an important role in the repertoire of Ukrainian politicians. Insults, accusations, intimidating statements incitement, and actual violence have been regular features in Ukrainian politics. What is the variation in the salience of nasty politics? Does it also peak around key time periods in Ukrainian politics like in the U.S.? Figure 3.4, presents quarterly time series data that shows variation in the salience of keywords associated with nasty politics using Ukrainian media coverage.[9]

There is quite a bit of variation in the data. But there are two key findings. Like in the U.S., the salience of nasty politics peaks before key events including the Orange Revolution (2004–2005), the trial of former Prime Minister Yulia

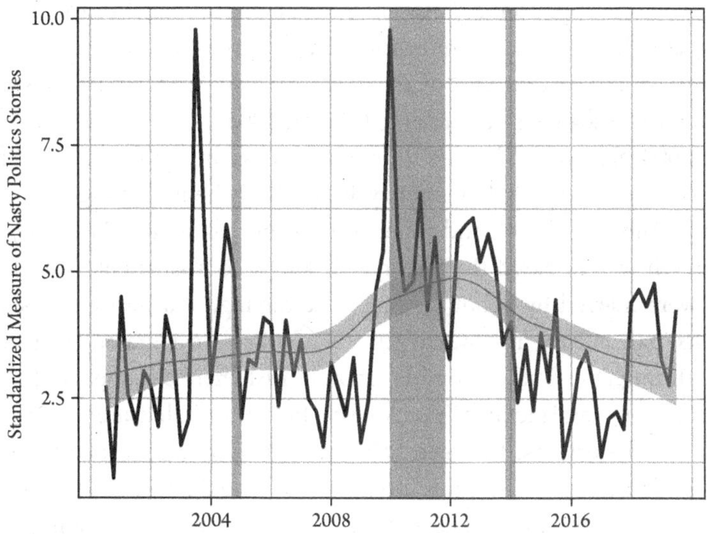

Figure 3.4 Salience of nasty politics in Ukraine peaks around key times of contention (2001–October 1, 2019).

Note: Shaded regions correspond to the Orange Revolution (2004–2005), the trial of former Prime Minister Yulia Tymoshenko (2010–2011), and the Euromaidan Revolution (2013–2014). Sources include *Ukrayinska Pravda*, *Ukr.net*, and *Korrespondent*. Y-axis is the average of the standardized number of stories containing nasty politics per 1,000 stories measured quarterly and transformed with a vertical shift so y-values are not negative.

[9] These search terms were drawn from a seed set of stories from stories about nasty politics in Ukraine. See Online Appendix for key words and disaggregated measures of nasty politics by news sources

Tymoshenko (2010–2011), and Euromaidan (2013–2014). The deeper trend in the data also shows that the salience of nasty politics in Ukraine increased from 2009–2013 following the trial, arrest, and imprisonment of former Prime Minister Yulia Tymoshenko[10] and in the lead up to the Euromaidan protests.

Below I discuss three crucial time periods in domestic Ukrainian politics: the Orange Revolution, the trial and imprisonment of Yulia Tymoshenko, and the events of Euromaidan.

3.2.1 Kuchma and the Orange Revolution (2004–2005)

The 2004 presidential election pitted incumbent Prime Minister Viktor Yanukovych of the Party of Regions—who enjoyed the support of incumbent President Kuchma and his allies, along with Russia—versus pro-Western candidate Viktor Yushchenko backed by Yulia Tymoshenko's political forces (Kuzio 2005). During the bitter campaign Yanukovych accused Yushchenko's father (who was imprisoned in Auschwitz) of being a "Nazi," and Yushchenko's wife of also having Nazi connections. Yanukovych's campaign also put up billboards in the eastern city of Donetsk that had Yushchenko dressed in a Nazi uniform and giving a Nazi salute (Haslett 2005).

The 2004 election had three rounds of voting. In the first round election held on October 31, 2004, Yanukovych and Yushchenko emerged as the top two candidates. In the second-round run-off on November 21, 2004, Viktor Yanukovych was declared the victor with 49.4% to Yushchenko's 46.7%. The results were marred by ballot stuffing, vote buying, and outright falsification of results, particularly in Yanukovych-friendly Eastern Ukraine (Wilson et al. 2005). Through the first two rounds of voting Yushchenko's supporters objected to the unfair electoral tactics of Yanukovych. Protests swelled after the fraudulent second-round elections. Between half a million to a million people gathered in Kyiv's Maidan Square to protest the results (Khokhlova 2004). Smaller, but sizable pro-Yanukovych protests were held in eastern parts of Ukraine.

Two days after the fraudulent second-round vote Yushchenko took the symbolic presidential oath in an emergency session of the Rada on November 23, 2004, to show his resolve. To further emphasize the stakes Yushchenko claimed that "Ukraine is on the threshold of a civil war" (Kyiv Post 2004). The 17 days of popular protests, along with international pressure from the United States and the European Union (McFaul 2007), as well as a Ukrainian Supreme Court

[10] See New York Times article: "Former Ukraine Premier Is Jailed for 7 Years" (Barry 2011) https://www.nytimes.com/2011/10/12/world/europe/yulia-tymoshenko-sentenced-to-seven-years-in-prison.html.

ruling, led to an election re-run, and a third round of voting on December 26, 2004. On the third vote Yushchenko emerged victorious with 52% of the vote. The popular protests, and constitutional changes that reigned in Ukraine's powerful president and tilted advantage to the Rada, are known as the Orange Revolution (the color of Yushchenko's campaign).

During this period Yanukovych and his allies ran a systematic campaign of harassment and intimidation against Yushchenko and his supporters (Kuzio 2010). These included two attempted assassinations against Yushchenko. The first, and the most famous, was the poisoning of Yushchenko in September of 2004 with dioxin. This almost killed him and badly disfigured his face. The second assassination attempt was a car bomb plot that targeted Yushchenko's headquarters. The poisoning and car bomb are widely presumed to be the work of Yanukovych's allies in the government with the help of his Russian backers (Kupchinsky 2006).

3.2.2 Trial and Imprisonment of Yulia Tymoshenko

The 2010 presidential election was a contest between Viktor Yanukovych and Yulia Tymoshenko. In the tightly contested second-round, Yanukovych won by 3% points. The campaign heightened regional divisions within Ukraine, with Tymoshenko representing a more pro-European outlook, and Yanukovych a more pro-Russian outlook (Levy 2010). The results reflected this, with Tymoshenko dominating in Western Ukraine, and Yanukovych winning handily in Southern and Eastern Ukraine.

From the outset of his presidency, Yanukovych sought to accomplish three tasks: (1) normalize relations with Russia, (2) secure a steady supply of Russian gas to Ukraine, and (3) sideline Tymoshenko. On April 21, 2010, he accomplished his first task, signing an agreement with Russia to extend the lease of the Russian Naval Fleet base in Crimean Peninsula in Ukraine for 25 years. Nationalists and supporters of the Orange Revolution viewed this as a betrayal of Ukraine. The April 27, 2010, Rada vote on the deal resembled a clash between rival soccer hooligan firms. Smoke bombs and eggs were thrown, piercing sirens were set off, and fights between supporters of Yanukovych and the opposition broke out on the floor (The Guardian 2010).

To go after Tymoshenko, Yanukovych and his allies started floating a legal case claiming that Tymoshenko had abused her office when she was prime minister and negotiated gas dealings with Russia in 2009. Tymoshenko had amassed a sizable fortune during the 1990s when she was the head of a gas and energy company, leading to her moniker the "gas princess." The gas princess nickname stuck. And it helped Yanukovych and his allies build support for the charges against Tymoshenko. The goal of the charges against Tymoshenko was to eliminate her as a political threat (Kudelia 2013).

Twisting the knife further, former president and one-time Tymoshenko ally, Viktor Yushchenko, testified against her at trial. During his testimony a supporter of Tymoshenko interrupted the proceedings and screamed that Yushchenko was a "bastard" (France 24 2010). Tymoshenko referred to the judge in her case as a "parrot," "a criminal," "a booby," and "an executioner" (Korrespondent 2011*b*). Tymoshenko was sentenced to seven years in prison. Outraged governments in Europe and the West viewed the trial and imprisonment as an authoritarian move by Yanukovych that would make political and economic integration with Europe and the West more difficult (Barry 2011).

A key part of Yanukovych's appeal was his staunch support in Eastern and Southern Ukraine. To his supporters Yanukovych was protecting them from encroaching Ukrainian nationalists. Yanukovych's critics accused him of being a hoodlum—he had been arrested as a youth twice for assault and robbery, and ran his political operation like a mafia. To his supporters he may have been a gangster, but he was their gangster (Shore 2018, pp. 29–30).

The trial and conviction of Tymoshenko was one of the most contentious times in Ukrainian politics. And the rhetoric reflects it—with some of the nastiest and hottest political rhetoric and fights. Tymoshenko's supporters regularly held mass protests in the street during the trial. To them her imprisonment made her a martyr and symbol of the corruption of the Yanukovych regime (Ioffe 2011).

This escalation was not confined to just rhetoric, but actual violence in and out of the Rada. At the beginning of this section I described the May 24, 2012, melee in the Rada over a law that would allow Russia to be used as an official language in many regions of Ukraine. This was a pivotal moment in Ukrainian politics, and one of the largest fights in the history of the Rada, with deputies cheering their side on from the balconies as punches were thrown and shirts were torn (The Economist 2012). Two days after the melee in the Rada, on the popular *Shuster Live* political chat show, two rival deputies—Vyacheslav Kyrylenko, a Tymoshenko supporter, and Vadim Kolesnichenko, a Yanukovych supporter—were called on to "investigate" what happened with the fight. Instead they ended up insulting each other and getting into a fight live on air (Korrespondent 2012*a*).

Yanukovych and the Party of Regions capitalized on the fights and rhetoric surrounding the language laws, calling it a "brutalized nationalist orgy" (Moser 2013, p. 343), and insinuating that their opponents were actual fascists. Helping Yanukovych's cause, the ultra-Ukrainian nationalist party Svoboda (Freedom)—the same party that the E.U. had referred to as openly xenophobic, racist, and anti-Semitic—made inroads in local elections. Svoboda provided a convenient bogeyman to Yanukovych and his supporters (Herszenhorn 2012).

3.2.3 Ukrainian Politics before and after the Euromaidan Revolution

From December 2013–February 2014, Kyiv's central square known as Maidan Nezalezhnosti (Independence Square) resembled an urban combat zone (Onuch 2015). Large swaths of cobble stones had been torn up, tents had been erected, and anti-Yanukovych protesters organized in quasi-military battalions were squared off against police and Ukrainian security services. Protests opposed to Yanukovych had popped up all over Ukraine starting in late November 2013. Protesters were angry at President Yanukovych's decision to spurn a European trade agreement, in favor of closer ties with Russia. They were also angry at the rampant corruption in Yanukovych's Ukraine.

Over several weeks in the cold Kyiv streets, a mix of Ukrainian nationalists, anti-corruption activists, and pro-European protesters, united in their anti-Yanukovych sentiment, engaged in pitched battles with the police. February 18–20, 2014, marked the worst violence, with close to 50 protesters killed by police snipers. In all nearly 100 people, including 17 police officers, were killed, and more than 2,000 were injured (Chivers 2014; RFE/RL 2019*a*) After the violence the European Union brokered a last-ditch deal to transfer power to the Rada and call for early elections. But shortly after the deal was signed Yanukovych fled Kyiv. A week later he surfaced in Russia and held a press conference saying: "I am eager, ready to fight for the future of Ukraine against those who are, with terror and fear, trying to rule Ukraine" (Shinkman 2014). Shortly after warrants were issued for his arrest, as well as for members of his government.

It's hard to overstate how much these three months changed Ukraine. Euromaidan would become a successful example of civil resistance (Chenoweth and Stephan 2011). The Euromaidan protests mobilized Ukrainians in numbers not seen since the Orange Revolution (Metzger and Tucker 2017; Onuch 2015). Yet the contentious events of 2013 and 2014 also broke with past mass protests in Ukraine in two important ways (Way 2019). First, the Yanukovych government was more aggressive in its willingness to use violence against protesters than past Ukrainian governments. Second, the protests had a more nationalistic bent, with far-right groups such as Right Sector (*Pravyi Sektor*) and Svoboda playing key roles, and protesters carrying banners of nationalist heroes such as Stepan Bandera.[11] Yanukovych and his supporters would use the more right-

[11] Bandera is a controversial figure in Ukrainian circles. He was a leader of the Ukrainian independence movement in the 1930s and 1940s and of the Organization of Ukrainian Nationalists (OUN), and leader of a Ukrainian militant partisan group during World War II. In much of Western Ukraine he is viewed as a hero for his struggles for Ukrainian independence against both the Soviet Union and Poland. However, Jews, ethnic Russians, and those in Eastern Ukraine tend to view him as a Nazi collaborator who supported massacre of Poles and Jews. In 2011 President Yanukovych stripped Bandera's posthumous status as a "Hero of Ukraine" following its conferral by his predecessor, Viktor Yushchenko. See Levy (2011).

wing members of the Euromaidan protests as a cudgel, referring to the protesters as fascists and Nazis. Russian media was highly critical of the protests. They played continuous clips of Right Sector and its outspoken leader, Dmitry Yarosh, whose anti-Russian rhetoric and ultra-nationalist ties made it easy for Russia to paint all of the protesters as "neo-Nazis."

By the time the presidential election in May 2014 rolled around, Ukraine was in crisis. A provisional government was in charge, and much of the Ukrainian military was in shambles following the Euromaidan revolution. Immediately following Yanukovych's exit, Russia sent special forces into the strategically important Crimean Peninsula to back local Crimean militias and "protect Crimeans" from "Ukrainian fascists." Banners went up in Sevastopol, the largest city and port on the Crimean Peninsula, that proclaimed "Sevastopol without Fascism" (Shuster 2014; Smale and Erlanger 2014). Despite international criticism, Russia put forth a sham vote in Crimea that led to its formal annexation by Russia in March of 2014.

Many in Ukraine were nervous about what would happen following the events of Euromaidan. Eastern Ukraine was a home base for Yanukovych's support, and a region with close economic and cultural ties to Russia. A large proportion of Eastern Ukrainians were anxious and skeptical about the pro-European/pro-NATO direction of Ukraine. Donbas, a region made up of the Donetsk and Luhansk oblasts and populated mostly by ethnic Russians, was a hotbed of separatist activity backed politically and militarily by Russia. In April of 2014, pro-Russian separatists occupied Ukrainian government buildings in more than 10 Eastern Ukrainian cities sparking the outbreak of the War in Donbas (Kramer 2014). The May 2014 presidential election led to Petro Poroshenko's victory in a first round election, albeit with much lower turnout in Eastern Ukraine and areas where the former Party of Regions previously enjoyed support (Kudelia 2014).

The October 2014 parliamentary elections brought several new faces into Ukrainian politics (Shevel 2015). Poroshenko's party (Petro Poroshenko's Bloc) finished second (21.8%) to center right party People's Front led by eventual Prime Minister Arseniy Yatsenyuk (22.1%). The remnants of Yanukovych's Party of Regions coalesced under the new Opposition Bloc party, which received only 9.4% of the vote. Tymoshenko's Fatherland party barely passed the 5% threhsold.

The Radical Party of Oleh Lyashko, often just referred to as the Radical Party received 7.4%. It combined Ukrainian nationalism with the old-fashioned Ukrainian pugilistic style. Lyashko and his cadre would bring their confrontational style to the Rada, being the main instigator in several feuds with deputies and numerous fights.

The far-right, ultra-nationalist parties associated with Svoboda and Right Sector didn't clear the threshold to enter parliament, but several prominent associated deputies did in single member districts. These included Dmytro Yarosh, the close-cropped leader of the ultra-nationalist Right Sector, who fought in the War in Donbas (Grytsenko and Walker 2014). In May of 2017, when news broke of a fire at a pro-Russian Opposition Bloc party offices, Yarosh responded on Facebook:

> The Opposition Bloc anti-government gangs obviously have fire safety problems.... The cleansing fire engulfed two more of their nests in Kryvyi Rih and my native Kamianske... Putin suckers in a panic.... And rightly so: Kremlin prostitutes have no place in Ukraine. God sees everything and punishes those who ignited this war.[12]

He was joined by fellow founder of the Azov Battalion militia, and notorious far-right provocateur Andriy Biletsky (Newman 2014).

In the wake of Euromaidan and the War in Donbas, several militias known as volunteer battalions were formed to fight against Russia and Russian separatists. Due to the poor readiness of the Ukrainian military, these volunteer battalions took front-line roles in the fighting at the outbreak of the conflict in 2014 (Marten and Oliker 2017). Many of the ranks of the volunteer battalions were filled with veterans from the Euromaidan protests. Yet, several volunteer battalions, particularly Right Sector and the Azov Battalion, also had large numbers of open neo-Nazis (Bellingcat 2019*b*). Many of their members had connections to the Ukrainian soccer hooligan groups known as *ultras* (Melkozerova 2016). The Russian media took great pains to paint Ukraine's volunteer battalions as filled with "little Nazis" (Akimenko 2018).

Several Ukrainian oligarchs also stepped in to finance these militias, including future Zelensky-backer Ihor Kolomoisky (Taub 2015). The militias had a two-fold benefit for the oligarchs. It provided them with positive coverage and political capital—"look at us defending Ukraine from foreign aggression." It also gave the oligarch-backers a private army that they could used to defend their business interests in Donbas and Eastern Ukraine, or be used as a muscle against rival business interests in other parts of Ukraine (Cohen 2015).

The strength of the far right in Ukraine lay not in their numbers in the Rada, but their ability to influence politics in the streets. Ukrainian authorities looked the other way, or in some cases tacitly endorsed the tactics of the far right in Ukraine. Arsen Avakov, the powerful Minister of the Internal Affairs in charge of internal security, was a prominent backer of the Azov Battalion and other volunteer battalions (Interfax Ukraine 2019).

[12] See Dniprovska Panorama (2017).

Having a large presence of experienced, armed, and motivated men gave these groups sway in protests and in other contentious actions.[13] They could also call on their broader network of veterans organizations who enjoyed cozy ties with the newly created Ministry of Veteran Affairs (as of 2018) (Bellingcat 2019*c*).

In August of 2015, far-right groups took a more direct and violent action against the government. During a debate in the Rada over a bill that would grant limited autonomy to the separatist regions in Donbas, protesters affiliated with Right Sector and Svoboda clashed with police outside of the Rada. During the clashes a protester lobbed a grenade towards the police, killing three and wounding more than a hundred (Quinn 2015).

As the War in Donbas dragged on, support for the Poroshenko administration flagged. By September 2017, only 15% of Ukrainians approved of his performance, and 67% felt the country was headed in the wrong direction, equaling anti-incumbent sentiments leading up to the Euromaidan protests. In 2019 and ahead of the presidential elections, Poroshenko was under investigation by the National Anti-Corruption Bureau (NABU). He and his allies were alleged to have run a scheme where they sold inferior smuggled Russian parts to Ukrainian defense contractors at inflated prices. This scandal was doubly bad for Poroshenko. Not only was he credibly accused of corruption, but it involved smuggling parts from the country Ukraine was at war with (Francis 2019).

In 2019, Zelensky experienced a meteoric rise to capture the presidency and control of the Rada. His ascension was just as much a protest vote against Poroshenko and the oligarchic system as it was in favor of Zelensky (Sasse 2019). Ukrainians thought that maybe the novice politician who could crack a joke could also fix this corrupt system—or at least he couldn't be worse than the others. Yet with the constants of Ukrainian politics remain: corruption, the influence of oligarchs, and the War in Donbas and tension with Russia.

As in the U.S., nasty politics in Ukraine is a leading indicator of heightened political conflict. It's also a way for politicians to grab attention, and signal that they will fight for their side. But there's some notable difference. Ukrainian politics is nastier and has much more actual violence. Its political parties are historically personality-based rather than rooted in partisan ideology like the U.S. Coupled with oligarchs pulling the strings behind the scene, this has led Ukrainians to have a very cynical view of the motives for nasty politics and politics in general.

[13] Experts estimate that several thousand Ukrainians volunteered to fight in War in Donbas (Käihkö 2018), and Azov's membership in its national militia is estimated in the "low thousands" (Miller 2019*b*).

3.3 Netanyahu and Nasty Politics in Israel

The story of modern Israeli politics is the story of Benjamin Netanyahu. In particular it's a story of how Netanyahu deployed nasty politics to become the longest-serving prime minister in Israeli history. The main political cleavages in Israel revolve around security (Schofield and Sened 2005; Tessler 2009). Security encompasses everything from willingness to negotiate with Palestinians (higher on the left than right), support for punitive responses to Palestinian violence (higher on the right than the left), support for settlements in the West Bank (higher on the right than left), and support for defining Israel as a nation-state of the Jewish people—the Nation-State Bill (higher on the right than left) (Berger 2018). Partisanship is not as sticky as in the U.S., but most Israeli voters identify as right, center, or left (Hermann et al. 2020).

The word "incitement" also holds particular significance for Israelis. Israeli Prime Minister Yitzhak Rabin was assassinated in 1995. The assassin was Yigal Amir, a right-wing, religious law student, who believed that Rabin was betraying the Jewish people by agreeing to a peace process with the Palestinians as part of the Oslo Accords (Zeveloff 2019). In the lead-up to Rabin's assassination, right-wing Likud and opposition leader, Benjamin Netanyahu, spoke at a rally in Jerusalem denouncing Rabin's peace deal. Those in the crowds held pictures of Rabin with a Nazi uniform or Arab headscarf and chanted "death to Rabin!" (AP 2016). Netanyahu and other right-wing politicians were seen as complicit in stoking violence towards Rabin. At a protest rally earlier in 1995, Netanyahu accompanied a black fake coffin that said "Rabin kills Zionism" (Freedland 2020).

Netanyahu would win a close election in 1996 to become Israeli prime minister. Following an electoral loss in 1999, he briefly left politics, but he would return in the mid-2000s, serving in Prime Minister Ariel Sharon's cabinet and resuming leadership of the Likud party. In 2009, Netanyahu capitalized on the fracture in the Israeli center and left to become prime minister for the second time. His second stint as prime minister lasted more than eleven years, and made him the longest leader in Israeli history. This led critics and admirers alike to dub him "King Bibi" (BBC 2019*a*).

How was Netanyahu able to maintain his stranglehold on Israeli politics for so long? Through a deft understanding of party politics, and his ability to exploit divides in the Israeli polity. Netanyahu used carrots and sticks to sideline any internal Likud challenge to his control over the party (Mualem 2018). He also was a skilled navigator of coalition politics, keeping a lock on religious right-wing Israeli voters and the ultra-Orthodox, while doing enough to appeal to more secular right-wing voters (Sharon 2020). Finally, Netanyahu was always quick to point out the relative security of Israelis under his leadership. Violence had ebbed in Israel since the Second Intifada in the early 2000s, and while there were periodic spikes in violence with Hamas in Gaza, for the most part Israelis, particularly Jewish Israelis, felt he was strong on security (Friedman 2019).

Rather than try to address secular-religious splits that could divide his bloc of religious and secular right-wing voters, Netanyahu and his Likud supporters attacked leftists, artists, and illegal immigrants. In 2018 there was a reading of a controversial draft bill for a "cultural loyalty law" that cut government funding for organizations and institutions not showing sufficient "loyalty" to Israel as a Jewish state. During the debate on the bill, Netanyahu's Likud ally and Minister of Culture, Miri Regev, accused opponents of the law of "voting with terrorists" (i24 News 2018).

Netanyahu was an expert at tapping into the very real resentment of many of his Mizrahi Jewish supporters.[14] They felt that the Ashkenazi Jewish elite had enjoyed too much power for far too long, and Netanyahu cultivated this view that leftist Asheknazi Jewish elite were all leftists trying to keep the Mizrahi down (Shindler 2015). It's slightly ironic, since Netanyahu himself is one of these Ashkenazi elites—he was educated in the U.S. and attended M.I.T.

The indictment in 2019 of Netanyahu on bribery and corruption charges coincided with a crisis in Israeli democracy. Israeli voters and politicians were deadlocked after three elections in less than two years (Halbfinger 2020*a*). Yet like an escape artist, Netanyahu once again emerged as prime minister by deftly striking a coalition deal with his centrist rival, Benny Gantz. Netanyahu was able to survive in office until spring of 2021, following the fourth election, when a broad coalition of anti-Netanyahu parties defeated him and his right-wing allies. This ruling coalition of parties included left, right, center, and, for the first time, an Arab-Palestinian party.

Netanyahu's skill as a politician and willingness to stoke outrage allowed him to survive repeated elections, indictments, cabinet reshuffles, and even protests during the COVID pandemic (Maor, Sulitzeanu-Kenan, and Chinitz 2020). All of these left their mark on Israeli politics. As Bassan-Nygate and Weiss (2020, p. 24) argues, Jewish Israelis have been increasingly polarized "into two hostile political camps: center-left- and right-wing supporters." And this polarization accelerated after Netanyahu assumed office for the second time in 2009.

To further see how Netanyahu changed nasty politics in Israel, I look at the salience of nasty politics in Israel using the frequency of articles on the *Ynet* news site containing nasty keywords (ynet.co.il).[15] *Ynet* is the most popular news site in Israel, and the fourth most visited website behind Facebook (Alexa 2021).

[14] Ashkenazi Jews are Jews of European origin, while Mizrahi Jews are from Arab and North African countries including Egypt, Iraq, Morocco, Tunisia, Yemen, etc.

[15] See the Online Appendix for a full list of words.

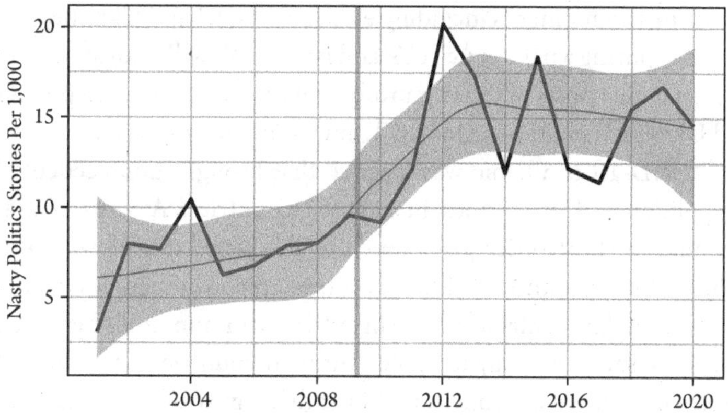

Figure 3.5 The salience of nasty politics in Israel increases following Netanyahu's becoming prime minister in 2009 (*Ynet* 2001–July 2020).
Note: Nasty politics stories per 1,000 "news" stories from ynet.co.il. Vertical shaded region correspond to Netanyhu becoming prime minister in March of 2009.

Figure 3.5 shows that the salience of nasty politics follows Netanyahu's rise, increasing by nearly three times since Netanyahu's election in 2009.

The Israeli case is important because it provides middle ground between the highly partisan polarized U.S., and the weak partisanship of Ukraine. It confirm our general findings that nasty politics increases in the lead up to heightened political contention. It also shows how nasty politics is a strategy that politicians can use to coalesce core supporters, and how the arrival of certain politicians like Netanyahu and Trump changed the level of vitriol in the political system.

3.4 Elections, Protests, COVID, and Nasty Politics

Our previous discussion showed how nasty politics peaks in the lead up to periods of heightened political contention, and provided historical evidence that it's a signal to ingroup voters that a politician will be tough and fight for them. But what it doesn't answer is who drives the uptick in nasty rhetoric? Is it mainstream politicians, who increase in their level of nastiness? Or is it outsider politicians who capitalize on the contention? And do voters reward nasty politics with increased attention?

To answer these questions we'll examine the social media posts of both key politicians and those that are more peripheral in the U.S., Ukraine, and Israel. Key politicians are party leaders who are actually govern or are leaders of the main opposition. In contrast peripheral politicians may include well-known politicians, but they have limited influence over governing, have smaller bases of support, or are leaders of more extreme factions. We'll look at how their rhetoric shifted during key moments including elections (Israel and Ukraine) and large-scale protests during a pandemic (U.S. and Israel). We will also take a closer look at the social media posts of the two prominent purveyors of nasty politics in the U.S. and Ukrainian politics—Donald Trump and Oleh Lyashko.

The COVID-19 pandemic was a shock that brought unprecedented strain on the politics and economics in affected countries. A virus that first hit China would in short order place much of the world in a state of economic and political limbo, with lock-downs, protests, record unemployment, all due to the novel, highly contagious cousin of the common cold. Yet, even if the threat was the same, the way it rippled through countries was unique. As *The Atlantic* science writer Ed Yong noted in early August of 2020, "few countries have been as severely hit as the United States, which has just 4 percent of the world's population but a quarter of its confirmed COVID-19 cases and deaths" (Yong 2020).

In contrast to the U.S., Israel was initially viewed as a COVID-19 success story. In March of 2020 it had closed its borders, shut down much of its economy and schools, and squelched the virus—all in the midst of parliamentary jockeying following the inconclusive March 2020 election. But as schools and shops reopened, the pandemic exploded. By August Israel had one of the highest case counts in the world (Kershner and Belluck 2020). Finally, Ukraine muddled along, closing down in early March of 2020, but following its reopening in June and July of 2020, the country's case count crept up. While neither as bad as the U.S. nor as much of a roller coaster as Israel, the pandemic deeply affected Ukraine both economically and politically (Kupfer and Talant 2020).

In Ukraine we focus on the period of March-July 2019. This was a decisive time. It contains the two rounds of the Ukrainian presidential election in March and April 2019, and the legislative election in July 2019 that determined whether Volodymyr Zelensky, the comedian and novice politician, would wrestle control from incumbent President Petro Poroshenko. Previous periods in which incumbents were faced with possibly losing power had been marred by violence and contention—for example, the 2004 presidential election and Orange Revolution, and the Euromaidan period. There was nothing settled about Ukraine's democracy going into the 2019 elections.

The COVID-19 pandemic, protests, and elections are important topics of study on their own. But it's not the main focus here. What we are really interested in are the heightened periods of political tension within the countries we're examining. And how these tensions in turn influence different politicians' use of nasty rhetoric. Economists like to explore what happens at the margins, because it lets them see how people behave when constraints are tightened or relaxed. Sociologists gravitate towards subcultures because like a negative in photography they shine a light on the boundaries of culture and what's socially acceptable mainstream behavior. Elections and pandemics play a similar role. When political tensions are ratcheted up, which politicians turn nasty and which don't?

We'll examine social media data from key politicians in the U.S., Ukraine, and Israel around these key periods (tweets and Facebook posts). The politicians we'll look at will be a mix of core politicians—heads of state, party leaders—and outsider politicians. This is by design to test the theory of nasty politics about whether core versus outsider politicians have different incentives to go nasty. Also we'll see if leaders like Netanyahu and Poroshenko are more likely to go nasty when faced with the prospect of losing power.

Before we dive into the analysis it's helpful to clarify how we are going to measure nasty rhetoric. Our goal is to take these politicians' social media posts and transform them into a measure of nasty rhetoric intensity for each politician. To do that we adapt the staircase model of nasty rhetoric from Chapter 1 (Figure 1.1). Each tweet or Facebook post was coded for whether it contained: (1) name-calling or insults, (2) accusations or conspiracy theories, (3) intimidating statements or veiled threats, or (4) incitement against domestic political opponents.

As Table 3.1 shows, each different kind of rhetoric corresponds to a different level of threat. Insults are the least threatening (score of 1), and incitement is the most threatening (4). To get a measure of threat intensity of a particular post we sum all the categories of the different types of nasty rhetoric included. So a social media post in which a politician called their opponent a "jerk" would receive a score of 1. But if they called their opponent a "jerk" (insult) and said they "needed to be investigated" (intimidating statement) that would be a 4 in terms of intensity (3 + 1). And finally, if they called their opponent a "jerk"

Table 3.1 **Measuring threat intensity of social media posts.**

Kind of Rhetoric	*Level of Threat*	*Definition*
Insults	1	Explicitly or implicitly name-calling or insulting opponents.
Accusations	2	Accusing the opponents of shady, criminal, or generally bad behavior. Pushing conspiracies.
Intimidating Statements	3	Intimidating, threatening, or coercing political opponents (e.g., with investigations, consequences, jail time, etc.) not in an explicitly violent manner. Veiled threats.
Incitement	4	Violent threats or encouragement of violent behavior.

(insult) who "needed to be eliminated" (incitement) that would be scored a 5 (4 + 1).[16] The intensity scale for each post or tweet spans from 0 to 10. For an individual tweet or post that contained nothing nasty, it would receive a threat intensity score of 0. The highest score would be a post that contained an insult, an accusation, an intimidating statement, and incitement (1 + 2 + 3 + 4) for a maximum value of 10.

The individual intensity scores for Facebook posts or tweets are then aggregated to daily or weekly measures to get an overall measure of how threatening the rhetoric is from different politicians around different time periods.[17] It also allows us to test whether intensity increases attention (likes, retweets, comments, emoji reactions, etc.). This measure of threat intensity from nasty politics is similar to measures of conflict intensity commonly used in international relations where news articles, reports, tweets, or other databases are coded and then aggregated to get a measure of conflict intensity (Bernauer and Böhmelt 2020; Brandt, Freeman, and Schrodt 2011; Goldstein 1992; Zeitzoff 2011).[18]

Throughout the book I will use this measure of threat intensity. But a skeptical reader might not agree with the coding of the scale or the way it's aggregated. To address this concern, I also use a coarser measure of threat—whether a post or tweet contains any insults, accusations, intimidating statements, or incitement. This binary measure of nastiness simply measures whether a post is nasty or not.

3.4.1 Protests, Pandemic, and U.S. Politics

On February 25, 2020, Trump tweeted out that the "CDC and my Administration are doing a GREAT job of handling Coronavirus. . . . So far, by the way, we have not had one death. Let's keep it that way" (Qiu and Bouchard 2020). Yet, this was wishful thinking. Cases which had initially been confined to Washington state soon spread to California and New York. Investors panicked. Over a four-day trading period in mid-March, U.S. stocks lost more than a quarter of their value—the worst losses since the Great Depression (Mazur, Dang, and Vega 2020). It was clear that the U.S. and President Trump's COVID task force, led by Vice President Mike Pence, did not have the pandemic under control. On March 13 President Trump declared a national state of emergency. By the end of April, the U.S. was approaching more than 2,700 deaths from COVID per day, particularly concentrated on the East Coast, with New York City as the

[16] Note, posts were only coded for whether they contained a particular type of rhetoric. Multiple instances of the same type of rhetoric were not double-counted. So a post with multiple insults ("jerk" and "asshole") would still only be coded a 1.

[17] I use absolute intensity rather than relative intensity because I want to differentiate between going from 1 nasty tweet a day to 2, versus 20 nasty tweets a day to 40.

[18] More information on coding and measuring threat intensity can be found in the Appendix.

epicenter. During this time period more than 90% of the U.S. population lived under some form of lockdown (BBC 2020*b*). The pandemic would recede in the worst hit areas across June, but it also spread to areas throughout the South including South Carolina, Alabama, Georgia, Florida, and Texas (IHME and Murray 2020).

Before the COVID-19 pandemic, the U.S. was already politically polarized and facing a bruising 2020 presidential election cycle. Trump had just been impeached by the House and acquitted in the Senate in February 2020. The allegations against Trump were that he had attempted to coerce Ukrainian President Volodymyr Zelensky of Ukraine into investigating Joe Biden and his son Hunter by withholding U.S. military aid to Ukraine. Several high-profile police shootings had exacerbated racial tensions, and so too did the Trump administration's pro-policing posture and antagonism towards the Black Lives Matter movement. The pandemic hit the U.S. worse than most other developed countries. By the beginning of August, the U.S. had more than a quarter of the world's COVID deaths, despite making up just 4% of the world's population. The U.S. response was plagued by a chaotic roll out of testing, and lack of coordinated federal response (Yong 2020). It also didn't help that President Trump was a fire hose of misinformation. He repeatedly lied—he said that COVID numbers were improving when they weren't, said 99% of the cases were harmless (also not true), and said that "anybody could get a test" when in fact there were widespread shortages (Paz 2020).

Democrats were vocal in their critique of the administration's response. Former Vice President Joe Biden and Democratic presidential candidate was blunt in his assessment: "The President should spend less time congratulating himself and more time doing his job."[19]

Republicans turned their criticisms on Democratic governors. In particular they homed in on New York Democratic Governor Andrew Cuomo's mishandling of the pandemic, including being slow to issue stay-at-home orders, and forcing nursing homes to accept COVID patients (Berman 2020). As Oregon Republican Representative Greg Walden said of Governor Cuomo, "horrible example of bad governance, bad leadership that not only was deadly but also unnecessarily put all of the workers at risk as well" (Republicans 2020). The critiques of Democrats weren't just elite-led. Diverse right-wing, anti-lockdown protests sprouted up across the U.S. In mid-May heavily armed protesters stormed Michigan's state house demanding that the lockdown orders be rescinded (Censky 2020). The anti-lockdown protests had the implicit

[19] Biden, Joseph (@joebiden). Twitter, April 28, 2020. https://twitter.com/joebiden/status/1255174436363268097?lang=en.

backing of President Trump who in mid-May tweeted out "REOPEN OUR COUNTRY!" (Rupar 2020).

Protests over COVID restrictions were not the only type of contention. On May 25, 2020, Derek Chauvin, a Minneapolis police officer, knelt on George Floyd's neck while Floyd was handcuffed and face down for several minutes and restrained by other officers. Floyd, a 46-year-old Black man, cried out several times that he couldn't breathe and would eventually be pronounced dead at the scene. Chauvin's killing of Floyd was caught on video, and it helped galvanize some of the largest protests in U.S. history throughout June and early July 2020. Protesters demanded an end to police brutality and racism across the country, and were linked to the larger Black Lives Matter movement. There were protests in more than 140 cities across the U.S., and the National Guard was activated in 21 states (Bryson Taylor 2021).

More than 90% of the protests were peaceful, but there were isolated incidents of looting, vandalism, and more serious violence (Chenoweth and Pressman 2020). One of the pivotal moments for the protests occurred in D.C. on June 1, 2020. Amidst large-scale, peaceful protests in Washington, D.C., the Trump administration ordered protesters in Lafayette Square to be forcibly cleared with tear gas and smoke and flash grenades. The motive behind the violent repression of protesters in D.C. was so that President Trump could pose for a picture in front of St. John's Church and burnish his law-and-order credentials (Baker et al. 2020). Trump's actions were heavily criticized by Democrats and even some former members of his administration.[20]

Republicans largely backed Trump's rhetoric and actions. They emphasized the threat posed by protesters, and in particular their favorite bogeyman, the loosely affiliated anti-fascist protesters known as Antifa. Florida Republican Rep. Matt Gaetz tweeted the following out the same day as the Trump photo-op (June 1): "Now that we clearly see Antifa as terrorists, can we hunt them down like we do those in the Middle East?" Gaetz's tweet was flagged by Twitter for "glorifying violence," and Gaetz responded, calling the warning a "badge of honor" (Lima 2020). Democratic House Speaker Nancy Pelosi expressed the sentiments of many Democrats on Twitter saying that: "Our country cries out for unification, this President is ripping it apart."[21] Fierce protests would continue in Seattle and Portland throughout much of July. In response the Trump administration sent in federal officers known as tactical teams (similar to SWAT teams) against the wishes of both cities' mayors. Federal tactical teams

[20] Former Secretary of Defense James Mattis strongly criticized Trump's actions for using the military for a photo-op. See Goldberg (2020).

[21] Pelosi, Nancy (@speakerpelosi). Twitter, June 1, 2020. https://twitter.com/speakerpelosi/status/1267648674491969536?lang=en.

used heavy-handed protest policing tactics that drew the ire of local politicians and the protesters. These tactics included crowd-control munition, and, most controversially, arresting and detaining protesters in unmarked vans (Baker and Kanno-Youngs 2020).

All of these issues—the COVID crisis and protests—were happening against the backdrop of the 2020 presidential election. In early June Biden clinched the Democratic nomination (Gambino 2020). President Trump's campaign attacks on candidate Biden could be summed up in this tweet: "Sleepy Joe Biden refuses to leave his basement 'sanctuary' and tell his Radical Left BOSSES that they are heading in the wrong direction" (Curl 2020). Biden focused on Trump's failure to contain the COVID pandemic as a larger failure of leadership.[22]

During this tumultuous period in American politics, I collected all of the tweets from eight key politicians from February 1–July 31, 2020.[23] The politicians include the main leaders of the Democratic Party: (1) House Majority Leader Nancy Pelosi, and (2) Democratic presidential candidate and former Vice President Joe Biden. Also included are the key leaders in the Republican Party: (3) President Donald Trump, and (4) Senate Majority Leader Mitch McConnell.

I also included several politicians with notable social media followings from the wings of each party. Included from the progressive and liberal wings of the Democratic Party are: (5) Vermont Independent and Democratic presidential candidate, Senator Bernie Sanders. I also included (6) New York Rep. Alexandra Ocasio-Cortez a leader in the young left progressive wing of the party. Also included are (7) conservative Senator Ted Cruz of Texas. Finally, (8) there's Rep. Matt Gaetz of Florida. Gaetz was a second-term representative who was one of President Trump's staunchest defenders in Congress. One of his most notable moments came back in February 2019. On the night before President Trump's former lawyer and fixer, Michael Cohen, was set to testify in front of Congress, Gaetz tweeted out the following threat:

> Hey @MichaelCohen212 Do your wife & father-in-law know about your girlfriends? Maybe tonight would be a good time for that chat. I wonder if she'll remain faithful when you're in prison. She's about to learn a lot. . . .[24]

[22] Biden, Joe (@joebiden). Twitter, June 17, 2020. https://twitter.com/joebiden/status/1273361303973900289?lang=en.

[23] Note if the politician had both a personal and an official Twitter account, I used the personal account, since that almost always had more followers, and contained more of the nasty rhetoric.

[24] A House ethics panel later admonished Gaetz over the tweet. See Zanona (2020).

Table 3.2 **Large variation between U.S. politicians in how often they tweet and how nasty they were on Twitter (February 1, 2020–July 31, 2020).**

Name	*# of Posts*	*Mean Intensity*	*Overall Nasty*	*Insults*	*Accuse*	*Intimidate*	*Incite*
Donald Trump (R)	5,813	1.7	50.6%	39.8%	47.0%	10.8%	1.3%
Joe Biden (D)	1,628	1.4	45.9%	33.0%	41.2%	9.2%	0%
Mitch McConnell (R)	354	0.9	32.5%	24.3%	32.5%	1.7%	0%
Nancy Pelosi (D)	719	1.1	37.3%	23.3%	36.4%	3.8%	0%
Ted Cruz (R)	2,569	1.7	56.3%	38.2%	54.2%	7.7%	0.7%
Bernie Sanders (I/D)	1,584	1.3	37.4%	35.7%	34.2%	7.6%	0%
Matt Gaetz (R)	1,727	1.8	58.8%	39.5%	55.2%	9.2%	1.2%
Alexandria Ocasio-Cortez (D)	1,256	1.6	52.0%	50%	50.0%	3.9%	0%

So how do these different U.S. politicians vary in their nastiness across the beginning of the COVID pandemic and the Black Lives Matter protests in the spring and summer of 2020? Table 3.2 shows the summary statistics. First, there's variation in how often people tweet. Trump tweeted more than 15 times as much as Mitch McConnell. There's also variation in how nasty they are. Approximately one-third of McConnell's tweets were nasty, whereas nearly 60% of Matt Gaetz's were. Across all politicians, insults and accusations were much more frequent than intimidating statements and incitement. Incitement is the rarest category, with only three politicians—Trump, Gaetz, and Cruz—using it, and none of them use it more than 1.5% of the time. Cruz, Gaetz, and Ocasio-Cortez are the three politicians who have the nastiest tweets in terms of mean threat intensity and overall percentage nasty—and all three are not key party leaders. Finally the nastiness of Trump's tweets resembles an outsider politician more than a partyleader.

Tweets that contained more threatening rhetoric like incitement or intimidation also tended to include less threatening rhetoric like insults. For instance, of the tweets that contained incitement in the U.S. sample, 62.5% also contained insults, 75.9% accusations, and 26% intimidating statements. Of the tweets that included intimidating statements, 61.8% also included insults, and 75.6% accusations.

How does the threat intensity of tweets vary around key events? These include the March 13, 2020, declaration of COVID as a national emergency, and June 1, 2020, when Trump had Lafayette Square in Washington, D.C., violently cleared of protesters during Black Lives Matter protests. Figures 3.6 and 3.7 present the time series plot for each politician.[25] Trump's weekly intensity and average intensity is many times higher than the others. But what we care about is the dynamics of nastiness—when are each politician's tweets particularly nasty and intense. If we used the same scale we wouldn't be able to see this. Democratic politicians like Sanders, Biden, and Pelosi reduced their nastiness in mid-March as the COVID pandemic spread. It's also where Biden consolidated his support and became the presumptive Democratic nominee when Sanders withdrew from the race on April 8. In contrast, Republicans like Trump, Gaetz, and Cruz all increase their intensity as the Black Lives Matter protests spread throughout the country. They all criticized the violence of the protesters and accused the

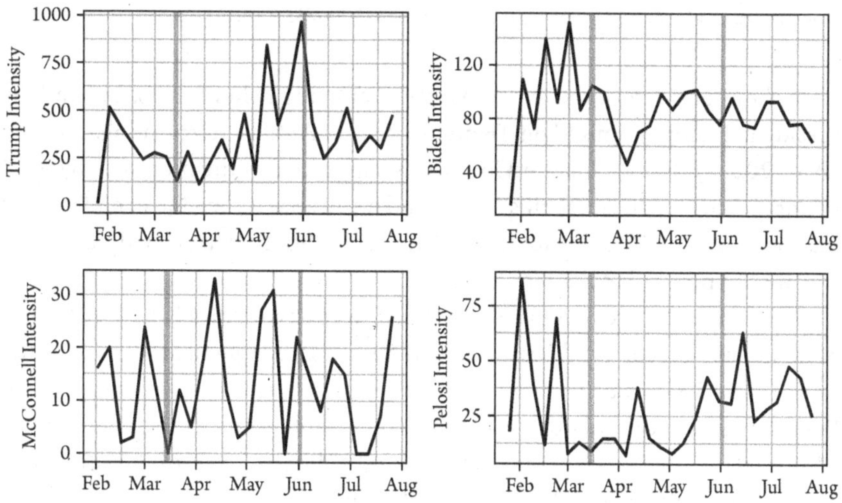

Figure 3.6 Democratic and Republican party leaders intensity of nasty tweets. Trump's peak around the D.C. Black Lives Matter protests (February 1, 2020–July 31, 2020).
Note: Trump (top left), Biden (top right), McConnell (bottom left), and Pelosi (bottom right). Graphs correspond to weekly sums of intensity of nasty tweets. Vertical shaded regions correspond to Trump's March 13 declaration of COVID as a national emergency, and June 1 when Trump had Lafayette Park violently cleared of protesters following the death of George Floyd for a photo-op.

[25] Note the y-axis scales are different for each politician.

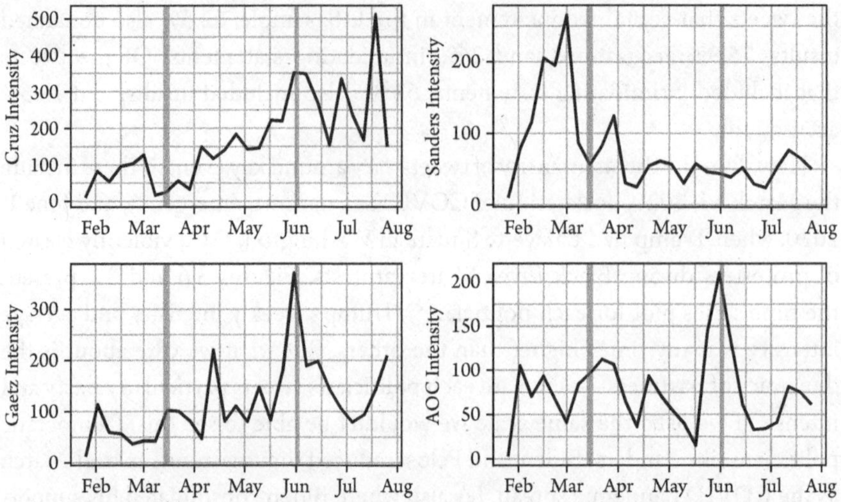

Figure 3.7 Democratic and Republican peripheral politicians and intensity of nasty tweets. Cruz, Gaetz, and AOC peak around the D.C. Black Lives Matter protests (February 1, 2020–July 31, 2020).

Note: Cruz (top left), Sanders (top right), Gaetz (bottom left), and AOC (bottom right). Graphs correspond to weekly sums of intensity of nasty tweets. Vertical shaded regions correspond to Trump's March 13 declaration of COVID as a national emergency, and June 1 when Trump had Lafayette Park violently cleared of protesters following the death of George Floyd for a photo-op.

amorphous anti-fascist movement (Antifa) of being behind them. In late May President Trump promised on Twitter to declare Antifa a terrorist organization (BBC 2020*a*). Finally, Ocasio-Cortez was supportive of the protests, saying "if you are calling for an end to this unrest, and if you are a calling for an end to all of this, but you are not calling for the end of the conditions that created the unrest, you are a hypocrite" (Michaels 2020).

One of the key predictions of the theory of nasty politics is that nasty, and more intense tweets should get more attention and engagement. But is this the case? Figure 3.8 shows that more intense and nasty tweets get more engagement. For instance, a one standard deviation increase in intensity increases the number of retweets by about 50% and favorites by 40% (Figure 3.8a). And nasty tweets overall get approximately 140% more retweets and 100% more favorites compared to non-nasty tweets (Figure 3.8b).

3.4.2 Comedians, Conflict, and Corruption in Ukraine's 2019 Elections

The period of time I focus on in Ukraine is March 1, 2019–July 31, 2019. This covers both rounds of the Ukrainian 2019 presidential elections (March 31 and April 21) and the 2019 parliamentary election (July 21). It's a period that saw Volodymyr Zelensky emerge as the main force in Ukrainian politics.

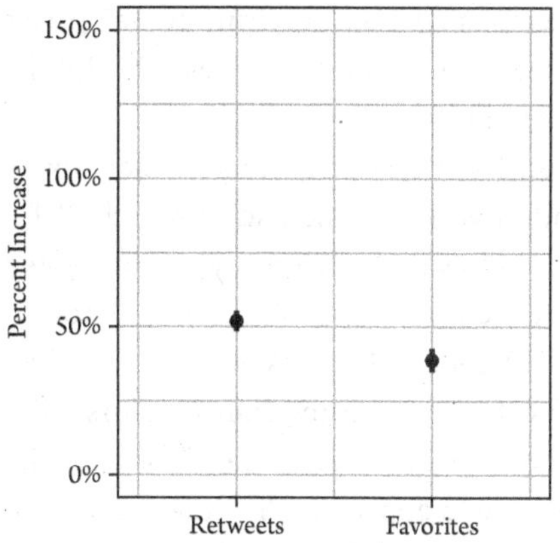

(a) Marginal effect of one standard deviation increase in intensity

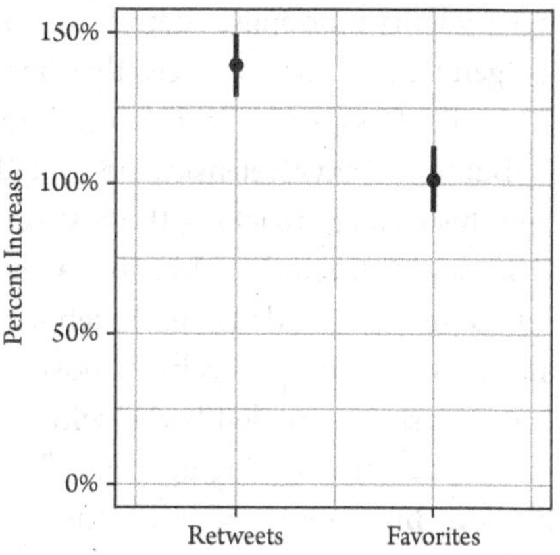

(b) Marginal effect nasty tweets (compared to non-nasty tweets)

Figure 3.8 Nastier tweets from select U.S. politicians during COVID and the Black Lives Matter protests in 2020 receive more engagement (February 1, 2020–July 31, 2020).
Note: Marginal effects with 95% confidence intervals from pooled OLS regressions on log of Retweets and log of Favorites. Plot on the left is from a regression using tweet intensity as the key independent variable. The plot on the right uses a dummy variable of whether a post was nasty or not as the key independent variable. All regressions contain fixed effects for politicians.

The 2019 presidential election pitted three main candidates against each other: incumbent Petro Poroshenko, novice politician and comedian Volodymyr Zelensky, and Yulia Tymoshenko. During the campaign Petro Poroshenko made a number of campaign promises designed to appeal to nationalists, including pushing for new language laws that would marginalize the Russian language in Ukraine, and supporting the new Ukrainian Orthodox Church–Kyiv Patriarchate in its bid for independence from the Moscow Patriarchate.[26]

Yet, Poroshenko's appeal to Ukrainian nationalism was not met with open arms by far-right supporters. On March 10, 2019, at a campaign stop in Cherkasy, Ukraine, a city 200 kilometers southeast of Kyiv, Poroshenko was almost chased off the stage when clashes erupted between police and far-right supporters of the National Corps party who were angry at corruption allegations against Poroshenko (Sorokin 2019). Later in March at a rally in Kyiv, far-right demonstrators wearing camouflage and affiliated with the far-right National Corps party fought with police and hurled toy pigs at them—the pigs were meant to represent Poroshenko's corrupt ways (Miller 2019*c*).

Tymoshenko was one of the early leaders in polls conducted in December 2018 and January 2019 (International Republican Institute 2019). She brought

[26] Poroshenko attended the formal service in Istanbul, Turkey, and said, "for us (it) is actually another act of proclaiming Ukraine's independence. . . . For Ukrainians, our own Church is a guarantee of our spiritual freedom. This is the key to social harmony." See Gall (2019).

her trademark populist rhetoric to the campaign trail, referring to gas prices as "genocide" and to charges that her rhetoric was too heated, as a hit job by "Poroshenko's corrupt mafia" (Williams and Polityuk 2019).

But Volodymyr Zelensky, the comedian, TV star, and novice politician slowly built his lead approaching the first round of voting in the end of March 2019. Zelensky distinguished himself with an offbeat campaign style. He posted self-deprecating videos on Facebook, toured with his old comedy troupe, and crowdsourced his cabinet positions (Miller 2019*a*). While Tymoshenko and Poroshenko traded barbs, with Tymoshenko accusing Poroshenko's allies in the Rada of "covering up crimes" for Poroshenko's "treasonous" behavior by blocking his impeachment, Zelensky was able to appeal to Ukrainian voters fed up with corruption and wanting someone who offered a break from traditional Ukrainian politics (RFE/RL 2019*b*). The first round reflected this dynamic. Zelensky won the first round with 30.2% of the vote, and Poroshenko finished in second with just under 16% to beat out Tymoshenko (11.7%) and advance to the second round run-off in April 2019.

The run-off in the 2019 presidential election was viewed as a showdown between competing oligarchs: incumbent President Poroshenko, known as the "Chocolate King" for his ownership in confectioneries, and worth nearly three-quarters of a billion dollars, versus the challenger Zelensky, who was backed by banking, energy, and media magnate Ihor Kolomoisky (Herszenhorn 2019). Zelensky's victory over Poroshenko also had a note of irony and revenge for Kolomoisky. It was just over four years prior that Poroshenko had fired Kolomoisky from his position as the Governor of Dnipropetrovsk in southeastern Ukraine. In 2016 the Ukrainian government accused Kolomoisky of defrauding PrivatBank—Ukraine's largest bank—of billions of dollars. Following the accusations and the Ukrainian authorities nationalization of PrivatBank, Kolomoisky fled the country (Davidzon 2015).

The campaign between Poroshenko and Zelensky was a heated, if unusual contest. Poroshenko sought to portray Zelensky as soft on Russia, inexperienced, and beholden to his oligarchic patron, Kolomoisky. Leaked recordings shortly before the April 21, 2019, second-round election showed that Kolomoisky had more influence on Zelensky's campaign than Zelensky had let on (Grytsenko 2019).

In contrast, Zelensky's campaign was a kind of anti-campaign. As one veteran Ukrainian pollster told me during the campaign, "Zelensky's best campaign strategy is when he doesn't actually answer any questions or talk about policy."[27] Zelensky was the candidate that voters could project their aspirations

[27] Interview #Ukr-P-A0219.

and frustrations with Ukrainian status quo onto—better to be a blank canvas than have defined policies.

The most surreal moment of the campaign was a televised debate at Ukraine's national Olimpiyskiy stadium—the largest stadium in Ukraine and home to the Dynamo Kyiv soccer team—on April 19, 2019 (Kyiv Post 2019). Poroshenko had been challenging Zelensky to a debate for months. Poroshenko was known as a strong debater and speaker and he believed he could easily best Zelensky. After repeatedly ducking the challenges, Zelensky posted on his Facebook page a short video. In the video Zelensky said, "I will debate. I'm speaking to Petro Poroshenko, you challenge me to debates, dreaming that I'll run away and hide. No. I am not you in 2014. I will accept the challenge." Treating the debate like a boxing match, Zelensky also stipulated that he would only debate Poroshenko in the Olimpiyskiy stadium, and that like in a prize fight, there would be a drug test and alcohol test to confirm that there were "no alcoholics or drug addicts among them, the country needs a healthy president" (UAWire 2019). Adding to the surreal stage for the debate, both Zelensky and Poroshenko took their drug and alcohol tests live on TV on April 5, 2019—both passed (Picheta and Polglase 2019). After much build up, the debate was somewhat anti-climactic. It did have its fair share of name-calling. Zelensky questioned Poroshenko's record, and during a dramatic moment in the debate he turned to Poroshenko and said, "I'm not a politician . . . I'm just an ordinary person who has come to break the system. I'm the result of your mistakes and (failed) promises." Poroshenko parried saying, "You'd (Zelensky) be a weak head of state who would be unable to defend yourself from Putin's blows" (Ivanova and Polityuk 2019). Poroshenko's efforts to try to sway opinion were not effective, as he was thoroughly drubbed in the April 21, 2019, vote. Zelensky received 73.2% to Poroshenko's 24.5%.

Zelensky sought to take advantage of the initial honeymoon approval rating he enjoyed with voters and called early parliamentary election for July 21, 2019. Zelensky's Servant of the People party won in a landslide taking 43.2% of the vote, which translated into a majority of the seats in the Rada.

Other political factions and politicians were also active in this time period. The remnants of Yanukovych's pro-Russian Party of Regions huddled under the banner of the Opposition Platform for Life and put forth Yuriy Boyko as their presidential candidate. This is the same Boyko who punched rival lawmaker Oleh Lyashko in November of 2016, when Lyashko accused Boyko of being a "Kremlin agent" (Reuters 2016). Boyko's campaign was largely premised on railing against the "ideological radicals in the Rada" (nationalists), reducing the size of the Rada, and promises to improve relations with Russia (112 Ukraine 2019). Boyko came in fourth in the first round of the March 2019 presidential elections. In the July 2019 Rada elections the Opposition Platform for Life took second place with 13.1%.

Tymoshenko's Fatherland took third with 8.2%, and President Petro Poroshenko's party was close behind at 8.1%. Reformist politician and Ukrainian musician Svyatoslav "Slava" Vakarchuk—a prominent supporter of the Orange Revolution and Euromaidan, and one of Ukraine's biggest rock stars—had teased a presidential run throughout much of 2018 and in early 2019 eventually declined to run. But his Voice (*Holos*) party did enter the Rada with 5.80%. Voice's platform emphasized anti-corruption and a liberal, pro-European orientation (Talant 2019).

Oleh Lyashko's Radical Party failed to clear the minimum electoral threshold of 5%. Before the election Lyashko had tried to drum up support for his party by sponsoring a controversial bill ahead of the July elections which would require sex offenders to be forcibly chemically castrated (Carroll 2019). In the end his party only received 4% of the vote.

Under the leadership of Oleh Tyahnybok a joint slate of far-right candidates from Dmitriy Yarosh, Svoboda, Right Sector, and the National Corps entered the July 2019 elections. Tyahnybok regularly referred to his Svoboda party as the worst fears of the "Russian-Jewish mafia" (who he claimed really control Ukraine), and called Jews "kikes" (JTA 2013). The far-right political parties were more focused on street politics—protests, or disrupting Petro Poroshenko's events—than traditional politics (Weir 2019). The 2019 Rada election was a low-point for the far right in Ukrainian politics. They only won 2.15% of the vote, and failed to enter the Rada. But the far-right still enjoyed a cozy relationship with law enforcement and veterans' organizations within Ukraine (Bellingcat 2019*b*).

How do these different Ukrainian politicians vary in their nastiness across the 2019 election period? Table 3.3 shows the summary statistics. First, there's variation in how often they post on Facebook. Poroshenko and Lyashko are prolific posters, both posting more than six times as much as Zelensky. There's also considerable variation in the level of nastiness. For instance, only one-quarter of Vakarchuk's—the pro-European reformer—posts are nasty. In contrast, more than 80% of far-right Tyahnybok's posts are nasty. Across all politicians, insults and accusations were more frequent than intimidating statements and incitement. But compared to the U.S. politicians, the prevalence of intimidating statements and incitement is also much more common. All of the politicians, save for Tymoshenko and Boyko engage in incitement. The mean threat intensity of posts from mainstream politicians like Zelensky (1.8) and Tymoshenko (2.4) are as high or higher than Matt Gaetz (1.8), the U.S. politician in the sample with the most threatening tweets on average. And then there are more peripheral politicians like Lyashko (2.6), Boyko (3.3), and Tyahnybok (4.2) who are much more threatening in their posts. All of this confirms the general idea, that nasty

Table 3.3 **Large variation between politicians in nasty posts on Facebook during the 2019 Ukraine elections (March 1, 2019–July 31, 2019).**

Name	*# of Posts*	*Mean Intensity*	*Overall Nasty*	*Insults*	*Accuse*	*Intimidate*	*Incite*
Volodymyr Zelensky	136	1.8	40.4%	21.3%	39.0%	25.0%	2.2%
Petro Poroshenko	866	1.4	31.4%	18.1%	24.9%	23.8%	0.7%
Yulia Tymoshenko	273	2.4	57.1%	25.6%	53.1%	35.2%	0%
Yuriy Boyko	155	3.3	78.7%	58.1%	71.6%	40.7%	0%
Svyatoslav Vakarchuk	235	1.1	26.4%	14.9%	20.0%	16.2%	0.9%
Oleh Lyashko	793	2.6	55.6%	39.3%	50.0%	32.6%	4.8%
Oleh Tyahnybok	199	4.2	80.9%	70.0%	74.9%	57.3%	7.6%

politics is indeed nastier in Ukraine. While incitement is still rare, it's more common in Ukraine than in the U.S.

As in the U.S., Facebook posts by Ukrainian politicians that contain more threatening rhetoric like incitement or intimidation also tend to include less threatening rhetoric like insults. More than 95% of instances of incitement also contain insults, accusations, and intimidating statements. And 84% of intimidating statements also include accusations, and 69% also contain insults.

How does the threat intensity of Facebook posts vary around key events like the two rounds of presidential voting (March 31 and April 21, 2019) and the July 2019 Rada parliamentary elections? Figures 3.9 and 3.10 show the results. For all of the Ukrainian politicians, the threat intensity of their Facebook posts peak around the various elections. Poroshenko's intensity peaks in between the first and second round, and Boyko before the first round of presidential election. For instance on April 19, just days before the second round of the presidential election, Poroshenko posted a message on Facebook that was directly addressed to Zelensky. Poroshenko accused Zelensky of treason by coordinating with the "Russian fifth column" (Yanukovych's old supporters) and "President of the Russian Federation" (Putin) to stoke violence in Donbas

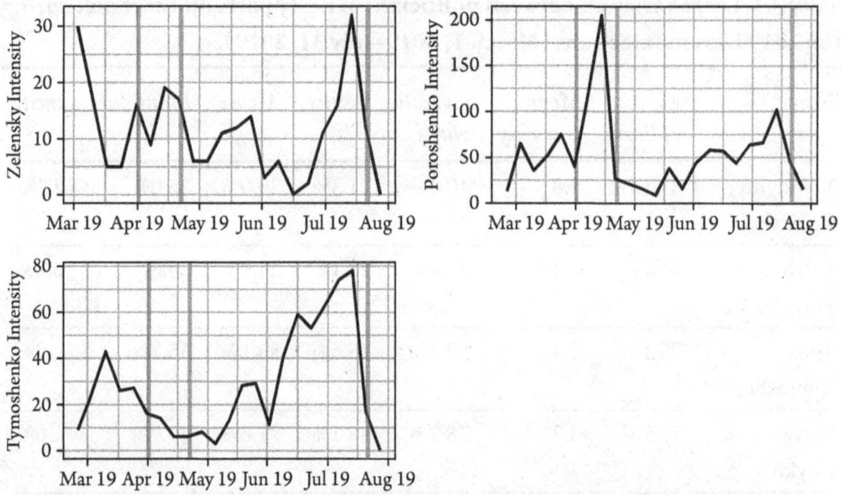

Figure 3.9 Key Ukainian politicians intensity of nasty tweets peak around elections (March 1, 2019–July 31, 2019).

Note: Zelensky (top left), Poroshenko (top right), and Tymoshenko (bottom left). Graphs correspond to weekly sums of intensity of nasty tweets. Vertical shaded regions correspond to the March 31 first round of presidential voting, April 21 second round of presidential voting, and July 21 Rada parliamentary elections.

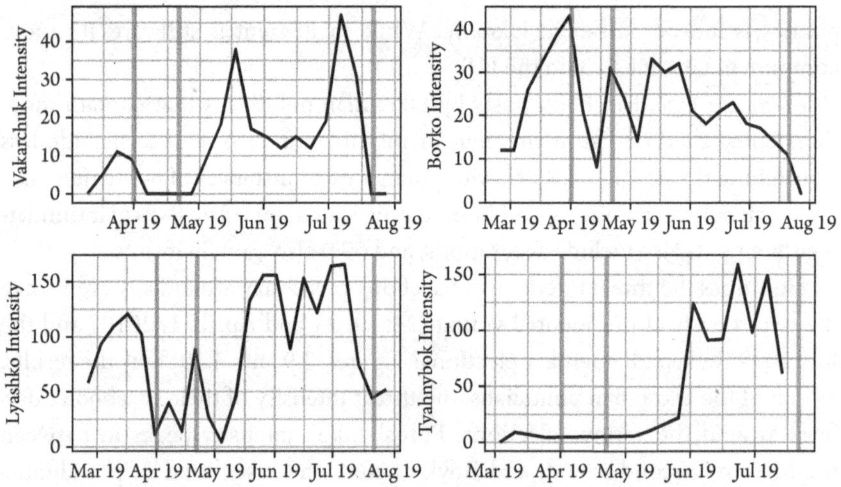

Figure 3.10 Peripheral Ukrainian politicians intensity of nasty tweets around the 2019 elections (March 1, 2019–July 31, 2019).

Note: Vakarchuk (top left), Boyko (top right), Lyashk (bottom left) and Tyahnybok (bottom right). Graphs correspond to weekly sums of intensity of nasty tweets. Vertical shaded regions correspond to the March 31 first round of presidential voting, April 21 second round of presidential voting, and July 21 Rada parliamentary elections.

and sabotage peace efforts and finished his post by saying, "The country is under threat! ... We have to save Ukraine!"[28] For Zelensky, Tymoshenko, Vakarchuk, Lyashko, and Tyahnybok their peak intensity is around the July Rada elections. For example, Zelensky in a July 18 post addressed to then Chairman of the Rada, Andriy Parubiy, a Poroshenko ally. Zelensky accused Parubiy and other Poroshenko allies of turning a blind eye to corruption "of indifference, inaction and failure. You all had a chance, but you've wasted it. Shame, gentlemen! We will change it on July 21 (election day)."[29] And in a July 19 post Lyashko uploaded a video ad that spoofed the old Soviet-era horror film *Viy* (Spirit of Evil). In the video Lyashko is an Orthodox priest who battles and cleanses a demonic-faced Zelensky in a church.[30]

Do nasty and more intense social media posts from Ukrainian politicians get more engagement like in the U.S.? Figure 3.11 shows they do. A one standard deviation increase in intensity increases the number of shares of posts by about 40%, and the number of angry reactions by 73% (angry emoji face) (Figure 3.11a). Nasty posts also receive approximately 80% more shares and

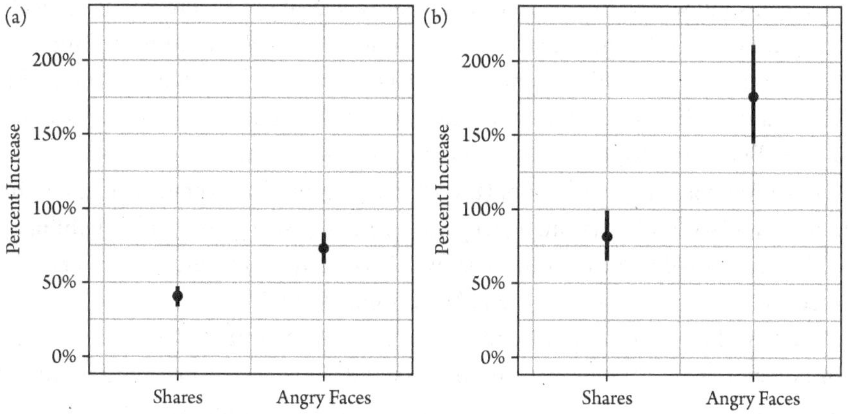

Figure 3.11 Nastier Facebook posts by select Ukrainian politicians during the 2019 elections receive more attention (March 1, 2019–July 31, 2019). (a) Marginal effect of one standard deviation increase in intensity. (b) Marginal effect nasty posts (compared to non-nasty posts).

Note: Marginal effects with 95% confidence intervals from pooled OLS regressions on log of Shares and log of Angry Faces. Plot on the left is from a regression using post intensity as the key independent variable. The plot on the right uses a dummy variable of whether a post was nasty or not as the key independent variable. All regressions contain fixed effects for politicians.

[28] Poroshenko, Petro (petroporoshenko). Facebook, April, 19, 2019. https://www.facebook.com/petroporoshenko/posts/272249033654861.

[29] Zelensky, Volodymyr (zelenskiy95). Facebook, July 18, 2019. https://www.facebook.com/zelenskiy95/posts/2291678517749178.

[30] Lyashko, Oleh (O.Liashko). Facebook, July 19, 2019. https://www.facebook.com/O.Liashko/posts/2283932261675358.

175% more angry faces than non-nasty posts (Figure 3.11b).[31] More intensely threatening posts, and nasty posts in general, get more reactions and engagement in Ukraine.

3.4.3 Corruption, COVID, and King Bibi

In late February of 2020, Israel's democracy was in crisis. Israel was on the cusp of holding its third national election in less than a year—previous elections had been held in April and September of 2019. Yet none of these previous elections had managed to break the stalemate. Incumbent Prime Minister Benjamin (Bibi) Netanyahu, the longest-serving prime minister in Israeli history, and his ruling Likud party were locked in stalemate with the centrist Blue and White alliance, led by former Israel Defence Forces (IDF) Chief of Staff Benny Gantz. Gantz had formed an alliance with other centrist parties including media personality Yair Lapid (Yesh Atid) and former IDF Chief of Staff Moshe "Bogie" Ya'alon. While Likud had won narrow advantages in the previous two elections, it had been unable to form a majority government.

Netanyahu was willing to do what it took to stay in power. From cutting deals with ultra-Orthodox members of his coalition, to his flirtation with annexing large chunks of the West Bank, Netanyahu was laser focused on managing his coalition. Avigdor Liberman, leader of the staunch right-wing and secular Yisrael Beitanu party, and a one-time Netanyahu ally turned rival, said of him, "(Netanyahu is) like Juan Perón, (the former Argentine autocratic leader) without values, without anything, except the desire to stay in power" (Halbfinger 2020*b*). This willingness to do whatever it takes to hold onto power, and his success in doing so, was what made Netanyahu "King Bibi."

Netanyahu's need to hold onto power also stemmed from self preservation. In November of 2019 he became the first sitting Israeli prime minister to be indicted while in office. The case against Netanyahu stretched back to 2016, with the most serious charges being that he gave favorable regulatory decisions to telecommunications companies worth hundreds of millions of dollars in exchange for positive news coverage of him (Estrin 2020). Netanyahu hoped to use the prime minister's office as a shield from the investigation, knowing that if he lost power, the probability of his imprisonment would increase. In addition to calling the cases "fraudulent" and built on lies, Netanyahu accused the media and law enforcement of engaging in an "attempted coup" (Halbfinger 2019).

Netanyahu's chief rival, Benny Gantz, was a former head of the Israeli Defence Forces (IDF). Ahead of the March 2020 election, Gantz painted Netanyahu as a

[31] Facebook also has many other reactions for people to respond to posts. In the Online Appendix, I show that more intense posts also receive significantly more likes, more loves, wow face emojis, haha face emojis, and more sad faces (all $p < 0.01$).

corrupt monarch seeking to avoid justice. Netanyahu stoked anti-Arab sentiment and tried to tie Gantz and his Blue and White party allies to "dangerous Arab parties" that represent Arab and Palestinian citizens of Israel (Times of Israel 2019). But following the March 2020 election neither Gantz's Blue and White nor Netanyahu's Likud emerged clearly victorious. The anti-Bibi bloc had grown, and Gantz appeared to be engaging in negotiations with several factions to form a large enough coalition to become prime minister (Weiss 2020). Yet, grumblings within Gantz's camp about possibly relying on the Arab Joint List party, backed by many leftists and Palestinian Israelis, caused these talks to slow down.

Then COVID-19 hit Israel, and by the end of March 2020 Israel was in stringent lockdown, and a new government still hadn't formed. In a series of controversial moves, Netanyahu and his Likud allies shuttered the courts and the Knesset under the pretext of health and safety. Critics charged that this was simply Netanyahu using the pandemic to delay his trial and cling to power (Horovitz 2020).

At the end of March 2020 Israeli politics took a shocking twist. Gantz was elected the Speaker of the Knesset with the backing of Netanyahu and his supporters (Holmes 2020). Gantz decided to break with half of his Blue and White coalition and form a unity government with Netanyahu who he would rotate with as prime minister—Netanyahu for the first eighteen months and then Gantz (Sachs and Huggard 2020). To say this was unexpected is an understatement. Gantz's whole political existence and support stemmed from being the anti-Bibi candidate, and as the one political force who could unite the opposition and legitimately challenge Netanyahu. By forming a unity government with Gantz, Netanyahu was able to stay on as prime minister and divide the opposition. A former ally of Gantz, Yair Lapid, referred to Gantz's decision to form a unity government with Netanyahu as a "betrayal," and even signaled he would support Netanyahu over Gantz as prime minister (Oster 2020).

Netanyahu appeared to be riding high. His grip on Israeli politics remained solid into April, and Israel was lauded as a COVID success story. The harsh early lockdown with closing of schools and the economy had crushed the virus, and Netanyahu's approval ratings reflected an appreciative public. In May of 2020 his approval ratings stood at 74% (Washington Post 2020). Yet following the opening of schools and businesses the virus roared back. By July Israel's COVID case count was as high as some of the worst-affected countries in Europe (Haaretz 2020*b*). The response to the renewed outbreak was chaotic. As infections reached 2,000 per day, Netanyahu flirted with possible annexation of the West Bank. Upset with the economic conditions, the government response, and Netanyahu himself, Israelis began demonstrating nightly outside of his Jerusalem residence and spread across the rest of the country in July. Netanyahu said the protests were trying to "drag the country into anarchy, violence, vandalism"

(Goldenberg 2020). Moreover, the honeymoon period of the Gantz-Netanyahu coalition deal was fraying, as Netanyahu signaled he might call early elections before Gantz could ever assume the role of prime minister, a break from their coalition deal (Wootliff 2020).

It's against this backdrop from February 1–July 31, 2020—elections, political crises, pandemic, and protests—that we explore how different Israeli politicians employed nasty rhetoric via Twitter. Tweets were collected from this 182-day time period of eight key politicians and Members of the Knesset (MKs) during this crisis. These included incumbent (1) Benjamin Netanyahu and his chief centrist rival (2) Benny Gantz. Included in this dataset is Gantz's former centrist ally turned rival, (3) Yair Lapid, who called Gantz's move to join Netanyahu in a coalition government "the worst act of fraud in the history of this country" (i24 News 2020).

Also included are MK and former Minister of Defense, (4) Naftali Bennett. Bennett led the Yamina alliance of right-wing and far-right parties in the Knesset, and would eventually succeed Netanyahu as prime minister in June 2021. He's a religious Zionist and staunch supporter of settler causes. Bennett was also a successful software entrepreneur and one-time Netanyahu ally. Yet throughout the summer of 2020 Bennett moved into the opposition. He used Netanyahu's stumbling response to the COVID crisis to cast himself as "right's anti-Netanyahu" and challenge him to be the next prime minister (Rettig Gur 2020).

(5) Avigdor Liberman is also included among the politicians. Liberman was a nightclub bouncer and manager while a student at the Hebrew University of Jerusalem. He's a staunch nationalist, right-wing politician who was once a close ally of Netanyahu. Liberman is also known for his controversial statements and policies, including advocating for a so-called "loyalty law" that he pushed in 2009. The proposed law would strip Arab and Palestinians of their Israeli citizenship if they refused to swear loyalty to a Jewish state (Reuters 2009). Liberman represented the interests of right-wing secular Jewish Israelis of Russian background and he broke with Netanyahu and his coalition in 2018. Part of this schism stemmed from Liberman's opposition to a ceasefire from the 2018 Gaza conflict. But at a deeper level Liberman wanted to push a more secular agenda, that was anathema to the ultra-Orthodox members of Netanyahu's coalition.

The lone leftist on this list is (6) Ayman Odeh, an Arab Palestinian MK and leader of the left-leaning, Arab Palestinian Joint List alliance. Under Odeh, the Joint List made huge gains, becoming the third largest party in the Knesset in the March 2020 elections. Odeh's charisma and ability to connect with both Arab Palestinians and also disaffected leftist Jewish Israelis made him an important voice (Kinglsey 2020).

The final two politicians in the dataset are two prominent right-wing firebrands: (7) Miri Regev, an MK with Likud, and (8) Bezalel Smotrich, party leader of the far-right, religious Zionist Nation Union. Regev was the Minister of Culture until May 2020, where she declared war on Israeli leftists and artist, who she deemed insufficiently loyal. Regev also is notable for famously referring to African migrants to Israel as a "cancer in the body," and in 2010 telling Palestinian Israeli MK Hanan Zoabi "Go to Gaza, you traitor!" (Margalit 2016). As both a religious Zionist and one of the most extreme right members of the Knesset Smotrich has made his career out of stirring up outrage. Some examples of this behavior include advocating that Israel become a fully theocratic state (Tress 2019), and saying he didn't like to be around Arabs in general because he considers them "enemies" (Douek 2016). Smotrich has stated his support for segregation in Israeli hospital wards between Arab and Jewish patients saying: "It's natural that my wife wouldn't want to lie down (in a bed) next to a woman who just gave birth to a(n Arab) baby who might want to murder her baby twenty years from now" (O'Grady 2016).

Table 3.4 shows the summary statistics for the Israeli politicians on Twitter. There's wide variation in how often they tweeted and how nasty they get. Bennett and Smotrich tweeted more than six times as often as Liberman and Regev. The proportion of Odeh's and Liberman's Twitter feeds that are nasty are more than two times that of Bennett's and Gantz's feeds, and nearly two times as nasty as Netanyahu's. This aligns with the findings from the U.S. and Ukraine—on average more peripheral politicians are more likely to use nasty rhetoric.

The average threat intensity of tweets also varies. The average tweet from Odeh and Liberman are nearly three times as threatening as Bennett's or Gantz's tweets. As in the U.S. and Ukraine, insults and accusations are much more common than intimidating statements, and incitement is quite rare. More threatening type of tweets also contain lower level insults and accusations. 65% of tweets containing incitement in Israel, also contain insults, 45.7% accusations, and 60% intimidating statements. For tweets that contain intimidating statements, 58.5% also contain insults and 62.5% contain accusations.

How does the threat intensity of tweets vary around key events like the lead up to Israel's third election on March 2, the surprise announcement of the Gantz-Netanyahu coalition on April 20, and the beginning of the anti-Netanyahu protests on July 7? Figure 3.12 shows the time series plots of key politicians. Approaching the pivotal third election, Gantz's and Netanyahu's intensity peaks right before the election, as does Bennett's. It's not surprising: the third election was incredibly contentious and Netanyahu was fighting for his political and legal future. During this time period, Netanyahu posted a series of tweets that highlighted a recording of one of Gantz's aides saying that Gantz "was a danger to the people of Israel" (Haaretz 2020*a*). Also of note is Lapid's spike in nastiness right after the surprise Gantz-Netanyahu deal in April. Lapid and Gantz had been political allies in their Blue White alliance with the stated goal of teaming up to

Table 3.4 **Large variation between Israeli politicians in how often they tweet and how nasty they were on Twitter (February 1, 2020–July 31, 2020).**

Name	*# of Posts*	*Mean Intensity*	*Overall Nasty*	*Insults*	*Accuse*	*Intimidate*	*Incite*
Benjamin Netanyahu	995	1.1	37.9%	29.4%	29.2%	4.8%	0.6%
Benny Gantz	724	0.7	26.9%	21.1%	16.0%	6.5%	0.4%
Yair Lapid	874	1.7	70.7%	59.1%	44.9%	7.7%	0.1%
Naftali Bennett	1,028	0.7	26.5%	22.8%	15.4%	3.3%	1.0%
Avigdor Liberman	167	2.0	62.9%	52.7%	52.1%	13.8%	0.6%
Ayman Odeh	288	1.9	67.5%	44.4%	37.8%	23.4%	0.4%
Miri Regev	172	1.1	47.1%	37.8%	23.3%	6.4%	1.2%
Bezalel Smotrich	1,086	1.5	55.8%	42.2%	33.8%	11.9%	1.2%

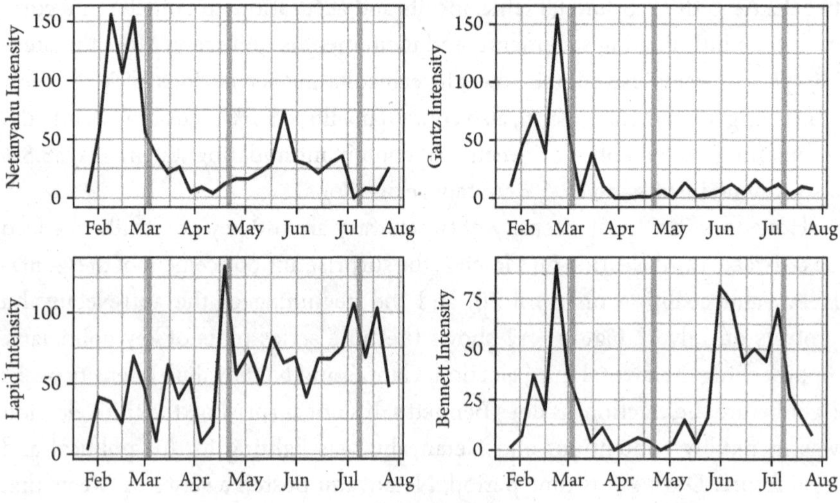

Figure 3.12 Key Israeli politicians and intensity of nasty tweets. Netanyahu's, Gantz's, and Bennett's intensity peaks around the election (February 1, 2020–July 31, 2020).

Note: Netanyahu (top left), Gantz (top right), Lapid (bottom left), and Bennett (bottom right). Graphs correspond to weekly sums of intensity of nasty tweets. Vertical shaded regions correspond to Israel's third election March 2, the April 20 announcement of the Gantz-Netanyahu coalition, and the beginning of the anti-Netanyahu protests on July 7.

defeat Netanyahu. But Gantz spurned that alliance when he struck a surprise deal to go into a coalition with Netaynahu. Lapid's Twitter feed reflected his sense of betrayal. On April 21 he tweeted out:

> I want to open with an apology. I apologize to anyone who I convinced to vote for Gantz and Blue and White. I could not believe someone would steal your vote (like Gantz) and give it to Bibi. You voted for people who promised to your children that they will never sit under a prime minister with indictments (like Netanyahu). Quite the opposite happened. There has never been a fraud like this in the country's history.[32]

Figure 3.13 shows the intensity of more peripheral politicians. Liberman, the staunch right-wing politician, harshly criticized the Gantz-Netanyahu coalition government and his intensity peaks following its announcement. Far-right MK Smotrich follows a different pattern of intensity (bottom left). The intensity of his tweets peak around the beginning of the anti-Netanyahu protests. Smotrich

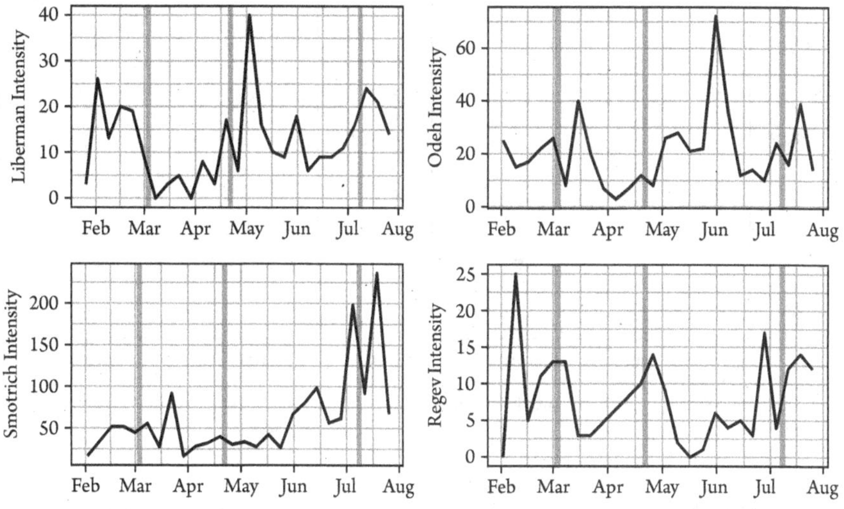

Figure 3.13 Peripheral Israeli politicians and intensity of nasty tweets (February 1, 2020–July 31, 2020).

Note: Liberman (top left), Odeh (top right), Smotrich (bottom left), and Regev (bottom right). Graphs correspond to weekly sums of intensity of nasty tweets. Vertical shaded regions correspond to Israel's third election March 2, the April 20 announcement of the Gantz-Netanyahu coalition, and the beginning of the anti-Netanyahu protests on July 7.

[32] Lapid, Yair (@yairlapid). Twitter, April 21, 2020. https://twitter.com/yairlapid/status/1252653761346129920.

took great pleasure in pointing out the perceived double standard of the media and police response to the left-leaning, anti-Netanyahu protests, compared to the police response to right-wing or religious Haredi Jews. In a series of tweets on July 17 and 18 he accused the media of being "leftist and biased," and sarcastically congratulated the police on showing great restraint towards the "left-wing anarchist media darling" protesters.[33]

Finally do nasty, and more intense tweets from Israeli politicians get more engagement? Figure 3.14 shows they do. A one standard deviation increase in intensity increases retweets by about 30% and favorites by 20% (Figure 3.14a). And nasty tweets get approximately 95% more retweets and 60% more favorites (Figure 3.14b). As in the U.S. and Ukraine, more threatening social media posts, and nastiness in general, gets more engagement.

There are four key findings from the social media posts of key politicians in the U.S., Ukraine, and Israel. These findings support the general theory of nasty politics. First, low-level nasty politics such as insults are relatively common, while incitement is rare. Second, nasty rhetoric tends to peak in the lead

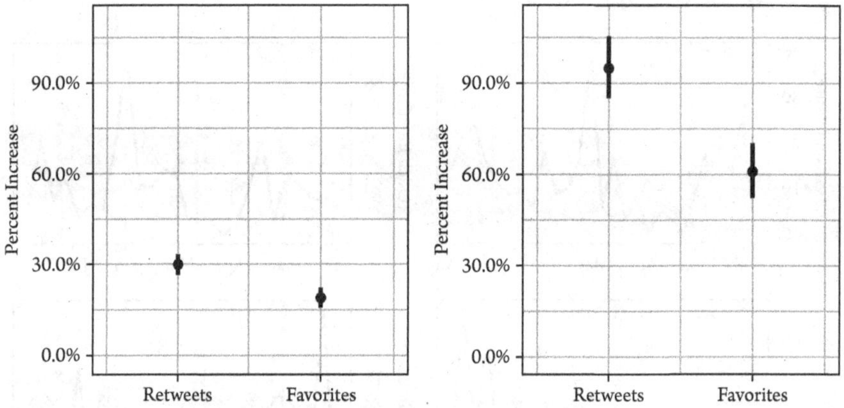

(a) Marginal effect of one standard deviation increase in intensity

(b) Marginal effect nasty tweets (compared to non-nasty tweets)

Figure 3.14 Nastier tweets from select Israeli politicians during COVID, March 2020 elections, and the beginning of the anti-Netanyahu protests receive more engagement (February 1, 2020–July 31, 2020).

Note: Marginal effects with 95% confidence intervals from pooled OLS regressions on log of Retweets and log of Favorites. Plot on the left is from a regression using tweet intensity as the key independent variable. The plot on the right uses a dummy variable of whether a post was nasty or not as the key independent variable. All regressions contain fixed effects for politicians.

[33] Smotrich, Bezalel (bezalelsm). Twitter, July 18–19, 2020. https://twitter.com/bezalelsm/status/1284614712190275584?lang=he and https://twitter.com/bezalelsm/status/128473584456640 1024?lang=he.

up to key events of contention like protests or elections. Third, there's wide variation in how nasty certain politicians are. For more peripheral politicians like Gaetz in the U.S., Tyahnybok in Ukraine, or Smotrich in Israel it is a core part of their communication strategy. Others like Biden in the U.S., Zelensky in Ukraine, or Gantz in Israel use it more sparingly around key events. Finally, across all three contexts, nasty rhetoric on social media gets more engagement. We want to be careful about placing too much credence on this select sample of politicians. But subsequent findings will show that these findings hold more broadly.

3.5 Trump and Lyashko: Peddlers of the Nasty Style

3.5.1 Donald Trump

Throughout his candidacy and presidency Trump's use of vulgar, nasty, and threatening language via Twitter and his omnipresent @realDonaldTrump account was front page news (Barbaro 2015). As a Republican outsider, Trump used nasty rhetoric in tweets and speeches to dominate media coverage in the 2016 campaign (Sides, Tesler, and Vavreck 2019). It was an easy story for the media: "Trump tweeted out X (or said Y) at a campaign rally . . . that's unprecedented, I can't believe he said it." And once elected he continued this pattern, raging against his opponents like the "Deep State (the bureaucracy)," "liberal Dems," "ANTIFA (protesters)," "Fake News (media)," "illegals (immigrants)," and other perceived enemies. Trump used his Twitter account to distract, reach out to his base, and intimidate opponents. In this sense, the defining feature of Trump's presidency was his full-throated embrace of the nasty style. Trump "weaponized rhetoric to captivate our interest, excite our emotions, and distract our attention" (Mercieca 2020, p. 20). As the figures presented earlier in this chapter show, his presidency coincided with a dramatic uptick in media coverage of nasty political rhetoric (Figures 3.1 and 3.3).

Do nasty tweets from President Trump's Twitter feed garner more attention? Anecdotal evidence would suggest they do. Some of his tweets with the highest engagement are quite threatening. For instance his tweet with the highest engagement in the spring of 2020 is the following: "The United States of America will be designating ANTIFA as a Terrorist Organization" (BBC 2020*a*). This garnered more than 324,000 retweets and more than 815,000 likes. Another of Trump's tweets from July 2017 contained a clip of him doing a pro-wrestling bodyslam on a man with the CNN logo in place of his head and calling it "Fake News." This tweet received 315,000 retweets and more than 535,000 likes and favorites, and also had some of the highest engagement of his presidency (Tweetbinder 2021).

I examined Trump's tweets from the @realDonaldTrump account for 172 days of his presidency, April 15–October 3, 2019. This was a particularly pivotal time in Trump's presidency. On April 18, 2019, the Department of Justice released to the public the redacted *Report on the Investigation into Russian Interference in the 2016 Presidential Election,* also known as the "Mueller Report." The Mueller Report stemmed from the investigation into Russian interference in the 2016 U.S. presidential election. The investigation also focused on President Trump and his team, resulting in convictions for several members of his campaign and former administration (Lerer 2019). The Mueller Report was the culmination of a nearly two-year investigation that had engulfed Trump's presidency. Trump had publicly raged against the report on his Twitter feed referring to it as "Witch Hunt" from the "Deep State," and disparaging it is a media and Democratic-perpetrated "hoax" (Shear and Fadulu 2019).

A second key event in Trump's presidency during this period was a direct results of one of his own tweets. On July 14, 2019, Trump attacked four progressive Democratic female members of Congress. He told Reps. Ilhan Omar of Minnesota, Alexandria Ocasio-Cortez of New York, Rashida Tlaib of Michigan, and Ayanna Pressley of Massachusetts—collectively known as "The Squad"—and told them to "go back to where they came from" (Sullivan 2019). In a series of three tweets, Trump tweeted out:

> So interesting to see "Progressive" Democrat Congresswomen, who originally came from countries whose governments are a complete and total catastrophe, the worst, most corrupt and inept anywhere in the world (if they even have a functioning government at all), now loudly (1) and viciously telling the people of the United States, the greatest and most powerful Nation on earth, how our government is to be run. Why don't they go back and help fix the totally broken and crime infested places from which they came. Then come back and show us how (2) it is done. These places need your help badly, you can't leave fast enough. I'm sure that Nancy Pelosi would be very happy to quickly work out free travel arrangements! (3).[34]

The anti-Squad tweets received more than 190,000 favorites, and more than 70,000 retweets, but also triggered a fierce backlash. Democratic House Speaker Nancy Pelosi said, that President Trump wants to "make America white again" and called his comments "xenophobic," and "divisive" (ABC 2019).

[34] See Cummings (2019).

One of the final key events during this time period was the emergence in mid-September 2019 of a scandal that alleged that President Trump withheld military aid from Ukraine unless they agreed to investigate former Vice President Joseph Biden and his son, Hunter Biden (Liptak, LeBlanc, and Mang 2019). This was seen by Democrats as a clear quid-pro-quo—"investigate my domestic opponents, or you can forget about U.S. military assistance." Democrats referred to Trump as acting like a "mob boss" while Trump said the call was "perfect" and that again it was all a big "hoax" (Baker 2019). The firestorm around the scandal would grow. It would eventually result in President Trump's impeachment by the House in December of 2019, before his acquittal in the Senate on February 5, 2020, for obstruction of Congress and abuse of power.

It's worth mentioning that the time period covered was the third year of Trump's presidency. Much of the novelty of Trump's language and Twitter feed had worn off, and data supports this view. Interactions with Trump's tweet slid significantly (almost 70%) since he was elected.[35]

Included in the dataset are 3,509 tweets from President Trump's account for 172 days of his presidency. Table 3.5 contains the descriptive statistics. During this time period, Trump is on average less nasty than he was in the spring and summer of 2020 amidst the COVID pandemic and Black Lives Matter protests. He has fewer nasty posts—only 39% are nasty compared to nearly 51% in the spring and summer of 2020. And his average threat intensity of posts is not nearly as threatening (1.1 compared, 1.7 mean intensity). He also engaged in incitement less frequently (0.5% compared to 1.3%).

Does the intensity of Trump's tweets peak around key events? And does audience engagement also match the patterns of Trump's Twitter intensity? The answer to both questions is, yes (see Figure 3.15). Variation in Trump's intensity (top plot) closely lines up with the vertical lines that indicate key events. His intensity reaches its peak following the revelations of the Trump-Ukraine phone call in mid-September 2019. And audience engagement follows. Retweets

Table 3.5 **Descriptive statistics of Trump's nasty tweets (April 15, 2019–October 3, 2019).**

Name	*# of Tweets*	*Mean Intensity*	*Nasty*	*Insults*	*Accuse*	*Intimidate*	*Incite*
Donald Trump	3,509	1.1	39.0%	26.4%	32.7%	4.3%	0.5%

[35] "The (interaction) metric measures retweets and likes per tweet divided by the size of his following" (Rothschild 2019).

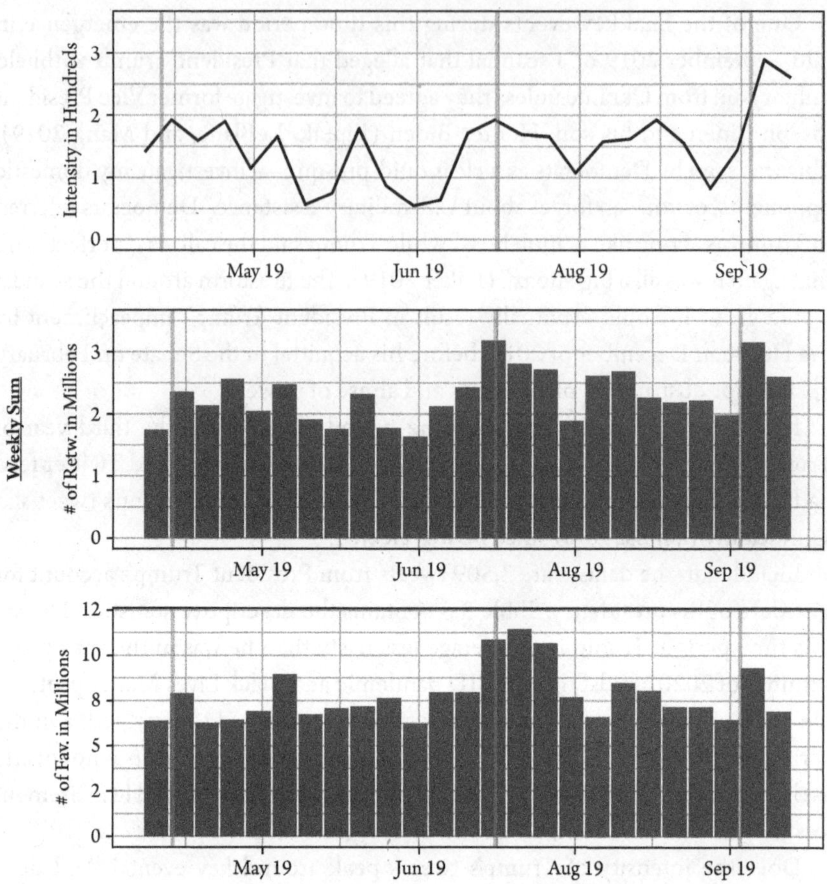

Figure 3.15 Trump's threat intensity of tweets and engagement peak around key events (April 15, 2019–October 3, 2019).

Note: Vertical shaded regions correspond to key events including: (1) the publishing of the "Mueller Report" (April 18, 2019), (2) President Trump telling four first-term, Democratic female members of Congress to "go back where they came from" (July 14, 2019), and (3) the breaking of the Trump-Ukraine "quid-pro-quo" scandal (September 18, 2019). Plots include weekly sum of the threat intensity of Trump's tweets (top), weekly sum of retweets in millions of his posts (middle), and weekly favorites (bottom).

closely track his intensity (middle plot, $r = 0.76$). Favorites are also positively correlated with intensity, though the relationship is not as strong (bottom plot, $r = 0.34$).

Do nasty and more intense tweets get more attention? Figure 3.16 shows they do. Nasty tweets get 28% more retweets (Figure 3.16a, $t = 10.6$, $p < 0.01$). They also get 8% more favorites (Figure 3.16b, $t = 3.8$, $p < 0.01$). A similar pattern holds when we look at our continuous measure of threat intensity. More intense tweets from Trump get significantly more retweets and favorites (Figure 3.17).

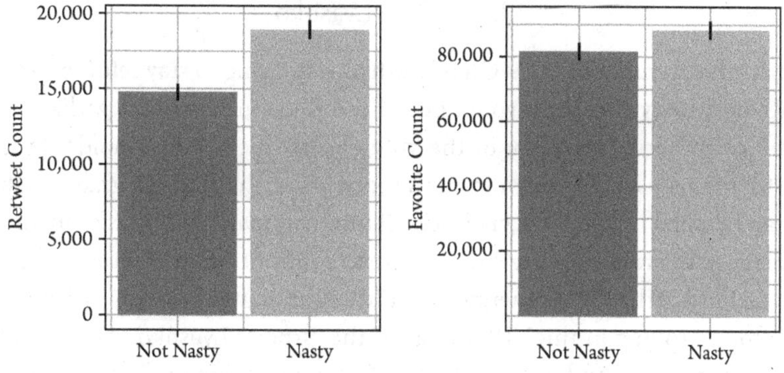

(a) Average number of retweets

(b) Average number of favorites

Figure 3.16 Trump's nasty tweets get retweeted more and generate more favorites (April 15, 2019–October, 3, 2019).

Note: Mean differences with 95% confidence intervals.

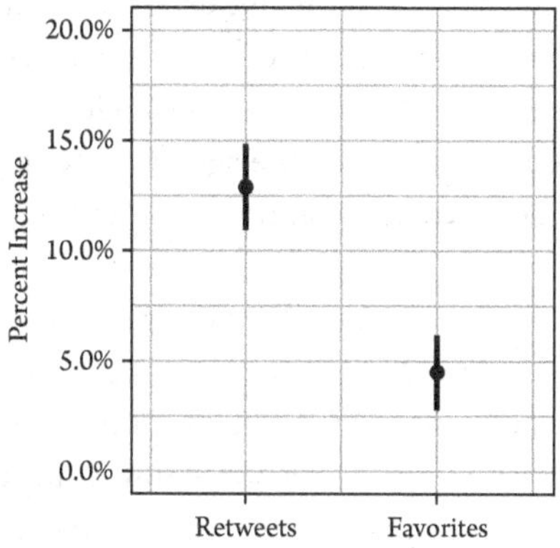

Figure 3.17 Trump's more intense tweets get more retweets and more favorites (April 15, 2019–October 3, 2019).

Note: Marginal effects with 95% confidence intervals from OLS regressions of a one standard deviation increase in a tweet's intensity on Log of Retweets and Favorite counts. Controls include whether the tweet was a quote tweet or retweet.

For all its exceptionalism, Trump's Twitter feed fits the broader pattern of what we found in our analysis of other politicians in the U.S., Ukraine, and Israel. Low levels of nasty rhetoric are quite common, but higher levels like incitement are relatively rare. The intensity of nasty rhetoric spikes during key contentious events like elections, protests, and scandals. Regardless of how we measure nastiness—a continuous measure of intensity, or a binary nasty or not measure—it gets more attention.

3.5.2 Oleh Lyashko

In Kyiv in November of 2019 Oleh Lyashko was trying to stay relevant. He and his Radical Party had been voted out of the Rada in July 2019 parliamentary elections, garnering only 4% of the vote (below the 5% threshold). Lyashko didn't have his usual platform from the rostrum in the Rada to grab headlines. Instead Lyashko trekked to Kyiv Boryspil International Airport accompanied by a camera crew. He and his crew were there to confront Andriy Gerus, a Zelensky ally, and head of the Rada's energy and utilities committee (Kossov 2019*a*). With the cameras rolling in the VIP lounge at the airport, Lyashko yelled at Gerus "who's paying you" and accused him of "selling Ukraine out" by enabling the possible import of electricity from Russia. Lyashko then grabbed Gerus's shirt and tore it while the two briefly tussled before being separated. Lyashko would later post the video on his Facebook:

> Today, I happened to see this "servant of the people" (Zelensky's party's name), Gerus, who opened up the import of Russian energy... When the Russian lobbyist (Gerus) ran out of arguments, he started waving his arms.... Because of Gerus's betrayal, Ukraine has fallen into a state of energy dependence from the aggressor country (Russia). This betrayal needs to be investigated and punished.[36]

Lyashko's post on Facebook got a lot of engagement for him—more than 5,000 likes, 3,000 shares, and 2,000 comments. Gerus responded on his Facebook calling Lyashko's actions a "show provocation" and a stunt on behalf of Ukrainian oligarch Rinat Akhmetov, a well-known oligarch with vast energy holdings who was considered one of the main financiers of Lyashko's political career (Democracy House 2019). Lyashko's airport confrontation was desperate even by the attention-hungry Lyashko's standards. And this was in part because his political fortunes had fallen so far.

Across my in-depth interviews in Ukraine, no politician was singled out more than right-wing firebrand Oleh Lyashko, whose name is synonymous in Ukraine with violent and inflammatory rhetoric. The story of his rise to prominence and eventual political failure is both fascinating and illuminating. It's fascinating because Lyashko was a politician who was willing to do or say most anything to win votes or attention. And it's illuminating, because he was the embodiment of the nasty style in Ukraine. His trajectory shows both the promise and pitfalls of the nasty style.

[36] Lyashko, Oleh (O.Liashko). Facebook, November 6, 2019. https://www.facebook.com/O.Liashko/posts/2492215337513715.

Lyashko was born in Chernihiv, a city in northern Ukraine along the Belarusian border. But he grew up and spent most of his time in an orphanage in Luhansk after his parents separated when he was two years old (Herszenhorn 2014). His youth was spent working on a collective farm (Marchenko 2015). Lyashko would later emphasize his agricultural roots and connection to Ukrainian villagers throughout his political career. After graduating from university he became a journalist. Lyashko ended up spending a year in prison in the early 1990's on charges of embezzlement, in what he claims was a political vendetta for his journalism. His time in prison would become fodder for his opponents who would compare him to a common criminal.

Lyashko used his journalism career and his business connections as a springboard to his political career. Lyashko's entered the Rada on former Prime Minister Yulia Tymoshenko's Fatherland party list in 2006 (Democracy House 2019). Events in 2010 would thrust Lyashko into the spotlight and also set him on his own independent political path. A video from Lyashko's youth surfaced that cast doubts upon Lyashko's sexuality. In the video a young Lyashko is seen in a police station talking about intimate relations with a man. Lyashko would claim the video was fake and deny that he was gay (Herszenhorn 2014). Shortly after the release of the video, Lyashko was expelled from Tymoshenko's Fatherland party for "cooperating with the majority coalition (Yanukovych)" on a series of bills (*Kyiv Post* 2010).

In August of 2011 he formed his own party, the Radical Party of Oleh Lyashko, or simply the Radical Party (*Kyiv Post* 2012*a*). Lyashko was still a bit player in Ukrainian politics, but his knack for getting attention was clear. He styled his speech patterns on those of ordinary Ukrainian villagers, playing up his rural time in Luhansk. He even adopted the pitchfork as his party's symbol—it was a nod to rural Ukrainian interests (his base), but it also served as a signal for Lyashko's desire to lead the people in a mob-like fashion. During this tumultuous period in Ukrainian politics, before Euromaidan, Lyashko picked fights with other deputies, ate soil in the Rada, and even brought sheep to various government buildings (Democracy House 2019). More concretely, he became an outspoken opponent of pro-Russian deputies. In March of 2012 he submitted a bill to strip the citizenship of several deputies in Yanukovych's Party of Regions over their support for Russian language in Ukraine, calling them "anti-Ukrainian" (Korrespondent 2012*b*). While the bill went nowhere, it did get a lot of attention for Lyashko.

But it wasn't until the Euromaidan protests that Lyashko's populist and nationalist rhetoric began to resonate. He became one of the loudest and brashest voices during the protests. Lyashko would invoke his omnipresent cry of "Glory to Ukraine, death to the occupiers"—always followed by a film crew (Amnesty International 2014). When war broke out in Donbas in 2014, Lyashko even formed his own volunteer battalion (militia) where he and its members were accused of kidnapping, torturing, and even executing suspected separatists in Eastern Ukraine (Miller and Webb. 2014).

He parlayed his notoriety and nationalist appeal amidst the War in Donbas to a third place showing in the 2014 presidential election (Balmforth and Zinets 2015). At his political height Lyashko's Radical Party held 22 seats and was part of President Petro Poroshenko's governing coalition from 2014–2015. Lyashko and the Radical Party left the ruling coalition and moved to the opposition over disagreements on a proposed government decentralization bill. Lyashko and his Radical Party acolytes, including the burly nationalist Ihor Mosiychuk, were more at home in the opposition picking fights, and provoking other deputies with name-calling and threats.

But by the spring of 2020 Lyashko was in political purgatory. His party was in shambles, and his only hope back to political relevance was to have his party win in the fall municipal elections. His form of pugnacious and confrontational nationalism had fallen out of favor with voters, and his usefulness to his oligarchic patron, Rinat Akhmetov, was in doubt (Bratushcak 2018). As one veteran Ukrainian journalist recounted in March of 2020:

> I think Lyashko has become an old story. There was a big demand for new faces during the last (2019) presidential and parliamentary campaigns. The strong showing of Zelensky and his party is an answer to this demand. Lyashko is obviously not a new face. He was first elected in parliament back in 2006, more than 10 years ago. In 2014, he was popular because he used the tragic events in the country for his political purposes and managed to become Number 3 at the presidential elections in 2014. But in 2019, scandals (his nasty brand of politics) were not enough and Lyashko lost.[37]

Yet, even in his lowest moments, Lyashko was scheming of ways to stay relevant. A seat opened up in the Rada in the Chernihiv region, after the deputy Valeriy Davydenko was found dead with a single gunshot to his head in his office in an apparent suicide (UNIAN 2020*b*). The opening of a seat in Lyashko's hometown was fortuitous and Lyashko jumped at the chance. He even managed to swing an endorsement from his old friend turned rival turned ally, Yulia Tymoshenko. The two were seen smiling and playing nice in an awkward Facebook video in July 2020 (UNIAN 2020*a*).

[37] Interview #Ukr-J-O0320.

But on October 25, 2020, Oleh Lyashko once again became a loser. His win should have been a sure thing. He had the backing of Yulia Tymoshenko and her party going into the election, and the seat in Chernihiv was one he had once held (Myroniuk 2020). He even made a music video for the campaign in classic Lyashko style. In the video Lyashko wears a red devil cape and carries his party's logo, a pitchfork. He is then summoned from a Ukrainian village to the city to subdue an overweight bald playboy, representing the Ukrainian oligarchs. Lyashko defeats the oligarch and is given a hero's welcome back in the village as he sings in front of an all-female rock band.[38]

Lyashko ended up losing the seat in a close election to the ruling Servant of the People party candidate, Anatoliy Gunko. Lyashko received 31.8% of the vote, while Gunko received 34.1%—less than 1,500 votes separated the candidates. Following the election, Lyashko accused Zelensky's "insignificant government" of having engaged in a "shameful and humiliating plot to steal the election."[39] Full of hyperbole and outrage in defeat, Lyashko's final role as the eternal victim was fitting.

Lyashko and his antics left their mark on Ukrainian politics. Some of his most famous moments in the Rada included calling politicians from the anti-Maidan Opposition Bloc "traitors" (BBC 2016; McPhedran 2014), referring to rival lawmakers as "parasites" (Oksana 2014), and foreign NGOs as "spies" (Yermolenko 2018). And then there's his favorite insult of calling his opponents *skotina*, or "animal-bastard," that has become synonymous with Lyashko (Kryvtsun 2014). Yet in Zelensky, Ukrainian politics had found a smoother, more charismatic populist that made Lyashko's antics look cheap in comparison.

During several of my interviews, Lyashko was referred to as a "clown"[40] or a "circus man."[41] Yet, even his detractors admired his ability to grab attention. Perhaps the most cynical view of Lyashko is that he was simply a tool of the oligarch Rinat Akhmetov. One veteran Ukraine journalist echoed this view:

> Lyashko only became who he is because of Akhmetov. Lyashko's job was to stir shit up (in the Rada) and rile up pensioner and disenfranchised folks, get them a little more politically active. He was also charged with attacking more veteran politicians in the Rada. It could be Yuriy

[38] Lyashko, Oleh (Oleh Lyashko). YouTube channel, October 22, 2020. https://www.youtube.com/watch?v=YnHMyUdj5Os.

[39] Lyashko, Oleh (O.Liashko). Facebook, October 28, 2019. https://www.facebook.com/O.Liashko/videos/3396764380392135.

[40] Interview #Ukr-NC-N0819.

[41] Interview #Ukr-O-V0819.

Table 3.6 **Descriptive statistics of Lyashko's nasty Facebook posts during his following election losses (August 1, 2019–November 1, 2020).**

Name	*# of Posts*	*Mean Intensity*	*Nasty*	*Insults*	*Accuse*	*Intimidate*	*Incite*
Oleh Lyashko	1,236	2.1	51.3%	32.4%	46.0%	20.5%	6.1%

> Boyko (one of the main leaders of the pro-Russian factions in the Rada) or Poroshenko. He doesn't really have a true belief system.[42]

So how did Lyashko use the nasty style? Did he put out a constant stream of nasty rhetoric? Or did he use nasty rhetoric around key times? And did the public respond in the same way to Lyashko as they did to other politicians, with his name-calling and threatening attacks garnering more attention? To answer these questions let's look at Lyashko's 1,236 Facebook posts that span his party's failure in the 2019 July election to his loss in the October 2020 special election (August 1, 2019–November 1, 2020).

About half of his posts were nasty during this period when he was trying to stay politically relevant while out of office (Table 3.6). More than 6% also contained incitement. How does the threat intensity of his posts vary across key events in Lyashko's bid to remain relevant and stage a political comeback? Does public engagement match these peaks in intensity? These key events include (1) Lyashko confronting Deputy Andriy Gerus of Zelensky's Servant of the People party at the Kyiv Airport (November 6, 2019), (2) earning the endorsement of Yulia Tymoshenko for the Chernihiv special election (June 15, 2020), and (3) confirmation that Lyashko lost the special election in Chernihiv (October 28, 2020).

Figure 3.18 shows Lyahsko's time series of the threat intensity of his social media posts stacked over measures of audience engagement, including shares (middle plot) and angry reactions (bottom plot). Lyashko's threat intensity reaches a crescendo with his physical attack on Gerus at the airport in November. And he continued to attack Gerus, Zelensky, and other members of their Servant of the People Party. For instance on the day of the attack on Gerus, November 6, Lyashko posted a video of the attack on Gerus, and justified his actions, accusing Gerus and Zelensky betraying the Ukrainian people by making Ukraine energy

[42] Interview #Ukr-J-C0120.

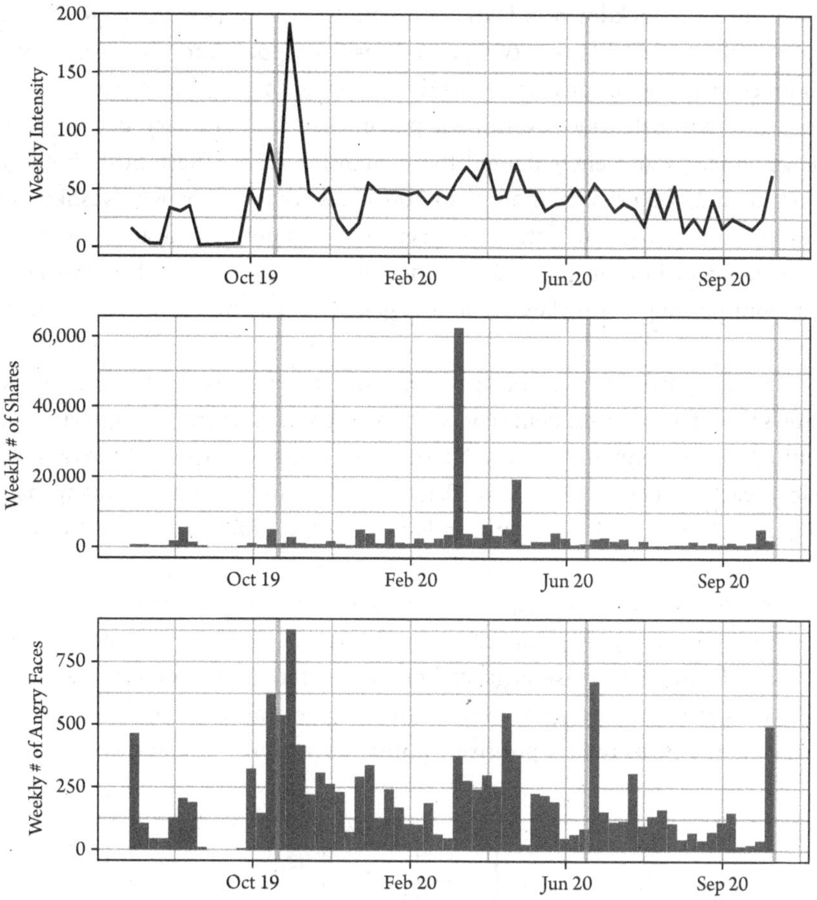

Figure 3.18 Lyashko's threat intensity of Facebook posts and engagement peak around key events (August 2019–November 1, 2020).

Note: Vertical shaded region corresponds to key events including: (1) Lyashko confronting Deputy Andriy Gerus of Zelensky's Servant of the People party at the Kyiv Airport (November 6, 2019), (2) Yulia Tymoshenko endorsing Lyashko via Facebook for the Chernihiv special election (June 15, 2020), and (3) confirmation that Lyashko lost the special election in Chernihiv (October 28, 2020). Plots include weekly sum of the threat intensity of Lyashko's Facebook posts (top), weekly sum of shares of his posts (middle), and weekly number of angry reactions (Angry Faces, bottom).

dependent on Russia. Lyashko closed his post by promising that "this betrayal must be investigated and punished!"[43]

Lyashko's intensity of posts remains relatively flat up to the special election. The number of times his posts get shared are positively correlated with his intensity, but only weakly so ($r = 0.18$). Two of Lyashko's posts in mid-March,

[43] Lyashko, Oleh (O.Liashko). Facebook, November 6, 2019, https://www.facebook.com/O.Liashko/videos/2492204254181490/.

right when the lockdown in Ukraine began, went viral (see the large spike in the middle plot).[44] In these two posts, Lyashko tapped into his populist base, and recorded a series of videos harshly criticizing the lockdown. He criticized fines that the Zelensky government put in place for ordinary people, while rich politicians and elites flouted the quarantine rules. These posts both got more than 25,000 shares, more than 200 times what an average Lyashko post would receive. The correlation between threat intensity and angry reactions (top plot and bottom plot) is considerably stronger ($r = 0.71$), with angry reactions peaking during key events and generally matching Lyashko's intensity of posts.

Do nasty posts from Lyashko get more engagement. Yes, they do. Figure 3.19 shows the effect of a post being coded as nasty, containing any insult, accusation, intimidating statement, or threat. Nasty posts get more than eight times as many angry reactions (Figure 3.19a, $t = 10.1, p < 0.01$), and three times as many shares (Figure 3.19b, $t = 2.3$, $p < 0.05$). In Figure 3.20, we further see that Lyashko's posts that are more intense, also receive more shares, angry reactions, more comments, wow face emojis, haha face emojis. But more intense posts don't influence how many likes, care emojis, or heart emojis. Nasty and more intense posts of Lyashko increase engagement. But in terms of emotional reactions, Lyashko's more intense posts only boost negative emotional reactions. In fact, more intense posts reduce positive emotional reactions (care and love emojis).

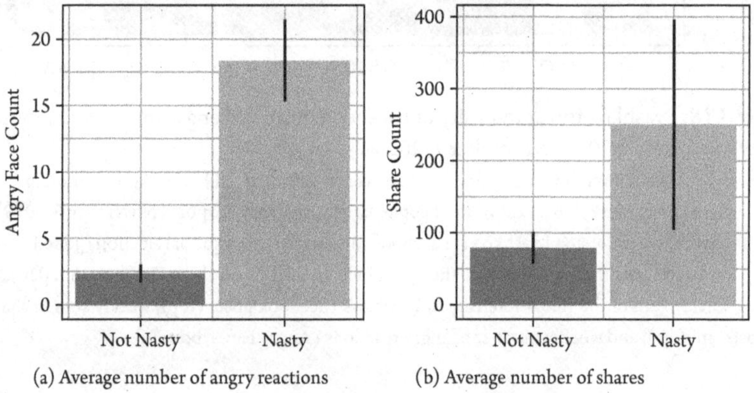

Figure 3.19 Lyashko's nasty Facebook posts get shared more and generate more angry reactions (August 1, 2019–November 1, 2020).
Note: Mean differences with 95% confidence intervals.

[44] Lyashko, Oleh (O.Liashko). Facebook, https://www.facebook.com/O.Liashko/posts/2785248004877112 March 16, 2020, and March 19, 2020, https://www.facebook.com/O.Liashko/posts/2791332797601966.

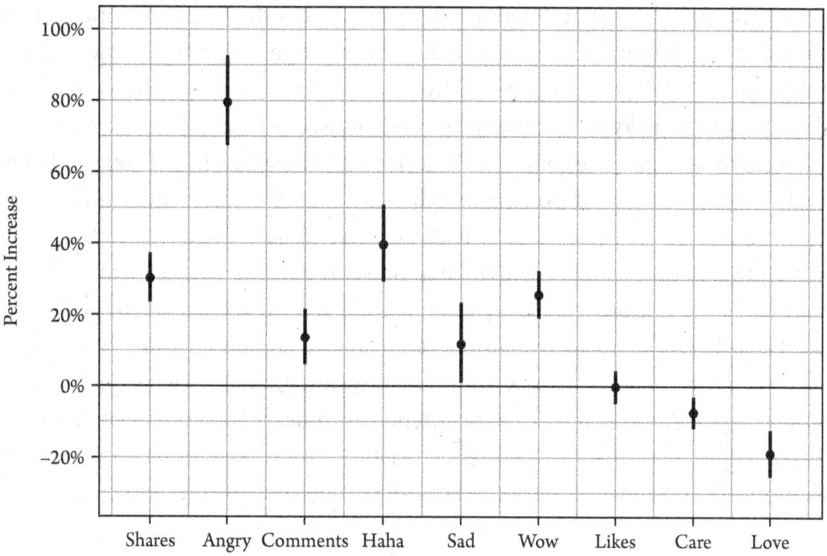

Figure 3.20 Lyashko's more intense Facebook posts get more engagement, and more negative emotional reactions (August 2019–November 1, 2020).

Note: Marginal effects with 95% confidence intervals from OLS regressions of a one standard deviation increase in a post's intensity on log of Facebook reactions including: Shares, Angry emojis, Comments, Haha emojis, Sad emojis, Wow emojis, Likes, Care emojis, and Love emojis.

This highlights Lyashko's strategy of deploying the nasty style to create negative emotions and stoke the outrage of his base.

3.6 Concluding Thoughts

One of the core arguments of nasty politics is that while the words and level of vitriol may be different it follows a similar dynamic in the U.S., Ukraine, and Israel. This chapter provided evidence in favor of this argument. There is a similar pattern in the relative frequency of different kinds of rhetoric across all three contexts: insults and accusations are much more common than intimidating statements, and incitement is quite rare. The salience of nasty rhetoric in all three countries peaks around periods of heightened elite competition. But there are also baseline differences in the level of nasty rhetoric across countries.

Another key finding is that nasty rhetoric grabs attention. Social media posts that are nasty get more engagement in all three countries. And the nastier and more threatening a post is the more engagement it gets as well. This is even true for populist politicians like President Trump and Oleh Lyashko—both of whom have made nasty politics a central part of their image.

Finally, the analyses of different politicians across the three countries during periods of heightened tension show that there's large variation in how different politicians use it. There are core politicians like Mitch McConnell in the U.S. or Volodymyr Zelensky in Ukraine who rarely engage in nasty rhetoric relative to others in their respective countries. You also have those like Matt Gaetz and Oleh Tyahnybok—peripheral politicians who are flamethrowers and regularly use nasty politics. Why do some politicians choose to use nasty rhetoric sparingly, while others embrace it? The evidence presented so far suggests that outsider politicians use it more frequently to grab attention. Also, incumbent politicians like Petro Poroshenko or Benjamin Netanyahu, who fear they are in danger of losing support, may turn nasty. But in the next few chapters we'll explore this in greater depth. We will also see how voters view different types of nasty rhetoric. Which types of voters are attracted to nasty rhetoric? Finally, what do insults, accusations, intimidating statements, and incitement signal to voters about the politicians that use them?

4

How Does the Public Respond to Nasty Rhetoric?

James Carville doesn't pull punches. Carville is a prominent Democratic political consultant and fixture on cable news channels who helped guide Bill Clinton's successful 1992 presidential campaign. His nickname—the "Ragin' Cajun"—stems as much from his thick Louisiana accent and love of LSU football, as his acerbic tongue. In early February 2020 he lamented the state of the Democratic presidential primary:

> The Democratic Party is out in some goofy la-la land waiting on Bernie Sanders' revolution or the proletariat to rise up or some other shit... (while) Trump and Trumpism is the most dangerous virus to affect this country since the fall of communism, and I think it has to be beaten badly and decisively at the polls. There is one moral imperative in the world right now, and that's to get this guy (Trump) outta there, open an investigation, have him arrested and have him put in jail.[1]

While lamenting Democrats' seeming embrace of progressive "left-wing fantasies" instead of winning elections, he called Trump a "dangerous virus" and said he needs to be arrested and thrown in jail. Carville was advocating for hardball, nasty politics.

Carville is not alone in supporting a confrontational style of politics. In May 2018, I was in Kyiv and interviewing a high-ranking member of the National Corps political party who I will call "Danylo."[2] National Corps was founded as the ultra-nationalist political wing of the Azov Battalion, one of the most powerful militias formed following Euromaidan and the outbreak of the War in Donbas (Miller 2018*a*). Historically, Azov and the National Corps espoused

[1] See Mills (2020).

[2] A pseudonym. Interview #Ukr-N-0318.

Nasty Politics: The Logic of Insults, Threats, and Incitement. Thomas Zeitzoff, Oxford University Press.
© Oxford University Press 2023. DOI: 10.1093/oso/9780197679494.003.0004

an extreme version of Ukrainian nationalism that led their critics to label them as fascists and neo-Nazis.[3] The views and actions of Azov and National Corps lent support to this view. Members of Azov and the National Corps favored a strong presidency that looks more like strong-man rule, supported bringing back the death penalty for treason and corruption, and favored Ukrainians openly carrying pistols (Kuzmenko 2019). Several Azov and National Corps members also openly espoused pro-Nazi views, sported Nazi tattoos, and if that weren't enough, the logo of Azov is the *Wolfsangel*, a key symbol of the Nazi Party and Nazi-SS armored divisions that is banned in Germany.

It was a beautiful spring day when I chatted with Danylo. We sat on a balcony overlooking a park and we were both drinking lemonade. Danylo was describing to me his political awakening. He started as member of an *ultras* group of hardcore soccer supporters for one of Ukraine's largest teams. In 2013 he became enraged at Yanukovych's corruption and overtures towards Russia, and joined in the protests in Euromaidan. He then volunteered and served in a combat role as part of the Azov Battalion in the War in Donbas. Danylo didn't give off the hardcore Nazi vibe. He wore a flannel shirt and a close-cropped beard, and looked like he belonged in a hipster bar in Brooklyn. Like many Ukrainians Danylo lamented the "corruption" of Ukrainian politicians. But where he showed his ultra-nationalist bona fides was when I asked him which tactics were acceptable for the Azov political movement and National Corps? Danylo responded:

> We are in a state of war (with Russia). This war is hybrid. Russia is not afraid of using different methods to continue the war (here) in Kyiv, and to kill our chances to be independent. If we know organizations or persons who take money from Russia, we will use force against them . . . (for example) Parties like the Opposition Bloc (the successor of Yanukovych's Party of Regions). They are writing bad things about our movement, and they are trying to destroy us as a country. . . . We are following our enemies closely and know what they're doing.

What's interesting about my conversation with Danylo was that he was very careful to not take credit for or explicitly endorse the actions of the Azov-affiliated National Militia who had engaged in racist attacks against Roma camps (Miller 2018*c*), and attacked several LGBT pride rallies (RFE/RL 2021*c*). These were referred to by him as "parallel actions." Yet even in his sanitized rhetoric, Danylo alluded to a very threatening style of politics. He talked about how hybrid

[3] This is especially true since the Russian invasion in 2022, where Putin sought to portray Russian actions as part of the "de-Nazification" of Ukraine. Azov also tried to soften its image and distance itself from its founder Andriy Biletsky and the National Corps party (John and Lister 2022).

war made necessary the "use of force"—a euphemism for violence, beatings, and worse—all of which the Azov movement were willing and capable of inflicting against their perceived political enemies, including rival politicians. And Danylo highlighted how the Azov movement and its political allies were "following our (their) enemies closely and know what they are doing." It was veiled but the threat was there. Azov and its affiliates have several thousand members. Many of their members have combat experience and a penchant for torch-lit marches and MMA fights (Miller 2018*a*). At the end of the interview, Danylo reminded me of his soccer hooligan roots and showed me clips of him and his fellow soccer ultras fighting other soccer partisans in the woods.

James Carville and Danylo have little in common. But their suggestion that the threat each of their groups and parties face justifies a heightened level of nasty rhetoric, even if the tactics they support for dealing with the threat are different.

In this chapter we explore how people make sense of this type of rhetoric by exploring the demand side of nasty politics. Do voters view all nasty rhetoric as unacceptable? And where do they draw the line? How do they view insults, accusations, intimidation, and incitement? Is calling an opponent an "asshole" viewed the same as calling them a "traitor?" Are certain personality types more willing to accept nasty rhetoric? Finally, are there situations where people become more supportive of nasty politics? To answers these questions we'll look at surveys and survey experiments from the U.S. and Ukraine.[4]

4.1 How Acceptable Is It for Politicians Be Nasty?

The first step to understanding the demand side of nasty rhetoric is to measure how people feel towards it. If people think that nasty rhetoric isn't a big deal, or if they find it generally acceptable then there's no puzzle. Politicians use nasty rhetoric because there is no penalty from voters for it.

Second, do people lump all nasty rhetoric together, or do they recognize that some types of rhetoric are more threatening than others? Calling an opponent a "jerk" is different than calling someone a "Nazi." And advocating for protests against an opponent is very different from saying they should "be eliminated." But does the public see it that way? Do they see insults as less threatening than threats or incitement? Are there major differences between Ukrainians and Americans?

To explore these questions, I turn to a series of surveys I conducted in the U.S. and Ukraine in the fall of 2018. I created a database of forty-two different phrases

[4] Demographics for the surveys and survey experiments can be found in the Online Appendix.

that politicians had previously uttered about their domestic opponents. This was constructed from existing news sources in Ukraine and the U.S.—and there was plenty to choose from in both countries. The database was divided between 23 examples of insults and accusations that ran the gamut from calling an opponent "corrupt" to calling them a "traitor" or a "parasite." And there were 19 examples of intimidating statements and incitement from saying political opponents should be "protested" to they "should be crushed." A few positive or neutral phrases were included as well, including saying that political opponents "be respected" or are "honorable." The same database was used in the U.S. and Ukraine for comparability. The U.S. survey was conducted via Amazon's Mechanical Turk (MTurk) online platform in November of 2018.[5] The Ukraine survey was carried out by the Kyiv International Institute of Sociology (KIIS) in the fall of 2018.[6]

Figures 4.1 and 4.2 present the average level of acceptability for different types of insults and accusations (4.1) and intimidating statements and incitement (4.2) in the U.S. and Ukraine.

The results fit the theory of nasty politics: Americans and Ukrainians have principled views on nasty rhetoric. Figure 4.1 shows most Ukrainians and U.S. respondents believe that most examples of insults and accusations are never, rarely, or only sometimes acceptable. U.S. respondents are consistently more accepting of negative rhetoric. Though this finding may be more due to the fact that people might be less willing to admit that they are OK with nasty rhetoric in a face-to-face survey (Ukraine) compared to an online survey (U.S.). Second, many of the least acceptable insults are dehumanizing phrases—calling an opponent an "animal," "rat," or "parasite." The notable exception is calling an opponent a "terrorist"—which is both an insult and an accusation, and one of the worst things you can say about a political opponent in both countries. Lest we think this kind of language never happens, many Democrats criticized President Trump for green-lighting a U.S. operation that assassinated the Iranian Revolutionary Guard commander, Qassem Soleimani, in Iraq in January 2020. Democrats viewed the assassination as an aggressive unilateral action that brought the U.S. closer to war with Iran and they pushed for greater House oversight over the president. In response, Georgia Republican Rep. Doug Collins responded that "Democrats are in love with terrorists" (Cole 2020). Collins did not outright say that Democrats are terrorists, but he did accuse them of terrorist flirtation.

[5] Following Huff and Kertzer (2018) and others, I re-weight the MTurk data to approximate the U.S. population on age, race, and ethnicity.

[6] See http://www.kiis.com.ua/?lang=eng&cat=about and was part of nationally representative, face-to-face omnibus survey.

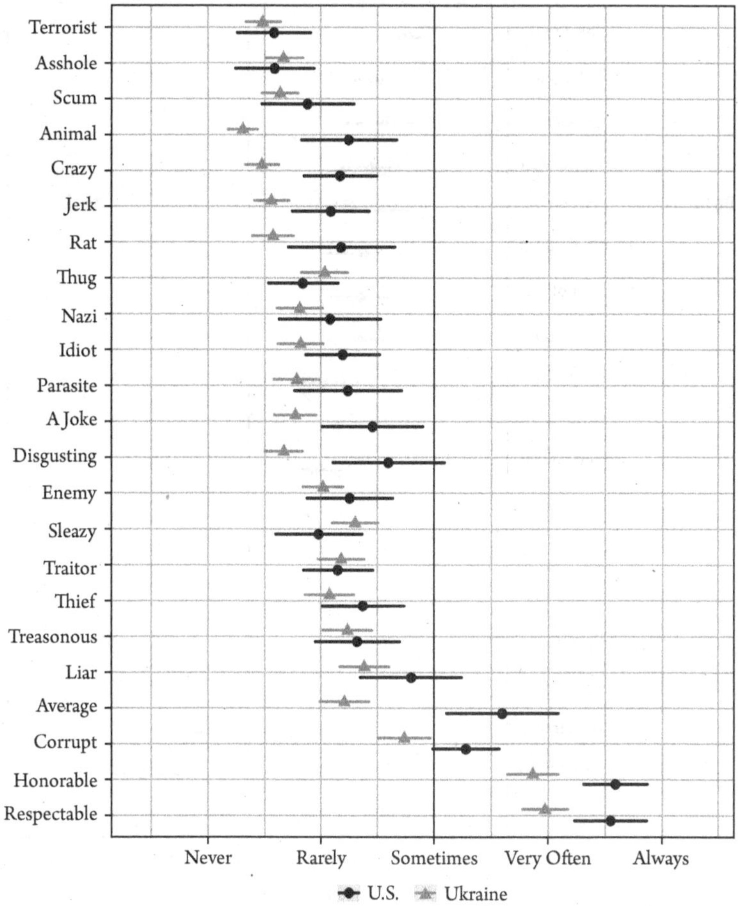

Figure 4.1 Wide variation in the perceived acceptability of different insults and accusations in the U.S. and Ukraine.

Note: Means with associated 95% Confidence Intervals. U.S. MTurk data is weighted to approximate U.S. population.

In official Ukrainian government communication there were no separatists in Donbas, only terrorists, and the zone of operations in the War in Donbas was called an "Anti-Terrorist Operation Zone" (NSDC 2015). Finally there are a few terms which have very different levels of acceptability (more acceptable in the U.S. than Ukraine), and these include calling an opponent "disgusting," "a joke," or "average."

There is less variation between Ukrainians and Americans views on intimidating statements and incitement (Figure 4.2). Most of the examples are rated as "rarely" or "never" acceptable. There's near-uniform agreement that advocating violence against an opponent—that they should "be beaten up," or the more vague but equally sinister "be eliminated or "be targeted"—are unacceptable.

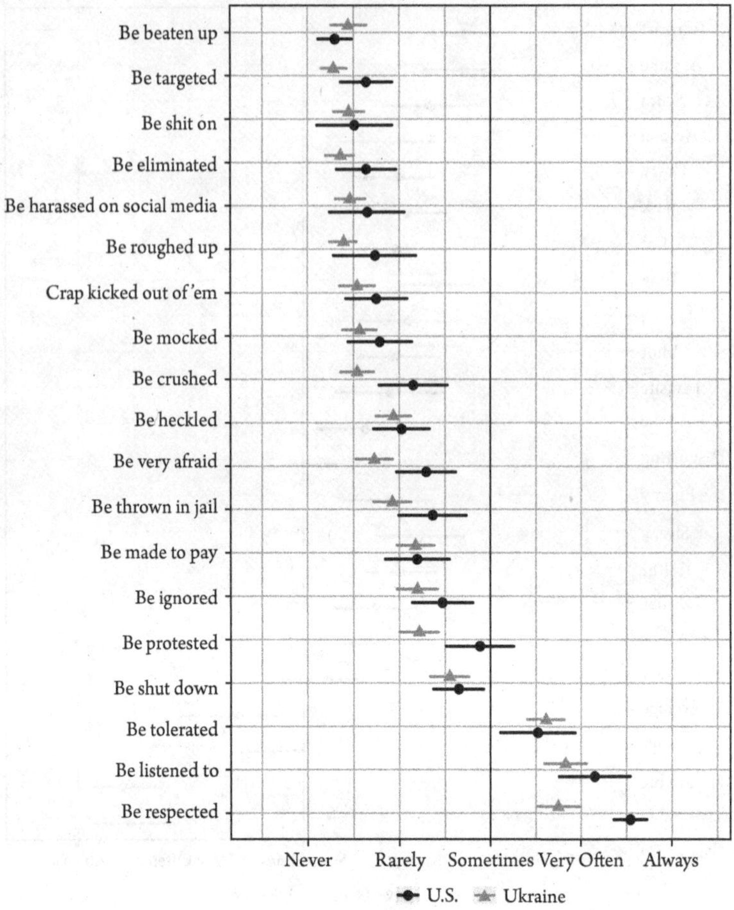

Figure 4.2 Most intimidating statements and incitement are viewed as unacceptable in the U.S. and Ukraine.

Note: Means with associated 95% Confidence Intervals. U.S. MTurk data is weighted to approximate U.S. population.

Though there is some disagreement over how acceptable it is to say their opponents to should "be protested." On average, U.S. respondents also seem slightly more accepting of violent threats—but again this may be a function of the survey mode.

While intimidating statements and incitement may be rarer, they still are a part of politics in both countries. In 2015, then candidate Trump said about a Black Lives Matter activist who was accosted at one of his rallies that "maybe he should have been roughed up" (Diamond 2015*a*). In 2018 in Ukraine, serious clashes erupted between anti-corruption protesters and counter-protesters over the actions of Minister of Internal Affairs, Arsen Avakov. Ilya Kiva showed up on behalf of the counter-protesters and Avakov (Cohen 2018). Kiva is the former head of the Narcotics Division in the Interior Ministry, a former far-right nationalist and member of Right Sector, and was leader of the Socialist Party of Ukraine. He was known for openly coming out as a "sexist" (Melkozerova 2017), and for posting semi-nude pictures of his bedroom escapades on his Instagram.[7] During the counter-protests Kiva said the following about then President Petro Poroshenko, "Here's what is evil, here's what's a betrayal. . . . Evil will be punished. Poroshenko will get what he deserves for his crimes to the Ukrainian people" (Ustinov 2018). The last part was a not so thinly veiled threat against Poroshenko, given that paramilitaries and paid muscle (*titushki*)[8] had just smashed up the office of the anti-corruption bureau (NABU) and thrown a green chemical into the eyes of one of the protesters (Cohen 2018).

Finally, one of the most frequently used forms of intimidation—and one that goes to the core of democracy and democratic erosion—are threats by politicians to throw their opponents in jail. From Trump's chants of "lock her (Hillary Clinton) up" to the actual jailing of Tymoshenko, and the investigation of former President Poroshenko by President Zelensky (Kramer 2020), these are serious threats. The public tends to view these threats to jail opponents as rarely to sometimes acceptable.

The findings show that the public generally doesn't like when politicians insult or make accusations against their opponents. Views on intimidating statements and incitement are even more uniformly negative. But not all threats or name-calling are viewed as equally prohibitive. Even given the different political histories and environments, and the different survey modes, the similar responses in Ukraine and the U.S. are surprising. It suggests that the negative reaction the public has towards nasty rhetoric isn't simply context dependent.

4.2 Who Supports It When Things Get Nasty?

It's clear that on average Americans and Ukrainians find it unacceptable when politicians engage in insults and accusations. And they especially dislike it when politicians make intimidating statements or use incitement against their opponents. Yet "on average" is masking a lot of the variation. Some people abhor it, while some tolerate it, and others may like it. Our theory argues that attitudes towards nasty rhetoric are not random. Rather they are related to their fundamental personality traits—how people feel about conflict, how aggressive they are, their attitudes towards hierarchy and authority.

[7] See Miller, Christopher (christopherjm). Twitter, June 17, 2017. https://twitter.com/christopherjm/status/876097063007772672?lang=en.

[8] The term *titushki* came out of the Euromaidan protest and it referred to groups of young, muscular guys in tracksuits whom Yanukovych hired to beat up peaceful protesters. Now it's a general term for thugs for hire. See Goncharenko (2014).

One open question is how are political identities related to attitudes towards nasty politics? Certain political parties tend to attract individuals with like-minded world ideologies and psychological traits (Hetherington and Weiler 2009; Jost 2017). Political identities also provide a sense of ingroup and outgroup. This is important for how politicians use nasty politics. By attacking an outgroup, politicians can be perceived as tough protectors of the ingroup. But this only works if there are salient political identities. In the U.S., with a strong two-party system this is straightforward. Partisan cleavages between Democrats and Republicans are highly salient. Yet things are less straightforward in Ukraine. Historically partisanship has been much weaker, with individuals having loose attachments to parties. Politics and political parties have been dominated by personalities like Zelensky, Tymoshenko, and Poroshenko. Yet one fault line that ran through Ukrainian politics was attitudes towards the Euromaidan Protests (2013–2014). Many supporters of former President Viktor Yanukovych believed that the Euromaidan was a nationalist coup d'état. In contrast, supporters of Euromaidan viewed the Yanukovych regime as corrupt, and believed that the protests were a popular movement to restore democracy (IFES 2017). Attitudes towards Euromaidan are strongly correlated with pro- and anti-European sentiment (Paniotto 2014). I use whether a respondent agreed with the statement that the Euromaidan (Maidan) Protests of 2013–2014 were a popular protest movement, as opposed to a nationalist coup d'état as measure of ingroup and outgroup status. Those who agreed with the statement were coded as pro-Maidan (Onuch, Mateo, and Waller 2021).[9]

Do personality traits and partisanship influence attitudes towards nasty politics? To find out, we'll look at this same survey data from Ukraine and the U.S. to see how personality traits and partisanship are correlated with attitudes towards politicians acting nasty.

4.2.1 Who Supports Nasty Politics in the U.S.?

To measure personality traits that might be associated with being more open to nasty rhetoric, we now turn to several standard psychological measures and questions.[10] This includes a three-question battery of preferences for a tough leader ($\alpha = 0.53$).[11] The authoritarianism child-rearing scale which measures

[9] Those who viewed Euromaidan as a nationalist coup d'état, or given social desirability bias, refused to answer, were coded as anti-Maidan.

[10] We'll use Cronbach's α as a measure of consistency. How closely related are a set of items—higher values (closer to 1) indicate a greater consistency.

[11] Whether they would prefer to have a leader who: (1) Takes quick action OR Works through the system; (2) Tough OR Diplomatic; and (3) Doesn't follow the usual rules OR Follows the usual rules.

how much people like uniformity and order, and dislike diversity and free-spirited individuals ($\alpha = 0.73$) (Hetherington and Weiler 2009; Stenner 2005). Included are three questions from social dominance orientation scale (SDO, $\alpha = 0.74$) which measures how people support a social hierarchy where some groups deserve to be on top and others should be on the bottom (Pratto et al. 1994).[12] Previous research has found that people that score higher on trait aggression—those that like to argue, get in fights, and make threats in their personal life are more receptive to violent language (Kalmoe 2014; Sydnor 2019). Included are three questions from the Buss-Perry trait aggression scale ($\alpha = 0.74$).[13] Finally, I also included a question drawn from the American National Election Study: "How often do you feel it is justified for people to use violence to pursue their political goals in this country?" (1-never to 5-always). All of these measures were then re-scaled to lie between 0-1 to make it easier to compare the magnitude of the effects.

We want to see how these personality traits correlate with propensity to support or oppose violent rhetoric. To create a general measure of acceptance of violent rhetoric, we'll examine a subset of the larger 42 items measured in the national survey. These include eight items—four drawn from the insults and accusations group, and four from the intimidating statements and incitement group—that were used in both the national surveys in Ukraine and the U.S., and the elite surveys that we'll discuss in Chapter 6. These eight items include how acceptable it is for a politician say their political opponent(s): (1) "is a traitor," (2) "is a parasite," (3) "should be harassed on social media," (4) "is corrupt," (5) "should be protested," (6) "should be crushed," (7) "should be afraid," and (8) "is an animal." I standardized these eight items and created an additive index that lies between 0 and 1 and is a measure of general acceptance of nasty rhetoric.[14] Higher values indicate a greater acceptance of nasty rhetoric.

Figure 4.3 shows the results for how different personality characteristics and attitudes correlate with acceptance of nasty political rhetoric. Positive values indicate that a personality trait, attitude, or identity are positively related to

[12] "Show how much you favor or oppose each idea below by selecting a number from 1 (strongly oppose) to 7 (strongly favor) on the scale below. You can work quickly; your first feeling is generally best." (1) Some groups of people are simply inferior to other groups; (2) No one group should dominate society (reverse coded); and (3) Group equality should not be our primary goal.

[13] "Please rate each of the following statements in terms of how characteristic they are of you, where 1 is extremely uncharacteristic of me, and 7 is extremely characteristic of me." (1) Given enough provocation, I may hit another person; (2) I have threatened people I know; and (3) My friends say I am somewhat argumentative."

[14] How much each respondent thought it was more or less acceptable than the mean response for each item to use this language he Cronbach's α from the general acceptance of violent rhetoric additive index shows that responses to different items about acceptability of rhetoric have fairly high consistency ($\alpha = 0.88$).

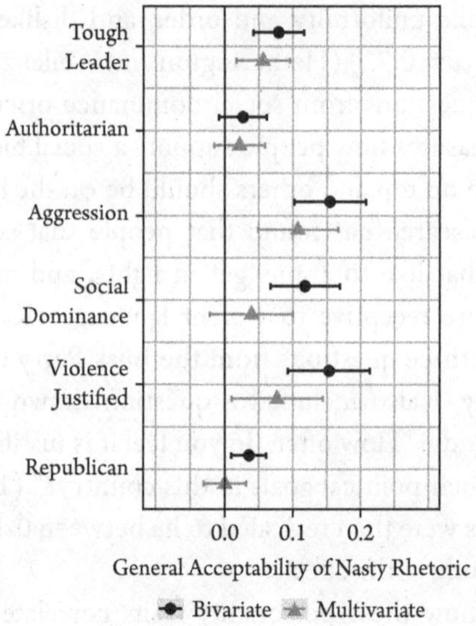

Figure 4.3 Personality traits and general attitudes predict support for nasty rhetoric in the U.S. (Amazon MTurk).

Note: Plot shows regressions coefficients. The dependent variable is general acceptance of nasty rhetoric (0-1). Each variable includes the bivariate relationship and also the full model with all variables included (multivariate). 95% Confidence Interval. Data weighted to approximate the U.S. population.

accepting nasty rhetoric. The results are in line with our theory. Certain individuals are more predisposed to accept violent rhetoric. People who have a preference for tough leaders are more likely to accept violent rhetoric. So are those who are more aggressive and believe that violence can be justified in politics. Believing that some groups are better than others (social dominance) also increases the acceptance of the nasty style. We see that there are partisan differences, with Republicans slightly more likely than Democrats to accept violent rhetoric. But this is only significant in the bivariate relationship. Trait authoritarianism has a weak correlation with attitudes towards nasty rhetoric. Finally, it should be noted that many of these traits and attitudes are positively correlated—Republican and social dominance ($r = 0.42$), aggression and violence justified ($r = 0.33$). This is in line with other research that certain personality traits and psychological predispositions are correlated with each other (e.g., authoritarianism and social dominance) and form the basis of political conservatism (Jost et al. 2003).

The key takeaway is that there is baseline variation in how much people will tolerate nasty rhetoric. Those who score higher on aggression, like tough leaders, believe some groups are better than others, and that violence is justified are more supportive of violent rhetoric. In later chapters I will present findings from a larger, more representative sample and show that the personality findings hold. So in sum, there are certain personalities that seem to be more accepting of violent rhetoric. The next question is whether we see a similar pattern in Ukraine?

4.2.2 Who Supports Nasty Politics in Ukraine?

What are the personality and partisan correlates of individuals who support the nasty style in Ukraine? Do they match the findings from the U.S.? To answer these questions, we'll examine several questions that were fielded as part of a nationally representative survey in Ukraine (N = 1,010). The survey contained similar psychological questions from the U.S. sample to those presented in Figure 4.3 with a slightly different dependent variable: a willingness to vote for a politician who uses threats and name-calls, but gets things done. The exact survey question was: "Suppose a politician is known for sometimes making violent threats and calling his opponents names, but they are also known as a politician that gets things done—fixes roads, builds hospitals, and attracts investments. How likely would you be to vote for such a politician?" 78% of the sample answered the question. Of those who answered it, 16% would definitely vote for, 31.7% probably would vote for, 18.4% probably would not vote for, and 34% definitely would not vote for a politician who uses violent rhetoric but got stuff done.[15] Which personality traits are correlated with supporting a nasty-talking politician?

These personality correlates included the same four questions to measure preferences for a tough leader ($\alpha = 0.37$);[16] the authoritarianism child-rearing scale ($\alpha = 0.46$) (Hetherington and Weiler 2009); the same three items from the Buss-Perry trait aggression scale ($\alpha = 0.64$); as well as the single item drawn from the American National Election Study question to measure their belief in the acceptability of political violence: "How often do you feel it is justified for people to use violence to pursue their political goals in this country?" (1-never to 5-always). Given the low α on support for a tough leader, each item of the scale is included separately. All of these measures were then rescaled to lie between 0–1 for comparability purposes. Also included are whether an individual was a supporter of the Euromaidan protests (49% of the sample), and of President Zelensky (88%). We are interested if certain personality traits and attitudes are positively correlated with support for a nasty politician.

The results are presented in Figure 4.4. Overall there's a similar pattern in Ukraine compared to the U.S. Certain psychological characteristics and political attitudes are associated with a greater willingness to support a politician who engages in name-calling and threats (but also gets things done). For instance those who prefer a leader that takes quick action, stands firm, and doesn't follow the usual rules are more supportive of a name-calling politician. One

[15] Rescaled to lie between 0 (definitely would not vote) to 1 (definitely would vote).

[16] (1) Takes quick action vs. Is patient, (2) Is diplomatic vs. Is tough, (3) Is willing to compromise vs. Stands firm on their positions, (4) Doesn't follow the usual political rules vs. Follows the usual political rules.

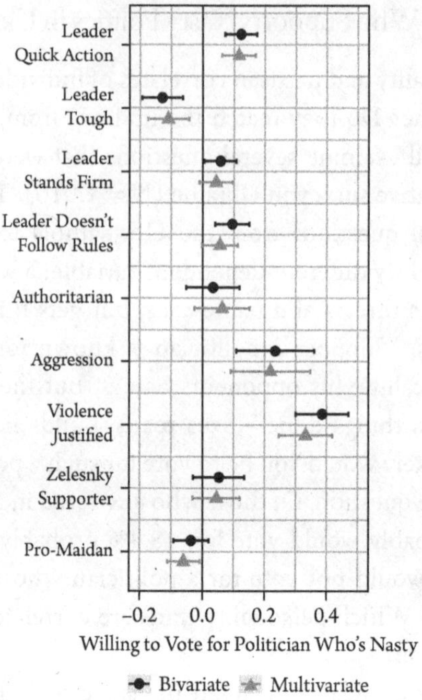

Figure 4.4 Personality traits and general attitudes predict support for a politician who uses nasty rhetoric in Ukraine (KIIS survey).

Note: Plot shows regressions coefficients. The dependent variable is willingness to vote for a politician who uses violent rhetoric (0-1). Each variable includes the bivariate relationship and also the full model with all variables included. 95% Confidence Interval.

curious exception is that individuals who prefer a tough leader (to one who is diplomatic) are *less* supportive of a politician who uses name-calling and threats. Nearly 81% of the sample preferred a tough to diplomatic leader. This findings may be due to Ukraine's political culture, whereby due to the legacy of communism Ukrainians hold both democratic and authoritarian values (Katchanovski 2012; Pop-Eleches and Tucker 2014). Or it could also be the fact that the Ukrainian word for "tough" we used in the survey (*mitsnyy*) also means sturdy and solid (much more positive connotation than in English). Those who hold more aggressive traits, as well as those who believe that violence is sometimes justified in politics are both more likely to support a politician who uses violent rhetoric. Finally, Euromaidan supporters are less likely to support a politician who uses nasty rhetoric.

Across both the U.S. and Ukraine we see that tolerance of politicians who use nasty politics is associated with a preference for strong and tough leaders, aggressive personality types, and those that think violence is acceptable to solve disputes. This is in line with our theory of the demand for nasty politics: certain personalities are more accepting of nasty politics.

Also, while partisanship is weakly related to tolerance and support of violence rhetoric in both contexts, it doesn't seem to be driving the results. This is an important point to emphasize. Imagine if most Republicans or Euromaidan supporters liked the nasty style of politics, and most Democrats and Euromaidan opponents hated it. Then an answer to our puzzle of violent rhetoric would be that one group of partisans like it, and the other side doesn't, so nasty political rhetoric is a purely partisan issue. But that's not the case.

4.3 Context, Threat, and Talking Tough

We've established that on average people don't like nasty political rhetoric, but certain personalities are more amenable to it. But one criticism is we're talking about nasty rhetoric in an abstract way. Yet, nasty rhetoric is never abstract. There's a politician using nasty language, and the target of the rhetoric. Nasty rhetoric also doesn't happen in a vacuum—there's political context. Is the rhetoric happening within the context of a back-and-forth between two politicians? Or is it part of a larger campaign of violence or intimidation? Do party leaders support or criticize it?

In this chapter, we've seen correlations that provide support for our theory of nasty politics and its implications for voters—it's generally not acceptable. However certain personality types are more accepting of it. One of the other key predictions of the theory is that perceived threats make voters more accepting of nasty politics, and more likely to view politicians who use it as tougher. To see whether this is the case we'll look at a series of survey experiments that manipulate different types of threats and see how that influences voters and their evaluations of the politicians who go nasty.

4.3.1 How Context Shapes Support for Nasty Rhetoric

Most times nasty politics is framed in protective language. Few politicians argue for outright aggression and violence. Rarely do they say, "I think we should just beat up the other side." It's usually framed as, "you should see what the other side wants to do to you. They are a threat and dangerous—and that's why I have to protect you." For example Hitler and the Nazis rooted their virulent antisemitism in protective language. They argued that German Jews (and leftists) had stabbed the German effort in World War I in the back (*Dolchstoßlegende*), and in doing so were responsible for Germany's humiliating defeat. This argument fit with the Nazis' broader narrative that Jews were "subhuman" (*Untermenschen*) cunning rats who needed to be exterminated to protect the Aryan nation (Smith 2011, p. 15).

Donald Trump's campaign for president began in 2015 with a speech that essentially said: "Mexico is sending rapists, China is killing us on trade, and the American dream is dying—so you need someone tough like me" (Phillips 2017). He continued this rhetoric in the lead up to the 2018 midterm elections, when he claimed, without any evidence, that the large group of Central American migrants that were traveling through Mexico to seek asylum at the southern U.S. border—known as the migrant caravan—was filled with "hardened criminals" who have "attacked others" (Yen and Long 2018).

In Ukraine in 2015 Serhiy Kaplin, the head of Social Democratic Party and member of Petro Poroshenko's Bloc, attacked then Prime Minister Arseniy Yatsenyuk (People's Front party) over Yatsenyuk's connections to former President Yanukovych and oligarchs. Kaplin said:

> Sooner or later in this life, everyone will be held accountable for all their crimes.... Sooner or later in life, the prime minister, his entourage, the robbing ministers and all members of the prime minister's mafia will answer.[17]

Politician's use nasty rhetoric to signal their toughness and willingness to fight for the ingroup in the face of outgroup threat. People might be willing to tolerate a bit of nastiness and unpleasantness if they feel that a threat demands it.

To test this argument we'll turn towards a series of survey experiments conducted in the U.S. and Ukraine. The experiments explore whether people do indeed equate nasty rhetoric with perceived toughness, and whether they are willing to reward politicians who use this kind of rhetoric.

At the beginning of both surveys respondents identified their ingroup and outgroup. In the beginning of the U.S. survey, respondents were asked whether they self identified as Republicans or Democrats.[18] Given the weakness of partisanship in Ukraine, I used whether a respondent agreed with statement that the Euromaidan (Maidan) protests of 2013–2014 were a popular protest movement, as opposed to a nationalist coup d'état as a measure of political identity. Those who agreed with the statement that the Euromaidan were popular protests were coded as Pro-Maidan, and everyone else Anti-Maidan.[19]

Also included in the U.S. survey experiments were psychological traits and predispositions that we've shown are correlated with acceptability of violent

[17] See *Obozrevatel* (2015).

[18] Note even those who identified as independent were forced to choose, "We know some people identify as independent, but do you think of yourself as closer to the Democratic or Republican party?"

[19] Respondents who viewed the Euromaidan as a nationalist coup d'état, or given social desirability bias, refused to answer, were coded as anti-Maidan.

rhetoric. This includes (1) their baseline levels of preferences for a tough leader ($\alpha = 0.53$); (2) the standard authoritarianism child-rearing scale ($\alpha = 0.76$) (Hetherington and Weiler 2009); (3) three items from the Buss-Perry trait aggression scale (Kalmoe 2014) ($\alpha = 0.84$); and (4) the single item drawn from the American National Election Study question to measure their belief in acceptability of violence in politics.[20] All of these measures were then rescaled to lie between 0-1 for comparability purposes.

In the Ukraine survey, because of space constraints, only two personality questions were abled to be included. One measure is whether they thought violence was a justified and acceptable part of politics. The other was a question on people's preference for a tough leader. "Some people prefer political leaders that are diplomatic and polite, while others like leaders that talk and act tough. On a scale from 0–100, where 0 is 'only diplomatic and polite,' 100 is 'only talks and acts tough,' and 50 is 'sometimes diplomatic and sometimes tough,' which kind of political leader would you prefer?" The mean response was 47.8.

Experiment 1: Does outgroup threat increase support for a nasty politician?

Our theory of nasty politics argues that aggressive, and threatening rhetoric is more attractive to voters when it's framed as protecting the ingroup from the outgroup. People are more willing to tolerate a nasty, junkyard-dog politician who insults and intimidates their rivals when the outgroup is viewed as a serious threat. The exact wording for the treatment in this experiments comes from prominent U.S. Christian conservative Jerry Falwell Jr.'s tweet that we previously discussed. In his tweet he argued that conservatives and Christians need more politicians as street fighters like Trump "because the liberal fascists Dems are playing for keeps & many Repub leaders are a bunch of wimps!" (Klein 2019).

Falwell's language fits with our theory of how politicians and political elites use nasty rhetoric. He emphasizes the threat posed by Democrats "playing for keeps," and how other Republicans were weak ("wimps") in the face of these threats. Finally, he advocates for more Republican "street fighters." It's a violent metaphor—politics as a blood sport—but it's ambiguous what Falwell is suggesting. In one interpretation, Falwell is saying that Republicans need to be more steadfast in their positions, something more in line with an intimidating statement. But it can also be read in a more sinister way. Given the stakes and what Democrats want to do Republicans must be willing to use all options, including actual violence.

[20] "How often do you feel it is justified for people to use violence to pursue their political goals in this country?" (1-never to 5-always).

Does threatening rhetoric where a politician advocates that the other side is "out to destroy" the ingroup increase support for nasty politics? This is our main question in Experiment 1. For example in the U.S. self-identified Democratic respondents were randomly assigned to: one in which a politician said it is necessary for politicians who are "streetfighters" to deal with members of the other party, and one in which they said the same thing, but also emphasized that the other side "wants to destroy us."[21] After the treatment, respondents evaluated how likely they were to vote for (0-not likely to 100-very likely), how strong of a leader (0-very weak to 100-very strong), and how much they would trust the nasty-talking politician (0-not trust a to 100-trust a lot).

The Ukrainian experiment wording closely followed the U.S. wording in Experiment 1, but Pro- and Anti-Maidan were substituted for Democrat and Republican.[22]

We are interested in whether voters are more willing to vote for, more likely to view as a strong, and more likely to trust a politician when they use nasty frames to argue that the outgroup is out to destroy the ingroup.

The findings in Table 4.1 show that this is the case. The average treatment effect (Columns 1, 3, and 5) and with controls (Columns 2, 4, and 6) all show that respondents were more likely to vote for, believe they are a strong leader, and trust a politician when nasty rhetoric towards the outgroup is framed in this existential way. The effect size for the treatment is significant too. It's equivalent to an approximately 1-standard deviation increase in trait aggression ($s = 0.26$). Across both treatment conditions respondents who have a preference for a tough leader and score higher on trait aggression are more likely to vote for, believe they are strong, and trust a politician that says they need street fighters. Those who believe violence is more justified are also more likely to vote and to trust a politician who advocates for a street fighting style of politics.

The findings in Table 4.2 show the results in Ukraine for the effects of framing nasty politics as protecting the ingroup from an outgroup that wants to destroy them. The effects are similar in terms of willingness to vote for a nasty-talking politician (Columns 1 and 2). Voters are about 4 points more likely on a (0–100)

[21] Self-identified Republicans received the exact same treatments just with partisanship switched (Democrat for Republican and vice versa).

[22] Since partisanship is a weaker issue in Ukraine, and the salience of corruption is high, I also split my sample in half. Half of respondents received a version of the treatment that refers to corrupt politicians instead of mentioning Euromaidan. The wording of the treatment was as follows for the corrupt politician versions, "Supporters of a strong Ukraine need to stop electing 'nice guys.' We need street fighters to deal with some of these corrupt politician assholes. Corrupt politicians don't just want to win, they want to destroy us." I found no difference in the direction of the treatment when the target of ire was a corrupt politician, or Pro-Maidan/Anti-Maidan politicians. So I pool these two versions of Vignette 2 together. Full wording of the treatments can be found in the Online Appendix.

Table 4.1 **Experiment 1: Threatening rhetoric increases support, perceived strength, and trust for a politician who uses nasty politics in the U.S. (Amazon MTurk).**

	Dependent variable					
	Willingness to Vote for (0–100)?		*How Strong of a Leader (0–100)?*		*How Much Trust in (0–100)?*	
	(1)	(2)	(3)	(4)	(5)	(6)
Treatment: Destroy Us	7.899** (3.114)	6.810** (2.844)	8.380*** (2.950)	7.315*** (2.734)	6.517** (3.005)	5.597** (2.714)
Violence Justified		19.990*** (7.015)		8.172 (6.742)		17.436*** (6.693)
Tough Leader		26.051*** (5.339)		26.379*** (5.132)		24.126*** (5.094)
Authoritarian		1.597 (4.150)		2.502 (3.989)		0.916 (3.960)
Aggression		18.524*** (6.868)		19.189*** (6.601)		25.233*** (6.552)
Republican		0.163 (3.313)		0.987 (3.185)		−1.076 (3.161)
Constant	39.468*** (2.200)	21.973*** (2.909)	46.507*** (2.083)	30.357*** (2.796)	41.473*** (2.123)	23.999*** (2.776)
Observations	409	409	409	409	409	409
R^2	0.016	0.193	0.019	0.173	0.011	0.208
Adjusted ^{2}	0.013	0.181	0.017	0.160	0.009	0.196

Note: *p<0.1; **p<0.05; ***p<0.01

scale to support the politician when the outgroup is framed as an existential threat. Yet, there's no effect of the treatment on how strong or how much they trust the politician (Columns 3–6). Across both treatment conditions, respondents who believe violence is always justified are also more likely to vote for a nasty politician, believe the nasty politician is a stronger leader, and have more trust in the nasty politician. Those who prefer a purely tough leader to a purely diplomatic leader are more likely to vote for, and view as strong and trustworthy the nasty politician. Euromaidan supporters are also slightly more likely to vote for and believe a politician is strong who uses nasty rhetoric.

Table 4.2 **Experiment 1: Threatening rhetoric increases support for a politician who uses nasty politics in Ukraine (KIIS).**

	Dependent variable					
	Willingness to Vote for (0–100)?		*How Strong of a Leader (0–100)?*		*How Much Trust in (0–100)?*	
	(1)	(2)	(3)	(4)	(5)	(6)
Treatment:	4.307**	3.791*	1.508	0.640	1.593	1.007
Destroy Us	(1.943)	(1.956)	(2.021)	(2.096)	(1.899)	(1.974)
Violence		29.421***		21.839***		17.435***
Justified		(3.850)		(4.124)		(3.884)
Tough		15.356***		10.323***		7.372**
Leader		(3.240)		(3.471)		(3.269)
Pro-Maidan		3.405*		3.820*		1.385
		(1.954)		(2.093)		(1.971)
Constant	23.754***	10.421***	32.904***	23.718***	26.774***	20.110***
	(1.400)	(2.341)	(1.456)	(2.507)	(1.369)	(2.361)
Observations	1022	942	1022	942	1022	942
R^2	0.005	0.094	0.001	0.045	0.001	0.030
Adjusted R^2	0.004	0.090	−0.000	0.041	−0.000	0.026

Note: *p<0.1; **p<0.05; ***p<0.01

Across both experiments we find support for the idea that framing nasty rhetoric as an existential threat increases support for the politician who uses this kind of language. It also increases how strong and tough politicians are viewed in the U.S. but not in Ukraine. Baseline attitudes and personality traits—aggression, acceptance of violence being justified in politics, and support for a tough leader—all are correlated with increased support for harsh language towards outgroups regardless of how nasty politics is framed.

Experiment 2: Does the threat of actual violence increase support for nasty politics?

Experiment 1 showed that people respond to the existential framing of outgroup threat. But what about actual violence—how does it shape how people view nasty politics? Experiment 2 explores whether the threat of actual violence influences how receptive people are to nasty rhetoric. Experiment 2 was carried out in both the U.S. and Ukraine. Respondents were randomly assigned to one of two treatments—one in which outgroup partisans are peacefully protesting (low threat), or one in which outgroup partisans are violently protesting (high threat). Across both treatments, one candidate advocated conciliation, saying "I wish we could all get along." The other candidate engaged in nasty politics by dehumanizing and engaging in incitement against the outgroup. The nasty candidate said: "Some of these [outgroup members] are animals who deserve to be roughed up."[23]

After the treatment, respondents evaluated whether they would vote for the nasty candidate over the more conciliatory candidate. They also evaluated how strong of a leader they thought the conciliatory and nasty candidates were. The key question is does violence by the outgroup make people more likely to support the nasty candidate and view them positively?

Table 4.3 presents the effects of high threat treatment compared to the low threat treatment among U.S. respondents. Columns 1 and 2 show that the threat condition has no effect on the likelihood of supporting the nasty candidate. However, respondents were more likely to view the conciliatory candidate as weaker in the high threat treatment (Columns 3 and 4), and that the nasty candidate was stronger (Columns 5 and 6). Across both treatment conditions, those who support tougher leaders were more likely to vote for the nasty candidate, view the conciliatory candidate as weaker, and the nasty candidate as stronger. Those who score higher on trait aggression were also more likely to vote for the nasty candidate and view them as a stronger leader.

Table 4.4 presents the effects of high threat treatment compared to the low threat treatment for the Ukraine respondents. Columns 1 and 2 show that the high threat condition marginally increases the likelihood of supporting the nasty candidate. Respondents were also more likely to view the candidate that called for reconciliation as weaker in the high threat treatment (Columns 3 and 4). Across both treatment conditions, those who support tougher leaders were more likely to vote for the nasty candidate, and view the conciliatory candidate as weaker. Those who believe violence is justified were more likely to vote for the nasty candidate, view the conciliatory candidate as weaker, and Candidate the nasty candidate as stronger. Interestingly, unlike in the U.S., there are partisan differences with Pro-Maidan supporters more likely to vote for the nasty candidate and view them as stronger.

Across both experiments in the U.S. and the Ukraine, threat makes people view leaders who use nasty rhetoric appear stronger (especially in the U.S.), and

[23] Self-identified Republicans received the exact same treatments just with partisanship switched (Democrat for Republican and vice versa). Self-identified Anti-Maidan respondents received the exact same treatments except "pro-Russian activists" was replaced with "nationalist activists," "Pro-Euromaidan political party" was replaced with "Anti-Euromaidan political party," and "pro-Russian supporters" was replaced with "nationalist people."

Table 4.3 **Experiment 2: When faced with outgroup violence, conciliatory politicians are rated weaker, and nasty politicians tougher in the U.S. (Amazon MTurk).**

	Dependent variable					
	Willingness to Vote for Nasty Cand. (0 = no, 1 = yes)?		*How Strong of a leader Conciliatory Cand. (0–100)?*		*How Strong of a leader Nasty Cand. (0–100)?*	
	(1)	(2)	(3)	(4)	(5)	(6)
Treatment: High Threat	0.029 (0.038)	0.038 (0.035)	−4.054* (2.382)	−4.213* (2.348)	5.966** (2.882)	6.801** (2.643)
Violence Justified		−0.010 (0.084)		−9.673* (5.585)		0.744 (6.287)
Tough Leader		0.370*** (0.066)		−13.735*** (4.369)		18.975*** (4.918)
Authoritarian		0.010 (0.051)		3.822 (3.404)		9.445** (3.832)
Aggression		0.251*** (0.085)		1.370 (5.654)		28.802*** (6.364)
Republican		0.003 (0.041)		−0.592 (2.730)		1.002 (3.073)
Constant	0.161*** (0.027)	−0.040 (0.038)	64.317*** (1.684)	69.454*** (2.516)	43.424*** (2.038)	24.694*** (2.832)
Observations	410	410	410	410	410	410
R^2	0.001	0.141	0.007	0.052	0.010	0.182
Adjusted R^2	−0.001	0.128	0.005	0.038	0.008	0.170

Note: *p<0.1; **p<0.05; ***p<0.01

those favoring reconciliation as much weaker. In sum, heightened threat makes people more willing to tolerate nasty politics, and view politicians who use it as tougher.

The results from Experiment 2 further confirm that personality traits and attitudes—such as supporting a tough leader, trait aggression, or believing political violence can sometimes be justified—increase support for and positively evaluate leaders who engage in nasty politics.

Table 4.4 **Experiment 2: When faced with outgroup violence, conciliatory politicians are rated weaker in Ukraine (KIIS).**

	Dependent variable					
	Willingness to Vote for Nasty Cand. (0 = no, 1 = yes)?		*How Strong of a leader Conciliatory Cand. (0–100)?*		*How Strong of a leader Nasty Cand. (0–100)?*	
	(1)	(2)	(3)	(4)	(5)	(6)
Treatment:	0.046^{**}	0.037	-3.808^{*}	-3.951^{*}	2.035	2.262
High Threat	(0.023)	(0.023)	(1.976)	(2.067)	(1.900)	(1.939)
Violence		0.139^{***}		-11.757^{***}		22.481^{***}
Justified		(0.046)		(4.080)		(3.828)
Tough		0.142^{***}		1.979		9.152^{***}
Leader		(0.039)		(3.436)		(3.224)
Pro Maidan		0.071^{***}		−1.145		4.594^{**}
		(0.023)		(2.068)		(1.940)
Constant	0.141^{***}	0.019	58.611^{***}	59.980^{***}	29.701^{***}	19.962^{***}
	(0.016)	(0.028)	(1.400)	(2.453)	(1.346)	(2.301)
Observations	1022	942	1022	942	1022	942
R^2	0.004	0.037	0.004	0.013	0.001	0.054
Adjusted R^2	0.003	0.033	0.003	0.009	0.000	0.050

Note: *p<0.1; **p<0.05; ***p<0.01

4.4 Summary of Findings

This chapter focused on the demand side of nasty rhetoric, and it provides part of the answer to the puzzle of nasty politics. Voters in both the U.S. and Ukraine have fairly consistent views on nasty politics. On average they don't like it. And they have a rank-ordering of nastiness. Incitement and threats of violence, such as threatening to beat opponents up are worse than insults and accusations.

But there are two important caveats. First, certain personality types are more accepting of nasty politics. Those who are more aggressive, like tough leaders, or believe violence can be justified are more accepting of violent nasty rhetoric. This is true in both the U.S. and Ukraine.

The context and framing of nasty politics matters. The two survey experiments show that respondents are more likely to support politicians who use nasty rhetoric, and view the politicians who use it as stronger leaders, especially when outgroups are framed as an existential threat, or engaged in actual violence. This confirms our theory of nasty politics that during periods of heightened threat or conflict, politicians have more leeway to use nasty rhetoric.

The picture we have now is that on average nasty rhetoric is costly for politicians to use because the public doesn't like it. But that's on average. Different personality types are more accepting of nasty politics. And if nasty rhetoric is framed as protecting the ingroup from threats from the outgroup, it also can increase support for the politician who uses it. In the next chapter, we'll explore when and how politicians use nasty politics.

5

Which Politicians Choose to Get Nasty and When?

On May 12, 2020, former White House physician to both President Obama and President Trump, Ronny Jackson, tweeted out the following: "President Obama weaponized the highest levels of our government to spy on President Trump. Every Deep State traitor deserves to be brought to justice for their heinous actions."[1] Jackson's tweet echoed President Trump's baseless claims that President Obama had tried to "take down" the Trump presidency. Jackson's tweet angered former Obama officials because Jackson had enjoyed a good relationship with many in the Obama administration including President Obama himself (Itkowitz 2020).

It's also a bizarre thing for a former White House doctor to tweet out. Yet, Jackson's tweet makes a lot more sense when we realize that he sent it while he was in the midst of a run-off in a Republican primary for an open seat in Congress representing the Texas Panhandle. After being criticized for his tweet from several of his former Obama-era colleagues, Jackson doubled-down on his comments in a statement he released saying: "I will never apologize for standing up to protect America's national security interests and constitutional freedoms, even if that means triggering liberals and the 'mainstream media.'" A former Obama National Security Council spokesman summed up the view of those who felt that Jackson was trying to trade in controversy for political gain: "Ronny Jackson was friends with Obama and his entire staff. I never heard him make a partisan statement. So it's really been sad to watch him debase himself by lying for Trump and promoting this toxic bullshit to win a Congressional primary. Truly shameful" (Liptak 2020). Jackson would win the Republican primary, and

[1] Jackson, Ronny (RonnyJackson4TX), Twitter, May 12, 2020. https://twitter.com/RonnyJackson4TX/status/1260313803297677312.

Nasty Politics: The Logic of Insults, Threats, and Incitement. Thomas Zeitzoff, Oxford University Press.
© Oxford University Press 2023. DOI: 10.1093/oso/9780197679494.003.0005

easily win the general election victory in November of 2020 with nearly 80% of the vote.

***

Former Georgian President Mikheil Saakashvili has enjoyed one of the most interesting journeys of a world leader. Before entering Ukrainian politics, he was best known as the leader of the Rose Revolution in Georgia in the early 2000s. The Rose Revolution was a popular uprising over fraudulent elections that led to the ousting of President Eduard Shevardnadze, and the ascension of pro-Western Saakashvili (Times 2008). As president, Saakashvili embarked on a broad pro-Western, anti-corruption platform. His turn towards the West and NATO irked Russia, who viewed NATO and Western infringement in Georgia as meddling in Russia's own sphere of influence (Trenin 2009). Saakashvili's anti-Russian policy spilled over into open-warfare when he initiated the disastrous (for Georgia) 2008 Russo-Georgian War over the breakaway region of South Ossetia (Traynor 2009). In 2013 he left Georgia at the end of his second term as president, and the new Georgia government subsequently issued a warrant for his arrest on human rights violations and embezzlement of government funds (Horowitz 2014). Following Euromaidan, and the election of his friend Petro Poroshenko as president, Poroshenko granted Saakashvili Ukrainian citizenship and appointed him as governor of the corruption-plagued Odesa Oblast.

From his perch in Odesa, Saakashvili began building his own political party and critiquing Poroshenko's anti-corruption effort. His confrontational style won him plaudits from some anti-corruption activists. But it did not sit well with Poroshenko and his allies who increasingly viewed Saakashvili as a political threat.

Saakashvili lasted only a year in the position before Poroshenko dismissed him. In 2017 Ukrainian police attempted to arrest Saakashvili on charges of "suspicion of assisting a criminal organisation." His supporters surrounded the police and were able to force Saakashvili's release. In a rousing speech from a rooftop, Saakashvili said, "The people of Ukraine must assemble and force the Rada to remove from power the criminal group led by the traitor to Ukraine, Poroshenko" (Polityuk and Zinets 2017). In February 2018, Poroshenko and the Ukrainian authorities were finally able to grab Saakashvili. Masked members of the Ukrainian security services apprehended Saakashvili while he was having lunch in a Georgian restaurant in Kyiv. They deported the now stateless Saakashvili to Poland. Once in Poland, held a press conference where he accused Poroshenko and state security services of "kidnapping" him and said, "(Poroshenko) is not a president and not a man, but a sly profiteer who wants to ruin Ukraine" (Higgins 2018).

Saakashvili was never able to drum up popular support in Ukraine, and his favorability ratings (12%) were even lower than Poroshenko (15%) (International Republican Institute 2019). In May of 2019, newly elected president Volodymyr Zelensky dismissed the charges against Saakashvili and invited him back to Ukraine. Saakashvili claimed he had "no interest" in returning to politics. In May of 2020, and Saakashvili accepted a position as head of Zelensky's National Reform Council (RFE/RL 2020*a*).

Yet Saakashvili was itching to maintain relevance in his native Georgia. In a move that surprised even his Georgian allies, Saakashvili returned to George in early October 2021 ahead of elections, to try to rally his supporters once more. He was promptly arrested by Georgian authorities. While in prison he began a hunger strike to protest against the incumbent Georgian government led by the Georgian Dream party. Saakashvili's political rival, and incumbent Georgian Prime Minister Irakli Garibashvili (Georgia Dream), said that Saakashvili's hunger strike was a staged "show," and accused him of trying to stoke tensions in Georgia (Agenda.ge 2021).

Why do politicians like Jackson and Saakashvili engage in nasty politics? How and why do the politicians use insults, accusations, intimidating statements, incitement, and even actual violence? What explains the supply side of nasty politics? These are the central questions that this chapter will answer. Jackson's tweets and Saakashvili's political brand all point to nasty politics as a disruptive strategy to garner attention and solidify core supporters. Saakashvili's approach to politics also shows how the nasty style can be a desperate attempt for politicians to stay relevant amidst declining support. To see whether these insights from Jackson and Saakashvili generalize, we will explore nasty politics in several different contexts in this chapter. We'll look at databases of nasty politics in the U.S. and Ukraine gathered from media sources. To see how nasty politics is used in legislatures, we'll explore a database of disruptions in the Ukrainian Rada. Finally, we will look at the use of incivility on Twitter from a large corpus of tweets from U.S. members of Congress.

5.1 Nasty Politics Database

Which politicians use nasy politics? What nasty things do politicians say about their opponents? Who are the targets of their ire, and where do they use nasty rhetoric? Answering these questions is key if we want to unlock the puzzle of nasty politics. We've already explored in Chapter 3 how key politicians in the U.S., Ukraine, and Israel use nasty politics on social media. But that precludes all of the other venues for nasty politics.

In the U.S. political rallies are important showcases for politicians to engage with supporters and stoke the base. Examples of this include President Trump calling California Democratic Rep. Adam Schiff a "pencil neck" at a rally in January 2020 (Walker 2020), or when Kamala Harris laughed and seemed to agree with a supporter that President Trump was "mentally retarded" at a New Hampshire rally in September 2019 (Taylor 2019). There also isn't anything in the U.S. comparable to the spectacle of Ukrainian political chat shows. For example, in August 2018 two deputies in the Rada—Ihor Mosiychuk of Oleh Lyashko's Radical Party, and Serhii Shakhov of the People's Will faction—got into a fight live on the *Pryamiy* TV channel. During the show, Shakhov accused Mosiychuk of attending gay pride parades. Shakov further implied that Mosiychuk himself was a closeted gay man, alluding to the leader of Mosiychuk's party—Oleh Lyashko and Lyashko's rumored homosexuality (Tuchynska 2010). Mosiychuk responded by promising he would do to Shakhov what he did to Serhiy Leshchenko, another deputy in the Rada who Mosiychuk had fought with previously. Shakhov responded by punching Mosiychuk, who then proceeded to use his cane to hit Shakhov. The host eventually stepped between the two of them. But the scuffle continued in the elevator after the show ended (Segodnya 2018).

Nasty politics does not just happen in Congress or the Rada, or on social media, but across all these different contexts. We want to capture as many of these instances of nasty politics. But if we only looked at tweets or Facebook posts,[2] or speeches in the Rada or Congress, we would miss many key incidents. We don't want to only focus on nasty politics on social media since that would miss what happens at political rallies or on talk shows. We would also miss the most threatening kind of nasty politics, which is not rhetoric but actual physical violence.

To get as wide a swath of nasty incidents as possible, I turned to media sources in both the U.S. and Ukraine. I created a database of nasty politics in both the U.S. and Ukraine from January 1, 2016–October 1, 2019, using Internet news websites in both countries.[3] In the U.S. I used five news websites: (1) nytimes.com (*New York Times*); (2) washingtonpost.com (*Washington Post*); (3) cnn.com (*CNN*); (4) politico.com (*Politico*); and (5) mailonline.com (*Daily Mail*). In Ukraine I used the following seven news websites: (1) znaj.ua; (2) ukr.net; (3) obozrevatel.com; (4) politeka.net; (5) korrespondent.net; (6) tsn.ua; and (7) segodnya.ua. These news websites represent a cross-section of ideological

[2] Facebook is more popular in Ukraine, while Twitter is extremely popular among political junkies, journalists, and politicians in the U.S. See Matviyishyn (2019) and Ingram (2017).

[3] More information on how I constructed the databases can be found in the Online Appendix. Many events had multiple news stories—particularly those involving Trump in the U.S., or Poroshenko in Ukraine. Stories were cross-referenced to avoid double-counting the same incident.

slants and types of coverage. For instance the *New York Times* and *Washington Post* are traditional newspapers, whereas *Politico* focuses more closely on the scoops and scandals of U.S. politics. Likewise while the *Washington Post* skews left, the *Daily Mail* is right-leaning.[4] In Ukraine, znaj.ua and politeka.net tend towards tabloid coverage, while segodnya.ua offers more traditional news coverage, and ukr.net is the largest news website in Ukraine, functioning as a news aggregator for other sites' stories.[5] In terms of ideological slant, obozrevatel.com leans more Pro-Euromaidan and Western in its coverage, while segodnya.ua, is owned by the oligarch Rinat Akhmetov and has a history of supporting former President Yanukovych and pro-Russian Ukrainian politicians (Faryna 2011).

To be eligible to be included in the database, the politician who instigated the nasty incident had to be a national-level politician. In the U.S. this is pretty straightforward. The eligible politicians included Congressional candidates and members of Congress, as well as the president, vice president, and presidential candidates. Governors, mayors, and state elected officials were excluded. Ukraine's semi-presidential system makes things a bit more complicated. In Ukraine I included in the database all People's Deputies in the 8th Rada (November 2014–July 2019), all People's Deputies in the 9th Rada (August 2019–2020), all presidential candidates from the 2019 presidential election, and the top-ten candidates from a list of major parties.

In order to understand a phenomenon we first have to document and catalog it (Tilly 2002). The databases of nasty politics in the U.S. and Ukraine gives us a systematic way to see what nasty politics looks like in both countries. What are politicians saying and doing? Who said or did what to whom, and when and where did they do it? Each instance of nasty politics includes the date it took place, where it took place (the context), who said or initiated the nasty politics (instigator), who it was targeted towards (target), and coded the nasty thing that was said or done (category of nasty politics). Note that if two politicians exchanged insults, or fought each other, this would be coded as two incidents—what politician A did or said to politician B, and what politician B did or said to politician A.

Each instance of nasty politics in the database also includes the level of threat intensity shown in Table 5.1. We have now added to our intensity scale a measure of actual physical violence. Recall that this level of threat intensity (intensity for short) lets us measure how threatening the rhetoric and actions are for an incident in our database. A pretty mundane instance of nasty politics that included an insult (1) and accusation (2) would receive an intensity score of 3 (1+2). A much more threatening incident that included an insult (1), an

[4] See AllSides (2021).

[5] See Churanova (2018) and All You Can Read (2021).

Table 5.1 **Measuring threat intensity in the nasty politics databases in the U.S. and Ukraine.**

Kind of Rhetoric	*Level of Threat*	*Definition*
Insults	1	Explicitly or implicitly name-calling or insulting opponents.
Accusations	2	Accusing the opponents of bad, shady, criminal, or illegal behavior. Pushing conspiracies.
Intimidating Statements	3	Intimidating, threatening, or coercing political opponents (e.g., with investigations, consequences, jail time, etc.) not in an explicitly violent manner. Veiled threats.
Incitement	4	Violent threats or encouragement of violent behavior by supporters.
Physical violence	5	Includes fist fights, wrestling, choking, violent protests, melees, stabbings, and using firearms or explosives perpetrated by politicians.

accusation (2), incitement (4), and actual physical violence (5) would receive an intensity score of 12 (1+2+4+5).

It's not enough to know nasty politics happened, and describe its intensity, but we also want to see the patterns in its usage. Where does it tend to happen? Is it mostly on social media or on TV shows? Who are the targets of nasty politics? Other politicians, members of the media, minorities? Finally, what nasty things are they actually saying? What frames or metaphors, if any, do they use to denigrate their opponents? Are they attacking their intelligence, their patriotism, or their sexual orientation? Or are they accusing somebody of being racist?[6]

Table 5.2 shows the different coding categories for the nasty politics databases in the U.S. and Ukraine.

There are drawbacks to using media sources to create a database of nasty politics. What is newsworthy depends not just upon what a politician says or does, but where they said or did it, and even more importantly who they

[6] It should be noted that charges of racism or xenophobia were only coded in the U.S., not in Ukraine. While racism and xenophobia are important issues in Ukraine, accusing rival politicians of being racist or xenophobic is not a regular part of elite political contention, and doesn't carry the same weight as calling someone a "Russian agent," or "traitor." See Karatnycky (2018).

Table 5.2 **Context, targets, and frames of nasty rhetoric.**

Context *Where did the nasty rhetoric or incident happen?*	*Target* *Who was attacked or targeted?*	*Frames* *What nasty frames or metaphors did they use?*
1. **Media**: In an interview on TV, or newspapers, or with journalists; at a press briefing, press conference, press release, or on political chat show 2. **Legislative Action**: In hearings, meetings, or floor speeches 3. **Social media**: On Facebook, YouTube, Twitter, or blogs 4. **Campaign**: During a speech, rally, campaign ad, debate, or political campaign event 5. **Other**: Court proceedings, restaurants, in public, or unclear	1. **Political**: Members of Congress or People's Deputies in the Rada, politicians, political parties, political bosses, oligarchs (Ukraine), partisans (Democrats, Republicans, Maidan supporters, opponents, etc.) 2. **Media**: Journalists, media, television stations, media owners 3. **Activists**: Protesters, activists, NGOs, civil society 4. **Government**: Specific governmental bodies or offices, bureaucrats, police, military, judges 5. **Minority groups**: Immigrants, LGBT, Roma, Jews, refugees, religious minorities, foreigners 6. **Other**: Criminals, academics, companies, religious figures	1. **Intelligence**: Calling target dumb, stupid, moron, imbecile, idiotic, low-intellect, fool, mentally ill 2. **Dehumanizing**: Comparing target to an an animal, scum, scumbag, sewer, garbage, disease, trash, plague 3. **Sexual**: Calling target a prostitute, whore, gay, woman, effeminate, or weak 4. **Patriotism**: Charging treason, calling someone a traitor, un-American, not a Ukrainian, Kremlin agent, terrorist, unpatriotic, anti-democratic, authoritarian, enemy of the people 5. **Criminal**: gang, bandit, corrupt, robber, thug, criminal, swindler, fraud 6. **Racist (U.S. only)**: Calling target a racist, White nationalist, antisemite, xenophobe

are (Groeling 2010). So a first-term People's Deputy in the Rada or first-term member of Congress who says that a rival politician is "being an idiot" might not get covered. But if either President Zelensky or President Trump said the exact same thing, it might lead the news. Extremist politicians are also more likely to be covered precisely because of their tendency to say or do more extreme things (Wagner and Gruszczynski 2018). But we can also use the fact that the media have an incentive to cover politics from a combative and salacious angle to our advantage (Atkinson 2017). Nasty things that are said and done are more likely to be deemed newsworthy and receive coverage. We shouldn't be too concerned that we are missing major instances of nasty politics. Finally, news outlets also have their own biases that influence coverage. Fox News is more likely to point out a controversial thing that a Democrat says compared to MSNBC (DellaVigna and Kaplan 2007; Groeling 2008). This bias is especially true when discussing contentious political events (Davenport 2009). We can also use this bias to our advantage. Slanted outlets have incentives to cover outrageous actions taken by the other side (Webster 2020; Zeitzoff 2011). By including sources with different slants, we can insure that even more modest incidents of nastiness appear in our dataset.

5.1.1 Database in the U.S.

The resulting database for the U.S. contains 1,407 unique instances of nasty politics. It's also apparent how much coverage of nasty politics revolves around Trump. 38% of the incidents are initiated by Trump himself, and in 42% he is one of the targets. So approximately 80% of the instances of nasty politics involve Trump as either the antagonist or the target. Republicans are the instigators in 54% of nasty politics stories, while Democrats are in 42%. But again, Trump is dominant. When we look at just the Republican-instigated incidents he is responsible for more than 70% of them.

Figure 5.1 shows the frequency of different types of nasty politics in the database. The average intensity of each incident was a 3.7. It should be noted that this is more than twice as intense as the average intensity of Republican Rep. Matt Gaetz's (FL) tweets—the U.S. politician with on average the nastiest tweets from the eight U.S. politicians we focused on in the analysis in Chapter 3 (Table 3.2). This suggests that the media covers more intense and threatening incidents. Many incidents contain multiple types of rhetoric. For instance, more than 75% contain insults and accusations. Intimidating statements account for a little more than 30% of incidents. Only 2% of the database incidents contain incitement. The only incident of direct physical violence perpetrated by a politician involved the case of Montana Republican Congressional Greg Gianforte who body-slammed Ben Jacobs, a reporter for *The Guardian*, in May 2017 (Keneally 2018).

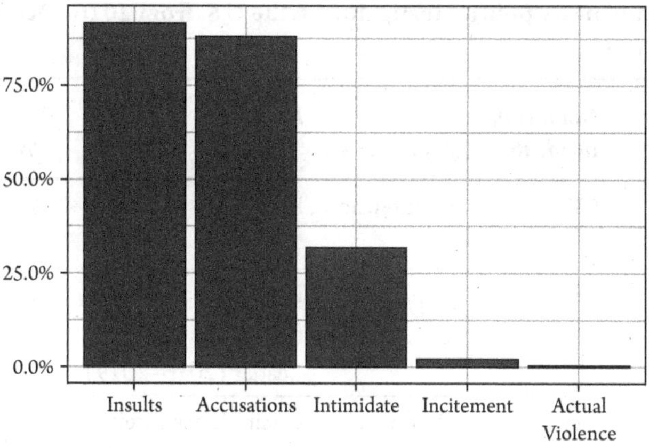

Figure 5.1 Insults and accusations are quite common parts of nasty politics in the U.S., while incitement and actual violence are rare (N = 1,407).

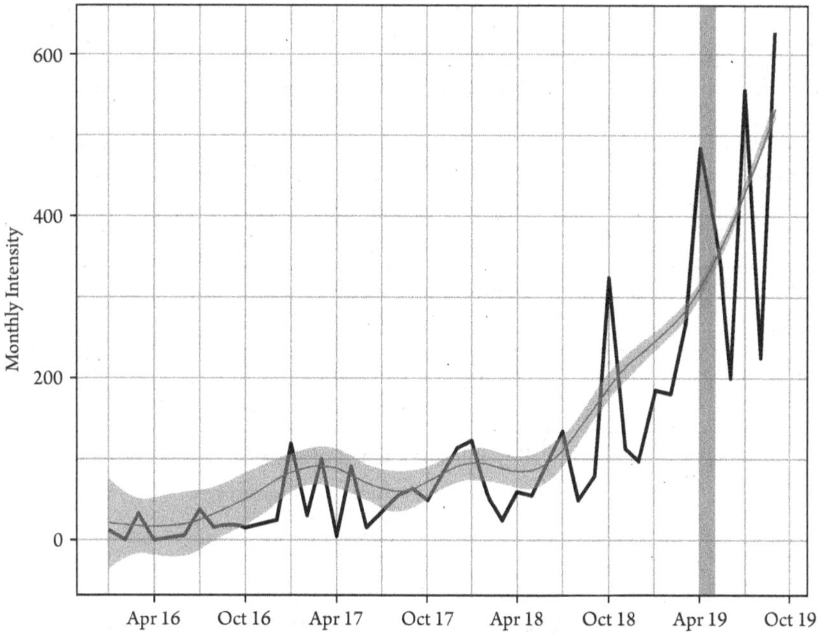

Figure 5.2 Intensity of nasty politics increases during the Trump presidency, particularly following the release of the Mueller report (2016–October 1, 2019).

Note: Vertical shaded region corresponds with the publishing of the "Mueller Report" (April 18, 2019).

Figure 5.2 shows the monthly time series of intensity in the U.S. from January 1, 2016–October 1, 2019. The graph makes clear how much the intensity of nasty politics increased during the Trump presidency, particularly following the release of the Mueller Report in April 2019. The intensity increased by more

Table 5.3 **Chief nasty politics instigators in the U.S. from 2016–October 1, 2019 (N = 1,407).**

Name	*Number of Incidents*	*Political Affiliations*	*Positions*	*Ran for President 2020?*
1. Donald Trump	532	Republican	President	Yes
2. Nancy Pelosi	64	Democrat	House Speaker (2019), Minority Leader (2016–2019)	No
3. Adam Schiff	29	Democrat	Chair House Intell. Committee (2019)	No
4. Elizabeth Warren	25	Democrat	Senator	Yes
5. Ilhan Omar	22	Democrat	Rep.	No
6. Chuck Schumer	21	Democrat	Senate Minority Leader	No
7. Jerrold Nadler	21	Democrat	Chair of the House Judiciary Committee (2019)	No
8. Joe Biden	20	Democrat	Vice President (until 2017)	Yes
9. Kamala Harris	19	Democrat	Senator	Yes
10. Lindsey Graham	18	Republican	Chair of Senate Judiciary Committee (2019)	No

than ten times, and the trajectory matches our findings from Chapter 3 about the upward trend in nasty politics in the U.S more generally (Figure 3.3).

Table 5.3 shows the key instigators of nasty rhetoric. It's not surprising, but President Donald Trump is at the top of the list with more than 532 incidents. This is nearly ten times the second-largest instigator, Democratic Speaker of the House, Nancy Pelosi. Part of the centrality of Trump to this database is his newsworthiness as president, and reflects a spin on the old adage that "when the president says it, it's news, regardless of how trivial." Trump's centrality reflects his unique predilection for insulting and making intimidating statements against varied groups (immigrants, Democrats, etc.), his perceived enemies (Mueller, Pelosi, and Schumer), and his prolific use of Twitter. One other key finding from the database, is that aside from President Trump and Republican Senator Lindsey Graham, eight of the ten biggest instigators are Democrats. And several of these Democrats were running for president in the Democratic primary, including Elizabeth Warren, Joe Biden, and Kamala Harris (Russonello 2020). The U.S. list also highlights two points about our theory of the nasty style. First, it tends to be more used by opposition politicians. And second, it can be a way to distinguish a politician with core supporters, especially in a crowded election field.

Where does nasty politics happen in the U.S.? Is it mostly at rallies? Interviews with journalists? Figure 5.3 shows the context. Reflecting the increasing primacy of social media in U.S. politics, more than 40% of nasty incidents happened on social media. The next two largest contexts are media interviews and press briefings, and campaign events and rallies, with each context accounting for more than 25% of the incidents. And while many decry the current political moment in the U.S. as echoing the "fields of blood" of Congress in the lead up to the U.S. Civil War (Freeman 2018), we don't see comparatively a lot of nasty politics being reported on during Congressional hearings, speeches, and meetings (less than 10%, legislative actions).

Who gets targeted by nasty politics? Figure 5.4 shows that more than 80% of the instances of nasty politics target other politicians, political figures, or political parties. Attacks on government officials, judges, and other members of the bureaucracy or law enforcement account for slightly more than 15% of all targets. Minority groups, including Jews, Blacks, LGBTQ, and immigrants,

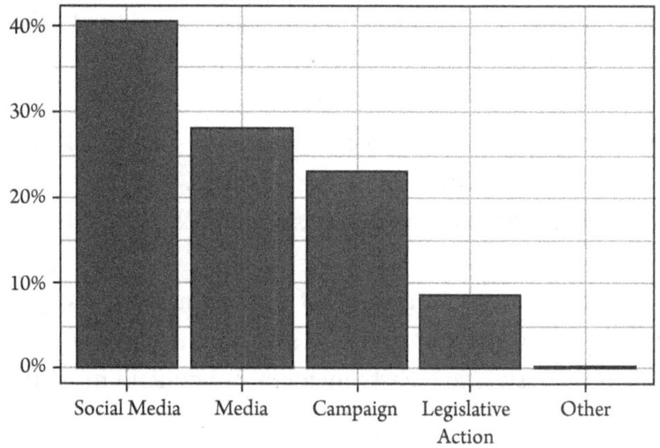

Figure 5.3 Nasty politics mostly happens on social media, via interviews and press releases (media), or on the campaign trail in the U.S. (N = 1,407).

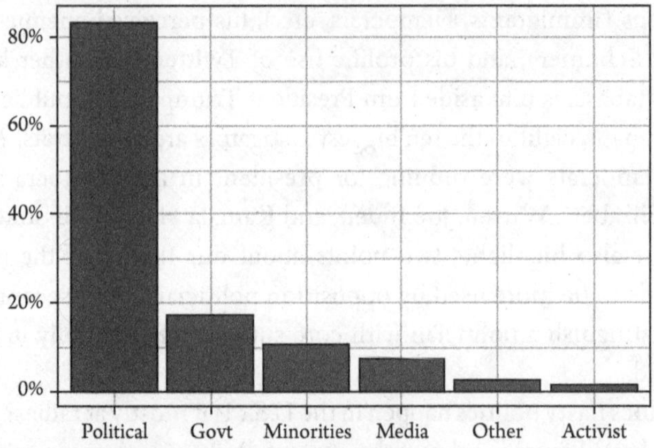

Figure 5.4 Political targets, including politicians, political parties, and their supporters, are the most common targets of nasty politics in the U.S. (N = 1,407).

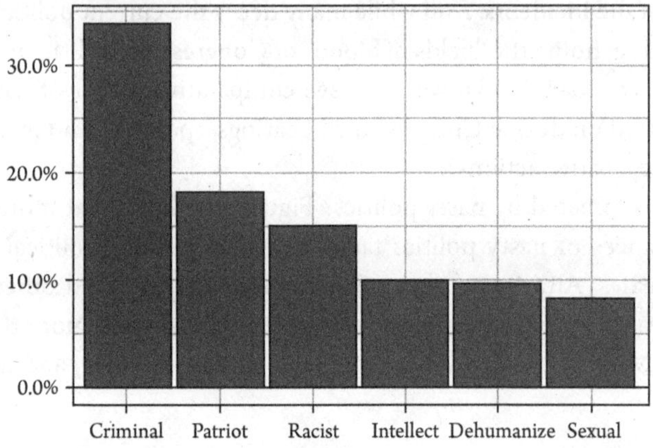

Figure 5.5 U.S. politicians most commonly use criminal, patriotic, and racist metaphors and frames when attacking their opponents (N = 1,407).

are the target in approximately 10% of all contexts, and attacks on media and journalists account for 7% of attacks. Big business, tech companies ("Other" category), as well as protesters and activists are each targeted less than 3% of the time.

It's also natural for us to wonder what kind of nasty metaphors or frames politicians choose to use (Figure 5.5).[7] It's important to note these categories are not mutually exclusive, so a nasty incident can contain more than one than

[7] Note, not all incidents contain a nasty metaphor or frame. In approximately 67% of the incidents in the U.S. database and 84% of incidents in the Ukraine database there was a nasty frame present.

metaphor or frame. For instance, at a rally in Texas in October 2018 in support for Republican Texas Senator Ted Cruz's reelection bid, President Trump said:

> Radical Democrats want to turn back the clock and restore corrupt, power-hungry globalists. A globalist is a person who wants the globe to do well but is not caring about our country so much. . . . I'm a nationalist.[8]

In this frame Trump is using a criminal frame against Democrats ("corrupt"), and also implying that they are unpatriotic, saying they are in favor of "power-hungry globalists" instead of Americans.[9]

Or the rhetoric may take a dehumanizing turn. At a rally to supporters in March 2017 Maryland Democratic Rep. Jamie Raskin made a pun with dehumanizing language comparing the Trump administration's contact with Russia to a "staff"/staph infection and questioning their patriotism:

> The Trump administration has a staff infection. . . . Every day we learn about another high-ranking Trump official who has been entangled with the highest levels of the Russian government, and Vladimir Putin, the former chief of the KGB.[10]

More than one-third of all incidents involve criminal allegations such as calling rivals "corrupt," "crooked," or a "conman." Questioning opponents' patriotism, or accusing them of treason was slightly less common, and present in a little less than 20% of incidents. Charges of racism, antisemitism, White nationalism, or xenophobia (Racist category) was present in 16% of violent rhetoric incidents. Less common was the use of dehumanizing rhetoric (10%), attacking an opponents' intellect by calling them "stupid" or an "intellect" (10%), or calling opponents weak, effeminate, or attacking their sexuality (8%).

What are the actual words U.S. politicians use to attack their opponents? Figure 5.6 shows a word cloud of the most commonly used nasty words. The most common word is "racist," reflecting the centrality that racism and racial appeals have played in Trump's presidency (Graham 2019). Several other key terms that were particular to the Trump era including threats to "impeach," "fake" (news), "witch," and "hunt" (witch hunt). Criminality or allegations of

[8] See de Moraes (2018).

[9] The Anti-Defamation League also consider the use of the term "globalist" as a code word for "Jews," and consider it an antisemitic dog whistle. See ADL (2018).

[10] See Martosko, Parry, and Chambers (2017).

Figure 5.6 Words used in nasty rhetoric in the U.S.
Note: Size, position, and color of word indicates frequency of this term mentioned in the U.S. database. Word stems are used, so idiotic/idiot/idiocy will all be under one term.

"crime," "illegal," "criminal," "crook," or "corrupt" are also quite common. Finally, allegations that opponents are "radic(al)" or "antisemit(ic)" were also common.

5.1.2 Database in Ukraine

The database in Ukraine contains 347 instances of nasty rhetoric and actual physical violence. The fact that the U.S. database contains nearly four times more incidents than the Ukraine database doesn't mean that U.S. politics is four times as nasty. It reflects the fact that nasty politics are much more central and common in Ukrainian politics, so the level of nastiness needed to make the news is a bit higher. Figure 5.7 shows the frequency of different types of rhetoric and actual violence in the Ukraine database and seems to support this view. More than 90% of the incidents contain insults and accusations. More than half of the incidents also contain intimidating statements. The biggest difference is the frequency of incitement and actual physical violence. More than 20% of the incidents in the database involve incitement, and more than 20% also involve actual violence, mostly physical fights between politicians. And the average intensity of each incident in Ukraine is a 6.3, more than 1.5 times higher than the average incident in the U.S. (average intensity is a 3.7). All of this confirms that Ukrainian politics are on average nastier and more violent than U.S. politics.

The monthly time series of intensity of nasty politics from January 1, 2016–October 1, 2019, is shown in Figure 5.8. The trend is fairly flat and constant. There are some small peaks around key events including the removal of Prime

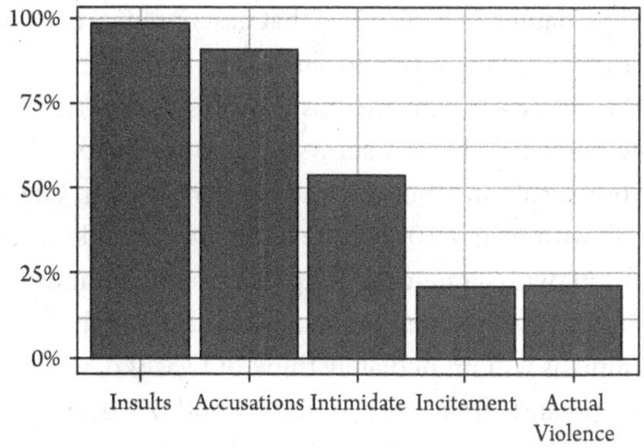

Figure 5.7 Most incidents in the Ukraine database contain insults, accusations, and intimidating statements. Incitement and actual violence is also quite common (N = 347).

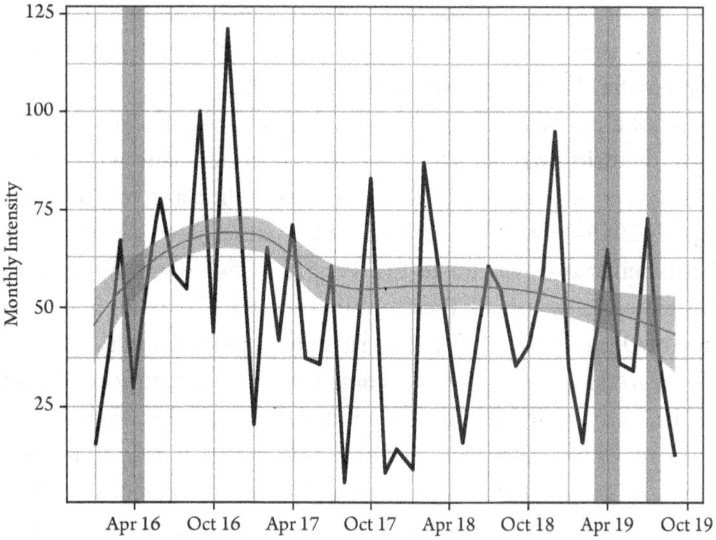

Figure 5.8 Intensity of nasty politics has some mini spikes, but is mostly flat (January 1, 2016–October 1, 2019).

Note: Vertical shaded regions capture three critical time periods: (1) the collapse of the Second Yatsenyuk Government in March and April of 2016; (2) the two rounds of presidential voting in March and April of 2019; and (3) the parliamentary elections in July of 2019.

Minister Yatsenyuk in April of 2016 following Yulia Tymoshenko and Oleh Lyashko withdrawing their support from President Poroshenko before a new government was formed (UNIAN 2016). While there is a small uptick in nasty politics around the 2019 presidential elections (March and April 2019) and the Rada elections (July 2019)—it does not deviate too much from the general flat trend. This in line from the time series analysis of media coverage of violent rhetoric shown in Chapter 3 (Figure 3.4) that nasty politics had fallen in Ukraine from its height in the lead up to the Euromaidan.

So who are the politicians who are most involved in the nasty style in Ukraine during this time period? Table 5.4 shows the top instigators who traffic in the nasty style. It's not surprising, but the Radical Party leader, Oleh Lyashko, is at the top of the list with nearly 10% of the incidents. Lyashko is the man whose name is synonymous with name-calling, fights in the Rada, and general rudeness. He so often used the insult *skotina* (animal bastard) that when you mention the word most Ukrainians will immediately think of Lyashko, much like Americans will connect Trump and "fake news."[11] The second politician on the list is also noteworthy. Borys Filatov was a deputy in the Rada from 2014–2015, and then elected Mayor of Dnipro in 2015. Filatov was a one-time ally of the oligarch, Ihor Kolomoisky. He also was one of the founding members of the right-wing nationalist party Ukrainian Association of Patriots (UKROP). Filatov had a tendency to call anyone he disagrees with an "idiot" (Glavnoe 2017). Echoing Trump, he also promised to "make Dnipro great again"—including taking on the city's trash mafia (Kovensky and Chernichkin 2018).

So besides a populist firebrand, and a tough-talking mayor, who is on our rogues of rhetoric list? For the most part it's politicians who are not key decision-makers or party leaders. Two of the politicians on the list ran for president in 2019—Lyashko and Kiva—but neither were serious contenders. There's Mikheil Saakashvili, the former President of Georgia (2004–2013) who famously fell out of favor with President Poroshenko after being appointed to be Governor of Odesa in 2015. Oleh Barna is another politician who is known more for his brutish style than legislative accomplishments. A deputy in the Rada from 2014–2019, Barna sported a handlebar mustache and had a penchant for calling his opponents "prostitutes" and "whores." He famously started a fight in the Rada when he gave former Prime Minister Yatsenyuk in December a bouquet of flowers and then tried to forcibly remove him from the speaker's podium (Reuters 2015).

Nadiya Savchenko is a former helicopter pilot who served in a volunteer battalion on the pro-Ukrainian side in the War in Donbas. She was captured by Russian separatist forces in Donbas and later taken to Russia. While imprisoned in Russia she was elected as a member of Yulia Tymoshenko's party. Savchenko was freed in a prisoner swap in 2016. But later her parliamentary immunity was stripped for plotting a coup against Poroshenko's government, and she spent nearly a year in prison (Kramer 2018). Savchenko has praised dictators and

[11] The word *skotina* literally means brute in Russian and livestock in Ukrainian. But its colloquial usage is closer to an animal or brutish bastard.

Table 5.4 **Chief instigators of nasty politics in Ukraine from 2016–October 1, 2019 (N = 347).**

Name	*Number of Incidents*	*Political Affiliations*	*Positions*	*Ran for President 2019?*
1. Oleh Lyashko	31	Radical Party	Party leader, and Deputy in Rada	Yes (5.5%)
2. Borys Filatov	21	Independent/Ukrainian Association of Patriots (UKROP)	Mayor of Dnipro	No
3. Oleh Barna	19	Petro Poroshenko/European Solidarity	Deputy in Rada	No
4. Arsen Avakov	18	People's Front	Minister of Interior	No
5. Mikheil Saakashvili	13	Independent, Movement of New Forces	Governor of Odesa/Head of the National Reform Council	No
6. Yuriy Lutsenko	12	Petro Poroshenko	Prosecutor General	No
6. Nadiya Savchenko	12	Batkivshchyna, Independent	Deputy in Rada	Tried to, but denied
8. Ilya Kiva	8	Opposition Platform For Life, Socialist Party	Deputy in Rada	Yes (0.03%)
8. Ihor Mosiychuk	8	Radical Party	Deputy in Rada	No

made no secret of her disdain for democracy and admiration for former Chilean dictator Augusto Pinochet (Maza 2018).

Ilya Kiva was elected to the Rada in 2019. He's the hulking former head of the Counter-Narcotics Division in the Ministry of Interior Affairs and a former member of the far-right political and paramilitary movement, Right Sector (Cohen 2017). Kiva appears on Ukrainian TV frequently. While I was having coffee with a veteran Kyiv-based journalist Kiva's name came up. The journalist's faced turned to disgust and he stated as a fact that, "Ilya Kiva is just a big brute, a muscly asshole."[12] Following the Russian invasion in 2022, Kiva was expelled from the Rada and charged with treason for supporting Putin and Russia. He fled to Russia where in a post on his social media Telegram channel in April 2022 he urged Putin to use nuclear weapons against Ukraine (Pleasance 2022).

Finally, there's Ihor Mosiychuk. Mosiychuk is a former member of Oleh Lyashko's Radical Party and a deputy in the Rada from 2015–2019. Mosiychuk was active in far-right nationalist circles before Euromaidan. He was a member of the Patriots of Ukraine, and was arrested in 2011 along with two of his fellow Patriots. They were accused of trying to blow up an already-dismantled statue of Lenin. Mosiychuk and his two compatriots became a cause célèbre for pro-European and nationalist forces in Ukraine while they spent two years in pretrial detention. They all were later convicted and sentenced to six additional years in prison in January 2014. Pro-European and nationalist Ukrainians deemed the process a show trial that was engineered by then-President Yanukovych and his allies.[13] The conviction was even more salient for its timing—right in the middle of the Euromaidan protests. Following Yanukovych's ouster and the Euromaidan revolution, Mosiychuk and his compatriots were freed. Mosiychuk then joined political forces with Lyashko. Mosiychuk's style combined brashness with the frequent use of his cane as a weapon to violently assault his opponents (Segodnya 2018). Mosiychuk is also well known for surviving an assassination attempt by an explosive device that killed his bodyguard in late October of 2017 (*Kyiv Post* 2017).

Most of the chief instigators in the Ukrainian list could be classified as provocateurs, agitators, and nasty personalities, but they don't necessarily control the levers of power in Ukraine. Yuriy Lutsenko is somewhat of a mixed bag. He has a long history in Ukrainian politics stretching back to the early 2000s where he was an active member of the Orange Revolution. Yet his tenure as Prosecutor General of Ukraine was tumultuous, and more notable for his failed investigations. His failure to prosecute anyone for the acid attack and murder of anti-corruption activist Kateryna Handziuk in November 2018 was roundly

[12] Interview #Ukr-J-C-0120.

[13] This was known as the "Vasylkiv terrorists case." See Coynash (2014).

criticized by activists in Ukraine (Colborne 2019). He said that critics of his handling of the Handziuk case were using Handziuk's "blood as a PR smear campaign" (UNIAN 2018). Lutsenko was forced out by Volodymyr Zelensky in August 2019. But he tried to resurrect his political career by feeding damaging information about former Vice President and Democratic Presidential Candidate Joe Biden to President Trump's personal lawyer Rudy Giuliani (Kramer, Higgins, and Schwirtz 2019).

One politician who does stand out on the list for their centrality to Ukrainian politics is Arsen Avakov. Avakov was the powerful Minister of Internal Affairs from February 2014 following the Euromaidan uprising until July 2021. He is also one of the founding members of the center-right nationalist People's Front party. He cultivated support among far-right volunteer battalions and militias that sprang up at the outbreak of the War in Donbas. Avakov regularly used his Twitter and Facebook to call protesters and rival politicians "trash" and "scumbags" (Rubryka 2018). Behind the scenes Avakov was seen as instrumental in organizing violent, far-right protests against President Poroshenko's reelection bid in 2019. Avakov calculated that he was more likely to stay in power if Poroshenko lost (Kuzio 2019). And in fact it worked. When Zelensky was elected in April 2019, Avakov remained on in the Zelensky administration, much to the surprise and outrage of those in civil society, who viewed Avakov as the main power behind far-right attacks on journalists and activists, and a saboteur of anti-corruption efforts in Ukraine. Like a Ukrainian J. Edgar Hoover, Avakov was able to initially survive because he had convinced people that he was indispensable, and was alleged to have the compromising inormation on many powerful figures (Skorkin 2020). However, Avakov eventually tendered his resignation in July of 2021 (RFE/RL 2021*b*).

Where does nasty politics happen in Ukraine? Figure 5.9 provides the breakdown of the different contexts. More than a third of incidents happens in the context of traditional media—whether it be interviews with journalists, press conferences, or political chat shows.

Political chat shows are very popular, appearing Thursdays and Fridays during prime time on most major channels (Korolenko 2018). These television spectacles are as a cross between edgy cable news and professional wrestling. The hosts typically bring on rival political guests in the hopes of sparking verbal and sometimes physical exchanges that drive ratings. My interview with a party worker for the pro-Russian Opposition Platform party highlights these points: "Chat shows are political theater, almost like a cheap form of PR."[14] Political chat

[14] Interview #Ukr-O-S0819.

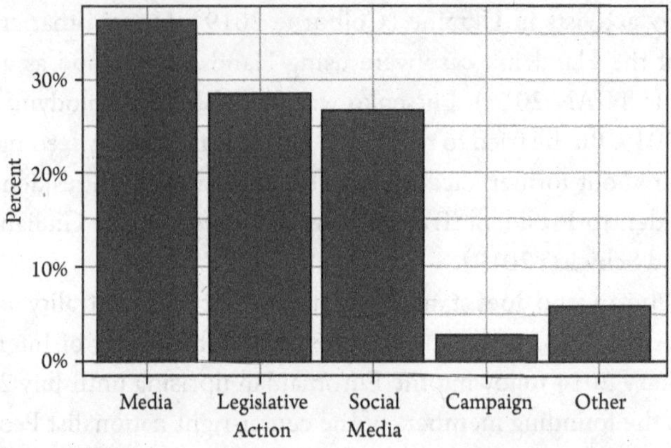

Figure 5.9 Nasty politics in Ukraine commonly happens in the media such as chat shows, in the Rada, and on social media (N = 347).

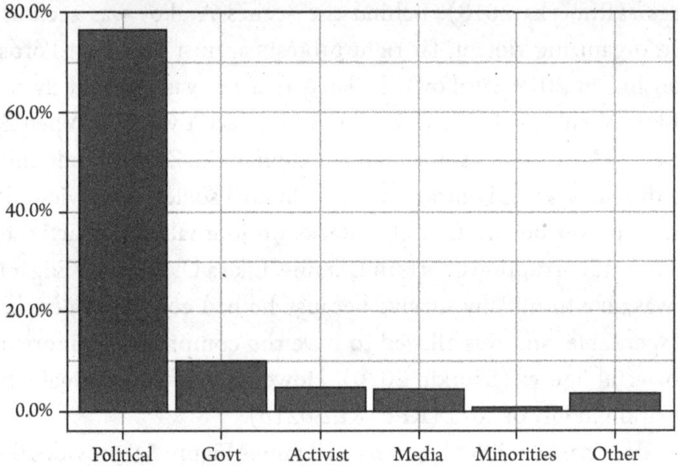

Figure 5.10 Frequency of different targets for nasty politics in Ukraine (N = 347).

shows are a major source of violent rhetoric in the media category, accounting for nearly half of all the media instances, and 18% overall of incidents.

The legislative action category captures any incident that occurs in one of the sessions of the Rada, government hearings, or other official government business, and it accounts for just over 28% of nasty incidents. Social media, including Facebook, Twitter, Instagram, and blog posts, also account for more than 25% of the incidents. Campaign events and rallies are a comparatively smaller overall part of the context for violent rhetoric (less than 3%).

Who are the targets of nastiness in Ukraine? Figure 5.10 matches our findings from the U.S. and shows that the most common target is the Political category that includes politicians and other political parties (more than 75%). The targets

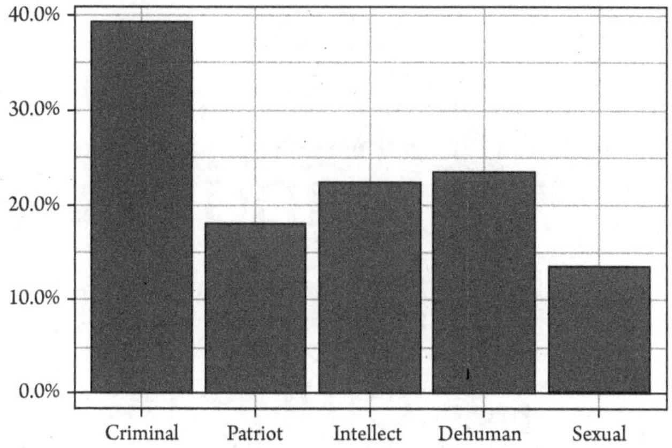

Figure 5.11 Ukrainian politicians use varied frames and metaphors to attack their opponents (N = 347).

of politicians are diverse. Within the Political category the most popular target is former President Petro Poroshenko and his political party, which account for 8% of all incidents. The next most popular targets are Yulia Tymoshenko and Oleh Lyashko who each are targeted 4% of the time. About 10% of nasty incidents are targeted at the military, government officials, police, judges, and other non-elected governmental officials (Govt). Protesters and civil society activists and organizations (Activist) and journalist and media (Media) each account for 5% of the targets.

What are the nasty frames and metaphors Ukrainian politicians use to verbally and sometimes physically attack their opponents? Figure 5.11 shows the distribution of different frames that are in the Ukrainian database. For instance, in May of 2019 Ilya Kiva was on a political chat show on channel *112 Ukraine* with People's Deputy Oleh Barna of Petro Poroshenko's party. Kiva accused Barna and Poroshenko of profiting and stealing from the war effort in Donbas. He then threatened to strangle and throw Barna in jail. Kiva said, "You (Barna and Poroshenko) are rascals, criminals, and looters. And your place is not in television studios, but in courtroom.... Also I have strong hands, and I should take you by the throat... and not let go" (Antikor 2019). This incident includes both patriotic attacks (profiting off the war) and accusations of criminality ("rascals, criminals, and looters"). It also includes two separate threats—one to have Barna tried in a courtroom (intimidating statement), and the other where Kiva actually threatens to physically strangle him (incitement).

Nearly 40% of all incidents of nasty politics include comparing a target to a "criminal," a "bandit," "gang," or "corrupt" (39%). This makes sense given the salience of corruption and charges of being corrupt within Ukrainian politics. A second common-line of attacks individuals' intellect, calling them "dumb,"

Figure 5.12 Commonly used nasty rhetoric in Ukraine.
Note: Size, position, and color of word indicates frequency of this term mentioned in the Ukrainian database. Word stems are used, so idiotic/idiot/idiocy will all be under one term.

"idiots," or "stupid" (22%). Dehumanizing language is much more common in the Ukrainian database than in the U.S. database. 23% of incidents involve dehumanizing language such as calling a politician an "animal" or "scum." A particularly vivid example of dehumanizing rhetoric occurred in August 2016 when Oleh Lyashko compared Petro Poroshenko's decision to give the Governorship of Odesa to Mikheil Saakashvili as inviting a "homeless sewer-dweller" into Ukraine (New Inform 2017). More than 18% of incidents involve questioning opponents' patriotism by calling them "traitors," "treasonous," or saying their allegiance lies to the Kremlin or Russia. Finally, 13% of the nasty rhetoric in our database is politicians attacking their opponents' sexuality, or gender by calling them "prostitutes," "whores," "gay," or questioning their manhood.

What are the most common words Ukrainian politicians use when talking nasty to their opponents? Figure 5.12 shows a word cloud of the most commonly used phrases. The most common phrase is "idiot" and its variations (idiotic, idiots), closely followed by "bandit," "gang," and "corrupt." Other common phrases include calling an opponent a "bastard," "scum," a "prostitute," or questioning their loyalty ("Kremlin" or "traitor").

5.2 Disruptions in the Ukrainian Rada

Historically behavior in the Verkhovna Rada sometimes better resembled clashes between rival soccer hooligans rather than the workings of a professional legislature. Blockades of the speaker's podium and shouting down speakers were all regular occurrences. But it's not just minor scuffles. Major fights and brawls also happened. In February 2015 deputies Yegor Sobolev (*Samopomich*) and Vadym Ivchenko (Yulia Tymoshenko's *Batkivshchyna* party), two coalition allies, had a nearly minute-long MMA-style fight. The fight started in the Rada session hall and then spilled out into the lobby, where the two repeatedly exchanged punches and kicks (Gordiienko 2015). Both had bloody faces before guards separated them. The fight was allegedly over disagreements on an anti-corruption bill, and Sobolev's claim that Ivchenko was smearing him in the press.

As crazy as the Sobolev-Ivchenko fight was, it probably wouldn't crack the top-10 of most chaotic moments in the Rada (Zavoyra 2016). In October 2017 a member of the far-right *Svoboda* (Freedom) Party threw a smoke grenade into the Rada protesting a bill on relations with Russia (RFE/RL 2017). And the Rada was actually shut down in May 2012, when a large group of supporters of Yulia Tymoshenko physically fought with supporters of then President Viktor Yanukovych's party over a draft bill on the status of Russian language.[15] The scene could best be described as legislative riot, with bodies literally flying over the rostrum (Chapple 2017). The surreal scene had rival deputies clashing, their clothes torn as they tried to choke and punch each other, while crowds above whistled and cheered. Vadim Kolesnichenko, drafter of the law and member of Yanukovych's Party of Regions, claimed that opponents of the law said to him: "You're a corpse, you have two days left to live, we will crucify you on a birch tree" (Roth and Goodman 2012). Finally many of these blockades, fights, and acts of vandalism are precipitated by insults, accusations, intimidating statements, and incitement. This means that disruptions in the Rada are a good proxy for the overall level of nastiness in Ukrainian politics.

Drawing on data from the Rada's official website,[16] and reports from news sources,[17] I worked with my Ukrainian research assistantships to construct a database of all disruptions (everything from blocking someone, to speaking, to wide-scale melees) in the Rada from 2001–October 1, 2019. We documented over 301 disruptive events. The database contains information on which kind of tactic was used, which faction instigated it, and who the target was.

Figure 5.13 shows the distribution of different types of disruptive tactics politicians employ. Note a single event can contain multiple types of disruptions—i.e., many physical fights in the Rada began with deputies blocking the podium. Blockades of the podium and presidium that prevent deputies from speaking are the most common type of disruption, and occur in nearly 80% of

[15] This took place during Yulia Tymoshenko's imprisonment and was briefly described in Chapter 3.

[16] See https://iportal.rada.gov.ua.

[17] See *Korrespondent* https://korrespondent.net and *Ukrainskaya Pravda* https://www.pravda.com.ua.

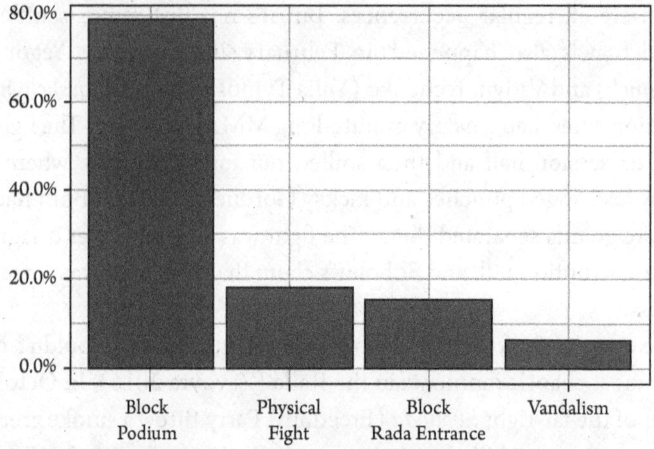

Figure 5.13 Frequency of different types of disruptions in the Ukrainian Rada from 2001–October 1, 2019 (N = 301).

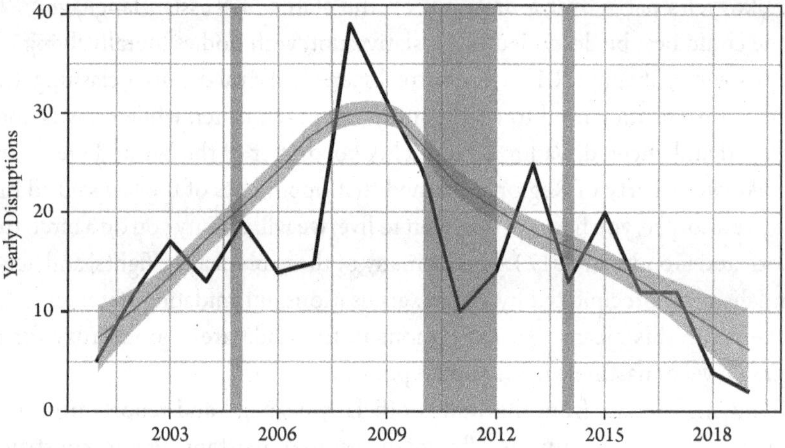

Figure 5.14 Aggregate disruptions peak in the lead-up to the arrest of Yulia Tymoshenko and increase again in the lead-up to Euromaidan from 2001–October 1, 2019 (N = 301). Note: Vertical shaded regions correspond to the Orange Revolution (2004–2005), the trial of former Prime Minister Yulia Tymoshenko (2010–2011), and the Euromaidan Revolution (2013–2014).

cases. Physical fights, including scuffles, melees, and spitting, are rarer and occur in 18% of the disruptive vents. Blocking of the entrance to the Rada session hall, or the Rada itself, is comparatively rarer, and present in only 15% of cases. The rarest type of tactic is vandalism (less than 6%), which includes unfurling large banners, hurling eggs, smoke bombs or grenades, and setting off noise sirens.

Are disruptions leading indicators of wider political conflict in Ukrainian? Figure 5.14 shows that this is in fact the case. Like the salience of nasty politics discussed in Chapter 3, disruptions in the Rada peaked in 2008–2009 in the period leading up to the arrest and trial of Yulia Tymoshenko. This was a period

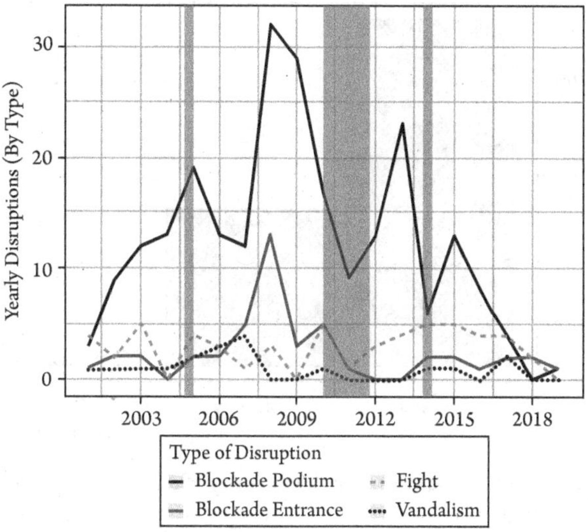

Figure 5.15 Blockades peak in the lead-up to the arrest of Yulia Tymoshenko and increase again in the lead-up to Euromaidan, while fights remain fairly constant from 2001–October 1, 2019 (N = 301).
Note: Vertical shaded regions correspond to the Orange Revolution (2004–2005), the trial of former Prime Minister Yulia Tymoshenko (2010–2011), and the Euromaidan Revolution (2013–2014).

of intense rivalry and competition between party elites and factions affiliated with Viktor Yanukovych and Yulia Tymoshenko. It also laid the groundwork for the tensions that would erupt during the Euromaidan Revolution (2013–2014). There were regular blockades in the Rada throughout much of 2008 and 2009. There are additional smaller peaks leading up to the Orange Revolution in (2004–2005). Disruptions drop off fairly quickly in the post-Euromaidan era. Figure 5.15 disaggregates the tactics by year and shows a similar pattern. Blockades of the podium and entrance peak just before Tymoshenko's arrest and imprisonment. Fights in the Rada are fairly rare, averaging only three fights per year, but the post-Euromaidan period, of 2014, 2015, 2016 (five fights each), also matched the highest number of fights in 2010.

Who instigates these disruptions? Is it more likely to be used as a tactic of opposition parties or those in the ruling coalition majority? Note these are not mutually exclusive, since sometimes it's unclear which party started a fight or disruptive tactic, so both parties may be involved in an incident, and both are coded as instigating. There's also a third category for extra parliamentary groups such as anti-corruption activists in July of 2017 who blocked deputies from exiting the Rada.[18] The results from Figure 5.16 shows the distribution of who instigated the

[18] See (Ukrainian) Center for Combating Corruption/ANTAC (antac.ua). Facebook, July 13, 2017. https://www.facebook.com/antac.ua/posts/1338234206275366.

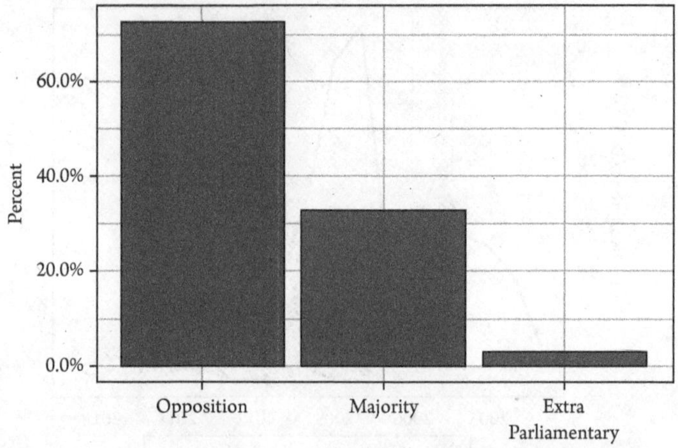

Figure 5.16 Opposition parties instigate the majority of disruptions in the Rada from 2001–October 1, 2019 (N = 301).

disruptive event. And it's not even close. More than 70% of disruptive events are initiated by opposition parties in the Rada, compared to only 33% by majority parties. This underscores how disruption is a tactic for opposition parties who don't have the same formal levers to gain attention and exercise power. Non-parliamentary groups account for less than 3% of disruptions.

Which political blocs or parties are most active in disrupting the Rada? Defining these blocs can be tricky because of the shifting party names, alliances, and the fact that smaller parties have a tendency to disappear from the Rada from one election to the next (Carroll 2015). During this period parliamentary factions can be divided into roughly seven groups based on a combination of personalities and political orientation: (1) Parties that are associated with Yulia Tymoshenko; (2) Pro-Russian and Eurosceptic parties that are associated with Viktor Yanukovych and his supporters including the Party of Regions, Opposition Platform For Life, Opposition Bloc; (3) Center-Right parties which are associated with Pro-Ukrainian, pro-European, pro-Orange Revolution, Pro-Euromaidan and includes a party allied with Viktor Yushchenko and Our Ukraine, Ukrainian Democratic Alliance for Reform (UDAR),[19] *Samopomich*, Self-Reliance, People's Front, People's Movement, and those allied with Saakashivili; (4) Communist and Socialist Parties of Ukraine; (5) far-right, ultra-nationalist parties such as Svoboda, National Corps, and Right Sector;

[19] Note UDAR was in alliance with Poroshenko from 2015–2019, before breaking away and becoming independent.

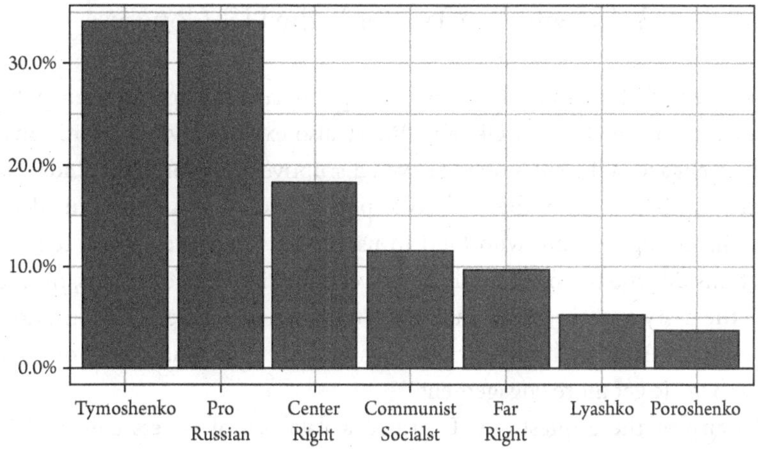

Figure 5.17 Parties and blocs allied with Tymoshenko and pro-Russian (Yanukovych) parties instigate many of the Rada disruptions from 2001–October 1, 2019 (N = 301).

(6) the Radical Party of Oleh Lyashko, and (7) political parties associated with Petro Poroshenko, mainly European Solidarity.

Figure 5.17 presents the results of disruptions broken down by faction. The two biggest instigators of disruptions are those associated with Yulia Tymoshenko's faction and Viktor Yanukovych's (pro-Russian factions). Each were involved in or instigated nearly a third of all disruptions. This tracks with the idea that much of Ukrainian politics from the Orange Revolution through Maidan was a fight between Tymoshenko- and Yanukovych-allied forces for power in Ukraine (Kudelia 2013). The next closest faction is the Center-Right bloc which was an instigator in half as many disputes as the Tymoshenko and pro-Russian parties (about 17%). Far-right parties have also been more active than their limited numbers of parliament would suggest. The far right has only cracked more than 5% of votes once in 2012, and have had only a few deputies in the Rada, but still instigated 10% of all the disputes. The case of Oleh Lyashko's Radical Party is also interesting. Lyashko's party entered the Rada at the same time as Petro Poroshenko's party (2014), and had one-sixth as many seats (22 to 132). Yet, Lyashko and his allies carried out nearly twice as many disruptions in a fairly short and comparatively calmer time in the Rada (post-Euromaidan). And if we restrict our time period to post-2014, Lyashko's Radical Party instigated more than a quarter of all disruptions in the Rada.

The findings from the disruption database show that disruptions, much like nasty politics in general, are a leading indicator of conflict and contention between elites. Furthermore, disruptions are a tool for opposition and fringe parties to try to influence the debate and grab attention, especially when formal legislative routes are blocked.

5.3 Incivility on Twitter in the U.S. Congress

We've seen what kinds of nasty language politicians use against their political opponents in the U.S. and Ukraine. We've also explored which politicians are likely to engage in the nasty style or even disruptive behavior in the Rada. Nasty politics tends to peak in the lead up to political conflict. And it's outsiders, or those in the opposition, who tend to use it. But there are several remaining questions. Maybe the media only covers certain kinds of politicians, or homes in on the nasty ones, so we are missing a swath of nasty rhetoric that just doesn't get covered? And finally, do our previous findings from Chapter 3 hold—does nasty rhetoric get more engagement?

To answer these questions, I turn to a database of tweets collected from Members of the 115th Congress. Twitter has become one of the most important communication platforms for members of Congress to communicate to their constituents, and has been used by several different scholars to study political behavior (Barberá 2015; Barberá et al. 2019; Russell 2018). The Twitter database I employ comes from a dataset collected by Theocharis et al. (2020).[20] Their dataset contains tweets from the general public and all members of Congress with a Twitter account from October 17, 2016, until December 13, 2017. This time period covers several contentious events including the November 2016 presidential election and the beginnings of the Mueller investigation into Russian hacking (May 2017).

While Theocharis et al. (2020) focuses on incivility directed at members of Congress from the general public, we're interested in the incivility of the members of Congress themselves. This database allows me to examine nasty politics among a wider swath of politicians. I examine 155,540 tweets sent by members of Congress. I use the civil-uncivil classification algorithm developed by Theocharis et al. (2020) to get a measure for each congressional tweet's incivility.[21] An incivility score closer to 0 indicates a tweet is highly likely to be civil and polite, while an incivility score closer to 1 indicates it's highly likely to be uncivil and nasty. About 4% of the 155,540 tweets sent had an uncivil classification of greater than 0.5, 0.6% greater than 0.75, and 0.1% greater than 0.9.[22] The use a different coding scheme (incivility) allows me to see if my

[20] And generously shared by the authors.

[21] From Theocharis et al. (2020, p. 7) they define incivility as: "(An) ill-mannered, disrespectful tweet that may contain offensive language. This includes threatening one's rights (freedom to speak, life preferences), assigning stereotypes or hate speech, name-calling ('weirdo,' 'traitor,' 'idiot'), aspersion ('liar,' 'traitor'), pejorative speak or vulgarity, sarcasm, ALL CAPS, and incendiary, obscene, and/or humiliating language.

[22] Theocharis et al. (2020) use 0.5 as their threshold.

findings on nasty tweets getting more engagement is simply an artifact of the nasty politics coding scheme, or a more general finding.

What do some of the tweets classified as uncivil look like? The following are a few examples. Rep. Frederica Wilson (Democrat, Florida) in August of 2017 after the violence at the Charlottesville "Unite the Right" White supremacist rally tweeted the following about President Trump: "If you support racists, you are racist. @realDonaldTrump supports racists because he is racist. #charlottesvilleterroristattack" (incivility score = 0.99).[23] Rep. Lou Barletta (Republican, Pennsylvania) tweeted out in November of 2017, "It's a disgrace to the Constitution some believe states can willfully ignore federal immigration law. #SanctuaryCities must cease & desist!" (incivility score = 0.93).[24] Or Rep. Steve Cohen (Democrat, Tennessee), who said, "Gregg Popovich (San Antonio Spurs basketball coach) calls Donald Trump a 'soulless coward'—SB Nation POP is a truth teller https://t.co/J68vbQDHUk" (incivility score = 0.82).[25] Finally, Rep. Adam Kinzinger (Republican, Illinois) in December 2017 attacked President Trump's strategist, Steve Bannon, saying, "Bannon is a RINO. His morally inept strategies are unwelcome here. #YoureFired" (incivility score = 0.64).[26]

Which members of Congress sent the most number of uncivil tweets? Table 5.5 provides a list of how many uncivil tweets these top offenders sent at different incivility score thresholds: greater than 0.5, greater than 0.75, and greater than 0.9. The ranking in the table reflects the number of uncivil tweets at a threshold greater than 0.75. There are several important takeaways. First, 18 out of the 20 members are Democrats. Given that this is a period in which Republicans had unified control of the House and Senate, and then won the presidency, it's in line with our previous findings that nasty politics tends to be perpetrated by those in the opposition. And 17 of the top 20 offenders are also members of the House. This echoes the reputation of the House as being a more raucous body compared to the more staid Senate (Ragusa 2016). The Republican leadership is completely absent from the list. Yet Democrats have several leaders in the list including Joe Crowley (13th place),[27] then-Minority Leader Nancy Pelosi in 14th place, and Hakeem Jeffries (15th place).

[23] Wilson Frederica (RepWilson). Twitter, August, 16, 2017. https://twitter.com/RepWilson/status/897932039319502849?s=20.

[24] See Barletta, Lou (RepLouBarletta). Twitter, November, 2017. https://twitter.com/RepLouBarletta/status/926552936544722944?s=20.

[25] Cohen, Steve (RepCohen). Twitter, October 16, 2017. https://twitter.com/RepCohen/status/920096858776760321?s=20.

[26] Kinzinger, Adam (RepKinzinger). Twitter, December 13, 2017. https://twitter.com/RepKinzinger/status/940927510207967233.

[27] He would later be defeated in a primary by Alexandra Ocasio-Cortez.

Table 5.5 **Top 20 uncivil tweet offenders in U.S. Congress (October 17, 2016–December 13, 2017).**

Name	*# Uncivil Tweets*			*Chamber*	*Incumb. Since*	*Leadership*
	(> 0.5)	(> 0.75)	(> 0.9)			
1. Jim McGovern	137	31	7	House (Dem. MA)	1997	
2. Steve Cohen	87	29	7	House (Dem. TN)	2007	
3. Jerrold Nadler	93	24	7	House (Dem. NY)	1992	
4. Keith Ellison	150	23	5	House (Dem. MN)	2007	
5. Brendan Boyle	64	22	2	House (Dem. PA)	2015	
6. Barbara Lee	113	21	3	House (Dem. CA)	1998	
7. Don Beyer	150	21	4	House (Dem. VA)	2015	
8. Eric Swalwell	107	20	2	House (Dem. CA)	2013	
9. Betty McCollum	86	18	5	House (Dem. MN)	2001	
10. Richard Blumenthal	90	17	2	Senate (Dem. CT)	2011	
11. Chris Van Hollen	69	16	4	Senate (Dem. MD)	2017	
12. Frederica Wilson	59	16	2	House (Dem. FL)	2011	
13. Joe Crowley	71	15	1	House (Dem. NY)	1999	Dem Caucus Chair
14. Nancy Pelosi	81	14	3	House (Dem. CA)	1987	House Minority Leader
15. Hakeem Jeffries	62	14	6	House (Dem. NY)	2013	Policy & Communication Co-Chair
16. Karen Bass	56	14	2	House (Dem. CA)	2011	
17. Ted Poe	49	13	5	House (Rep. TX)	2005	
18. Nydia Velazquez	95	13	2	House (Dem. NY)	1993	
19. Jackie Speier	60	13	1	House (Dem. CA)	2008	
20. John McCain	83	13	2	Senate (Rep. AZ)	1987	

In the tables and regressions below, I examine first who sends uncivil tweets, and whether the public responds to uncivil tweets with greater attention in terms of retweets and favorites.

Table 5.6 looks at the correlates of a tweet being uncivil or not (a binary variable). It looks at this across thresholds: an incivility score greater than 0.5 (column 1), greater than 0.75 (columns 2), and greater than 0.9 (column 3). Across the different thresholds, tweets from Republican are between 0.1% to 2% less likely to be classified as uncivil compared to Democrats. Independent politicians are also much more likely to use uncivil language in their tweets rhetoric compared to the average Democrat.[28] More ideological extreme mem-

Table 5.6 **The correlates of a tweet being uncivil (OLS regressions).**

	Dependent variable		
	Civil = 0 and Uncivil = 1		
Incivility Score	(>0.5) (1)	(>0.75) (2)	(>0.9) (3)
Independent	0.074***	0.053***	0.011***
	(0.006)	(0.002)	(0.001)
Republican	−0.020***	−0.006***	−0.001***
	(0.004)	(0.001)	(0.0003)
Male	−0.005	0.00004	0.001***
	(0.004)	(0.001)	(0.0002)
Senator	−0.005	−0.001*	−0.0003
	(0.003)	(0.001)	(0.0003)
Ideological Extremism	0.023	0.010***	0.002*
	(0.016)	(0.003)	(0.001)
Constant	0.045***	0.004***	0.0004
	(0.008)	(0.001)	(0.0004)
Observations	154,410	154,410	154,410
R^2	0.003	0.002	0.0004
Adjusted R^2	0.003	0.002	0.0004

Note: Standard errors clustered at the user account.
*p<0.1; **p<0.05; ***p<0.01

[28] Note, being an independent is really a proxy for independent Vermont Senator Bernie Sanders, one of two independents in Congress at the time. Maine Senator Angus King also counts as an independent, but he rarely tweeted.

bers of Congress are also more likely to send uncivil tweets, especially when we restrict the threshold to a higher level of incivility (Columns 2 and 3).[29] Again, this supports the idea that outsiders (more extreme politicians) and opposition members (Democrats and independents) are more likely to send uncivil tweets.

Do uncivil tweets get more attention and attention? Tables 5.7 and 5.8 look at whether uncivil tweets get more retweets (5.7) or more favorites (5.8). Both tables also control for the fact that certain members of Congress are likely to receive more or less attention. I control for this with a dummy variable for each member of Congress's Twitter handle (fixed effect). The results are clear. Uncivil tweets get between 38% to 155% more retweets and favorites as civil tweets.[30] Also, the effect is stronger when we restrict the threshold of uncivil to tweets with higher incivility scores. You can see this by the higher coefficients on Incivility >0.9 in column 3 compared to Incivility >0.50 in column 1 and Incivility >0.75 in column 2 in both tables. The straightforward interpretation is that uncivil tweets get more attention, and the more uncivil the tweet is, the more attention it gets on average. Nastiness gets attention.

Table 5.7 **Uncivil tweets get more retweets. Fixed effects of incivility on natural log number of retweets (OLS).**

	Dependent variable		
		ln (Retweet Counts + 1)	
	(1)	(2)	(3)
Incivility >0.5	0.346***		
	(0.035)		
Incivility >0.75		0.635***	
		(0.055)	
Incivility >0.9			0.937***
			(0.123)
Constant	2.191***	2.191***	2.191***
	(0.000)	(0.000)	(0.000)
Fixed Effects	✓	✓	✓
Observations	154,410	154,410	154,410
R^2	0.565	0.564	0.564
Adjusted R^2	0.564	0.563	0.562

Note: Standard errors clustered at the user account.
*p<0.1; **p<0.05; ***p<0.01

[29] Ideological extremity is the absolute value of the DW-Nominate voting score.

[30] Since the dependent variables are transformed by its natural log, we exponentiate the coefficient to get the marginal effect $\implies \approx e^{0.324}$ (Table 5.8 column 1) to $e^{0.937}$ (Table 5.7 column 3).

Table 5.8 **Uncivil tweets get more favorites. Fixed effect regression on natural log number of favorites (OLS).**

	Dependent variable		
	ln (# of Favorites + 1)		
	(1)	(2)	(3)
Incivility >0.5	0.324***		
	(0.027)		
Incivility >0.75		0.600***	
		(0.052)	
Incivility >0.9			0.865***
			(0.116)
Constant	2.124***	2.124***	2.124***
	(0.000)	(0.000)	(0.000)
Fixed Effects	✓	✓	✓
Observations	154,410	154,410	154,410
R^2	0.587	0.586	0.586
Adjusted R^2	0.585	0.585	0.584

Note: Standard errors clustered at the user account.
*p<0.1; **p<0.05; ***p<0.01

Tables 5.9 and 5.10 examine how incivility predicts how many retweets and favorites a tweet receives, while also controlling for politician-specific factors (random effects). Tables 5.9 and 5.10 match those from the fixed effects only regressions. Uncivil tweets get approximately 66% to 260% more retweets and favorites than civil ones, and the effect is even stronger the more restrictive we are about what we consider as uncivil tweets. Independents—i.e., Bernie Sanders—also get more engagement, and Republicans less engagement than Democrats. Finally, the most ideologically extreme candidates receive more than five times more retweets and favorites compared to moderates.[31] Senators also get more favorites and retweets than members of the House (approximately 260% more retweets and favorites).

The are four main findings from the analysis of incivility on Twitter by members of Congress. First, this is a period of remarkable Republican control. Republicans controlled the House, Senate, and with Trump's election in November 2016, the presidency. Republicans during this time period are less likely to send uncivil tweets than Democrats. Second, ideologically extreme members of

[31] Someone who is a moderate would have a score of 0 on DW-Nominate, while a score of −1 or 1 would be extremely liberal or conservative.

Table 5.9 **What predicts retweets (OLS random effects).**

	Dependent variable		
	ln (# of Retweets + 1)		
	(1)	(2)	(3)
Incivility > 0.5	0.533***		
	(0.067)		
Incivility >0.75		0.811***	
		(0.083)	
Incivility >0.9			1.280***
			(0.165)
Independent	4.087***	4.083***	4.113***
	(0.299)	(0.301)	(0.302)
Republican	−1.413***	−1.420***	−1.423***
	(0.208)	(0.209)	(0.209)
Male	0.101	0.099	0.098
	(0.219)	(0.221)	(0.221)
Senator	1.273***	1.272***	1.271***
	(0.256)	(0.257)	(0.257)
Ideological Extremism	2.032***	2.036***	2.042***
	(0.765)	(0.769)	(0.770)
Constant	2.203***	2.224***	2.227***
	(0.382)	(0.386)	(0.387)
Observations	154,410	154,410	154,410
R^2	0.205	0.203	0.202
Adjusted R^2	0.205	0.203	0.202

Note: Standard errors clustered at the user account.
*p<0.1; **p<0.05; ***p<0.01

Congress are more likely to send uncivil tweets. These two findings mesh with our theory that nastiness and incivility are a strategy for outsiders and opposition politicians. Third, those who are more ideologically extreme also get more retweets and favorites on average than less extreme members. This points to the idea that being ideologically extreme can provide some cache and attention. Finally, the most important finding is that incivility drives attention. Uncivil tweets get more favorites and retweets. And this is increasing in the threshold used to measure incivility. Tweets that have a higher predicted probabilities of being uncivil (greater than 0.75 or 0.90) get more engagement than those at a lower threshold. This matches our general findings that nastiness grabs attention.

Table 5.10 **What predicts favorites (OLS random effects).**

	Dependent variable		
		log (# of Favorites + 1)	
	(1)	(2)	(3)
Incivility >0.5	0.507***		
	(0.054)		
Incivility >0.75		0.787***	
		(0.087)	
Incivility >0.9			1.220***
			(0.168)
Independent	4.167***	4.163***	4.192***
	(0.289)	(0.290)	(0.291)
Republican	−1.373***	−1.379***	−1.382***
	(0.201)	(0.202)	(0.202)
Male	0.101	0.098	0.098
	(0.206)	(0.207)	(0.207)
Senator	1.467***	1.466***	1.465***
	(0.271)	(0.271)	(0.271)
Ideological Extremism	2.014***	2.018***	2.024***
	(0.736)	(0.739)	(0.739)
Constant	2.996***	3.016***	3.018***
	(0.342)	(0.345)	(0.345)
Observations	154,410	154,410	154,410
R^2	0.201	0.199	0.199
Adjusted R^2	0.201	0.199	0.199

Note: Standard errors clustered at the user account.
*p<0.1; **p<0.05; ***p<0.01

5.4 Summary of Findings

We've explored databases from Ukraine and the U.S. of nasty politics reported from media sources. We've also looked at disruptions in the Rada, and finally incivility in U.S. Congressional tweets. Even given the different data sources and contexts, the results paint a unified picture of nasty politics that supports the theory. Insults and accusations are quite common, while incitement and actual violence are rarer—though both are more common in Ukraine. The nasty style of politics tends to be carried out by more extreme politicians, and those in the opposition. This points to the strategic role of nasty politics as a way for opposition parties to gain attention when conventional political avenues may be blocked. Increases in nasty politics tend to precede contentious events and political conflict. Finally, nasty rhetoric gets attention from the public. So we now know why politicians may choose to use nasty politics, even when the public says they don't like it. It's a Faustian bargain some outsiders and opposition members are willing to make—accept some reduction in likability, in exchange for getting noticed.

It's also important to emphasize the key difference between the U.S. and Ukraine in which politicians engage in nasty politics included in the databases. In both countries nasty politics is mainly a tactic of opposition politicians, with the gigantic caveat being President Trump himself. During the period of coverage in the Ukraine, nasty politics is more a strategy of peripheral politicians, not generally associated with party leaders. While in the U.S. the list of top-ten instigators of nasty politics include President Trump, and most of the key party leaders of the Democratic Party (Chuck Schumer, Nancy Pelosi, and Joe Biden). Much of the nasty rhetoric of Democratic politicians during this time period is calling out Trump's rhetoric and behavior. This highlights a conundrum for opposition and marginalized groups who risk being tarred as nasty for calling out the nasty behavior of incumbent politicians.[32]

One explanation for the finding that nasty politics isn't carried out as much by Ukrainian political leaders (Zelensky and Poroshenko compared to Trump and Pelosi) is that the coverage of nasty politics is simply different in the two countries. Ukrainian politics is baseline more violent, so a nasty comment by leading politicians won't get covered like it does in the U.S., and we are just missing some of those stories in our database of nasty incidents happening by party leaders. An alternative explanation that better matches the data is that nasty rhetoric and disruptions within Ukraine ebbed from their peak pre-Euromaidan levels (see Figures 3.4 and 5.14). In the pre-Euromaidan time period in Ukrainian politics (2008–2014), there were intense cleavages in Ukrainian politics and lots of name-calling and threats exchanged between the two leading politicians, Yanukovych and Tymoshenko.

In contrast, Trump's election accelerated polarization in the U.S., and brought nasty politics to new heights (see Figure 3.1 and 5.2). This means that nasty politics is no longer relegated to outsiders and fringe opposition politicians within U.S. politics. Rather it is part of mainstream party politics carried out by leaders.

[32] This was a constant debate within the Democratic Party during Trump's presidency (Martin 2018).

6

What Do the Experts Think about Nasty Politics?

If you spend some time following Ukrainian politics you will hear people use the Ukrainian word "*politoloh*." The direct translation is politologist, but it's a catch-all term for a political scientist, political expert, campaign strategist, or pollster (Shamota 2013). It's anyone who has expertise or knowledge in the dark arts of politics. And what these political experts think about nasty politics matters a lot. They're the ones who design strategies on how to communicate to voters. These experts decide which campaign strategies or messages are acceptable and effective, and which cross a line. It's their job to know.

Political experts and campaign strategists determine which rhetoric brushes up against the line of acceptability, and which crosses it. But sometimes they design strategies to intentionally polarize the populace. Former Trump campaign manager and convicted felon, Paul Manafort, was brought to Ukraine by Rinat Akhmetov, Viktor Yanukovych's billionaire oligarch-backer. Manafort's job was to help burnish the image of Yanukovych and his Party of Regions. Part of Manafort's strategy from 2006–2010 was a delicate dance of expanding Yanukovych's party's base beyond Eurosceptic Russian-speakers in Eastern Ukraine, all while also delivering on issues his base cared about. Yanukovych and his allies signaled that they would like Ukraine to be a part of Europe—something that had wide approval in Ukraine—while also pushing to make Russian an official second language. The status of Russian was a core issue for Yanukovych's supporters in Eastern Ukraine, but a flash point for those in Western Ukraine who staunchly opposed making Russian an official second language (Abou-Sabe, Winter, and Tucker 2017; Moser 2013). Manafort was also instrumental in pushing anti-NATO messaging and demonstrations in Ukraine and using it as a wedge issue (Haaretz 2016). While becoming part of Europe was broadly popular in Ukraine, opposition to NATO united Russian-speakers, nationalists, and those who were concerned that Ukraine would become a pawn between the West and Russia (Zhurzhenko 2010).

Nasty Politics: The Logic of Insults, Threats, and Incitement. Thomas Zeitzoff, Oxford University Press.
© Oxford University Press 2023. DOI: 10.1093/oso/9780197679494.003.0006

Political strategists and elites like Manafort are crucial in shaping whether politicians choose to engage in nasty rhetoric (Lilleker, Tenscher, and Štětka 2015; Nelson and Thurber 2018). So a key question is what kinds of nasty rhetoric do elites think the public finds acceptable? What about unacceptable? And what insights can they provide about answering our central puzzle of nasty politics—the public says they don't like nasty politics, yet why do politicians use it, and many of them win?

A second question is whether our scale of nasty politics tracks with how experts (political scientists) think about nasty politics. Do they see a similar rank ordering of the threat posed by different types of nasty rhetoric, with insult, followed by accusations, then intimidating statements, and incitement the most threatening?

Finally, how do different campaign strategists think about the strategies of nasty politics? What are the goals of politicians with it?

Before we continue, it's helpful to define what we mean by "elites." Elites are those who have the ability to influence politics through their wealth, power, connections, or knowledge. They can come from a variety of backgrounds: business, politics, media, military, academia, etc. (Hafner-Burton, Hughes and Victor 2013; Kertzer 2020). There's two reasons why care what elites think about nasty politics. First, it's the jobs of political elites and campaign strategists to know what helps and hurts campaigns. So they can provide unique insights into what they have found works versus what doesn't. Second, one potential explanation for the puzzle of nasty rhetoric is that maybe politicians and elites simply overestimate voters appetite for nasty politics For instance, Rosenzweig (2017) argues that elites overestimate the electoral benefits of violent campaigning and "heated rhetoric" in Kenya leading them to engage in more of it than voters tolerate. In the context of American politics, other find that politicians and elites may hold biased views of the American public, viewing them as consistently more conservative than they actually are (Broockman and Skovron 2018). So if there is a large gap between how acceptable the public finds violent rhetoric and what elites think the public finds acceptable, it might explain our puzzle of violent rhetoric. Yet more recent research by Kertzer (2020) casts doubt on these gaps between elites and the general public. He finds that elites respond similarly to experimental stimuli, that the size of the gap between elites and the general public is overstated, and what gap there is related to the demographics of the elites rather than elite-specific knowledge.

In this chapter we'll examine several different analyses. These include surveys of elite perceptions of the acceptability and strategies behind nasty politics in the U.S. and Ukraine. We'll also discuss the results of an expert survey of political scientists to see which types of nasty rhetoric they find particularly threatening. Finally, we'll explore in-depth interviews I conducted with both U.S and Ukrainians political experts and campaign strategists to examine the strategies behind nasty politics.

6.1 Elite Surveys

6.1.1 Political Elites

To understand how elites think about the effectiveness and acceptability of violent rhetoric, let's turn to two surveys of elites—one in the U.S. and one in Ukraine—fielded in March and April of 2019. The surveys sought to answer two questions. First, if a politician said "X" about their political opponents—how acceptable would the public find this kind of rhetoric? Second, what is the strategy of name-calling and threats by politicians against their political opponents?

The U.S. elite survey was fielded by the CivicPulse, a non-profit organization of researchers that runs online national surveys of local and municipal U.S. officials via email.[1] 520 respondents completed the survey. The Ukrainian survey was fielded by the Kyiv International Institute of Sociology (KIIS). I worked with KIIS to create a diverse database of both pro- and anti-Euromaidan elites (activists, politicians, and political consultants) across the various regions of Ukraine.[2] 165 individuals completed the elite survey in Ukraine.

The survey asked elites how often they thought the public would find it acceptable for a politician to say or call their opponent a: (1) "traitor," (2) "parasite," (3) "be harassed on social media," (4) "corrupt," (5) "be protested," (6) "be crushed," (7) "be afraid," and (8) "animal."[3] Figure 6.1 compares elite perceptions in the U.S. and Ukraine to that of the actual response of the general public in each country to nasty politics drawn from the previous results presented in Chapter 4 (4.1 and 4.2). The first thing to notice is that elites in Ukraine generally think it is more acceptable to use nasty rhetoric compared to their American counterparts. Calling opponents "traitors" or "corrupt" is perceived to be much more acceptable in Ukraine than the U.S. This might also be due to the fact that the Ukrainian elite sample has a fair number of activists,[4] and that corruption is understood to be common in Ukraine, and a regular complaint of the public against politicians. There's less of a gap between the two countries on the more extreme rhetoric ("animals" or "parasites") or incitement ("be crushed" or "harassed on social media").

Figure 6.2 takes the data from Figure 6.1 and shows the size of the gap between elites and masses. Elites in the U.S. systematically underestimate the public's

[1] The survey was fielded as a module as part of an omnibus survey between March 12–April 12, 2019. See https://www.civicpulse.org/.

[2] The invitation was emailed out to the Ukrainian elites, along with reminder emails, to nearly 2,000 activists, politicians, and political consultants, and was completed between March 5–April 19, 2019.

[3] These were drawn from a subset of the insults, accusations, intimidating statements, and incitement and threats from the survey of general public in Ukraine and the U.S. See Figures 4.1 and 4.2.

[4] Nearly 75% are members of an NGO, and activists. On average, activists were more supportive of violent rhetoric by ≈ 0.20 points more on a 5-point scale, but this was not significant (95% confidence interval, $-0.15, 0.54$).

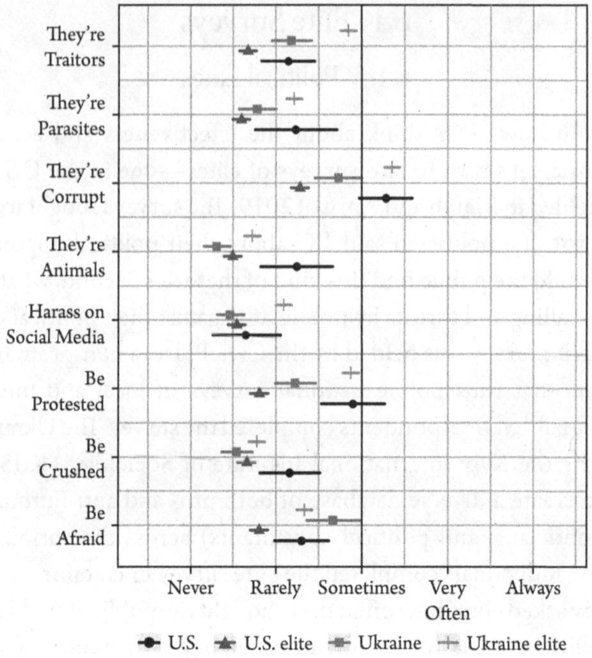

Figure 6.1 There's general agreement that the public doesn't like nasty politics, and in particular incitement. Comparing elite perceptions and actual mass opinion of nasty politics in Ukraine and the U.S.

Note: Means with associated 95% Confidence Intervals from 10,000 bootstraps. U.S. MTurk data is weighted to approximate U.S. population.

appetite for nasty politics. In contrast elites, in Ukraine systematically overestimate the public's appetite. Yet the size of this gap in Ukraine is fairly small—most within a half point on the five-point scale. The only notable exception are calls for protests, which U.S. elites and the Ukraine general public perceive as rarely acceptable, but are viewed as acceptable by Ukraine elite and U.S. general public. The gap is also fairly small for the most serious type of intimidation and incitement: "be afraid," "be crushed," and "harass on social media." The takeaway here is that elites in the U.S. do not overestimate the public's appetite for nasty politics. The case in Ukraine is different, with elites slightly overestimating the public's appetite, but again this gap is relatively small, and might also stem from the more activist sample of elite we have in Ukraine.

Does political identity shape perceptions of acceptability of different types of rhetoric among elites, and actual levels of acceptability in the masses? Among the Ukrainian general public, there are no statistically significant differences between elite Pro-Euromaidan and Anti-Euromaidan supporters. For the elite Ukrainian sample, Pro-Euromaidan supporters have significantly lower perceptions of the public's acceptability of calling an opponent a parasite

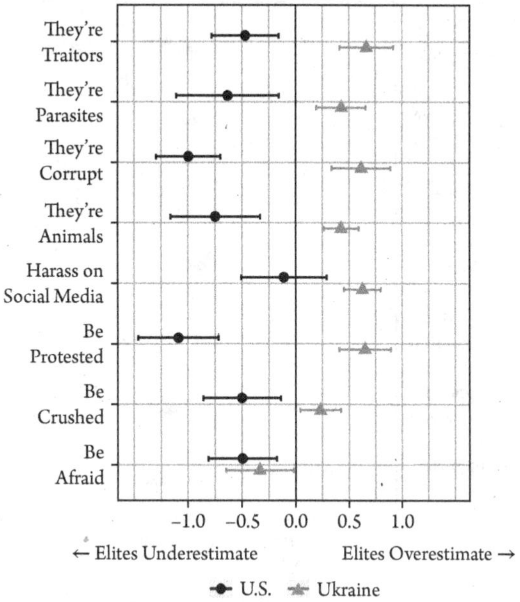

Figure 6.2 Elites in the U.S. underestimate the public's appetite for nasty politics, while those in Ukraine slightly overestimate.

Note: Means differences between elites and masses on 5-point scale (1-never acceptable to 5-always acceptable) with associated 95% Confidence Intervals from 10,000 bootstraps. U.S. MTurk data is weighted to approximate the U.S. population.

($D = -0.47, t = 2.15, p = 0.04$). In contrast in the U.S. elite sample, Republicans (compared to Democrats and Independents) are significantly less likely to view calls for protesting an opponent as acceptable ($D = -0.83, t = 3.20, p = 0.002$); more likely to view it as acceptable to say an opponent "should be crushed" ($D = 0.48$, $t = 2.29$, $p = 0.02$); and more likely to view calling an opponent an "animal" as acceptable ($D = 0.91, t = 2.77, p = 0.01$). Republican elites are also less likely to believe the public thinks it is acceptable to say an opponent "should be protested" ($D = -0.19, t = 2.03, p = 0.04$).

What do elites view as the strategy for politicians to name-call (Figure 6.3a) or threaten their political opponents (Figure 6.3b). I asked this question in both a closed-ended, and open-ended format (see word clouds in Figures 6.4a and 6.4b). While elites perceive some differences in the perceptions of the acceptability of violent, nasty rhetoric in the U.S. and Ukraine, there is strong agreement on the strategies behind politicians using name-calling and threats. Elites in both countries think nasty rhetoric is about media attention and core supporters, and much less about politicians sending a message to members of their own party.

These sentiments are also reflected in the free responses shown in the word clouds (Figures 6.4a and 6.4b), where both in the U.S. and Ukraine elites believe

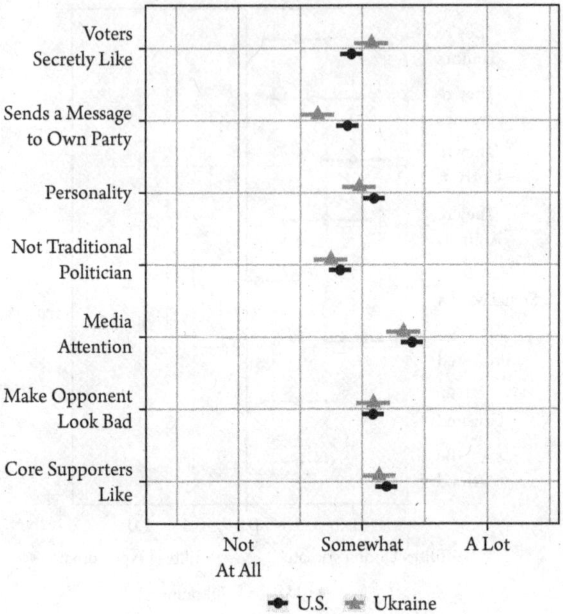

(a) Insults and accusations

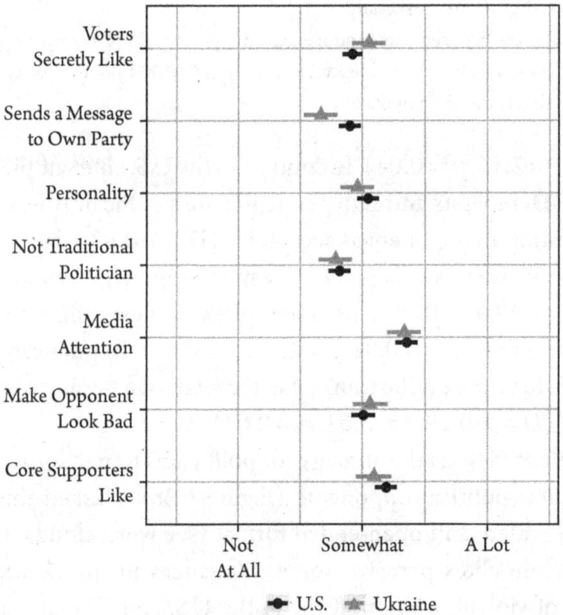

(b) Intimidation and incitement

Figure 6.3 Elite explanations for nasty politics.
Note: Means with associated 95% Confidence Intervals from 10,000 bootstraps.

(a) U.S. elites

(b) Ukraine elites

Figure 6.4 Elites in both the U.S. and Ukraine argue nasty rhetoric is mostly about media attention (open-ended response).

Note: Size, position, and color of word indicates frequency of this term mentioned in free response questions for "what do you think best explains why a politician may engage in name-calling or use threatening language against their political opponents."

the main motive behind politicians using nasty rhetoric is to attract media and general attention (two of the most repeated, and largest words in the free response). Ukrainians elites also talked about the "low culture" and "bad culture" of Ukrainian politics stemming from the use of violent rhetoric.

The findings of the elite surveys are clear. There are different levels of perceived acceptability of the nasty style writ large. It's perceived to be more acceptable to use nasty language in Ukraine compared to the U.S. This is likely a reflection of the fact that Ukrainian politics are more rough and tumble compared to the U.S. But among elites in both countries there's broad agreement that incitement is never or rarely acceptable. Yet, even given all the differences between the U.S. and Ukraine, elites in both countries are remarkably in agreement about what they think are the strategies behind violent rhetoric—it's about attention, and coalescing core supporters.

The story of whether elites in the U.S. and Ukraine systematically overestimate the public's appetite for nasty politics is more mixed. If anything, elites in the U.S. underestimate the public's appetite for nasty politics. In Ukraine elites tend to overestimate the public's appetite, but the level of overestimation is quite small (half a point on a five-point scale), and smallest for rhetoric containing incitement. In sum, there's not strong evidence that the puzzle of nasty politics is simply a case of misguided elites in both countries telling politicians to engage in nasty politics.

6.1.2 What Do Political Science Experts Think about Nasty Rhetoric?

How do political science experts view nasty politics? Which types of rhetoric do they see as particularly threatening? Given concerns about the link between nasty rhetoric, democratic backsliding, and political violence the opinion of political science experts is an important one.[5]

To answer these questions, I conducted a survey with 180 political scientists in March and April of 2021. These are academic experts whose research touches on nasty politics during political campaigns and political violence in the context of American Politics, Comparative Politics, and International Relations.[6]

As part of the survey, the political science experts were asked to rate how threatening they viewed different types of nasty rhetoric used by politicians. The scale was from 0 to 10, with a 0 not threatening at all, and 10 extremely threatening and corresponding to actual violence against domestic political opponents. There were 30 different examples of nasty rhetoric contained in the survey: seven insults, seven accusations, nine intimidating statements, and seven examples of incitement (see Table 6.1). Each expert rated five examples from each category.

[5] This is the approach of the "Bright Line Watch" project which regularly surveys "a group of political scientists to monitor democratic practices, their resilience, and potential threats." http://brightlinewatch.org/.

[6] The survey was conducted via an email invitation. See Appendix for sample details.

Table 6.1 **Examples of nasty rhetoric used in political science expert survey (March–April 2021).**

Insults	***Calling their opponent...*** idiots; jerks; corrupt; scum; parasites; animals; traitors
Accusations	***Accusing their opponent of...*** buying influence; being a liar; encouraging violence; being a sexual harasser; engaging in voter fraud; being a sellout; engaging in secret coup
Intimidation	***Saying their opponents...*** should be banned from social media; should be banned from holding office; should be investigated; should be heckled; are their enemies; should be made to pay; need to watch out; who knows what might happen; should be jailed
Incitement	***Saying their opponents should be...*** harassed on social media; crushed; afraid; pointing weapons at images of their opponents; eliminated; beaten up; their supporters should come armed and ready

On average how threatening did political scientists rate insults, accusations, intimidate statements, and incitement? Did they recognize the rank ordering proposed in the theory of nasty politics, with incitement being the most threatening, then followed by intimidating statements, accusations, and insults?[7] Figure 6.5 presents the results, and shows mostly "yes." Incitement was rated as the most threatening ($\bar{x} = 7.9$), and nearly 2 points higher than the next highest intimidating statement ($\bar{x} = 6.1$). The one area where there is some disagreement is that political science experts rated accusations ($\bar{x} = 4.7$) as slightly less threatening than insults ($\bar{x} = 4.9$).[8] Finally, perhaps the most important takeaway is that the political experts think nasty rhetoric matters and is threatening. The average level of threat for the least threatening categories (insults and accusations) is close to a 5, the mid-point of threat-level scale, and incitement is close to an 8 on the ten-point scale.

Figure 6.6 shows how political science experts rated each of the individual nasty rhetoric examples. There's quite a bit of variation within categories. For example the least threatening insult—calling an opponent an "idiot"

[7] There was higher internal consistency across the different categories based on the examples experts rated: insults ($\alpha = 0.91$), accusations ($\alpha = 0.88$), intimidation ($\alpha = 0.89$), and incitement ($\alpha = 0.83$).

[8] $D = 0.22, t = 1.77, p < 0.07$.

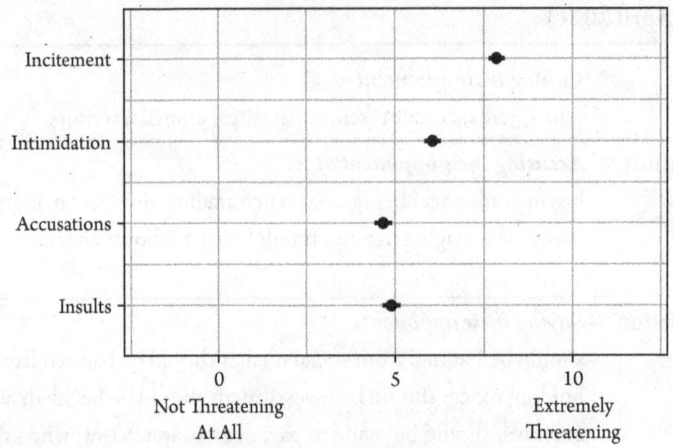

Figure 6.5 On average most political science experts view incitement as quite threatening. Intimidating statements slightly less so. Accusations and insults are viewed similarly (N = 180).

Note: Means with associated 95% Confidence Intervals from 10,000 bootstraps.

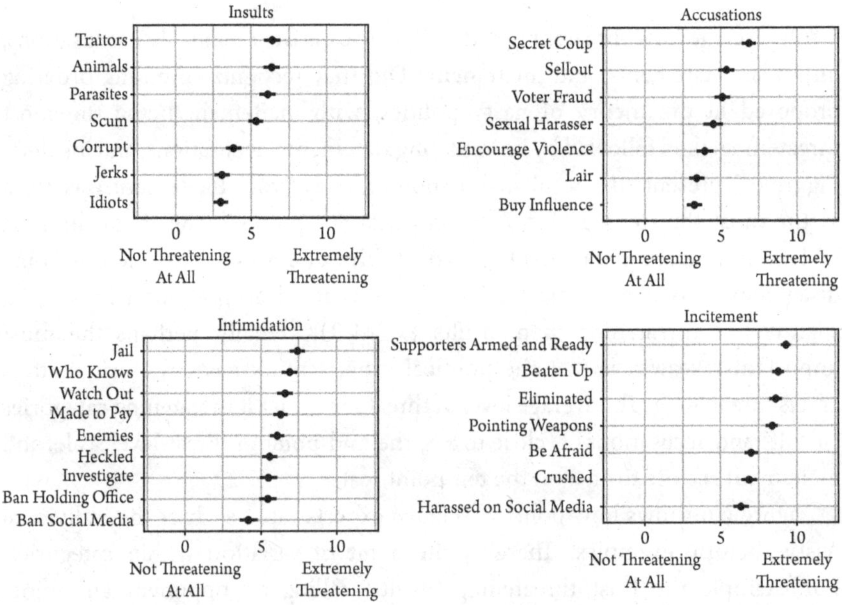

Figure 6.6 Most political science experts agree different types of incitement are highly threatening. There's more variation within the intimidation, accusations, and insult categories (N = 180).

Note: Means with associated 95% Confidence Intervals from 10,000 bootstraps.

($\bar{x} = 3.0$)—is viewed as half as threatening as calling an opponent a "traitor" ($\bar{x} = 6.4$, top left plot). A similar dynamic is at work with accusations. Accusing an opponent of a secret coup plot ($\bar{x} = 6.9$) is viewed as twice as threatening as accusing them of buying influence ($\bar{x} = 3.3$, top right plot). Intimidating statements have less variation, with all the examples except for supporting a ban on the opposition on social media rated above 5, the mid-point of threat (bottom left). The incitement examples also point to the kinds of nasty rhetoric experts find most threatening and likely to lead to violence (bottom right). The most threatening kinds of nasty rhetoric are those that contain explicit threats. These include telling supporters "to come armed and ready" ($\bar{x} = 9.3$), or saying their opponents should be "beaten up" ($\bar{x} = 8.8$), "eliminated" ($\bar{x} = 8.6$), or pointing weapons at images of their opponents ($\bar{x} = 8.4$).

Which type of nasty rhetoric is most threatening of all? The experts' response to this open-ended supports the idea that there is a unique threat posed by incitement.[9] More than 78% of open-ended responses singled out calls to violence and incitement as the most threatening. As one political scientist who studies political communication and political violence said alluding to the insurrection on January 6 at the U.S. Capitol:

Figure 6.7 Most political science experts view direct calls or threats of violence as the most threatening (open-ended).

Note: Size, position, and color of word indicates frequency of this term mentioned in the free response question for political science experts: "Which type of rhetoric that politicians use against their domestic political opponents do you think is the most threatening?"

[9] 66% of the 180 experts filled out the open-ended response.

> Open calls for violence, veiled or direct threats to their lives (these are the most dangerous). The past months (2020 U.S. election, and the January 6th insurrection at the Capitol) have shown that there are followers "out there" willing to act on these threats.

Second, 24% of answers also argued that dehumanizing insults such as calling opponents "animals" or "parasites" pave the way for future violence. An expert who studies international relations and political violence emphasized the following point: "Dehumanizing language—parasites, animals etc. (is the most threatening). As this has been shown to be a power tool for stoking divisions among the population and leading to mass human rights atrocities."

6.2 Going In-Depth with Campaign Experts

The surveys of political elites and political science experts give us a general sense of how they think about nasty politics, and which kind of language is particularly threatening. But it's incomplete. Campaign strategists, political operatives, and journalists have spent much of their careers thinking about how people respond to different types of rhetoric and messages. Which types of rhetoric and behavior do they think qualifies as nasty politics? What are the strategies behind its use? How do they think voters feel about it, and which kind of politicians do elites think are likely to turn to the nasty style? I conducted 59 in-depth interviews from May of 2018 to April 2020: 21 in the U.S. and 38 in Ukraine. The bulk of the interviews were with campaign strategists, and party activists, but also included some journalists, and civil society members.[10] In order to make respondents feel comfortable speaking frankly, all interviews were done as "not for attribution." The campaign experts are only identified by their political leaning and position.

We touched on several topics during the interviews. But the main focus was on what campaign experts see as nasty politics. What are some prominent examples? And most importantly what do they see as the strategies behind it?

One of the first questions I asked in my interviews is what type of language do they see as nasty and violent? How do they think about the difference between insults and accusations, and intimidating statements and incitement? In Ukraine, respondents could easily come up with several examples of nasty politics. For example one party worker for Petro Poroshenko mentioned an incident when in 2011 then President Yanukovych called journalist Mustafa Nayyem an "enemy" and also threatened his family (Resende 2018,

[10] Sample demographics for the elite in-depth samples are shown in the Appendix.

pp. 118–119).[11] Ukrainian elites understood that name-calling was a regular feature in Ukrainian politics, and something much more common than threats of violence. As one Anti-Euromaidan activist said, "There is a difference between name-calling and threats (of violence). Sometimes politicians may shout and name-call just to make attention. But sometimes threats may be real, such as when they promise to throw their rivals in jail."[12] One other important point was that threats that were made in public were not perceived to be as threatening as those that happened in private. My interview with a veteran of both the Euromaidan and War in Donbas, and member of a center-right party emphasized this point: "If a politician really wants to crush his opponent in real life, he will do so quietly, and not make a big publicity. Our politicians are first of all businessmen, and that's why they protect their own interest."[13] Thus in Ukraine the public-facing calls for violence may be used more to attract media attention. Whereas private threats carry the weight of violence, particularly for journalists and activists (Theise 2019). Finally, more than 70% of Ukrainian elites interviewed cited Oleh Lyashko as being a key purveyor of the nasty style. A party operative for the far-right National Corpus party described that, "The best example of a politician who uses violent rhetoric is Lyashko—it's core to his image."[14]

In the interviews in the U.S. there was more uncertainty and debate about what was meant by nasty, violent rhetoric. For instance, a Democratic strategist said:

> I didn't think violent rhetoric was that common pre-Trump . . . I see violent language as threatening and encouraging physical violence. I think name-calling can take somewhat different forms. Saying "impeach the motherfucker" (as Democratic Rep. Rashida Tlaib did in 2019)[15] or yelling "liar" during the State of the Union Address (as Republican Rep. Joe Wilson (South Carolina) did in 2009)[16]—it's name-calling. It's norm-breaking, but it's not violent rhetoric.[17]

A Republican strategist also referred to much of the nasty rhetoric employed by Trump as hyperbole.

[11] Interview #Ukr-P-N0219.
[12] Interview #Ukr-AM-D0219.
[13] Interview #Ukr-S-S0219.
[14] Interview #Ukr-NC-N0819.
[15] See Stracqualursi (2019).
[16] See Kleefeld (2009).
[17] Interview #US-D-S0719.

> I don't always like it (Trump's rhetoric)—it's not always a positive development. Voters have a way of being pretty sophisticated at filtering things. They don't hear the promise to put her (Hillary Clinton) in jail as a real promise. Or, "lock her up." Much like, at the football game/or baseball "ump you suck," It's hyperbole.... Trump is a real estate guy who is prone to hyperbole.[18]

In fact every interview but one (95%) mentioned Trump's rhetoric. But again, there was a general agreement that name-calling was less serious than threats.

What do elites think is the strategy behind the nasty style, and how do they make sense of the fact that voters seem to dislike it? Elites in both Ukraine and the U.S. had a lot of thoughts on what they saw as the strategic purpose of "going to the gutter,"[19] or "acting like a clown"[20]—all things campaign experts used to describe nasty rhetoric. These arguments can be classified into five different strategies behind nasty politics. First, nasty politics may be financially motivated. Saying nasty things about your opponent can be a way to raise money (*Get Money*). A second strategy is that voters like politicians who talk like them, and use the coarse language of the common people. Some people prefer the language of a bartender to that of a polished aristocrat and think that the nastier language is a signal that a politician is speaking their mind, and not just pretending (*Authenticity*). A third strategy of nasty rhetoric, is that it's not meant to persuade, but rather serves as a rallying cry for the base and core supporters in polarized times (*Core Supporters Like It*). Fourth, and one of the most prominent goals of the nasty style, is that it's largely about drawing attention and media coverage to the politician (*Media Attention*). And finally, perhaps voters aren't as opposed to nasty politics as they claim to be—perhaps they may secretly like or enjoy it (*Voters Secretly Like It*).

6.2.1 Strategies behind Violent Rhetoric

So which factors did elites mention as being important for explaining nasty politics? Table 6.2 shows the percentage of interviews which mentioned each strategy during the interviews.[21] First, elites in both countries believe that nasty rhetoric is done for media attention. More than 95% of interviews in both countries mentioned how politicians say nasty things for attention. There are

[18] Interview #US-R-B0619.
[19] Interview #US-D-M0319.
[20] Interview #Ukr-Z-L0819.
[21] I transcribed notes during each interview. I then used the NVivo software to tag and code the transcripts.

Table 6.2 **Which strategies of nasty rhetoric were mentioned in the elite in-depth interviews (March 2018–April, 2020)?**

Explanation	*Ukraine* (N = 38)	*U.S.* (N = 21)
Get Money	3.3%	23.8%
Authenticity	30.0%	38.1%
Core Supporters Like It	40.0%	95.2%
Media Attention	96.7%	95.2%
Toughness and Dominance	40.0%	57.1%
Voters Secretly Like It	6.7%	38.1%

however some notable differences between how Ukrainian and U.S. elites and campaign strategists perceive things. In the U.S. more than 95% of the interviews touched on the role that core supporters and polarization play in perpetuating violent rhetoric, compared to only 40% in Ukraine. Given the strong two-party system in the U.S. and growing concerns about polarization, that's not surprising. U.S. elites were also more likely to mention nasty rhetoric as a tool to raise money (23.8% to 3.3%), about being viewed as authentic (38.1% to 30.0%), and about being perceived as tough and dominant (57.1% to 40.0%).

Get the Money

Politicians, particularly in the U.S., have to be attuned to donors. Campaign strategists in the U.S. argued that fundraising can explain some of the nasty language politicians use. As a Democratic campaign strategist told me, "You see it (nasty rhetoric) in fundraising emails—'it's a fight to the death, the world is ending if you don't send in your $5.' They (campaigns) pull out every trick to get you to give to give a small modicum of money. There's always a need to create an urgency, and social media has amped it up."[22] This sentiment was echoed by a Republican strategist, "If you are going to do any email fundraising. . .you need to say something to get people to pay attention and click. If you say something a bit on the edge (use violent rhetoric) it is far more likely to get someone to open it."[23] So even though it's about fundraising, there's a symbiotic relationship between gaining attention and money. A Democratic strategist discussed this even more explicitly:

[22] Interview #US-D-M0319.
[23] Interview #US-R-M0919.

> Anyone in politics who is looking to stand out, is looking to raise a lot of money, gain notoriety, one of the ways to do this—is to engage in the very type of violent rhetoric we are talking about.... [O]ne of the places that you see the most partisan, vitriolic, incendiary rhetoric is fundraising emails. You are appealing to a subset of a subset of a subset for contributions. People are not trying to win over the hearts or minds.[24]

Nasty rhetoric attracts attention and can be tailored to core supporters—and this can be an effective way to raise money. After Democrat Rep. Rashida Tlaib's (Michigan) controversial outburst where she pledged to "impeach the motherfucker (President Trump)" her campaign began fundraising off of it, selling t-shirts that said "Impeach the MF" (Neavling 2019).

The politics of money in Ukraine is much more opaque. Parties raise money, but much of the money in Ukraine gets funneled from oligarchs to politicians through back channels (UNIAN 2019). One Pro-Euromaidan journalist and anti-corruption activist describes how oligarchs use nasty and populist rhetoric for their own business interests:

> In Ukraine, we have a business-criminal political system. It's a situation where a criminal is connected to politics and vice versa. We have this relationship between business and politics—they are not separate as they should be.... Populism is impossible without violent rhetoric—it depends upon it. Oligarchs hire politicians to use violent rhetoric and to implement "populist" policies all to protect their own interests.[25]

Authenticity

One of the common refrains that several of the campaign strategists mentioned was how nasty rhetoric was seen as more authentic, and not just a politician being fake in front of the cameras. Several Republican strategists in the U.S. mentioned this as one of Trump's key rhetoric strengths when he engaged in name-calling. "He's (Trump's) out there raising hell. He's not a traditional politician or rational fellow, he's cagey. I think he's a master at being politically off the throttle."[26] Another Republican strategist echoed these sentiments:

[24] Interview #US-D-S0919.
[25] Interview #Ukr-PE-I0120.
[26] Interview #US-R-B0419.

> Voters take him (Trump) seriously not literally, but the media takes him literally and not seriously. Voters have been looking for candidates that don't give them pre-scrubbed sound bites.[27]

Several of my interviewees in the U.S. also pointed out how distrust in institutions fosters the idea that being civil equates with being inauthentic. One Democratic strategist described it, "Being indirect is a form of being an elite. So violent rhetoric is a way to fight against the elites—it's direct. Academics and eggheads (use civil rhetoric), whereas someone who is (more of the people is) going to call a spade a spade."[28]

Many in Ukraine argued that nasty language is a way for a politician to signify that he or she is one of the people, and not just another slick-talking politician. A campaign worker for Yulia Tymoshenko's party said this explicitly, "Ordinary people use bad words in their communication—(so when politicians do it) it connects them to the people."[29] Politicians like Lyashko may intentionally cultivate this tough-talking, man-of-the-people style. A freelance Ukrainian journalist described Lyashko's rhetorical appeal, "His (Lyashko's) supporters are mostly low-educated, rural people, who like his blunt remarks and his showman's style. Lyashko likes to travel to some remote villages and take photos with so-called babushkas, the elderly women."[30] One party worker for Petro Poroshenko's European Solidarity party described her own experience of when one of her candidates lost to a tough-talking candidate:

> I worked for a local candidate—an educated person, a lawyer, and he had money to finance a good campaign. Yet another candidate won. Why? Because the constituency was filled with uneducated, poor people. My candidate had nice suits, expensive shoes, and spoke well—but it didn't matter. Because the people wanted something different. The guy who won was a local hairdresser who used all sorts of coarse language and talked like the locals talked.[31]

Core Supporters Like It

Two of the common refrains I heard in my conversations with U.S.-based elites was that nasty rhetoric was a product of two interrelated ideas. First, it's a result of increasing levels of partisan polarization. And second, a need to talk to the

[27] Interview #US-R-B0619.
[28] Interview #US-D-D0719.
[29] Interview #Ukr-T-O0219.
[30] Interview #Ukr-J-O0320.
[31] Interview #Ukr-P-N0219.

base, or core supporters. This idea was hammered home by both Democratic and Republicans. One Democratic strategist said:

> It (nasty rhetoric) polarizes. Polarization is an efficacious political strategy.... The stronger the name-calling, the more the polarization, and the more likely it is to be memorable. Calling someone a "violent radical" sticks. With polarization (and violent rhetoric) you don't allow a mushy middle, you force them to pick a side.[32]

Another Democratic strategist emphasized the need for party leaders to match the intensity of their bases. "Both Republican and Democratic leaders want to reflect the emotions and intensity of the base. These partisans who are most likely to vote in the primaries are the loudest on Twitter, and politicians feel like they have to match the intensity of the base."[33]

A strategist for Bernie Sanders and other progressive causes also described how social media and polarization both are increasing the incentives for nasty political rhetoric:

> All of this (nasty language) is geared towards base voters, core supporters. And it's not just coming from politicians. This is coming from a shitty media culture, reality TV, influencers, people watching bloodsports on YouTube, and the rise of UFC/MMA.... If you are a politician and want to lead a beer-hall type of a humanity, you used to show an educated type of leadership, but now it's guttural instinct and basic id.[34]

Core supporters and polarization takes on a different flavor in Ukraine. Historically parties are much weaker and more ephemeral in Ukraine. Nonetheless, many of those interviewed discussed how the nasty style plays to core supporters in Ukraine, and in particular around events leading up to and following Euromaidan. One Euromaidan participant and activist described this dynamic: "(Euro)Maidan changed some things—but it couldn't change Ukrainian culture. Violence is part of our society and culture.... Ukrainian society is very very polarized and split. That's why violent language is a consequence of this polarization due to multiple factors—split by ideas, language, etc."[35] Another journalist echoed this sentiment for how Euromaidan polarized society, "Now, post-Maidan, it's (rhetoric) more about posturing

[32] Interview #US-D-D0719.
[33] Interview #US-D-D0919.
[34] Interview #US-P-S0319.
[35] Interview #Ukr-PE-A0219.

and you need to signal that you are more nationalistic, patriotic and a better Ukrainian."[36]

A political commentator and journalist who supported Euromaidan connects the level of nasty rhetoric to key points of contention in Ukrainian politics:

> This kind of rhetoric is quite common for Ukrainian politics. The peaks of violent rhetoric tend to appear when society is under pressure. When there is some political crisis or there is some revolution (such as Euromaidan). In these periods of time, there is a fight for people's attention and their sympathy.[37]

One veteran Ukrainian pollster suggested that much of the appeal of Zelensky in 2019 was his rejection of the polarizing rhetoric of the Pro-Euromaidan versus Anti-Euromaidan. "A lot of people supported Zelensky because of his more integrative discourse, and not his fiery rhetoric."[38]

Media Attention

Politicians have a fundamental need for attention and recognition. People can't support you if they don't know who you are. A Republican strategist put it more colorfully when discussing Trump's appeal, "It (Trump's appeal and rhetoric) all stem from media attention. The public views him as a TV show not a businessman, and they view him as a TV star. . .as someone who has been in the public life, next to survival and sex being on TV is the next best thing."[39] Attention is a currency that is important to politicians and many including Trump recognize this. One left-leaning journalist was even more critical of the media's role in Trump's rise:

> An almost visceral insight that Trump gets, is that attention is everything and behaving outrageously is a way to get attention and drown out everything else. And if there's one thing he knows how to do it's get attention. To the extent that it's all talk, the media could cover it less. . . . then keep day-to-day focus on the policy. But as a cable news producer the easier thing to do is to put up Trump's "crazy tweet of the day" and then talk about it from both sides.[40]

[36] Interview #Ukr-J-C0120.
[37] Interview #Ukr-PE-AR0120.
[38] Interview #Ukr-P-A0120.
[39] Interview #US-R-B0419.
[40] Interview #US-LW-D0120.

A Republican strategist echoed the financial incentive for the media to cover the outrage and critiqued the Fox News model:

> Media are a profit-making machine—they have ads and they need to "sell" (their) viewers. Fox is one of the most profitable media companies, and they gin up anger and outrage as they essentially operate like a state-run media network.[41]

A Democratic strategist who has run campaigns both in the U.S. and abroad highlighted how politicians can exploit this media dynamic:

> The public hates the sensationalism and the punditry (of the media). The public wants the media to stop doing ambulance chasing, and fire chases, and the floods, and stop doing the Hannity/Maddow (partisan cable news shows) extreme-opinion making. Yet, there are clicks and eyeballs for the sensationalist and extreme. Politicians are willing to trade-off a bit of their reputation to get noticed, get eyeballs, get money and support.[42]

The story in Ukraine was also about attention, but political elites and strategists were much more cynical of politicians' intentions. Many of my interviews touched on the role of Ukrainian political chat shows. One Pro-Euromaidan activist captured a common sentiment about the nasty style in Ukraine: "it's all (violent threats and name-calling) just a show, politicians fight on camera, and then grab drinks and dinner afterward."[43] A long-time Tymoshenko supporter and party worker talked about how when politicians do or say outrageous things it's beneficial for both politicians and the media. "The media gets ratings and so do the politicians with attention. This is food for the people—conflict is food for the general populace, and people are hungry for events and rhetoric."[44]

This same interviewee also brought up the role that oligarchs play in controlling the media. "Different (oligarchic) groups own TV shows and media, they can manipulate public opinion." This point was echoed by several interviews who saw politicians doing the bidding of oligarchs. "These oligarchs use the media and political actors to win these (inter-) oligarchic conflicts. Politicians that work under an oligarch are told to emphasize certain topics (on the media and use nasty language)."[45] Another veteran pollster in Ukraine emphasized the

[41] Interview #US-R-J0220.
[42] Interview #US-D-J0319.
[43] Interview #Ukr-PE-E0219.
[44] Interview #Ukr-T-N0120.
[45] Interview #Ukr-PE-AR0120.

incentive for politicians to do or say crazy things to get invited back onto these channels:

> Why are there stupid videos on the Internet or TV? You remember stupid shit. Violent rhetoric is the same. It's like the saying, "any PR is good PR." It's the easiest way to draw attention. The more people who know you, the more TV channels invite you on. And if you behave unpredictable, it will increase the TV channel ratings, so they invite the most unpredictable politicians who are willing to say crazy shit.[46]

This confluence of attention-seeking politicians, ratings-seeking media, and oligarchic control leads to heightened incentives for the nasty style of politics.

A second common refrain among Ukrainian elites is that these provocations—fights, threats, and name-calling—were not genuine. Rather they were calculated moves to distract the Ukrainian public and grab media attention. One party worker from the center-right who participated in Euromaidan said, "This type of rhetoric gets widely discussed among ordinary people. That is the way to remove people's attention from the really important issues. Violent rhetoric is hiding the really important issues that are being discussed (behind closed doors)."[47]

In both the U.S. and Ukraine insults, accusations, intimidating statements, incitement, and actual fights in Ukraine, are all part of a strategy to draw attention to a candidate. This is because the media have incentives to chase ratings—and this makes them more likely to cover conflict, controversy, and outrageous behavior. But there are also several key differences in the way political elites in Ukraine and the U.S. view attention as a currency in the polarized and partisan media environment. Ukrainian elites are even more cynical than their U.S. counterparts, pointing out that much of the media and politicians are affiliated with the different oligarchic factions. Nasty rhetoric and behavior become a way to grab attention and strategically manipulate media coverage towards or away from oligarchic interests.

Toughness and Dominance

Politics and elections are ways of resolving disputes peacefully. Yet, "violence lurks in the back of politics."[48] Politicians may want to signal that they can represent their constituents, and being "tough enough" is one litmus test for certain voters. The demand for strong and tough leaders also spikes when voters feel

[46] Interview #Ukr-P-A0120.
[47] Interview #Ukr-S-S0219.
[48] Interview #US-D-J0319.

threatened (Stenner 2005). Nasty, violent language can be a way for politicians to signal strength and that they are tough enough to deal with threats. One Republican strategist said that being perceived as strong was as important as having good policy proposals, and said that "In executive races, strength has always been the (main) currency."[49] The need to project strength is particularly of concern for a politicians' supporters. A Republican strategist explained how this logic plays out with core supporters:

> The bases of both parties think they're losing. They can't believe what the other side is doing. They need tougher people that won't put up with it. They feel that candidates that don't use this kind of language aren't tough enough.[50]

This need to be seen as tough creates incentives for politicians to go nasty, and play to their core supporters. A politician is supposed to represent and channel the passions and hopes of their supporters. "Partisans see someone expressing or validating their anger. 'He or she gets me' when they use this language. You hear this a lot. What I hear from voters is not about policy, it's that 'they are scrappy, a fighter, or tell the truth.'"[51]

But not all candidates are equally able to play up their toughness. Several U.S. elites highlighted how tricky it was for female candidates to appear both tough but not "shrill."[52] For example, "People want their office holders to be tough enough to stand up for evil forces. We want presidents to be tough and fighters. But it's tough for women." The strategist further elaborated on focus groups they had conducted where female candidates like Kamala Harris or Elizabeth Warren attacked Trump, and where Democratic male voters worried if she was "tough enough" to take on Trump, while the female voters were worried that female candidates wouldn't be likable.[53]

A Republican strategist connected the gendered effects of nasty rhetoric to the way aggression signals a politician's ideology:

> What's interesting is ideology is in the mind of voters on the policy spectrum. Now it's on the aggression spectrum. Some people might be very conservative in their views but not use this kind (nasty) of rhetoric, and they would be viewed as a moderate. Quite often in a Republican primary, if there is a woman running, the female running

[49] Interview #US-R-B0619.
[50] Interview #US-R-M0919.
[51] Interview #US-D-D0919.
[52] Interview #US-D-K0919.
[53] Interview #US-D-K0919.

> gets labeled as a "moderate," even if she has more conservative views than her challengers. A lot of this comes back to tone. Just by being a woman there's an attached perception with their gender, of being less aggressive than a man. Every woman has this problem in both parties. When a woman says something tough "she's a bitch" but if a guy says it "he's tough."[54]

Several interviews in Ukraine also singled out Yulia Tymoshenko as having to walk a fine line. As one of the few prominent, female political leaders in Ukrainian politics, Tymoshenko has had to both embrace traditional feminine roles in Ukraine—and she has done so deftly with her dress, speech, and manner—while also showing that she is tough enough to be a leader (Kis 2007). One of her supporters argued that she engenders criticism from her rivals because of this, "politicians who are males like to attack Tymoshenko—because they are afraid of a woman leader."[55] As if to underscore this point, a high-ranking member of the far-right, ultra-nationalist National Corps party said about her, "The Tymoshenko block. . . . they do not have any ideology other than scandal-plagued female populism."[56]

In Ukraine, the need for toughness was similar to the U.S., but not viewed as much through the lens of partisan politics. Politicians that spoke or acted tough were more likely to take actions or do something on behalf of the people.[57] A former public relations specialist who was active in Yanukovych's Party of Regions, argued that Zelensky was able to walk a fine line between signaling toughness and avoiding outright violent rhetoric in his 2019 presidential campaign against Poroshenko:

> During Zelensky's debate at the soccer stadium, Zelensky said to Poroshenko (paraphrase) "I am the outcome of the trial for you. Because of me, you are done. I am your judgment." It was not a direct threat or name-calling, Zelensky showed who he was and people decided to vote for Zelensky. Zelensky was signaling that he was tough but not violent.[58]

Voters Secretly Like It

One point that American elites were quite sure of is that nasty, violent rhetoric works to some extent. And when voters say they abhor it, they aren't being

[54] Interview #US-R-M0919.
[55] Interview #Ukr-T-L0819.
[56] Interview Ukr-N-0318.
[57] Interview #Ukr-L-L0819.
[58] Interview #Ukr-Y-D0120.

completely honest with themselves. Many, such as one Republican strategist, connected it to the supposed dislike of the public to the long tradition of negative advertising in American politics:

> The public is lying. I don't think they're being venal in their lying. . . . they're just trying to say they aren't the kind of person attracted to this stuff. In general negative advertising works, but you'll never get a poll saying they like this.[59]

Another Republican strategist mentioned the disconnect between Republican voters not liking Trump's tweets but liking that he's being authentic when he uses nasty language. "It's social pressure. 'I don't approve of his tweeting, but I like his end results.' It's a double edged sword—they (Republican voters) say they don't like his tweeting—they don't agree with everything he says, but they still agree with his thrust and authenticity."[60] A Democratic strategist also echoed this social pressure, "Voting is a social act. You are getting a social response (when people say they don't like violent rhetoric). I do think there is a genuine desire for civility and decency, but it's a lot smaller than what you would find in a poll."[61]

Ukrainian elites generally didn't emphasize this social desirability bias. But a Pro-Euromaidan journalist drew an important distinction that holds for both Ukrainian and U.S. politics, "People may claim they don't like such kind of nasty, violent rhetoric. Yet, people are attracted to scandals, provocations and violence."[62]

So the idea that voters secretly like nasty politics might be a bit strong. But at the same time they are drawn to it. And this attention-grabbing aspect of the nasty style helps explain a large part of our nasty politics puzzle.

There were additional insights from the interviews that were unique to both countries. In the U.S., there was a debate about how much the powerful invoked claims of civility to shield themselves from criticism from the less powerful. Ukraine's politics also led to some unusual insights related to the oligarchs in Ukrainian politics, what role fights play, and how Ukrainian politics resembles a circus.

The Civility vs. Incivility Debate in American Politics

Centrist Republican and Democratic strategists I interviewed decried the erosion of civil discourse, and the emergence of "raging flamethrower" politicians

[59] Interview #US-R-B0419.
[60] Interview #US-R-B0619.
[61] Interview #US-D-D0719.
[62] Interview #Ukr-PE-AR0120.

on both sides.[63] This uncivil political discourse reinforces polarization. For example one Democratic strategist decried how the "public has become a lot more frustrated and hostile with each other."[64]

Yet some elites who I interviewed saw this framing of civility versus incivility as centrist grandstanding. They pointed the finger at the media as being a chief instigator of the civility police, while ignoring pressing problems. "The press is playing out the David Broder fantasy of politics as sports, as we should all get along, whereas politics since Nixon has been about transferring pain."[65]

Many of the leftists and Bernie Sanders supporters I interviewed were just as enraged at the mainstream media as the faux arbiter of discourse as they were at Trump. A leftist journalist and Sanders supporter described this belief:

> The media has a long-standing belief of "both sides" and "balance" and this longstanding problem with the media has been exacerbated by the media. Because Trump is so insane and unrestrained in his speech that accurately characterizing what he says is really difficult. It fundamentally challenges the media's quixotic idea of objectivity.[66]

Another leftist journalist connected the media's desire for perceived fairness between the left and right, with journalists drawing false equivalence and civility-policing politicians on the left:

> They (the media) got madder at her (Michigan Democratic Rep. Rashida Tlaib for saying "impeach the motherfucker") than at Trump for banning Muslims. The media finger wags at incivility, but will "both sides" policies that hurt refugees.[67]

Leftists elites in the U.S. believe that the media didn't feel comfortable criticizing Trump's or the Republicans' policies, so the media fell back on policing civility. Many of the Sanders supporters and progressives I interviewed believe this made it harder for marginalized groups to challenge the powerful, as they got accused of using "violent" rhetoric or being "uncivil" whenever they call out injustice. A leftist academic and activist wanted to emphasize this point:

[63] Interview #US-R-F0419.

[64] Interview #US-D-M0619.

[65] David Broder was a long-time *Washington Post* columnist and pundit who was known for his commitment to centrism in U.S. politics. Interview #US-D-L1219.

[66] Interview #US-LW-DD0120.

[67] Interview #US-LW-D0120.

> Who is considered "violent" is a deeply political thing. . . . I can't deal with this civility discourse—this has been used to set the parameters of acceptable speech. . . . Civil discourse is totally unmoored from reality, because the reality is quite unequal. . . . I'm OK with saying the 1% is bad. There are moments to rile people up against the powerful society, and it's totally OK for the Davids to be angry at the Goliaths.[68]

One of the unexpected takeaways from the U.S. interviews was how similar Trump-supporting Republican strategists and leftist Sanders supporters viewed the nasty style. Elite Trump supporters and strategists described Trump's rhetoric as "gritty"—but viewed it as authentic way of expressing ire at targets, like the media, that mostly deserved it.[69] Another Republican strategist emphasized this point:

> You have to understand that people have a tremendous amount of distrust in institutions. And most of that stems from 2008—the big banks got a bailout, the politicians got a bail out, and Detroit got a bailout. And it took 8–10 years for the recovery to come into place. Some people just wanted to burn them down. They (politicians talking nasty) are just tapping into what people feel.[70]

Leftists Sanders supporters in the same way found that incivility could be a useful weapon against powerful interests. To both elite supporters of Trump and Sanders the strategic use of nasty politics was less of an issue than the perceived transgressions of the targets. Centrists Republicans and Democratic elites meanwhile bemoaned the decline in the quality of political discourse and its role in polarization. The acceptability of the nasty style was thus one of the defining things that split elites in both parties.

Of Oligarchs, Fights, and the Circus in Ukraine

Elites in Ukraine were nearly uniform in decrying corruption, and in particular the influence of various oligarchic factions. Unlike in the U.S., where partisan polarization was viewed as motivating the harsh rhetoric, several of the elites connected the nasty, violent style of politics practiced in Ukraine to more cynical ploys by oligarchs. For instance, a Ukraine-based journalist described this belief:

[68] Interview #US-D-T0202.
[69] Interview #US-R-B0619.
[70] Interview #US-R-J0220.

> These politicians are used by oligarchs. And they use the politicians as attack dogs to defend their interests without saying the oligarch's name publicly. Kolomoisky recently has been the exception. A lot of politicians and public servants get paid a bunch of money and live lavishly because they are paid by oligarchs. (For example) Lyashko (was an attack dog) for Akhmetov (his oligarchic patron).[71]

Politicians in Ukraine use name-calling and threats as a way to distract and "do work" for their oligarchic patrons. But elites don't simply view politicians' behavior as idle threats. Many politicians also have businesses themselves, and are willing to protect them viciously. A Pro-Euromaidan activist and journalist argued that many Ukrainian politicians are "corrupt criminals" who see politics as a money-making enterprise.[72]

Perceptions that financial interests motivate nasty politics is not just common among traditional politicians but even among far-right nationalist groups like the Azov Battalion and Right Sector. Many of these group have been involved in attacks on Roma and LGBT groups, and harbor White supremacists and neo-Nazis (Hume 2019; Miller 2018*b*). Yet even for these ideological hard-line groups there's a widespread feeling that "they are basically a tool of oligarchic groups."[73] Another Pro-Euromaidan journalist who has covered the far-right extensively in Ukraine said that "the far right is likely hired muscle, and oligarchs point them in the direction they want."[74]

Many connected the corrupt influence of the oligarchs to the pugilistic nature of politics in the Rada. Why were there so many fights? One campaign strategist from the pro-Russian Opposition Bloc argued that these fights are strategic in nature to change the conversation, and that parties employ enforcers:

> It's not a secret that there are some (deputies who are) sportsmen from a fighting backgrounds who are sometimes used offensively and sometimes defensively (during these fights). Mainly the fights are strategic to change attention from legislation that politicians don't want attention on.[75]

[71] Rinat Akhmetov is the richest man in Ukraine, and a former member of the Party or Regions and the Rada. Interview #Ukr-J-C0120.

[72] Interview #Ukr-PE-A0219.

[73] Interview #Ukr-P-A0120.

[74] Interview #Ukr-PE-O020.

[75] Interview #Ukr-O-L0819.

The ritualistic nature of these fights and coverage have led to jaded views of Ukrainian politics. When your politics are akin to professional wrestling it's not surprising that elites and voters have low evaluations of the political culture:

> Mostly people laugh at such fights in the Rada. They laugh and cry, and because they can see that it's not normal, but politicians do it, and when they see fighting in the Rada, they think to themselves "what kind of people did we vote for?[76]

A party worker for Zelensky commented that while these fights in the Rada are strategic and designed to distract, they turn politics into a spectacle. "People are just laughing at such events. What do people think? These deputies (in the Rada) they make us laugh, it's like a circus."[77]

This theme of Ukrainian politics as a carnival-like atmosphere with politicians play-acting was a common subject brought up by the interviews. "Fights in the Rada are the logical conclusion of using name-calling and threats, it's like a continuation of the show—the circus must go on."[78] Several viewed Lyashko's antics as being particularly egregious. According a party worker for Zelensky, "Lyashko is a clown and he creates a circus (wherever he goes)."[79] A campaign strategist for the pro-Russian Opposition Platform for Life put it succinctly: "politicians are just clowns in a circus."[80]

Among elites with familiarity with Ukrainian politics, three insights explain Ukrainian politics and the nasty style. First, oligarchs control many political parties and the media. Second, fights in the Rada reflect real political differences, but they were also a tool for oligarchs and politicians to stir things up for their own private benefit. Finally, since politicians are pawns and controlled by business interests and many fights were staged, Ukrainian politics resembles a cross between the circus and American professional wrestling. So what gets reported on in the news and what the public observes is all for show, and the real dealings happen behind closed doors. This all leads to a very cynical view of Ukrainian politics.

[76] Interview #Ukr-O-V0819.
[77] Interview #Ukr-Z-P0819.
[78] Interview #Ukr-AM-A0219.
[79] Interview #Ukr-Z-L0819.
[80] Interview #Ukr-O-A0819.

6.3 What Have We Learned from Elites?

The elite and expert surveys find support for our general theory of nasty politics. Direct calls for violence (incitement) is in a category of its own—and considered both rarely acceptable and likely to trigger violence. Intimidating statements are also quite threatening, if slightly less than incitement. But accusations and insults are more ambiguous. Some insults, particularly the dehumanizing kind, such as calling opponents "animals" or "scum," are considered very threatening. While others, such as calling opponents "idiots" or "jerks" are more mundane. Likewise some accusations come in the quite threatening variety—"they're engaged in a secret coup"—versus the more pedestrian, "they use money to buy influence."

When I first started this project I was prepared to tell a very different story about nasty politics in the U.S. and Ukraine. But the elite surveys and interviews show that there are strong similarities in the strategy and response to the violent rhetoric in both countries. Yes, the U.S. has high levels of partisan polarization and Trump, while Ukraine has a more personalized politics that revolves around oligarchs. But even with these differences, the nasty style of politics still draws outsized attention, making it an attractive strategy for politicians who are willing to sacrifice some of their reputation for headlines. And nasty politics can be a way to signal how tough you are to your core supporters.

The next chapter will discuss the implications of nasty politics for democracy in Israel, Ukraine, and the U.S.

7

Nasty Politics and Its Implications for Democracy

In July of 2004, Oleh Tyahnybok, a deputy in the Rada, gave a speech in the Carpathian Mountains. He didn't choose just any mountain outlook. As leader of the far-right, ultra-nationalist Svoboda party, and a member of Viktor Yushchenko's Our Ukraine opposition bloc, Tyahnybok was a savvy operator in Ukrainian politics. And he knew which buttons to press to stoke outrage. Tyahnybok chose to speak from the grave of a prominent commander of the Ukrainian Insurgent Army (UPA) during World War II (Kuzio 2004). To Ukrainian nationalists and many in Western Ukraine, the UPA served as a bulwark of Ukrainian nationalism against the Soviets. To its critics and those in Eastern Ukraine, the UPA were Nazi collaborators and Ukrainian fascists. During his speech Tyahnybok, speaking to a crowd, said that "Ukraine ought to be finally returned to Ukrainians. (You are the ones) that the Moscow-Jewish mafia ruling Ukraine fears most." He then implored the crowd to act like the UPA, who "took their automatic guns on their necks and went into the woods, and fought against the Muscovites, Germans, Jews and other scum who wanted to take away our Ukrainian state" (Kuzio 2004).

Tyahnybok's speech immediately caused an uproar in Ukraine. Yushchenko expelled him from the Our Ukraine opposition bloc. Prosecutors charged Tyahnybok with inciting ethnic hatred, though the charges would later be dropped (Shekhovtsov 2011). Tyahnybok would continue his proclivity for trafficking in antisemitism. In 2007 he said that "kikes and the Russian Mafia now rule Ukraine." When questioned by reporters about his penchant for antisemitic statements, he replied with the classic, "I have Jewish friends so I can't be an antisemite" defense. "I personally have nothing against common Jews, and even have Jewish friends, but rather (I'm) against a group of Jewish oligarchs who control Ukraine and against Jewish-Bolsheviks (from the past)" (Matveyev 2009).

Nasty Politics: The Logic of Insults, Threats, and Incitement. Thomas Zeitzoff, Oxford University Press.
© Oxford University Press 2023. DOI: 10.1093/oso/9780197679494.003.0007

By 2012, Tyahnybok had revamped the image of Svoboda from Nazi street thugs to a legitimate protest party. Tyahnybok claimed: "Svoboda is not a xenophobic party. Svoboda is not an anti-Russian party. Svoboda is not an anti-European party. Svoboda is simply and only a pro-Ukrainian party. And that's it" (Herszenhorn 2012). Tyahnybok and Svoboda received fresh support from Ukrainians who were ambivalent about their far-right policies, but who liked their anti-corruption and anti-system stance, as well as their tough rhetoric (Stern 2012). In the 2012 election, Svoboda went from receiving 0.8% support in 2007 (not enough to gain entrance into the Rada), to 10.4% and 37 seats in the Rada. Finally, Tyahnybok and Svoboda would also play a key role in the Euromaidan protests. Svoboda was one the key political factions involved in the Euromaidan protests and battles (2013–2014), during which they cooperated with more moderate factions (Ishchenko 2016).

So why were Tyahnybok and Svoboda and their harsh rhetoric radioactive in the mid-2000s? But by the time of the Euromaidan, why did a sizable chunk of Ukrainian voters and political actors embrace them, and shrug off the worst of their antisemitism? And what does it mean for democracy?

In this chapter we will look the implications of nasty politics for democracy. We'll use data collected from surveys in Israel, Ukraine, and the U.S. to answer the following questions. When do voters see nasty politics as justified? How do voters evaluate ingroup versus outgroup politicians who use nasty politics? Does nasty politics lead voters to be more cynical and less willing to participate in politics? Finally, we will turn to case studies of politics in Ukraine, Israel, and the U.S. to see how nasty politics influences which politicians run for offices, and which drop out.

7.1 What Voters Think about Why Politicians Go Nasty

How do voters think about nasty rhetoric in very different contexts? Do they think that politicians are just using it to grab attention? Are they concerned that nasty rhetoric can lead to actual violence? These are all potential effects of nasty politics. But are voters willing to excuse nasty rhetoric, or think it's necessary? Do they think politicians who use it are more likely to speak the truth, and signal they'll fight for what they believe? And do voters think there are certain dangerous groups or people who need to be called out for what they are?

To answer these questions I conducted surveys in October and November 2020 in Israel, Ukraine, and the U.S. Nasty rhetoric was not some abstract concept when the surveys were conducted. This was a period of intense polarization and uncertainty, and COVID cases were surging across all three countries.

The U.S. was in the midst of the heated 2020 presidential election between Joe Biden and Donald Trump. In Israel, Prime Minister Benjamin Netanyahu was facing daily protests, and mounting legal pressure from his corruption cases. And in late October 2020 Ukraine held closely contested municipal elections which would serve as a barometer of support for incumbent President Zelensky.

Across the three different contexts, I fielded the exact same survey question. This allows us to see whether the public responds similarly to nasty politics in each country. The first set of questions focused on how individuals respond to various statements that stress the negative motivations and effects of nasty rhetoric (see Figure 7.1).

The results are striking. Large majorities of respondents in all three countries view nasty politics as a cynical ploy, and that it turns them off from politics. More than 80% of respondents in all three countries agree with the idea that nasty words can lead to violence.

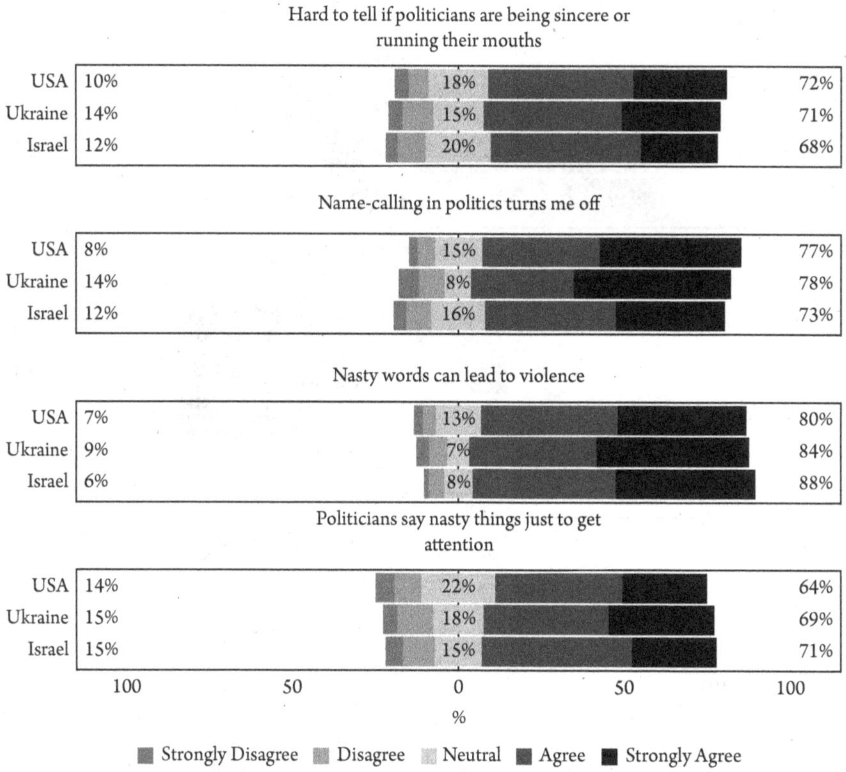

Figure 7.1 The public takes a dim view of nasty politics and the politicians that use it (October–November 2020).

Note: Surveys were conducted online by iPanel in Israel ($N = 1,342$), via telephone by CSI/KIIS in Ukraine ($N = 804$), and online by LUCID in the U.S. ($N = 1,399$).

People in general don't like nasty rhetoric for a variety of reasons—they see politicians using it cynically, it turns them off, and they even worry it can spark violence. If politicians just did something that turned voters off that would be the end of the story, and we wouldn't have a puzzle, because voters would vote politicians who use it out of office. But we know that's not the whole story. There are benefits to politicians using nasty rhetoric, and in particular what it signals to voters.

This is where things get interesting. Our respondents are fairly uniform in their agreement about the negative effects of nasty rhetoric. But on the potential arguments in favor using nasty rhetoric there is a lot more variation (see Figure 7.2). For instance, while most people disagree with the sentiment that they trust a politician who uses coarse language, there's considerable variation between countries (51% in the U.S. to 81% in Israel). Most nasty rhetoric isn't simply aggressive for aggression sake. Rather, nasty rhetoric is framed as protective. "Look at what the other side is trying to do, and that's why I need to

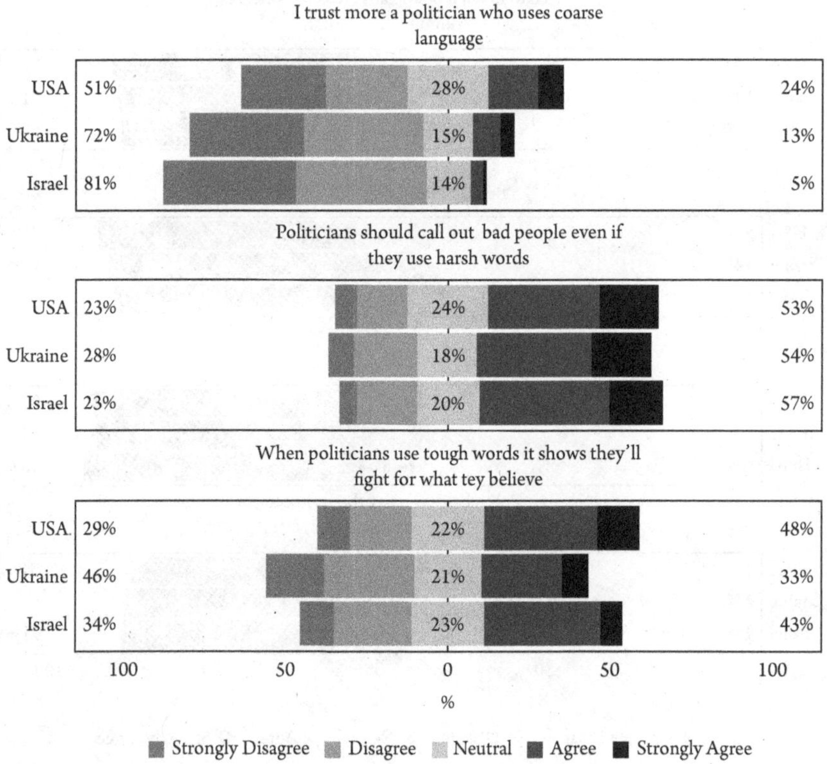

Figure 7.2 The public is more split on arguments in favor of using nasty rhetoric (October–November 2020).

Note: Surveys were conducted online by iPanel in Israel ($N = 1,342$), via telephone by CSI/KIIS in Ukraine ($N = 804$), and online by LUCID in the U.S. ($N = 1,399$).

be tough for our side." Or as Texas Republican Rep. Dan Crenshaw put it in a June 2020 tweet about the Black Lives Matter protests following the death of George Floyd: "The far left won't stop until they tear the American story apart. We need to hold the line. #CancelCancelCulture."[1] So nasty rhetoric is justified when it is couched as calling out a threat. That's exactly what we find. A slight majority in all countries think that "politicians should call out bad and dangerous people for what they are even if they use harsh language to do so." Finally, there's the idea that politicians can use harsh or tough words to signal that they will fight for the ingroup and true believers. This question split respondents the most, with between 30% to 50% of respondents agreeing and disagreeing with it. It's not a surprise, given the Ukrainian public's cynicism with politicians that they were most likely to disagree with this sentiment. Voters appear divided on this idea of whether nasty rhetoric equates with toughness.

Part of the answer to the puzzle of nasty rhetoric is that the public has mixed feelings towards nasty rhetoric. Some think politicians are cynically using it for attention and it turns them off. They're also concerned that nasty words can spark violence. But at the same time, people are divided about whether they feel violent rhetoric can be a useful tool to call out threats or for a politician to signal their toughness.

7.2 Nasty Politics Is Different When It's Coming from the Outgroup

The previous survey questions were agnostic about the identity of the perpetrator and the target of nasty rhetoric. Politicians don't just pick random opponents to target. They find targets that are likely to unite the ire of the ingroup. Right-wing politicians in Israel are more likely to target leftists and academics. Likewise Euromaidan supporters are more likely to attack politicians and groups associated with former President Yanukovych, or that express pro-Russian sentiment.

To get at the intergroup effects of violent rhetoric, we first need to see who people think is to blame for violent rhetoric. Do they think nasty rhetoric comes more from ingroup or outgroup politicians? I use partisan divisions in each country to divide the sample into ingroup and outgroup: right-wing and left-wing Jewish Israelis, Euromaidan supporters and opponents in Ukraine, and Republicans and Democrats in the U.S. Figure 7.3 shows that across all three

[1] Crenshaw, Dan (RepDanCrenshaw). Twitter, June 23, 2020. https://twitter.com/RepDanCrenshaw/status/1275418602871623682.

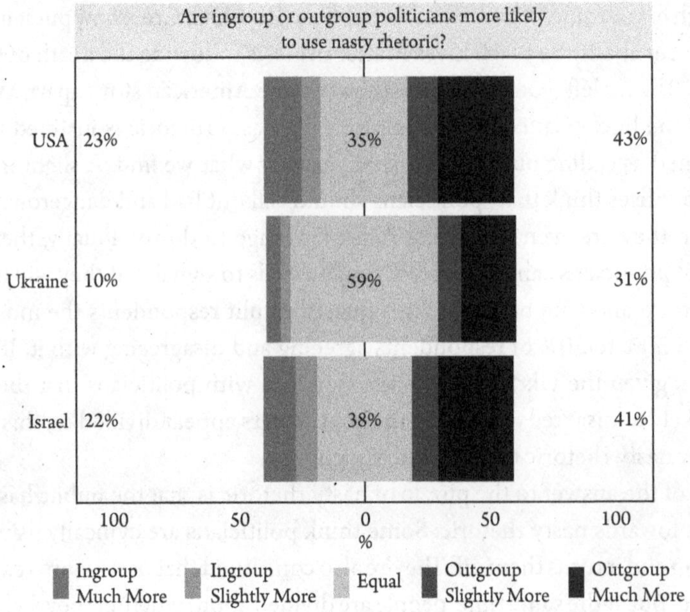

Figure 7.3 Americans, Ukrainians, and Israelis more likely to believe outgroup politicians are to blame for nasty politics (October–November 2020).

Note: Surveys were conducted online by iPanel in Israel ($N = 1,342$), via telephone by CSI/KIIS in Ukraine, ($N = 804$), and online by LUCID in the U.S. ($N = 1,399$).

countries respondents were more than two to three times as likely to say that the outgroup was more likely to engage in violent rhetoric.

There are also partisan differences in strength of this belief that the outgroup was to blame for nasty politics. In Ukraine, the weakest case of partisanship, there is no statistical difference between how much pro-and anti-Maidan respondents blamed the outgroup for promulgating nasty rhetoric. In contrast, in Israel, left-wingers blame right-wingers 1.43 points more ($t = 20.57$) on a 5-point scale for nasty rhetoric compared to Israeli right-wingers blame for left-wingers. Likewise Democrats have stronger beliefs that Republicans are behind the bulk of violent rhetoric compared to Republicans (0.93 points more, $t = 13.35$). It's also worth pointing out that a sizable portion of the population in each country thinks that both sides are equally to blame.

Israelis, Ukrainians, and Americans all think that outgroup members are more likely to use nasty rhetoric. But we want to further explore what people think about the reasons behind why ingroup versus outgroup politicians use it. Figure 7.4 show the difference in perceptions of motivations for nasty rhetoric between outgroup and ingroup politicians. Respondents in all three countries are more likely to ascribe sinister motivations for nasty rhetoric to outgroup politicians compared to ingroup politicians. For instance in Israel and the U.S.

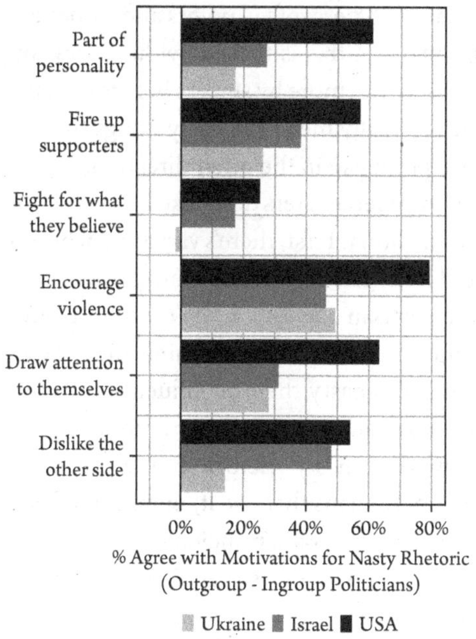

Figure 7.4 Americans, Israelis, and Ukrainians believe outgroup politicians that use nasty rhetoric are driven more by negative motivations compared to ingroup politicians (October–November 2020).

Note: Measure is a difference in percentage net agree (agree minus disagree) in perceptions of motivations for outgroup politicians engaging in nasty politics minus net agree for ingroup politicians. *Question: The following are statements about why some [ingroup/outgroup] politicians use violent rhetoric such as threats and name-calling against their political opponents. Please select how much you agree or disagree* Surveys were conducted online by iPanel in Israel ($N = 1,342$), via telephone by CSI/KIIS in Ukraine ($N = 804$), and online by LUCID in the U.S. ($N = 1,399$).

respondents are more likely to agree with the idea that outgroup compared to ingroup politicians are saying nasty things because they dislike the other side (by more than 40 percentage points in both countries). By a gap of more than 45 percentage points in the Ukraine and Israel, and more than 75 percentage points in the U.S. are more likely to agree that outgroup politicians are using nasty rhetoric to encourage violence.

There's also a rank ordering in the size of this outgroup politician versus ingroup politician perception gap for nasty rhetoric. This perception gap is a good proxy for how bad people think the other side's politicians are. The perception gap is largest in the U.S. and smallest in Ukraine, with Israel somewhat in the middle. This mirrors the level of polarization in our case selection—Ukraine the lowest, Israel in the middle, and the U.S. highest. One other important finding is that in both the U.S. and Israel, outgroup politicians are thought to be driven to use nasty rhetoric because they are fighting for what they believe more than ingroup politicians (25 percentage points and 17 percentage points respectively). One way to interpret this is that individuals view outgroup politicians' use of nasty rhetoric as driven more by sincere beliefs than ingroup politicians—the outgroup politicians really mean the nasty things they say. In Ukraine there is only a 2 percentage point gap in the other direction.

We've shown that in general voters don't like nasty rhetoric. But there are two important caveats to this story. First, there's variation in how much people accept arguments in favor of nasty rhetoric. And second, voters' views of nasty rhetoric are colored by their partisan identity. They're more likely to think outgroup politicians use it, and are more likely to think they are doing it for sinister motivations. But how does nasty rhetoric influence broader political attitudes? How do voters react to politicians using nasty rhetoric as part of calls for violence and incitement? How does nasty rhetoric frame the way voters think about political violence, the politicians that use it, outgroup threat, and perhaps most critically, attitudes about democratic principles?

To test these questions I fielded a series of survey experiments in Israel, the U.S., and Ukraine that utilized the exact same questions and wording to allow a comparison across countries. Across the three surveys I also included attitudes towards four key personality traits and views (measured pre-treatment). (1) How often they believe political violence is justified, from never to always justified (Violence Justified)?[2] (2) Do they prefer tough leaders to those who are more diplomatic (Tough Leader)?[3] (3) Are they an aggressive, argumentative person scoring high on trait aggression (Aggression)?[4] The aggression measures were omitted in Ukraine due to survey space constraints. (4) Finally, a key part of this study is dividing respondents into their ingroup and outgroup based on the main political cleavages in each country (Partisanship). In Israel this is whether a respondent identifies as a right-wing (1) or center-left (0). In Ukraine, I use the standard Euromaidan cleavage, dividing voters by whether they thought that the Euromaidan protests were a popular protest movement against a corrupt government (Pro-Maidan, 1) or a nationalist coup (Anti-Maidan, 0). Finally in the U.S., I divide voters by whether or not they self-identify as Republicans (1) or

[2] "How often do you feel it is justified for people to use violence to pursue their political goals in this country?" on a 5-point scale.

[3] "Some people prefer political leaders that are diplomatic and polite, while others like leaders that talk and act tough. Which kind of political leader would you prefer?" on a 5-point scale.

[4] The three items drawn from the Buss-Perry Aggression Questionnaire (Buss and Perry 1992). $\alpha = 0.58$ in Israel and $\alpha = 0.86$ in the U.S. "(1) Given enough provocation, I may hit another person. (2) I have threatened people I know. (3) My friends say I am somewhat argumentative." These were on a 7-point scale from 1-extremely uncharacteristic of me, to 7-extremely characteristic of me.

Democrat (0).[5] All of these items and the dependent variables are rescaled to lie between 0 and 1 to make it easier to compare items and interpret effect sizes.

In the first experiment all respondents saw the same context about a hypothetical incident of political violence:

> An [ingroup] protester threw a firebomb (Molotov cocktail) into the headquarters of the local [outgroup] political party.

What was varied between the treatments is the follow-up statement from an ingroup politician.

In the "Deserve it" treatment condition it was: "Afterward, an [ingroup Member of the Knesset/Rada/Congress] said, 'Look I don't condone violence. But let's be honest many [outgroup members] are scum and deserve it."

In the "Protect Ingroup" treatment: "Look I don't condone violence. But let's be honest many [outgroup members] are scum and we have to protect ourselves from them."

So between the two treatments, the nasty rhetoric was held constant, but the justification was varied. The idea behind this experiment is to test whether voters are more accepting of nasty rhetoric when it's framed as protecting the ingroup from an outgroup threat.

There are two questions that we want to know. First, does framing the violence as "the outgroup deserves it" versus "protecting the ingroup" influence support for the ingroup protester throwing the Molotov cocktail? Second, are people more or less likely to agree with what the politician said based on how they frame the violence?[6]

Support for the protester who threw a Molotov cocktail is fairly low. Less than 10% of respondents in Israel, and around 36% in both the U.S. and Ukraine, agree with what the protester did, or at least sympathize with it.[7] Likewise, few respondents agree with what the politician said (5% in Israel, 31% in Ukraine, and 22% in the U.S).

Are people more willing to support violence when it's framed as protecting the ingroup versus the outgroup deserved it? From Figure 7.5 the answer is no. The difference in the effect between the two conditions is approximately zero.

[5] Note, I forced centrists in Israel and independents in the U.S. to pick which way they lean to classify them. In Ukraine, given social desirability bias surrounding EuroMaidan, and following best practices I code "Don't Know"/refusal as pro-Maidan.

[6] Average Treatment Effect plots are presented in the Appendix.

[7] Sympathize with the protester was a response option, where a respondent disagreed with what the protester did, but understood why someone would do it.

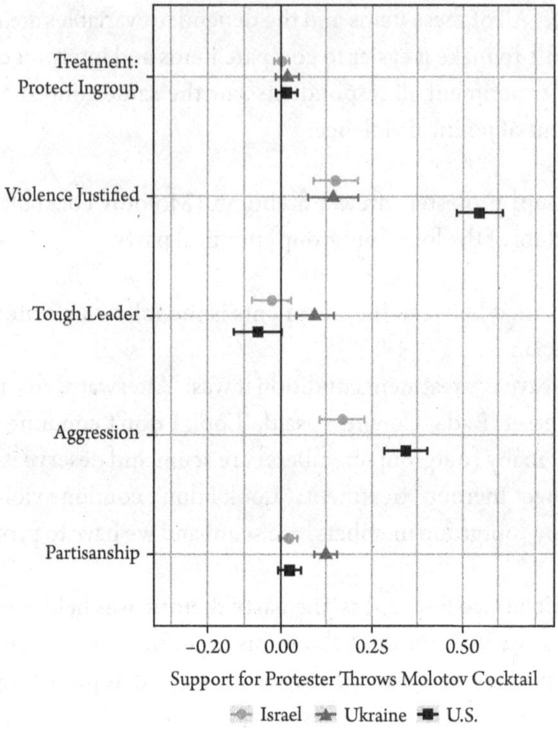

Figure 7.5 Framing violence as protecting the ingroup does not increase support for the violence (support for throwing Molotov cocktail, October–November 2020).

Note: Plot shows regression coefficients. Dependent variable is level of support for protester on a 3-point scale (0-disagree with his actions, 0.5-disagree with his actions but sympathize with it, 1-agree with his actions). Partisanship is a dummy variable for right-wing (Israel), Pro-Maidan (Ukraine), and Republican (U.S.). Baseline case for treatment comparison is that the outgroup "deserved it." Surveys were conducted online by iPanel in Israel ($N = 1,342$), via telephone by KIIS/CSI in Ukraine ($N = 2,004$), and online by LUCID in the U.S. ($N = 1,399$).

In contrast, a belief that violence can sometimes be justified and trait aggression are all correlated with an increase in support for the protester. Curiously support for a tough leader is associated with increased support for protester violence in Ukraine and decreased support in the U.S. And only in Ukraine is partisanship associated with increased support for violent rhetoric, with pro-Maidan Ukrainians showing higher levels of support.

We now turn to support for what the politician said in justifying violence in Figure 7.6. Here there is a small, positive and significant effect of the treatments. In both Israel and Ukraine, framing violence as protecting the ingroup leads respondents to be more accepting of nasty rhetoric, and in particular incitement. The effects of trait aggression and people who believe violence is justified are

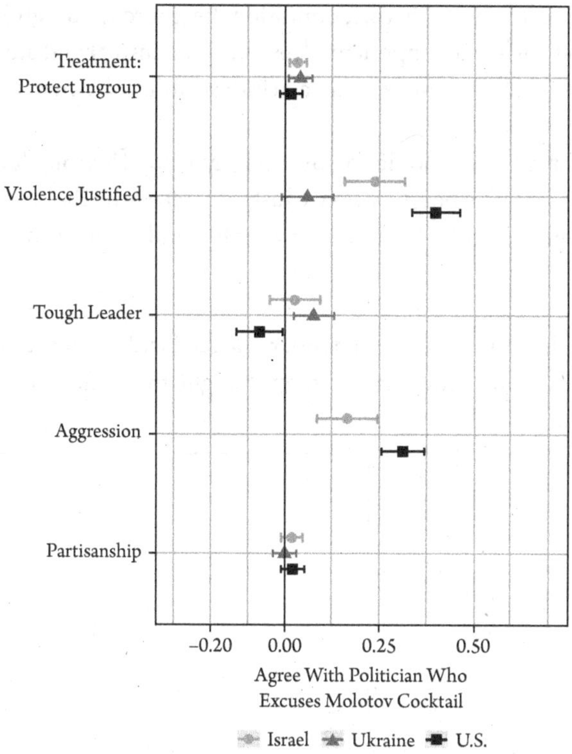

Figure 7.6 Framing violence as protecting the ingroup increases agreement with a politician who advocates violence (October–November 2020).

Note: Plot shows regression coefficients. Dependent variable is level of agreement with a politician who advocated violence on a 5-point scale rescaled to lie between 0 (strongly disagree) and 1 (strongly agree). Partisanship is a dummy variable for right-wing (Israel), Pro-Maidan (Ukraine), and Republican (U.S.). Baseline case for treatment comparison is that the outgroup "deserved it." Surveys were conducted online by iPanel in Israel ($N = 1,342$), via telephone by KIIS/CSI in Ukraine ($N = 2,004$), and online by LUCID in the U.S. ($N = 1,399$).

also associated with an increase support for nasty rhetoric which excuses political violence.

A second set of survey experiments sought to tease out how individuals respond to conciliatory or nasty rhetoric when it comes from ingroup versus outgroup politicians. The experimental vignette began with an ingroup or outgroup party leader appearing on a TV talk show and talking about their opinion on the other side. In the conciliatory condition respondents saw:

> Look, many [ingroup/outgroup] politicians are nice people who we just disagree with. This is the nature of politics.

Conversely in the nasty rhetoric condition the [ingroup/outgroup] politician uses nasty rhetoric to call opponents "enemies" (an insult) and advocate throwing politicians from the other side in jail (intimidating statement).

> Look I can sit here and lie to you, and say many [ingroup/outgroup] politicians are nice people who we just disagree with. The truth is [outgroup/ingroup] politicians are our enemies and some of them should be thrown in jail.

Figure 7.7 shows how much respondents agreed with what the politician said, and Figure 7.8 shows how violent they thought the politician's rhetoric was.

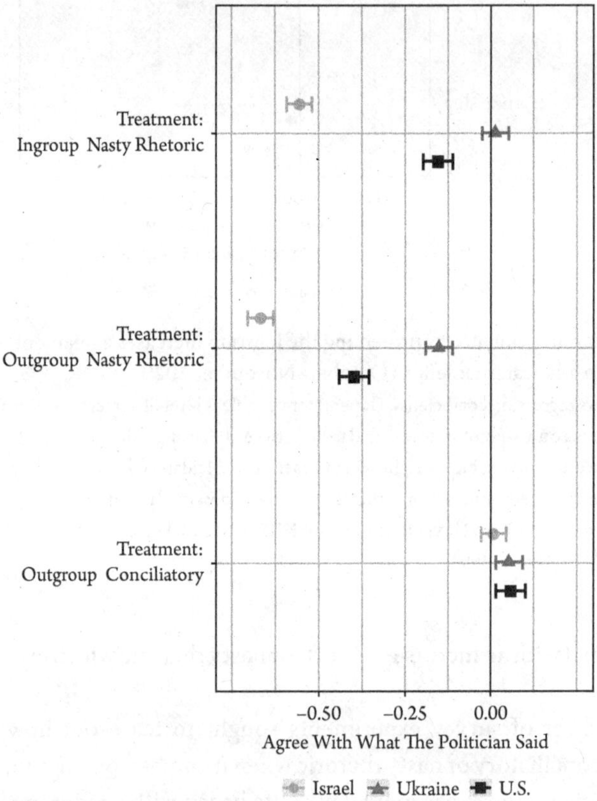

Figure 7.7 Most people disagree with violent, nasty rhetoric, but especially when it's coming from outgroup politicians (October–November 2020).

Note: Dependent variable is the level of agreement with what the politician said on a 5-point scale rescaled to lie between 0 (strongly disagree) and 1 (strongly agree). Baseline case for comparison is an ingroup politician that makes a conciliatory statement. Surveys were conducted online by iPanel in Israel ($N = 1,342$), via telephone by KIIS/CSI in Ukraine ($N = 2,004$), and online by LUCID in the U.S. ($N = 1,399$).

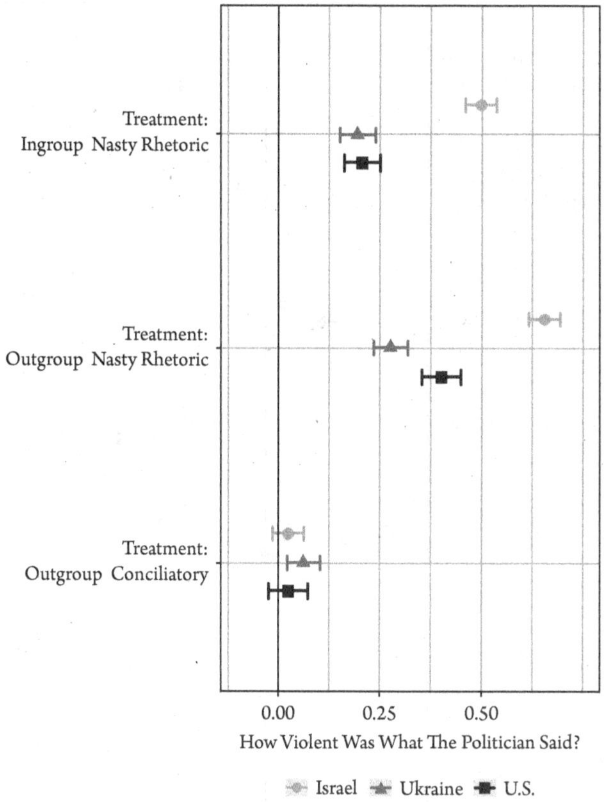

Figure 7.8 Nasty rhetoric is considered violent, especially when it's coming from outgroup politicians (October–November 2020).

Note: Dependent variable is how violent a respondent rated the politician's words on a 5-point scale rescaled to lie between 0 (not at all violent) to 1 (extremely violent). Baseline case for comparison in ingroup politician makes a conciliatory statement. Surveys were conducted online by iPanel in Israel ($N = 1,342$), via telephone by KIIS/CSI in Ukraine ($N = 2,004$), and online by LUCID in the U.S. ($N = 1,399$).

Compared to when politicians make a conciliatory statement, Ukrainians, Israelis, and Americans all strongly disagree with both ingroup and outgroup politicians that employ nasty rhetoric. But there is a key difference. Respondents in all three countries are significantly more likely to disagree with nasty rhetoric when it comes from the outgroup compared to the ingroup. The same is true for how respondents rate how violent the rhetoric is. Nasty rhetoric from both ingroup and outgroup politicians is rated as more violent than conciliatory rhetoric. But nasty rhetoric from the outgroup is seen as more violent compared to nasty rhetoric from the ingroup. Across the three countries there is an outgroup penalty, or ingroup bonus, whereby voters are more likely to agree with and less likely to rate nasty rhetoric as violent when it's coming from the

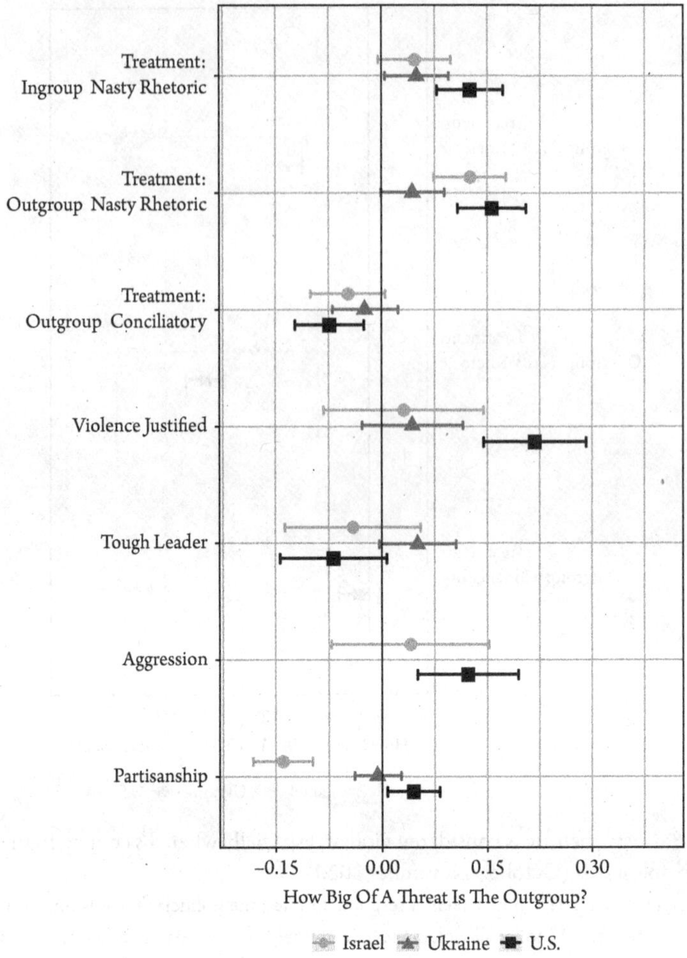

Figure 7.9 Nasty rhetoric from both the ingroup and outgroup politicians increases threat perception of the outgroup (October–November 2020).

Note: Plot shows regression coefficients. Dependent variable is given the scenario, how big of a threat does a respondent think the outgroup is on a 5-point scale rescaled to lie between 0 (not a threat at all) and 1 (extreme threat). Partisanship is a dummy variable for right-wing (Israel), Pro-Maidan (Ukraine), and Republican (U.S.). Baseline case for comparison is an ingroup politician that makes a conciliatory statement. Surveys were conducted online by iPanel in Israel ($N = 1,342$), via telephone by KIIS/CSI in Ukraine ($N = 2,004$), and online by LUCID in the U.S. ($N = 1,399$).

ingroup compared to the outgroup. Nasty rhetoric is just seen as worse when it's coming from the outgroup.

Does nasty rhetoric also increase perceptions of outgroup threat? Figure 7.9 shows that it does. The substantive effect is large and significant. The effect size of nasty rhetoric is as large as fundamental traits and views such as partisanship, belief violence is justified, preference for a tough leader, and trait aggression.

What's perhaps most interesting is there is no statistical difference in threat perception stemming violent rhetoric when it's coming from the ingroup or outgroup. They both amp up perceptions of intergroup threat.

The public disagrees with nasty rhetoric, but more so when it comes from the outgroup. They are also more likely to view nasty rhetoric that comes from outgroup politicians as violent. Regardless of where nasty rhetoric is coming from it boosts perceptions of outgroup threat. The nasty rhetoric in this experiment is also not mild. The politician is calling rival politicians the "enemies" and advocating throwing rival politicians in jail—a particularly egregious violation of democratic norms.

What effect does nasty rhetoric coming from ingroup politicians versus outgroup politicians have on willingness to support subverting democratic principles more generally? To answer this question, I created an additive index from four questions respondents saw after they read what the ingroup and outgroup politician said.[8] These questions were designed to see whether respondents agree with sacrificing democratic principles by supporting punitive action against outgroup partisans. The questions were phrased as agree-disagree with the taking the following steps to subvert democracy and punish an outgroup, "Suppose an (ingroup) politician says":

1. Outgroup politicians should have their social media accounts (on YouTube, Facebook, etc.) banned.
2. If the outgroup won an election they wouldn't respect the results.
3. Certain outgroup politicians should be banned from running for political office.
4. It should be illegal for radical outgroup members to hold protests or rallies.

The index spans from 0 (strongly disagree with all of the actions of democratic subversion) and 1 (strongly agree with all of the actions). Higher values are associated with more support for democratic subversion. The mean on the index in Israel is 0.30, in Ukraine 0.41, and in the U.S. 0.48.

Figure 7.10 shows the effect of nasty rhetoric when it comes from the ingroup and outgroup, as well as fundamental attitudes and traits on support for democratic subversion. Even though the nasty rhetoric treatments ramp up perceptions of threat, they have limited to no effect on democratic subversion. There is a small positive effect of both ingroup and outgroup violent rhetoric on support for democratic subversion in the U.S. This is perhaps due to the fact that the U.S. is the most politically polarized of our cases, and was in the midst of a bruising

[8] $\alpha = 0.75$ in Israel, $\alpha = 0.67$ in Ukraine, $\alpha = 0.86$ in the U.S.

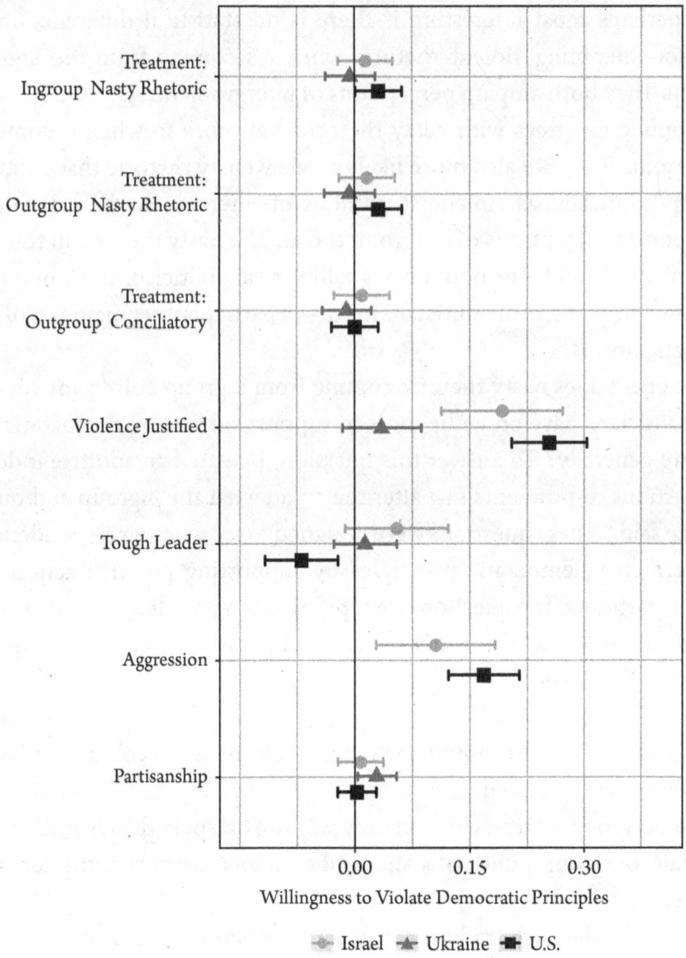

Figure 7.10 Nasty rhetoric doesn't have a large effect on support for subverting democratic principles (October–November 2020).

Note: Plot shows regression coefficients. Dependent variable is an additive index of agreement with various statements made by an ingroup politician who advocates: (1) banning certain outgroup politicians from social media, (2) disputing elections where the outgroup wins, (3) banning certain outgroup politicians from the running for office, and (4) making it illegal for radical outgroups to protest. This index was rescaled to lie between 0 (strongly disagree with all of these) and 1 (strongly agree with all of them). Partisanship is a dummy variable for right-wing (Israel), Pro-Maidan (Ukraine), and Republican (U.S.). Baseline case for comparison is an ingroup politician that makes a conciliatory statement. Surveys were conducted online by iPanel in Israel ($N = 1,342$), via telephone by KIIS/CSI in Ukraine ($N = 2,004$), and online by LUCID in the U.S. ($N = 1,399$).

presidential election. Also support for Democratic subversion on average was the highest in the U.S. (0.48 on 0 to 1 scale). In contrast, fundamental traits and attitudes—like a belief that violence is justified and trait aggression—are more strongly correlated with support for democratic subversion.

7.3 What Does It Mean for Democracy?

The portrait here goes a long way to answering our question about what nasty rhetoric means for democracy. Across surveys and experiments in three different countries we find that on average voters don't like nasty rhetoric, and think it has corrosive effects. But that's not the whole story. There's considerable variation in attitudes about when nasty rhetoric can be justified. The public in all three countries reacts less negatively to ingroup politicians using it compared to outgroup politicians. Respondents were also divided on whether respondents should call out bad and dangerous groups. Furthermore nasty rhetoric boosts perceptions of threat from the outgroup, but doesn't directly translate into increased support for democratic subversion. However, the findings for the U.S. are a notable exception. Politicians use nasty language to cast aspersions on the outgroup, and they pay a penalty—but it's asymmetric. Ingroup politicians are more likely to be viewed as fighting for what's right and calling out bad characteristics.

But this craving for attention can lead to the public to grow cynical of the intentions of politicians. A September 2020 Ukraine survey conducted by KIIS found that nearly 70% of voters thought that politicians were using nasty rhetoric only for attention, or mostly for attention, and less a way to fight for what is right. It follows that the constant use of nasty rhetoric has the effect of increasing cynicism. But ingroup politicians, particularly those on the periphery, will be more willing to sacrifice a bit of their reputation for attention, and have a higher incentive to use it garner to attention.

There are competing effects of nasty rhetoric on democracy. In one sense nasty rhetoric may be a purely cynical ploy for attention. But it also can be a legitimate way for politicians to signal their toughness and call out bad people. And some voters or elites may not even care that a politician is being cynical, as long as they are doing what they want. For instance, Rich Lowry was an early Republican critic of Trump from his perch as editor of the *National Review*, a prominent American conservative magazine. But by 2019 he had become a Trump supporter. In an interview Lowry explained his shift towards Trump:

> He (Trump) doesn't respect the separation of powers in our government, he doesn't think constitutionally, and says and does things no president should do or say. And I and my colleagues call him out on that.
>
> But at the end of the day, we're asked to either favor Trump or root for Elizabeth Warren or Bernie Sanders or Joe Biden or Mayor Pete, who oppose us on basically everything. So it's a pretty simple calculation.[9]

[9] See Illing (2019).

Here Lowry starts off by saying he doesn't particularly like Trump's nasty rhetoric—"he says and does things no president should do or say." And then there's his euphemism for Trump's authoritarian impulses: "doesn't think constitutionally." But Lowry goes on to say that it's all worth it because the other side—the Democrats—are so awful. In the process he highlights an answer to our puzzle. People may dislike the nasty style. They may even wring their hands at ingroup politicians with authoritarian impulses. But some voters in a highly polarized context—like the U.S. in the Trump-era, Israeli politics under Netanyahu, and Ukrainian politics in the lead-up to Euromaidan—may hate the other side even more.

Another key finding across Israel, Ukraine, and the U.S. is that nasty politics has very different effects when it's coming from the ingroup versus outgroup. Ingroup politicians who say the exact same vile thing are viewed as much less violent, and much less likely to be motivated by hatred or cynical motivations than their outgroup counterparts. This mirrors findings from social psychology that ingroup members tend to view their fellow members as driven by ingroup love, while outgroup members are driven by hate (Brewer 1999; Mernyk et al. 2022; Waytz, Young, and Ginges 2014). It also points to a potential driver of political conflict—when ingroup politicians talk about threats from the outgroup, and the need to protect the ingroup it is viewed as defensive. Yet this same rhetoric coming from the outgroup is viewed as explicitly threatening (De Figueiredo et al. 1999; Posen 1993).

7.4 The Effect of Nasty Politics on Participation and Candidate Selection

7.4.1 Nasty Politics on Voter Participation

Does the cynicism generated by nasty rhetoric translate into voter apathy? Do voters take a cynical view on the nasty style, and are they less likely to vote and participate more generally? Or does nasty politics mobilize and increase participation? The theory of nasty politics argues for the former—over time, nasty politics breeds cynicism and makes people less likely to participate. There's some evidence for this cynicism breeding apathy from the qualitative interviews, particularly in Ukraine.

To see whether nasty politics decreases voters' political participation or not, let's turn to a series of survey experiments I conducted in September and October of 2021 in Ukraine and the U.S. In the survey experiment respondents were randomly assigned to two conditions. In the Conciliatory Condition a politician (Candidate A) is talking about the outgroup:

Candidate A is a [Democratic/Republican] candidate running for Congress who recently said on a TV talk show:

In the Conciliatory Condition the candidate said:

> Look, many [Republican/Democratic] politicians are nice people who we just disagree with. This is the nature of politics.

The Nasty Condition proceeded with the exact same set-up as the Conciliatory Condition. However, what Candidate A said was quite different and violent:

> Look, I can sit here and lie to you, and say many [Republican/ Democratic] politicians are nice people who we just disagree with. The truth is [Republican/Democratic] politicians are animals, and some of them should be thrown in jail . . . or worse.

Respondents were randomly assigned to whether Candidate A was an ingroup or outgroup politician talking about their (a respondent's) outgroup or ingroup. The experiment proceeded the exact same way with the exact same wording in Ukraine, except Republican and Democrat were replaced with Pro-Maidan and Anti-Maidan, and Congress with Rada.

One other thing to note is that the Nasty condition is not mild. The politician is calling opponents "animals" (dehumanizing language), and advocating they should be "thrown in jail" (intimidating statement) or "worse" (incitement).

Figure 7.11 shows the effect of nasty rhetoric on political participation. The top left plot shows the effect of the treatment on the likelihood of voting in an election involving in Candidate A. All of the treatments reduce the likelihood of voting relative to the base condition (Ingroup Conciliatory). On average, U.S. respondents who received the treatment where an outgroup politician talked nasty (Outgroup Nasty) were significantly less likely to participate relative to all the other conditions. The effect size is particularly large—a reduction in the stated likelihood to vote between 0.10–0.27 on a scale from 0 (not at all likely) to 1 (extremely likely). Receiving either a nasty treatment from the ingroup or the outgroup (Either Nasty) reduces likelihood of voting by approximately 0.12 points. In contrast, the treatments don't have an affect on Ukrainians likelihood of voting.

When we examine the effects of the nasty versus conciliatory treatments on likelihood of protesting we see the reverse (top right). Nasty treatments reduce the likelihood of Ukrainians protesting in an election involving Candidate A by 0.03–0.06 points on a scale from 0 (not at all likely) to 1 (extremely likely). We don't see any effect in the U.S.

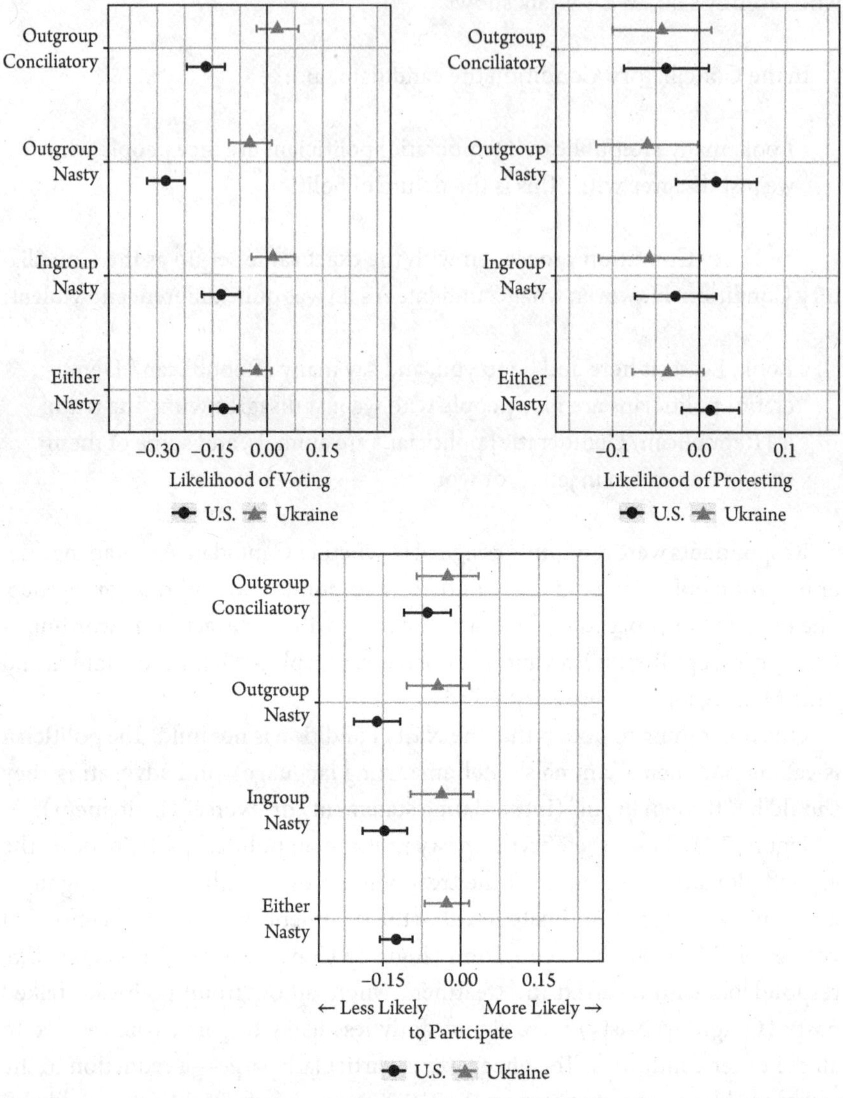

Figure 7.11 Nasty politics reduces the likelihood of voters participating in politics (September–October 2021).

Note: Plot shows regression coefficients from treatments (average treatment effects). Dependent variables are likelihood of voting (top left), protesting (top right), participating in general (bottom left) on 5-point scale rescaled to lie between 0 (not at all likely/much less likely) and 1 (extremely likely/much more likely). Base case is conciliatory rhetoric from the ingroup (Ingroup Conciliatory). Either Nasty is average treatment effect of receiving either nasty treatment (combining Ingroup Nasty and Outgroup Nasty). Surveys were conducted online via telephone by CSI/KIIS in Ukraine ($N = 1,012$), and online by LUCID in the U.S. ($N = 1,467$).

Finally, I asked respondents if all politicians spoke like Candidate A, how much more or less likely they would be to participate in politics more generally (bottom left). The effects of the nasty politics treatment in Ukraine are negative but insignificant. In the U.S., the effects of the nasty treatments are between a 0.06–0.15 point reduction in participation in general again on 0 (much less likely) to 1 scale (much more likely).

The findings from the experiment show that nasty politics significantly reduces the reported likelihood of voting and participating in politics in general in the U.S., and reduces the likelihood of protests in Ukraine. In sum, nasty rhetoric has a demobilizing effect on participation, in line with our theory.[10]

The weaker findings in Ukraine also support the idea that sustained exposure to the nasty style of politics breeds mistrust in politics in general. For example turnout in presidential elections in Ukraine averaged between 75–80% from 1999–2004 and Rada turnout averaged about 70%. In the 2019 turnout had slid to 63% in the presidential election, and 49% in the Rada elections (IFES 2019).

In the next section we will explore how nasty politics influences which candidates choose to run for office.

7.4.2 Nasty Politics and Who Runs for Office

Ukraine

Perhaps the most underappreciated part of nasty politics is how it influences the kind of people who run for office, and those who drop out. A 2019 Gallup poll found that only 9% of Ukrainians had confidence in the Ukrainian government—the lowest number they recorded for any country (Bikus 2019). Historically, the cynical nature of Ukrainian politics was a product of the prominence of the nasty style married with endemic political corruption (Kuzio 2015). Who wanted to run for office in Ukraine when you are likely to be attacked and smeared in the oligarchic-controlled press, and have to endure the threat of actual physical violence? As one Ukrainian journalist and Euromaidan activist said, "There is a low-level of culture and democracy in Ukraine. Our society doesn't have real debates. So yes, in Ukraine politicians who use more aggressive and radical way of behavior—they are more recognizable, they are more well-known."[11] A party worker for Zelensky's Servant of the People party was more blunt, "There are many dumb people who paid for their position in the Rada,

[10] The benefit of this experimental approach is that nasty rhetoric tends to occur during periods of heightened threat which can *increase* participation (Miller and Krosnick 2004), and thus confounds the relationship between nasty politics and participation. The survey experiment allows us to isolate the effect of nasty politics on participation.

[11] Interview #Ukr-PE-A0219.

and they don't have a (high) level of culture. They can only discuss things with their fists."[12]

The person who's political career best exemplifies the effects of Ukraine's low political culture is, like President Zelensky, another celebrity turned politician. Svyatoslav "Slava" Vakarchuk is one of Ukraine's biggest rock stars. He's been a prominent supporter of anti-corruption and pro-European protests including the Orange Revolution and Euromaidan in 2013–2014. He even briefly served in the Rada from 2007–2008, but left after becoming disillusioned with Ukrainian politics (France 24 2019). During the 2019 presidential election Vakarchuk flirted with running and actually polled better than Zelensky early on, but opted instead for a seat in the Rada with his Voice (*Holos*) party. The party received 5.8% of the vote and won 20 seats. Vakarchuk's Voice party was unique in many respects. It did not have any oligarchic backing (Haring 2020). Vakarchuk also filled the party list with young, Western-educated professionals. He didn't want to taint Voice, so he also banned previous lawmakers from joining the party. Finally, Voice also had a clear ideological orientation—pro-Western/European, anti-corruption, and Pro-Euromaidan—that was not driven by oligarchic or personal interests.

In March of 2020, Vakarchuk stepped down from his post as the leader of Voice. In a video posted to the party's website Vakarchuk said that:

> The (Zelensky) government, under the guise of new faces, actually installs old ones. We, by example, demonstrate the opposite: we elevate new professional people to leadership roles in the party and parliament. . . . My mission is to continue bringing new, honest, professional people into politics.[13]

Vakarchuk resigned from the Rada in June 2020. A year after his resignation, Voice began to fall apart. In July of 2021 7 of the 20 Voice deputies in the Rada were expelled from the party for internal criticism of the party leaders (Mazurenko 2021). Some critics said that Vakarchuk simply didn't have the stomach for the bruising nature of Ukrainian politics.[14] Supporters counter that Vakarchuk had a built model for honest politicians to enter the Rada. Regardless of the view, the nasty, cynical nature of Ukrainian politics influenced Vakarchuk's decision to enter, and likely his desire to leave.

[12] Interview #Ukr-Z-I0819.
[13] See RFE/RL (2020*b*).
[14] Survey #Ukr-P-A1120.

Israel

Benny Begin is Likud royalty. He is the son of the former prime minister of Israel, Menachem Begin, who co-founded the right-wing Likud party. Benny Begin served as a Likud Member of the Knesset and cabinet member off and on for more than 30 years. But by 2019 he was done with Likud. In September 2019 he said the he could no longer support Likud under Netanyahu's leadership given the seriousness of the criminal charges against Netanyahu alluding to Netanyahu's involvement in corruption and bribery schemes (Hoffman 2019).

Who took Begin's spot in the new Likud? It was politicians like Micki Zohar who entered the Knesset in 2015. Zohar was a tireless defender of Netanyahu. In a radio interview in June 2018 criticized the criminal investigations into Netanyahu, Zohar and said that the "Jewish race" is the smartest in the world and possessing of the "highest human capital," which is why the Israeli public did not believe the allegations against Netanyahu (Winer 2018). Zohar was interviewed by Israeli police for attempting to extort and threaten Israeli Attorney-General Avichai Mandelblit (Beeri and Jeremy Bob 2020). During a radio interview in October 2020 Zohar threatened to release personal audio conversations of Mandelblit if he didn't drop the charges against Netanyahu. After the interrogation, Zohar would claim on his Facebook page that he was targeted for being "right wing" and that the police interview was part of a broader "dangerous phenomenon to silence an entire political camp. A phenomenon that is located in dark regimes and surely not in a glorious democracy like Israel."[15]

Zohar is not alone. The Netanyahu years have brought a slew of young and more confrontational lawmakers to the right-wing bloc in the Knesset. Lawmakers like May Golan of Likud, who started as a South Tel Aviv blogger protesting against the effects of illegal immigration in South Tel Aviv. Golan referred to African immigrants in South Tel Aviv as "infiltrators" and said of the "extremist" label: "If to be extreme it is to make sure that Israeli girls can walk around at night without fear of being raped (by immigrants)—then they are called 'extreme.' And if that's extremism, then I'm an extremist too, and I'm proud to be such an extremist" (Makor Rishon 2012). Golan has even made appearances on Sean Hannity's show on Fox News, and was quoted as saying, "a Palestinian state is a terror state" (Adkins and Sales 2019). This is the downstream effect of Netanyahu's use of nasty rhetoric and nasty politics to maintain his stranglehold on the Likud party and purge rivals (Shalev 2018).

[15] Zohar, Micki (MikiZoharLikud). Facebook, November 5, 2020. https://m.facebook.com/story.php?story_fbid=4947623301922030&id=977353718949028.

U.S.

In the U.S. there have been more academic studies on who runs for office and who doesn't. Nasty campaigns and heated elections are at least part of the reason why women are less likely to run for office in the U.S. (Kanthak and Woon 2015; Preece and Stoddard 2015). In recent years the financial and reputation costs of running for and staying in Congress have risen. As Hall (2019) argues this means that the only people willing to run and bear these costs are die-hard partisans, leading to worsening polarization. More moderate members choose to retire and "die in their ideological boots" (Poole 2007).

The Trump-era has accelerated trends of the nastiness of politics and partisan polarization, particularly on the Republican side. Trump's takeover of the GOP led to a changing of the party's faces. For instance by July 2020, "115 have either retired, resigned, been defeated or are retiring in 2020 (48% of House Republicans)" (Dezenski 2020). Why the changeover? Dave Wasserman of Cook Political Report chalked it up to three reasons:

(1) Being in the minority can suck, esp. w/ committee term limits;
(2) Hyper-partisan, investigation-driven Hill atmosphere;
(3) Dealing w/ POTUS (Trump) many in House GOP still privately say is unfit for office.[16]

The last point in particular was that many moderates in the GOP were tired of defending President Trump's nasty rhetoric or behavior on Twitter (Zanona, Everett, and Levine 2019).

Republican members were also scared of drawing President Trump's ire. Trump used his Twitter feed as a tool to keep Republican members in line like when he repeatedly called Trump critic, and Utah Republican Senator Mitt Romney a "LOSER" (Wagner 2020).

Who were the new Republicans that gained office since 2016? Many were even Trumpier than Trump, copying his communication style down to the use of all caps on Twitter (Mark 2020). For instance, Republican Marjorie Taylor Greene won a seat in the House representing Georgia. Greene is an open supporter of QAnon, a pro-Trump conspiracy theory that alleges without evidence that President Trump and his allies are battling a deep state cabal of pedophiles (Vox 2020). During the general election campaign in September 2020, Greene posted a picture on Facebook in which she held a gun up to the pictures of three progressive Democratic representatives, Alexandria Ocasio-Cortez, Ilhan Omar,

[16] Wasserman, Dave (Redistrict). Twitter, August 2, 2019. https://twitter.com/Redistrict/status/1157253088136314880?s=20.

and Rashida Tlaib. The caption to the photo said that she "Hate(s) American leftists who want to take our country down." Facebook took down Green's post saying it violated their "violence and incitement" policy (Stracqualursi 2020).

Back in the spring during the primary, many in the GOP leadership came out against Greene, calling her comments and views "divisive" (Mitchell and Kallis 2020). But following her victory, President Trump tweeted out that Green was a, "future Republican Star . . . strong on everything and never gives up—a real WINNER!" Any major Republican opposition to Greene's candidacy evaporated. One of the few Republican willing to speak out was Michigan Rep. Paul Mitchell who said, "How can we warmly receive someone that's publicly stated some of the things she stated in her videos?" Why would Mitchell speak out? It just so happens he was retiring that year in Congress (Bade and Stanley-Becker 2020). It was clear who now was calling the shots in the GOP.

Journalist Tim Murphy was blunter in his assessment of the hold that the nasty style has taken on Republicans. In an article entitled "Donald Trump's Parting Gift to Washington Was a Party of Shitposters"[17] Murphy argues that for Republicans:

> The performance of politics became the purpose of it, and the grind of governance became secondary to the responsibilities of posting.[18]

To summarize the findings, we've now seen that voters generally have negative views of nasty politics. But they sometimes think it can be acceptable to use it as a way to call out dangerous people and show that they are tough. The surveys and survey experiments further showed that ingroup politicians have more leeway to engage in nasty politics, especially when they are protecting the ingroup. Nasty politics increases threat from the outgroup, but it doesn't increase support for democratic subversion.

Nasty politics affects political participation in two ways. First, it makes voters less likely to participate in politics. Second, when it becomes a core part of a political party (Trump's GOP, or Netanyahu's Likud), or in the system in general (Ukraine), outrage and attention become the currency of politics. Thus nasty politics has long-term effects on who runs for office and who leaves politics altogether.

[17] Shitposting (noun): "The activity of posting deliberately provocative or off-topic comments on social media, typically in order to upset others or distract from the main conversation." See https://www.lexico.com/definition/shitposting.

[18] See Murphy (2021).

8

Prelude to War, a Coup and an Insurrection, and Concluding Thoughts

Ukrainian politics in early 2022 was a kaleidoscope of crises: everywhere you looked there were political conflicts and threats of uncertain magnitude. Former President Petro Poroshenko was under investigation and charged with treason for allegedly allowing Russian-backed separatists to profit from coal sales in occupied areas. Many suspected that President Volodymyr Zelensky and his allies were using Poroshenko's trial to sideline a key Zelensky opponent. By late January 2022 there were more than 100,000 Russian troops on Ukraine's borders. While some in Kyiv initially sought to downplay the threat of a large-scale Russia invasion and to keep the public calm, as January turned to February the threat became real (Forgey 2022).

Following the Russian invasion on February 24, 2022, Ukrainian politics were up-ended. Poroshenko and Zelensky temporarily buried their hard feelings and met in person to show a unified front. Poroshenko said, "The world before the 24th of February and the world after the 24th of February, this is completely different . . . We united not around Zelensky or around Poroshenko. We united around Ukraine" (Reed, Chazan, and Olearchyk 2022). Even Yuriy Boyko, a former Yanukovych ally and a main leader of the pro-Russian bloc in the Rada, heavily condemned the Russian invasion and encouraged his supporters to enlist in the Ukrainian Territorial Defence Forces.[1]

***

In July 2022 the Democratic-led U.S. House Select Committee tasked with investigating the January 6 attack on the U.S. Capitol held its seventh hearing.

[1] Boyko was leader of the Opposition Platform–For Life, but that party was banned after the 2022 invasion. He then became leader of the successor party: Platform for Life and Peace. Boyko, Yuriy (official.yuriy.boyko). Facebook, March 8, 2022. https://www.facebook.com/100044611081411/posts/486743752822657.

Nasty Politics: The Logic of Insults, Threats, and Incitement. Thomas Zeitzoff, Oxford University Press.
© Oxford University Press 2023. DOI: 10.1093/oso/9780197679494.003.0008

The committee used this hearing focus on how President Trump used his rhetoric to incite the insurrection at the Capitol. Maryland Democratic Rep. Jamie Raskin said, "The problem of politicians whipping up mob violence to destroy fair elections is the oldest domestic enemy of constitutional democracy in America." Raskin then went on to lay the culpability at Trump's feet: "And how do you mobilise a crowd in 2020? With millions of followers on Twitter, President Trump knew exactly how to do it" (Smith 2022).

The first two sections of this chapter focus on how threats shape nasty politics. In the case of Ukraine we will examine how the external threat of the Russian invasion of February 2022 sharply reduced the level of nasty politics in Ukraine. In the U.S. we will look at the dynamics of nasty politics between key Republican politicians involved in efforts to overturn the election and President Trump in the lead up to the insurrection and attempted coup on January 6. Finally, I'll provide a summary of the book, and areas for future research.

8.1 Nasty Politics before and after the Russian Invasion of 2022

This book opened by describing Petro Poroshenko's strange journey home in January 2022. After being abroad for nearly a month, Petro Poroshenko flew back to Ukraine from Warsaw to appear in a Kyiv courtroom to face treason charges. The intrigue was even more heightened given the precarious geopolitical context for Ukraine—more than 100,000 Russian troops were massed on its borders. U.S. and other intelligence services pointed to a high probability of a large-scale Russian invasion with as many as 175,000 troops (Harris et al. 2022). After his court appearance Poroshenko posted on his Facebook feed and thanked his supporters who rallied for him outside the court and those "who refused to execute criminal orders (opposed his treason trial)."[2] In a follow-up Facebook post a few days later, Poroshenko explicitly compared the criminal threat he faced to the Russian threat faced by Ukraine: "Zelensky and his surroundings are trying to return Ukraine now in the worst times of Yanukovych. Our task is to defend the European future and unite Ukraine before the threat of the Russian invasion."[3]

Other politicians, like Yulia Tymoshenko, were concerned that Zelensky would capitulate to the Russian military threat on the Ukrainian border. She warned Zelensky to avoid being pressured into a Minsk-like agreement.

[2] Poroshenko, Petro (petroporoshenko). Facebook, January 18, 2022. https://www.facebook.com/watch/?v=470245657940841.

[3] Poroshenko, Petro (petroporoshenko). Facebook, January 21, 2022. https://www.facebook.com/watch/?v=3449142278646123.

This would involve giving up Ukrainian territory to Russia and Russian-backed separatists, referring to any such agreements as "state betrayal," "shameful agreements with terrorists (Russian-backed separatists)," and that this would amount to "treason."[4]

Pro-Russian politicians like Yuriy Boyko had the opposite concern. Boyko criticized Zelensky's perceived warmongering and called for peace. In a Facebook post in mid-January 2022 he said: "The current (Zelensky) government is not ready for decisive steps in world politics.... it drove itself into a corner with warlike rhetoric, loud statements and accusations."[5]

Dmytro Razumkov also criticized Zelensky's dealing. Razumkov was a one-time ally of Zelensky. He was formerly the leader of Zelensky's Servant of the People party and the Chairman of Rada. But following a rift with Zelensky over the anti-oligarch bill that Zelensky had made a centerpiece of his agenda, he was kicked out of the Servant of the People and dismissed as Chairman in early October 2021 (Reuters 2021). In a January 25, 2022, Facebook post Razumkov criticized Zelensky's dealing with the Rada and the Russian invasion:

> Last Friday, I invited Volodymyr Zelensky to the walls of parliament for a report. The country needs clear answers to the questions that is happening in the field of security and defense and energy.... You (Zelensky) should at least forget about political ratings, your own ambitions and start working for the benefit of the nation. Unfortunately, what we see and hear today does not give confidence to people. Unlike diplomats that are evacuated by embassies, Ukrainians have nowhere to be evacuated.[6]

While he was accused of being too dovish on the Russian threat (Poroshenko and Tymoshenko), being too hawkish (Boyko), or lacking transparency with the public and the Rada (Razumkov), Zelensky sought to project an aura of calm. In a February 12, 2022, Facebook post he said: "We are not afraid or panicking (over the Russian threat). We are conducting (military) training and keeping the situation under control. Everything will be Ukrainian (i.e. no concessions to Russia)!"[7]

[4] Tymoshenko, Yulia (YuliaTymoshenko). Facebook, February 8, 2022. https://www.facebook.com/100043915910253/posts/495415735265619.

[5] Boyko, Yuriy (official.yuriy.boyko). Facebook, January 18, 2022. https://www.facebook.com/watch/?v=1127327701139315.

[6] Razumkov, Dmytro (dmytro.razumkov). Facebook, January 25, 2022. https://www.facebook.com/watch/?v=585372489300067.

[7] Zelensky, Volodymyr (zelenskiy.official). Facebook, February 12, 2022. https://www.facebook.com/zelenskiy.official/posts/3009252932658396.

Yet, as the likelihood of an actual Russian invasion increased in late January 2022, a noticeable shift occurred in the general nastiness of Ukrainian politics. Oleh Lyashko, out of a job but always the political opportunist, was one such person whose rhetoric shifted. Lyashko had heavily criticized Zelensky and his Servant of the People party—many times referring to the party as a "green plague" (Servant of the People's main color).[8] In November 2021 he said on a popular TV show that "Zelensky deceived people and together with his partner (and patron, the oligarch Ihor) Kolomoisky robbed the country."[9] Yet sensing the increasing probability of an invasion, Lyashko started to be significantly less critical of Zelensky in late January of 2022, shifting his focus to Putin and the Russian threat whenever asked about Zelensky.[10]

This shift was also apparent in the focus of Petro Poroshenko's post on February 21, 2022, who focused on collaborators and infiltrators within Ukraine. In it Poroshenko said:

> It is necessary to adopt laws to combat collaboration (with Russia) and counteract Russian propaganda within Ukraine. This issue needs to be on the agenda. We emphasize that the "fifth column" (collaborators) should be detained and have their hands and legs bound.[11]

One notable exception to this shift to rally around Zelensky was Yevhen Murayev. Murayev was a former deputy in the Rada and the founder of the pro-Russian Nasi party. Throughout his political career Murayev had pushed pro-Kremlin talking points saying that the 2013–2014 Euromaidan revolution was a Western-backed coup, that Zelensky is a puppet of the West, and accused Ukraine of provoking Russia into war. The U.K. Foreign Secretary even released a public report in late January 2022 that the Russian government was planning to install a puppet government in Ukraine, and Murayev was their leading candidate (Schwartz 2022).[12]

During the lead up to the invasion Murayev accused Zelensky of provoking Russia. He posted threatening and ominous Facebook posts. "Two days ago,

[8] Lyashko, Oleh (O.Liashko). Facebook, July 31, 2019. https://www.facebook.com/O.Liashko/posts/2305694566165794.

[9] Lyashko, Oleh (O.Liashko). Facebook, November 3, 2021. https://www.facebook.com/O.Liashko/posts/575563856837772.

[10] Lyashko, Oleh (O.Liashko). Facebook, January 21, 2022. https://www.facebook.com/O.Liashko/posts/4761979987203894.

[11] Poroshenko, Petro (petroporoshenko). Facebook, February 21, 2022. https://www.facebook.com/petroporoshenko/videos/474597230818135/.

[12] Murayev's candidacy was seen as bizarre and even ridiculous, given that most ordinary Ukrainians saw him his as Russian stooge and held very negative views of him (Politi, Seddon, and Olearchyk 2022).

I wrote how this green circus will end, and today I want to finish their non-renewal... #TimeToSayGoodbyeToGREEN (anti-Zelensky hashtag)."[13] And in early February 9, 2022, he even began a post with: "When I become president...."[14] Given the open rumors that Murayev was Russia's preferred puppet, this was a particular, dark post.

On February 24, 2022, Russian began its full-scale invasion of Ukraine. Putin declared it a "special military operation." Pointing to conspiracy theories and propaganda stoked by his own Russian government, Putin said the Russian invasion was necessary because the Zelensky-led government was infiltrated by Nazis and engaging in an ongoing genocide against ethnic Russians in Ukraine—two baseless claims (Veidlinger 2022). Air strikes pounded cities across the country including Kyiv; Odesa, Mariupol, and Kherson in the south; Chernihiv in the north; and Kharkiv, and targets in Donetsk and Luhansk in the east (Associated Press 2022). Russian troops also invaded along multiple fronts: from Belarus and Russia in the north towards Chernihiv and Kyiv, from Crimea in the south towards Odesa, Kherson, Mariupol, and in the east towards Kharkiv and Ukrainian-controlled territories in the Donbas (Kirvy 2022). Ukrainian resistance was much stiffer than anticipated, and Russia's goal of a swift collapse of Ukrainian military and a capture of Kyiv evaporated. Russian forces continued to attack civilian targets, including striking a children's hospital, and violating ceasefires for humanitarian evacuation, prompting the International Criminal Court to launch an investigation. In the opening weeks of the war, Ukraine and Russia held several peace talks on the Ukraine-Belarus border, but the talks failed to produce any meaningful change in the course of the conflict (Axios 2022). After the first weeks of the war the fear that Kyiv and Ukraine would fall quickly gave way to a grinding war of attrition, as the front shifted to the east and Donbas.

It was clear from Putin's words and actions that one of the main Russia goals was the removal of Zelensky. There were reports that Russian forces were trying to assassinate him during the early weeks of the war (Harris et al. 2022). Zelensky did not flee Ukraine as some thought he might, instead he remained in Ukraine. On the first day of the Russian invasion, President Zelensky tweeted the following out in English (clearly meant to signal to an international audience):

> Russia treacherously attacked our state in the morning, as Nazi Germany did in 2WW years. As of today, our countries are on different sides of world history. Russia (Russian flag emoji) has embarked on a path of

[13] Murayev, Yevhen (e.murayev). Facebook, January 19, 2022. https://www.facebook.com/100044411920056/posts/472251527598574.

[14] Murayev, Yevhen (e.murayev). Facebook, February 9, 2022. https://www.facebook.com/watch/?v=284423733779220.

evil, but Ukraine (Ukraine flag emoji) is defending itself & won't give up its freedom no matter what Moscow thinks.[15]

One of the major themes and surprise of the conflict itself was the emergence of Zelensky as a wartime leader, who caught admiration of many around the world for his defiance in the face of Russian threats (Applebaum and Goldberg 2022). The comedian candidate had become the face of Ukrainian steadfast resistance, and enjoyed close to 95% approval of the Ukrainian populace by early May 2022, as Ukrainians rallied around him (IRI 2022). It's all the more surprising, given that Ukrainian politics and polling before the war suggested that there were deep fissures within Ukraine, and support for Zelensky had declined markedly since his peak back in 2019 when he was elected (Minakov 2021). Before the invasion, Russia thought that enough Ukrainian politicians and ordinary Ukrainians would defect to their side following the actual invasion, and that the Zelensky government would collapse quickly (Reynolds and Watling 2021). But that didn't come to pass.

To analyze the dynamics of nasty rhetoric in Ukraine in the lead up to and the early stages of the Russian invasion, we'll turn to Facebook posts from key Ukrainian politicians. The time period covered in the analysis is November 1, 2021, though March 10, 2022. This includes the Russian build-up through late 2021 and early 2022, the treason charges levied against former President Poroshenko in December 2021, and the first two-weeks following the initial invasion. The key politicians covered in this dataset include the key factions and personalities in Ukrainian politics: (1) President Zelensky, (2) Petro Poroshenko, (3) Yulia Tymoshenko, and (4) Yuriy Boyko. I also included (5) the populist-nationalist Oleh Lyashko and (6) the former Zelensky-ally-turned-rival, Dmytro Razumkov. Finally, (7) I also included the pro-Russian provocateur and presumed Russian puppet-leader-in-waiting, Yevheniy Murayev.

The resulting dataset contains 1,509 Facebook posts. Table 8.1 shows the summary statistics for each politician, and Figures 8.1 and 8.2 show the time series for each politicians' nasty rhetoric during this time period. As in our previous analyses the Facebook posts were coded for whether they contained any type of nasty rhetoric and which type of rhetoric they contained: insults (1), accusations (2), intimidating statements (3), and incitement (4). An additive measure of threat intensity was constructed that summed up all the types of nasty rhetoric contained in a particular post.[16]

[15] Zelensky, Volodymyr (ZelenskyyUa). Twitter, February 24, 2022. https://twitter.com/ZelenskyyUa/status/1496787304811315202?s=20&t=K3N2MbIoUTbRL9P5Wv8NLw.

[16] Insults = 1 + accusations = 2 + intimidating statements = 3 + incitement = 4. So if a post contained all these types of rhetoric it's intensity would be a 10.

Table 8.1 **Nasty rhetoric from Zelensky and other key Ukrainian politicians in the lead up to and following the Russian invasion in February 2022 (November 1, 2021–March 10, 2022).**

Name	*# of Posts*	*Mean Intensity*	*Overall Nasty*	*Insults*	*Accuse*	*Intimidate*	*Incite*
Volodymyr Zelensky	140	0.1	2.1%	0.0%	2.1%	2.1%	0.0%
Petro Poroshenko	483	1.0	26.1%	15.7%	25.3%	8.9%	1.0%
Yulia Tymoshenko	160	1.1	32.5%	12.4%	32.5%	8.8%	0.6%
Yuriy Boyko	118	2.1	55.9%	33.9%	55.1%	22.0%	0.0%
Oleh Lyashko	254	0.9	24.0%	15.0%	22.8%	8.7%	0.4%
Dmytro Razumkov	217	0.8	27.3%	11.6%	26.4%	5.6%	0.0%
Yevheniy Murayev	137	2.1	58.4%	35.8%	52.6%	19.0%	3.7%

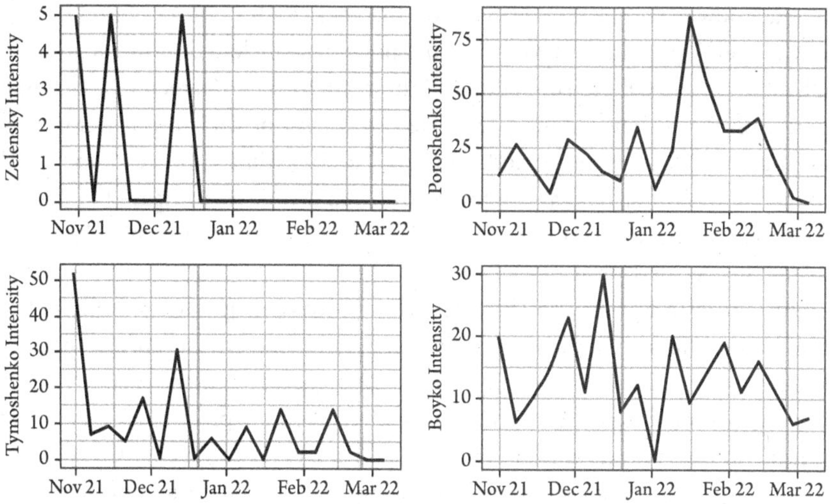

Figure 8.1 The threat intensity from Zelensky and other key Ukrainian politicians decreases following the Russian invasion in February 2022 (November 1, 2021–January 20, 2021).

Note: Zelensky (top left), Poroshenko (top right), Tymoshenko (bottom left), and Boyko (bottom right). Graphs correspond to weekly sums of intensity of nasty Facebook posts. Vertical shaded regions correspond to the announcement of treason charges against Petro Poroshenko on December 20, 2021, and Russia's large-scale invasion on February 24, 2022.

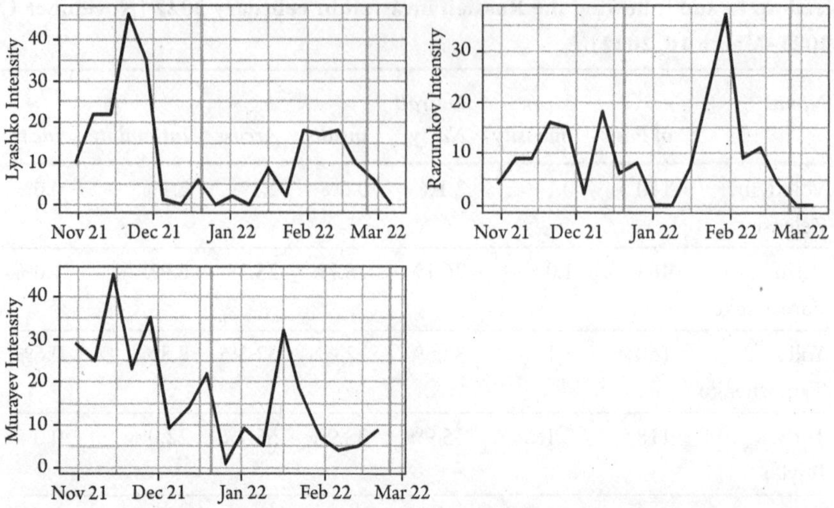

Figure 8.2 The threat intensity from other Ukrainian politicians decreases following the Russian invasion in February 2022 (November 1, 2021–January 20, 2021).

Note: Lyashko (top left), Razumkov (top right), and Murayev (bottom left). Blue lines correspond to weekly sums of intensity of nasty Facebook posts. Note Murayev's last post is on February 25, 2022. Vertical shaded regions correspond to the announcement of treason charges against Petro Poroshenko on December 20, 2021, and Russia's large-scale invasion on February 24, 2022.

There are two key takeaways from the analyses. First, domestic nasty rhetoric is much lower during this time period than the 2019 election period shown in Chapter 3 (see Table 3.3). All of the politicians included in the analysis in Chapter 3 have decreased their domestic nasty rhetoric compared to the electoral period in 2019. For instance, for Zelensky 40.4% of their posts were nasty during the 2019 election period, compared to 2.1% during the lead-up to and following the Russian invasion; for Poroshenko it's 31.4% compared to 26.1%, Tymoshenko 57.1% to 32.5%, Boyko 78.7% to 55.9% and Lyashko 55.6% to 24.0%. It's decidedly less nasty.

As Figures 8.1 and 8.2 make clear, nasty rhetoric drops dramatically in the build-up and following the Russian Invasion. On average, posts are significantly less intense by 1.2 points ($t = 10.5$) on our 10-point threat intensity scale following the Russian invasion on February 24, 2022. And the probability that a post is nasty drops by a one-third ($D = -0.33$, $t = 12.4$) post invasion. Every single politician has a statistically significant decrease in the intensity and nastiness of their posts.[17] This is true with the exception of Murayev, who's last post on

[17] Individual decreases in intensity and probability a post is nasty: Zelensky intensity ($D = -0.23, t = 2.6$) and nasty ($D = -0.05, t = 1.9$); Poroshenko intensity ($D = -1.11, t = 4.9$) and nasty ($D = -0.30$, $t = 5.6$), Tymoshenko intensity ($D = -1.33$, $t = 3.93$) and nasty

Facebook (as of August 2022), was on February 25, 2022, one day after the invasion. The post was a rambling critique of the past eight years of Ukrainian foreign policy.[18] By early April 2022 he was rumored to have fled Ukraine to Russia with the help of Russian special forces (Shevchuk 2022).

This doesn't mean that there wasn't quite a bit of violent and aggressive rhetoric on Facebook post-invasion. There most certainly was. It was just directed mostly at Russia and Putin. Recall that our definition of nasty politics was that it must be directed at *domestic political opponents*—so insults, accusations, or incitement directed against foreign adversaries don't count. For instance, on March 10, 2022, Oleh Lyashko posted the following:

> Good morning, invincible Ukraine! During the last day of the war, the Russian Nazis have not achieved any success in any of the directions.... No matter how much the Kremlin Führer (Putin) throws at us, he will never win Ukraine. This is a fact that the whole world has already recognized! Death to the fascist invaders! Glory to the heroic defenders of Ukraine! Glory to Ukraine![19]

On March 9, 2022, President Zelensky posted a video of the bombed out Mariupol children's hospital and maternity ward where a Russian strike had happened and imploring action:

> People under the rubble. Children under rubble. It's atrocity! How many more will the world be the accomplice by ignoring terror? Close the sky immediately!...ATROCITY! How Much Longer Will The World Be ACCOMPLICE IGNORING TERROR? Close The Sky Right Now! Stop The Killings![20]

Yulia Tymoshenko echoed a similar sentiment, posting a video of the rubble outside the Mariupol hospital on March 9, 2022. She called on world leaders to declare a no-fly zone over Ukraine in response to the Russian attack: "All boundaries have been crossed (by Russia's airstrikes). It's pure fascism and

($D = -0.41$, $t = 4.7$); Boyko intensity ($D = -1.23$, $t = 2.2$) and nasty ($D = -0.27$, $t = 2.1$); Lyashko intensity ($D = -1.74$, $t = 9.1$) and nasty ($D = -0.48$, $t = 10.9$); and Razumkov intensity ($D = -1.07$, $t = 4.6$) and nasty ($D = -0.36$, $t = 5.4$).

[18] Murayev, Yevheniy (e.murayev). Facebook, February 25, 2022. https://www.facebook.com/100044411920056/posts/495170005306726.

[19] See Lyashko, Oleh (O.Liashko). Facebook, March 10, 2022. https://www.facebook.com/O.Liashko/posts/4917511558317402.

[20] Zelensky, Volodymyr (zelenskiy.official). Facebook, March 9, 2022. https://www.facebook.com/zelenskiy.official/posts/3027366947513661.

genocide!"[21] Facebook even relaxed its normal ban on calls for violence, and allowed Ukrainians to post threats of violence against the Russian military. (Wagner 2022)

This was a remarkable time period in Ukrainian politics. A former president was charged with treason. Yet, even in the fractious nature of Ukrainian domestic politics, the threat of and eventual invasion by Russia on February 24, 2022, had a huge impact on Ukrainian politics. It reduced the nastiness that had been ingrained in Ukrainian politics, and led Ukrainians to rally behind Zelensky.

As of August 2022, Ukraine was on a war-time footing. Martial law was still in effect. Opposition parties that had alleged links to Russia were banned, and national TV channels were placed into a single platform controlled by the government to maintain a "unified information" front and counter Russian propaganda (Sauer 2022). But domestic politics was starting to return to Kyiv (Baer 2022). The Poroshenko-Zelensky truce was tenuous, as the treason case continued to hang over Poroshenko. In May 2022, Poroshenko was blocked from leaving Ukraine to attend a NATO meeting due the pending charges (Reuters 2022*b*). Before the Russian 2022 invasion, the main fissure in Ukrainian politics were attitudes towards the Euromaidan Revolution—was Euromaidan a nationalist coup, or a democratic revolution? Attitudes towards the existential war Ukraine is currently fighting against Russia, and security in general, will likely reshape Ukrainian politics in the future. But how that affects the nasty style in the rough-and-tumble world of Ukraine's oligarchic democracy remains to be seen.

8.2 Nasty Politics in the Lead up to January 6

"We ain't fucking leaving either. We ain't fucking leaving.... What (do) patriots do? We fuckin' disarm 'em and then we storm the fuckin' Capitol!" (Anderson 2021). The man screaming in the video recorded outside of the U.S. Capitol is Scott Fairlamb, a New Jersey gym owner. In the tapes released by the U.S. Department of Justice in June of 2021, Fairlamb can also be seen carrying a baton, and pushing and punching a U.S. Capitol Police officer in the lead up to the storming of the Capitol.[22] What led thousands of Trump supporters to storm the U.S. Capitol, and some like Fairlamb to use flag poles, pipes, pepper spray, and their own fists to attack the U.S. Capitol Police?

[21] Tymoshenko, Yulia (YuliaTymoshenko). Facebook, March 9, 2022. https://www.facebook.com/watch/?v=660302575255252.

[22] Fairlamb was charged with multiple felonies, including assault on a federal officer, and was sentenced to 41 months in prison in November of 2021. See Fischer, Flack, and Wilson (2021).

The violence wasn't spontaneous. It was part of a coordinated campaign and coup attempt orchestrated by Trump and his allies to stop the certification of Joe Biden as president, and maintain Trump's hold on power. As Fiona Hill, a former member of Trump's National Security council wrote shortly after January 6:

> The storming of the Capitol building on January 6 was the culmination of a series of actions and events taken or instigated by Trump so he could retain the presidency that together amount to an attempt at a self-coup.
> (Hill 2021)

During the 2020 U.S. presidential election period the quantity of violent tweets on Twitter peaked in the lead up to the attempted insurrection on January 6 (Kim 2022). On Reddit, Parler, Telegram, and other social media chat platforms, far-right supporters of President Trump had promised to show up on January 6 and "storm the Capitol," and said that they were "ready for blood" (Lytvynenko and Hensley-Clancy 2021). This nasty rhetoric was being stoked at the elite level. Republican politicians and President Trump had engaged in a months-long campaign of baseless accusations saying that the vote was "rigged" and "stolen" by the Democrats. They claimed that there was "fraud that has never been seen like this before" (Yen, Swenson, and Seitz 2020). Chairman of the Joint Chiefs General Mark Milley became increasingly concerned that Trump and his political allies' were using incendiary rhetoric to stoke violence, and engineer it so Trump could invoke the Insurrection Act and stay in office. Milley and other military officers were so alarmed about a potential self coup that they made preliminary plans to resign one-by-one to avoid carrying out illegal or dangerous orders (Gangel et al. 2021).

How did Trump and his Republican allies use nasty rhetoric in the lead up to January 6 and the failed coup? We focus here on the interplay between President Trump and a group of Republican members of Congress from October 1, 2020, through January 20, 2021. This period covers the lead up to the 2020 election, the election on November 3, the attack on the U.S. Capitol on January 6, and Biden's eventual inauguration on January 20.

During this time period Trump and a group of Republicans engaged in a concerted campaign of nasty politics to try to subvert and overturn the results of the election. This group was instrumental in pushing unfounded conspiracies that Biden and Democrats had stolen the 2020 presidential election. These Republicans supported lawsuits objecting to different states' certification of Biden's victory, and promised to formally object to his election in Congress during the vote counts on January 6, 2021. They organized protests and mobilized supporters around the "StoptheSteal" hashtag. Finally, they were instrumental in promoting the Save America Rally on January 6 in Washington, D.C., that would serve as the launch point for the insurrection (Armus 2021*b*). Critics of this group of Republicans in Congress labeled them the "Sedition Caucus" (Nichols 2021). We'll refer to this group collectively as the "Republican Objectors." We'll focus on the rhetoric of eight key Republican Objectors on Twitter and President Trump during this time period (see Table 8.2 for a list). Was Trump taking inspiration from the Republican Objectors and heightening the intensity of his rhetoric in the lead up to January 6? Or did the Objectors take their cues from Trump? Figuring out "who was following whom" can help us understand the dynamics of elite nasty rhetoric, and the eventual violence at the Capitol.

The first ten days of October 2020 were a dicey period for President Trump. He had been severely ill with COVID, and was even taken to Walter Reed National Military Medical Center when his oxygen levels plummeted. By the time Trump was released from the hospital and resumed campaigning in mid-October, he began telling his supporters that the vote was going to be "rigged." By mid-November 2020 following election day, it became increasingly clear that Biden would prevail as mail-in ballots were counted. Trump tweeted out the following accusation: "He (Biden) only won in the eyes of the FAKE NEWS MEDIA . . . I concede NOTHING! We have a long way to go. This was a RIGGED ELECTION!" (Freking 2021). At the same time, Trump and his allies were operating behind the scenes. They were pressuring Vice President Mike Pence and elected officials in key swing states to overturn the election results (Collinson 2022).

As states began certifying the results in early December 2020, Trump began holding rallies and telling his supporters, "You can't let another person steal that election from you" (Yen, Swenson, and Seitz 2020). Trump and his allies also pressured state and local election officials to throw out the results. Gabriel Sterling—the chief operating officer for Georgia Secretary of State's office and a lifelong Republican—became a favorite target of Trump supporters. They believed he was secretly stealing the election for Democrats, and it resulted in Sterling receiving a torrent of abuse and violent threats. Sterling received so many threats that he had to have police protection (Dovere 2020). In the weeks leading up to the January 6 Save America Rally in Washington, D.C., Trump encouraged his supporters to show up for the "big protest," and implored his supporters "we're going to take what they did to us on Nov. 3. We're going to take it back" (Sherman 2021). President Trump's speech on January 6 that preceded the insurrection at the Save America Rally exhorted his supporters to take action. As the Associated Press documented:

> For more than an hour, Trump made the case that he and his supporters at the rally had been "cheated" and "defrauded" in the "rigged" election by a "criminal enterprise" made up of some of the "weak" legislators the insurrectionists were about to confront.[23]

Following the insurrection, Facebook and Instagram banned Trump indefinitely on January 6, 2021, for his perceived role in instigating the insurrection and "undermin(ing) the peaceful and lawful transition of power to his elected successor (Biden)" (Denham 2021). Twitter locked Trump out of his personal account briefly on January 6, and then banned him indefinitely two days later citing "the risk of further incitement of violence (from Trump)" (Twitter Inc. 2021).

Trump was not alone in his push to discredit the election and mobilize his supporters. He had a cadre of Republican politicians fanning baseless election fraud claims and encouraging their supporters to fight the election, and they were led by the Republican Objectors. For instance, Rep. Paul Gosar (Arizona) and Rep. Mo Brooks (Alabama) were two of the chief ringleaders of the Save America Rally. Gosar had been instrumental in organizing and speaking at protest rallies outside of ballot-counting sites in Arizona throughout November 2020, spreading unfounded accusations about "voter fraud" and declaring "this is our Alamo" (MacDonald-Evoy 2020). Brooks, speaking to the crowd at the Save America Rally on January 6, said: "Today is the day American patriots start taking down names and kicking ass! . . . Our ancestors sacrificed their blood, their sweat, their tears, their fortunes and sometimes their lives. . . . Are you willing to do the same?" (Tolan et al. 2021).

On the same day, Gosar sent out the following tweet an hour before protesters breached the Capitol: "Biden should concede. I want his concession on my desk tomorrow morning. Don't make me come over there. #StopTheSteal2021."[24]

Gosar and Brooks were joined by several new members of Congress. These included Florida Rep. Matt Gaetz. Mere hours after the insurrection had been put down, Gaetz cited a baseless conspiracy theory in a speech on the House floor, "some of the people who breached the Capitol today were not Trump supporters. They were masquerading as Trump supporters and in fact, were members of the violent terrorist group Antifa." Gosar echoed Gaetz's comment on Twitter, saying "This has all the hallmarks of Antifa provocation" (Armus 2021*a*).

[23] See Woodward (2021).

[24] Gosar, Paul (DrPaulGosar). Twitter, January 6, 2021. https://twitter.com/DrPaulGosar/status/1346865455571599363.

First-term Rep. Marjorie Taylor Greene (Georgia), the ardent QAnon conspiracy-supporter, met with President Trump, Rep. Brooks, Rep. Gosar, and Rep. Andy Biggs (Republican, Arizona) in December 2020 to plot a path to overturn the election results (Edmondson and Broadwater 2021). Greene was joined by fellow first-term representative and QAnon supporter, Lauren Boebert from Colorado. Boebert in her election ads vowed to carry her Glock handgun on the House floor.[25] In the lead up to January 6 both Boebert and Greene referred to the Save America Rally as a "1776 moment" (Edmondson and Broadwater 2021). The final member of this younger group of Republican Objectors was first-term North Carolina Rep. Madison Cawthorn. Cawthorn became one of the youngest Republicans ever elected to the U.S. Congress, comfortably winning his North Carolina House seat over Democratic rival, Moe Davis by more than 12 percentage points. Cawthorn's first tweet after being elected was the following taunt at liberals and Democrats: "Cry more, lib."[26] Cawthorn was one of the main speakers at the January 6 Save America Rally. At the rally he said, "This crowd has some fight in it. . . . The Republicans hiding and not fighting (and not objecting to the count), they are trying to silence your voice. . . . We're not doing this just for Donald Trump, we are doing this for the Constitution." When asked later if he regretted speaking at the rally, Cawthorn said "no" (Castronuovo 2021).

There were fewer Republican Objectors in the Senate compared to the House. But two notable Republican senator Objectors stand out. First, there was Texas Republican Senator Ted Cruz. While speaking at a January 3, 2021, rally for Georgia's special Senate election with President Trump, Cruz encouraged supporters to show up on January 6: "We will not go quietly into the night. We will defend liberty. And we are going to win" (Goodman, Dugas, and Tonckens 2021). Cruz had even called into right-wing radio host Mark Levin's show, two days before the insurrection. On Levin's show he accused Republican members of Congress who didn't support the campaign to block Biden's certification of being "piously and self-righteously preening" (Samuels and Svitek 2021). Missouri Senator Josh Hawley was the earliest senator to state his plans to object to the certification of Biden's victory, saying in a tweet in late December 2020: "Millions of voters concerned about election integrity deserve to be heard. I will object on January 6 on their behalf."[27] The photograph taken of him pumping his fist in exhortation to the protesters before they would storm the

[25] She caused a kerfuffle with Capitol Police a week after the insurrection when she attempted to carry her Glock handgun on the House floor where guns are banned. See Kim (2021*a*).

[26] See Cawthorn, Madison (CawthornforNC). Twitter, November 3, 2020. https://twitter.com/CawthornforNC/status/1323813315169165313.

[27] Hawley, Josh (HawleyMO). Twitter, December 30, 2020. https://twitter.com/HawleyMO/status/1344307458085412867.

Capitol on January 6 was widely condemned. Former Republican Missouri Senator John Danforth said after the January 6th insurrection: "Supporting Josh Hawley . . . was the worst decision I've ever made in my life. . . . He has consciously appealed to the worst. He has attempted to drive us apart and he has undermined public belief in our democracy" (Beaumont and Salter 2021).

Table 8.2 shows the descriptive statistics of the nastiness of the eight Republican Objectors' rhetoric plus President Trump's rhetoric on Twitter during the 2020 pre-election period through Joe Biden's eventual inauguration. Like the previous analyses, the tweets were coded for whether they contained any type of nasty rhetoric and which type of rhetoric they contained: insults (1), accusations (2), intimidating statements (3), and incitement (4). An additive measure of threat intensity was also constructed that summed up all the types of nasty rhetoric contained in a tweet.

Table 8.2 shows that the level of nastiness and intensity of tweets from these politicians during this time period is quite high. Cawthorn has the lowest percentage of nasty tweets at 62.6%, and others like Boebert, Brooks, Gosar, and Greene are closer to 80%. The level of intensity is also quite high. Brooks, Gosar, and Greene all have an average threat intensity in their tweets greater than 3. In fact Brooks (3.5) and Gosar (3.6) have higher intensities than all of the Ukrainian politicians during their 2019 election period, sans the extreme far-right Oleh Tyahnybok (4.2, see Table 3.3). This high level of intensity and nastiness of tweets is not simply because these are the nastiest members of the Republican Party. Both Trump's (2.1 to 1.7, and 64.2% and 50.6%) and Gaetz's (2.1 to 1.8, 64.6% to 58.8%) tweets were on average more intense and a greater percentage nasty during this 2020 election compared to the early stages of the COVID pandemic and the Black Lives Matter protests in the spring and summer of 2020 (see Table 3.2 in Chapter 3).

Figures 8.3 and 8.4 show the time series plots of daily intensity of Trump and the Republican Objectors on Twitter during the 2020 election period. Trump's intensity peaks before the election on November 3. However others such as Brooks, Cawthorn, Gaetz, Gosar, and Greene peak in the period between the election and the January 6 insurrection.

The findings in Figures 8.3 and 8.4 show that several of the Objectors—Brooks, Cawthorn, Gaetz, Gosar, and Green—were deploying their nastiest rhetoric (highest intensity) in the nine-week period between the November 3, 2020, election and the January 6, 2021, insurrection.

Yet an important question is who was setting the agenda for nasty rhetoric during this time period? Was Trump simply responding and feeding off the Republican Objectors and the most extreme elements of his party? Or were the Objectors taking their cues from Trump and following his rhetorical lead? To answer these questions, we'll turn to a vector autogregression (VAR). VAR

Table 8.2 **The rhetoric of Trump and Republican Objectors on Twitter was particularly nasty during the 2020 elections and in the lead up to the January 6 insurrection (October 1, 2020–January 21, 2021).**

Name	*# of Posts*	*Mean Intensity*	*Overall Nasty*	*Insults*	*Accuse*	*Intimidate*	*Incite*
Donald Trump	3,054	2.1	64.2%	40.4%	59.7%	15.2%	0.7%
Lauren Boebert (Rep. R–CO)	984	2.8	78.8%	67.9%	66.2%	24.9%	1.2%
Mo Brooks (Rep. R–AZ)	242	3.5	80.1%	63.6%	79.9%	43.1%	0%
Madison Cawthorn (Rep. R–NC)	164	2.5	62.6%	52.8%	60.7%	23.3%	1.2%
Ted Cruz (Sen. R–TX)	1,202	2.4	71.0%	60.7%	61.2%	19.3%	0.3%
Matt Gaetz (Rep. R–FL)	820	2.1	64.6%	58.7%	58.1%	10.3%	0.1%
Paul Gosar (Rep. R–AZ)	496	3.6	76.8%	66.8%	72.5%	44.3%	4.0%
Marjorie Taylor Greene (Rep. R–GA)	1,708	3.2	76.9%	66.2%	69.7%	36.4%	0.3%
Josh Hawley (Sen. R–MO)	454	2.4	65.6%	51.8%	59.6%	24.0%	0%

is a time series approach that looks at how multiple time series can influence each other (Brandt and Williams 2006). It allows us to disentangle whether the Objectors were following and reacting more to Trump's nasty rhetoric or vice versa.[28]

[28] This is a similar type of analysis to Barberá et al. (2019) that examines which actors set the agenda in the U.S. Congress using a VAR as well.

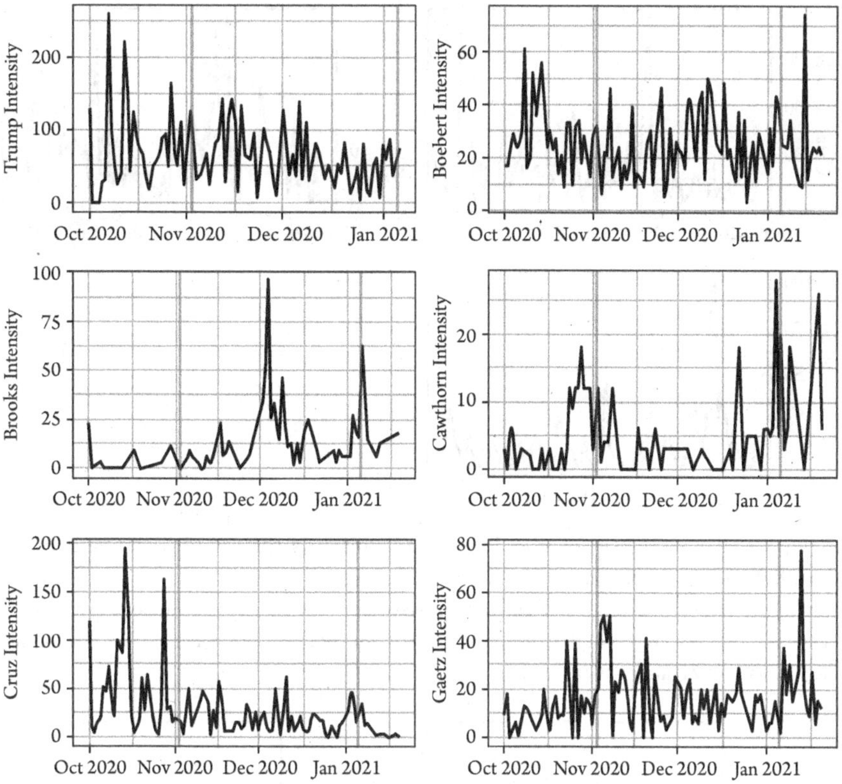

Figure 8.3 Threat intensity of Trump's and Republican Objectors' rhetoric on Twitter around the 2020 election (October 1, 2020–January 20, 2021).

Note: Trump (top left), Boebert (top right), Brooks (middle left), Cawthorn (middle right), Cruz (bottom left), and Gaetz (bottom right). Trump's tweets stop on January 8 following his ban by Twitter. Graphs correspond to daily sums of intensity of nasty tweets. Vertical shaded regions correspond to the November 3, 2020, election and the January 6, 2021, insurrection.

The findings plotted in Figure 8.5 present the results from the VAR model tracing out how Objectors' respond to an increase in Trump's intensity (nastiness), and how Trump responded to an increase in the Objectors' intensity (nastiness).[29] The results provide evidence that the Objectors were taking their cues from Trump, but Trump was not taking cues from the objectors. Figure 8.5a shows that nine days after an increase in Trump's intensity, the Republican Objectors increase their intensity by 17.0% (95% Confidence Interval: 1.0%, 32.6%). In contrast, Figure 8.5b shows that an increase in the Objector's intensity had a negligible impact (3.3% increase) on Trump's intensity after nine days

[29] This is known as an impulse response function (IRF), which traces how "surprise" shocks in one variable influence the other variable. It provides us a measure of which time series was reacting to which.

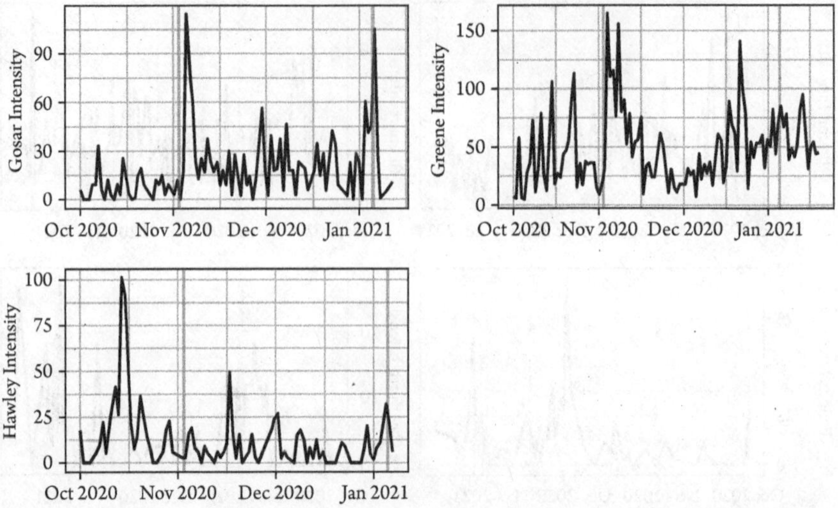

Figure 8.4 Threat intensity of other Republican Objectors' rhetoric on Twitter around the 2020 election (October 1, 2020–January 20, 2021).

Note: Gosar (top left), Greene (top right), and Hawley (bottom left). Graphs correspond to daily sums of intensity of nasty tweets. Vertical shaded regions correspond to the November 3, 2020, election and the January 6, 2021, insurrection.

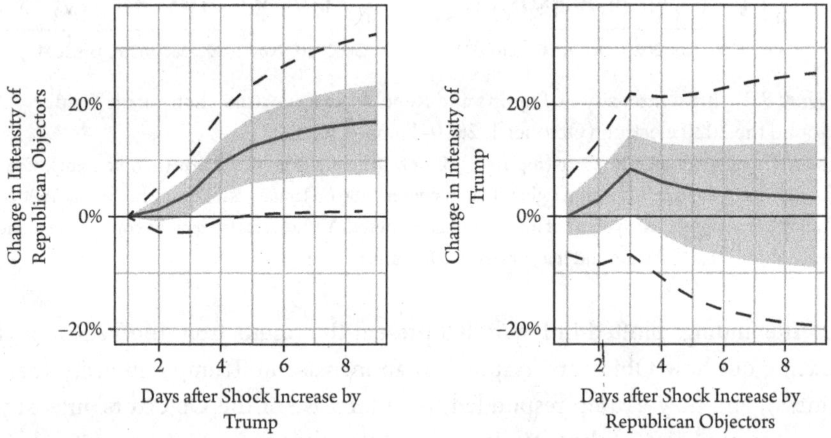

(a) Republican Objectors' response to an increase in intensity in Trump's rhetoric

(b) Trump's response to an increase in intensity in Republican Objectors' rhetoric

Figure 8.5 Republican Objectors' rhetoric increases in intensity in response to increases to Trump's rhetoric, but not vice versa.

Note: Results are cumulative impulse response function (IRF) plots from a 3-lag vector autoregression (VAR) following a shock standard deviation of the disturbance term. The Republican Objectors' time series is the average of the eight Objectors' time series that have been standardized. Both the Trump and Republican time series had their minimum values set at 1 and log transformed so the IRF results can be interpreted in percentage terms. Grey regions represent 68% confidence intervals that show the overall shape of the IRF, and dashed lines represent 95% confidence intervals (Sims and Zha 1999).

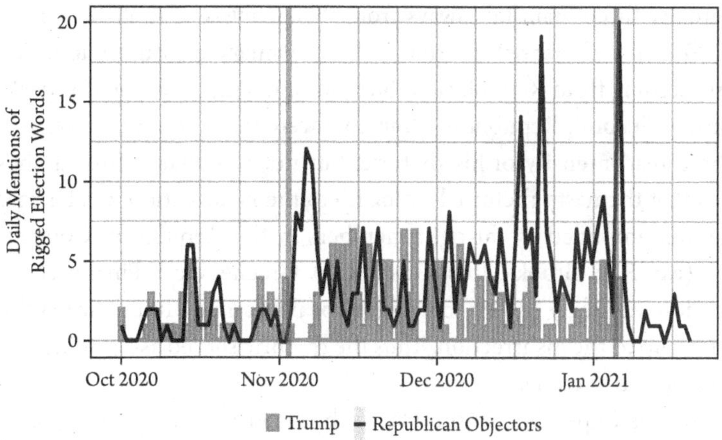

Figure 8.6 Trump's use of rigged election rhetoric on Twitter peaks before the November election, while Republican Objectors' use of rigged election rhetoric peaks in the lead up to the January 6 insurrection (October 1, 2020–January 20, 2021).

Note: Daily frequency of rigged election rhetoric includes daily counts of "steal, stole, coup, sedition, treason, corrupt, rigged, fraud" for Trump (gray bars) and sum of the eight Republican Objectors (black lines). Vertical shaded regions correspond to the November 3, 2020, election and the January 6, 2021, insurrection. Total mentions during this time period: Trump 209, Boebert 25, Brooks 56, Cawthorn 7, Cruz 35, Gosar 89, Greene 128, and Hawley 15.

(95% Confidence Interval: −19.0%, 24.7%).[30] So Trump was influencing the Republican Objectors' nastiness more than the Objectors were influencing him.

But what about accusations that the vote was "rigged" specifically? How did the dynamics of Trump's claims that the election was rigged on Twitter evolve during the election period and in the lead up to the insurrection? What about among the Republican Objectors? Figure 8.6 shows the daily frequency of rigged election rhetoric coming from Trump and the Objectors. In the pre-election period, Trump's accusations that the election was "fraudulent" and "rigged" match the levels of all eight of the Republican Objectors combined. However, after the November 3 election, and in the lead up to the insurrection, the frequency of Republican Objectors' rigged language increases dramatically. It peaks right at the insurrection on January 6.

[30] The Portmanteau Test for this 3-lag VAR model suggests that serial correlation is not a big concern: $\chi^2 = 46.109$ DF $= 52$, p-value $= 0.7036$. Sometimes impulse response function (IRF) results are sensitive to the ordering of the variables. When we reverse the order of the variables (putting Trump's time series first), the results are largely the same: Trump $\Longrightarrow$ Objectors 17.0% increase 95% CI (−1.1%, 33.9%) and Objectors $\Longrightarrow$ Trump 3.3% increase 95% CI (−18.2%, 22.8%). Or if we take a longer lag length (5-lag VAR and expand our results to 10 days) the uncertainty is greater, but the point estimates are similar in direction: Trump $\Longrightarrow$ Objectors 9.7% increase 95% CI (−6.9%, 25.3%) and Objectors $\Longrightarrow$ Trump −8.6% (decrease) 95% CI (−31.1%, 15.7%).

There are three main takeaways from this analysis of rhetoric surrounding the 2020 U.S. presidential election and the January 6 insurrection. First, the rhetoric coming from Republican Objectors and Trump during this period was quite nasty. Second, Republican Objectors were taking their cues from Trump and the threat intensity of his rhetoric, but not vice versa. This meshes with the idea that the nasty rhetoric leading up to the insurrection was instigated by Trump, but amplified by far-right members in the Republican Congressional Caucus (e.g., Rep. Brooks, Rep. Gosar, Rep. Greene, etc.). Finally, claims that the election was being "stolen" or "rigged" peaked among Republican Objectors in the lead up to the insurrection. Thus the rhetoric served as a leading indicator for the violence to come.

Trump was impeached in the House, but later acquitted during his Senate trial on February 13, 2021, on charges of incitement of insurrection. Shortly after he was acquitted Trump and his allies plotted his revenge on Republicans they viewed having wronged Trump (Smith 2021). In a show of how much sway Trump still had with the GOP rank-and-file, Trump-backed state Republican parties censured Republican members of Congress that voted for his impeachment (Carr Smyth 2021). Eight of the ten Republican representatives in the House who voted to convict Trump after January 6 either retired or lost their primary (Gedeon 2022). Liz Cheney, the third highest ranking Republican in the House from Wyoming, who voted to convict Trump and was critical of his baseless electoral fraud claims, was pushed out of her leadership role for her lack of fealty to Trump (Beauchamp 2021*a*). In August 2022 Cheney lost by nearly 40 percentage points to her Trump-backed challenger in the Republican primary—a race she had won just two years prior with more than 70% of her party's support.

For the GOP, Trump's baseless claims that the 2020 election had been stolen had become a key Republican litmus test. A Reuters/Ipsos poll from March 2021 showed how deep Trump's election claims had penetrated the GOP rank-and-file. More than 60% of Republicans believed that the 2020 elections had been stolen from Trump. More than half of Republicans also believed the following two false claims about January 6: (1) that the insurrection was mostly peaceful; or (2) that the insurrection was led by left-wing protesters to make Trump look bad (Oliphant and Kahn 2021).

By the end of July 2021, conspiratorial views about January 6 and the 2020 election had taken root in the right-wing of the Republican Party. The most prominent Republicans in Congress promoting these conspiracies were Reps. Matt Gaetz (Florida), Marjorie Taylor Greene (Georgia), Paul A. Gosar (Arizona), and Louie Gohmert (Texas). These Republicans decried the conditions of defendants being accused of taking part in the January 6 insurrection. They referred to them as "political prisoners" (Flynn 2021).

Trump campaigned as an outsider using the nasty style. But he continued to use incendiary rhetoric as president and after he left office. Trump reshaped the Republican party, and his nasty and conspiratorial style became the Republican Party brand (Lerer and Herndon 2021). Trump helped usher in a new era where anti-democratic attitudes weren't confined to the extreme. Rather, mainstream discourse in Trump's Republican Party was that contested elections where Republicans lost to Democrats were "stolen" or "rigged." To suggest otherwise was to risk being labeled a "Republican in Name Only" (RINO), being primaried, and censured.[31] Most concerning for the future of U.S. democracy, Trump-allied Republicans have used the baseless allegations about the 2020 election to restrict voting, take over election administration by installing loyalists, and subvert the democratic process. Republican partisan elites are not simply shrugging their shoulders as their elected representatives turn towards democratic subversion, but actively cheering it on (Rosenfeld 2022).

It's ironic that shortly after Trump exited office while decrying fraud, his right-wing populist ally Benjamin Netanyahu would do the same. Following a March 2021 election, the fourth election held in two years, Israeli politics were still deadlocked. However, in late May 2021 Netanyahu's rivals from across the political spectrum struck a deal. Right-wing leader Naftali Bennett and centrist Yair Lapid—along with several other parties—agreed to join a coalition government. The biggest surprise was that an Arab party (Ra'am) would be in the coalition for the first time in Israel's history (Times of Israel 2021*c*). With Netanyahu supporters leveling charges against the coalition as perpetrating "a big fraud" and vowing to do "anything possible" to stop the anti-Netanyahu coalition government from forming, Israel's head of Shin Bet (security service) became increasingly concerned. He issued a public warning in early June 2021 about "extremely violent and inciting discourse" and about a possible January 6-type insurrection in Israel (Rubin 2021). In an impassioned exit speech before the coalition was formally sworn in, Netanyahu accused Bennett of perpetrating the "greatest fraud" in the history of democracy, and vowed to fight daily to topple the Bennett-led government (Times of Israel 2021*b*). Netanyahu, like Trump, would lose. But not before scorching his political rivals with nasty rhetoric and vowing to return again—which he would do when he became prime minister once more in December 2022 following new elections.

Both Trump and Netanyahu increased insults, accusations, and threats when their hold on power was threatened. This is perhaps the most insidious and dangerous incarnation of nasty politics. Leaders have more access to levers

[31] The Arizona party censured and labeled their fellow Republicans—Governor Doug Ducey and Speaker of the Arizona House of Representatives, Rusty Bowers—RINOs for saying that the 2020 election was legitimately won by Joe Biden (Draper 2022).

of power and security services to make their accusations—even the baseless ones—appear legitimate, and carry out their threats.

Turkish President Recep Tayyip Erdoğan fits this dynamic. In mid-July 2016 a faction of Turkish military officers attempted a coup, using tanks and helicopters to try to control Istanbul and the capital city, Ankara. Approximately 300 people were killed before it was crushed by the Turkish armed forces loyal to the government. Hours after the coup was quashed, Erdoğan declared: "this uprising (coup) is a gift from God" and "it will be a reason to cleanse our army" (Dolan and Solaker 2016). Within days, thousands of military officers and judges suspected of supporting the coup and U.S.-based Turkish cleric, Fetullah Gülen, had been rounded up and arrested. Erdoğan blamed Gülen and Gülen-backed military figures for masterminding the coup and accused Gülen allies of infiltrating the Turkish government and society. Erdoğan's allies pushed the conspiracy theory that the U.S. government had allowed Gülen to live freely in the U.S. and thus was the real power behind the coup (Arango and Yeginsu 2016; Guiler 2016).

Following the coup attempt Erdoğan and his allies declared a state of emergency and engaged in a wide campaign of arrests and purges (Hansen 2017). Judges, doctors, academics, teachers, politicians, police officers, and any other public servants alleged to be connected to Gülen were put on lists and fired. An estimated 80,000 people were held in pretrial detention, and 150,000 were fired. In April 2017, in the midst of the state of emergency, Erdoğan won the support of Turkish voters for a controversial constitutional referendum that turned Turkey into a presidential system and concentrated power in the hands of the president—President Erdoğan's hands (Shaheen 2017).

On the one-year anniversary of the failed 2016 coup attempt Erdoğan promised to a crowd of his supporters that he would "rip off the heads of those traitors (his opponents)" (Tharoor 2017). As Human Rights Watch documented, Erdoğan had done much in the six months following the coup:

> (The Turkish) government carried out mass arrests of journalists, closed multiple media outlets, and jailed elected opposition politicians. It dismissed or detained without due process over 100,000 civil servants including teachers, judges and prosecutors, suspended hundreds of nongovernmental groups, and consolidated government control over the courts.[32]

[32] See Human Rights Watch (2017).

Erdoğan's nasty rhetoric was part of a larger orchestrated campaign. He used the threat and fallout from the coup to purge his political enemies, consolidate his power, and kill Turkey's fragile democracy.

8.3 Summary of the Findings

To answer the puzzle why politicians use nasty rhetoric this book developed a supply and demand theory of nasty politics. It focused on voters' responses to nasty rhetoric (the demand side), politicians' incentives to go nasty (the supply side), and the implications for democracy. One of the core findings is that voters on average don't like nasty politics. This dislike is increasing in the threat of violence it poses. Incitement is viewed as more threatening than intimidating statements, which are more threatening than accusations and insults. It's not simply a country-specific finding. Voters in Ukraine, Israel, and the U.S. all have an aversion to nasty politics.

So why then do politicians go nasty? First, there's an important caveat with the phrase "voters on average." Certain voters—those who like tough leaders, are more aggressive, or favor violence—are more open to and supportive of nasty rhetoric.

Second, nasty politics is about attention and signaling. One of the key currencies for politicians is attention. Politicians are willing to sacrifice likability to get it. Being willing to break civility norms and use nasty language can get a politician media coverage and stir up conflict. That conflict then draws even more attention from both media and voters. The social media data supports this argument. Whether on Twitter or Facebook, or in Ukraine, Israel, or the U.S., nasty social media posts get more attention, and the more intense a post is the more engagement it gets. Nasty rhetoric also signals to voters that a politician is willing to fight for their beliefs and voters. They may come off like a jerk, but they will fight for the ingroup.

The findings here are also not specific to one country or context. Ukraine, Israel, and the U.S. all have their own political institutions, history, and levels of partisan polarization. Yet how politicians deploy the nasty style and how voters respond is a more universal story. This has implications for both scholars of American and Comparative Politics.

In aggregate voters view nasty politics as a cynical appeal to grab attention, or even a dangerous one to stoke violence. But these concerns are not equally weighted across the ingroup and outgroup. Outgroup politicians using violent rhetoric are more likely to be viewed as motivated by cynical or sinister motivations. In contrast, ingroup politicians are more likely to be perceived as fighting for what's right. This intergroup penalty for violent rhetoric provides one motivation for how nasty rhetoric can spiral into violence. Voters excuse ingroup politicians who use it, but feel threatened when outgroup politicians use it.

Nasty politics can be both a strategic choice and a style. Social media data from the U.S., Ukraine, and Israel, as well as disruptions in the Rada, all show that the nasty style tends to be used more by outsiders and opposition politicians. These are the kinds of politicians that are willing to make a trade-off. They are willing to suffer a hit to their reputation that comes with using nasty politics to get attention, and signal their toughness with voters. Politicians are also mindful of not going too nasty. Insults and accusations are relatively common, while intimidating statements are rarer, and incitement and actual physical violence are the rarest of all. Why does all this matter? If nasty rhetoric "worked" for everyone then we would see all politicians use it and use it regularly. Instead, the findings suggest that certain politicians are able to use it effectively. But like the political career of Oleh Lyashko, there's sometimes a shelf-life for such theatrics.

Nasty politics also has several important implications for democracy. On the positive side, it can be a tool for marginalized groups and politicians to get noticed and fight for their group. But it also breeds cynicism in the long-term and can reduce political participation. It also influences which politicians run for office—sustained periods of nasty politics lead good politicians to retire and nasty ones to replace them.

How does nasty politics lead to violence? The evidence presented in this book shows that inciting rhetoric doesn't directly persuade people to commit violence. Even when nasty rhetoric comes from the ingroup, or is framed in defensive ways to make it more amenable, voters still dislike it more than civil rhetoric. Rather, what nasty rhetoric does is garner attention—the nastier the more the attention—signal toughness to members of the ingroup, and coordinate the ingroup around a particular threat. But there's an important caveat. As the findings in Ukraine post-Russian 2022 invasion show, nasty politics towards domestic opponents can be tempered in the face of external threats.

Coordination is an important component connecting nasty politics to violence. The most insidious version of nasty politics is a concerted campaign of accusations, intimidation, and incitement by political and party leaders against a domestic outgroup. These campaigns are the most likely form of nasty politics to spiral into violence. Our discussion in this chapter of the events surrounding the January 6 insurrection at the U.S. Capitol supports this argument. President Trump and the Republican Objectors (#StoptheSteal) engaged in a concerted effort to promote conspiracies and baseless allegations. They signaled to their supporters that the other side (Democrats) were so bad that all strategies were on the table including violence. They coordinated supporters who were already primed to dislike the outgroup to be ready to act violently against them. In doing so, Trump and the Republican Objectors weakened two of the key guardrails of democracy—toleration of political opponents and willingness to exercise self-restraint when holding power (Levitsky and Ziblatt 2018).

These concerted campaigns are part of a broader menu of political tactics by political leaders to polarize the populace into supporters and opponents. Politicians repeatedly tell their supporters that if they don't take action against the outgroup first—sometimes violent and anti-democratic action—the outgroup will do it to them. Leaders amp up their supporters' fears, and use it to justify sidelining their political opponents (Braley et al. 2021). These concerted campaigns that mix accusations, conspiracies, and incitement against the outgroup are not solely the province of Trump in the U.S., Netanyahu in Israel, or Erdoğan in Turkey. Rather we also have seen it emerge with other leaders like Viktor Yanukovych in Ukraine (*Kyiv Post* 2012*b*), Hugo Chavez in Venezuela (Moffitt 2013), and Jair Bolsonaro in Brazil (Londoño, Milhorance, and Nicas 2021). When leaders themselves become the main axis of political competition and polarize society into their supporters and opponents, nasty politics, violence, and democratic erosion are likely to follow.

8.4 Future Work

Democracy is a system of government in which parties lose elections (Przeworski 1991). In liberal democracies political elites defer to fair elections to peacefully settle disputes. The model of nasty politics discussed in this book covers low-level insults and accusations that are part and parcel of democratic competition. But it also includes incitement and actual violence which violate the norms of democracy. When a candidate says their rival is an "idiot" who "shouldn't be elected to political office, let alone dog catcher" it's definitely nasty, but it's not anti-democratic. Yet baselessly accusing your political opponents of fraud, engaging in treason, or bringing the "country to its knees" while brandishing an assault rifle is not a part of the democratic process. It's anti-democratic.[33] Thus shifts in the kind and quantity of nasty politics portend shifts in the quality of democracy.

As we've seen throughout the book, nasty politics appears to be on the rise in the U.S and in other advanced countries. Why is this the case? Why is the public now more amenable to nastiness and tough-talking politicians? Tentative research suggests a myriad of reasons: fears of changing demographics

[33] These are examples of the behavior drawn from some of the prominent Republican candidates running for office in the 2022 elections (Weigel 2022).

and culture (Mason, Wronski, and Kane 2021; Mutz 2018; Norris and Inglehart 2019), increased outsourcing of jobs and exposure to trade (Autor et al. 2020), inequality (Hacker and Pierson 2020), and the weakening of parties (Ignazi 2020).

Or is the increasing use of nasty politics a side effect of new, more aggressive forms of social communication that come with the increasing use of social media?[34] More work should be done to tease apart which factors are leading the public to increasingly take solace in the nasty style.

The previous chapters provided evidence that nasty rhetoric shapes which candidates select into office and how they communicate. More work should be done on how nasty politics influence who runs for office, and its effect on political conflict.

Throughout this book we've seen how politicians seek attention by using nasty rhetoric and appeals to get likes, clicks, views, and attention more generally. The public is not passive in the story of nasty politics. Many times fringe citizens can egg on their politicians to engage in the nasty style. For instance the original driving force behind the Stop the Steal campaign that preceded the January 6 insurrection was not a Republican politician. Rather it was Ali Alexander—a 35-year-old convicted felon[35] turned right-wing social media personality and conspiracy theorist. Alexander did much of the early promotion and coordination of Stop the Steal rallies (Sommer 2021). More work should be done on how citizens and activists can push politicians and the public towards or away from the nasty style of politics.

Many of the data sources here are drawn from social media. But more work should be done to disentangle how social media and the traditional media interact to shape how politicians use the nasty style. How do tweets, Facebook posts, Instagram, or even Tik-Tok usage by politicians' influence the way the media covers politics? And how does this in turn shape traditional media coverage?

Memes, video, and other visual images play an increasing role in political communication (Joo and Steinert-Threlkeld 2018). There are also increasing concerns about deepfakes and manipulated video and how they may mislead the public (Barari, Lucas, and Munger 2021; Vaccari and Chadwick 2020). All of this suggests that nasty politics is changing with the technology, and future research should seek to study these issues. Given concerns about disinformation on social media and the increasing role of social media in political campaigns and communication this is an important next step (Tucker et al. 2018; Zeitzoff 2017).

My final thoughts are that democracy is always contentious. Nasty politics is part of that contention. Yet as the fallout from January 6 in the U.S. and the

[34] This is the argument Kevin Munger makes in a March 2022 Substack post (Munger 2022).

[35] Theft and credit card abuse.

2022 Russian Invasion of Ukraine show, politicians respond to new threats with changes in the quantity and type of nasty politics. The nasty style of politics is not going away. It will morph and change as new political threats emerge. But the core logic that nasty politics is fundamentally about attention and signaling will remain.

Appendix A

UKRAINIAN POLITICS OVERVIEW

A.1 Ukrainian Political System

Ukraine is a semi-presidential system with power split between the parliament—Verkhovna Rada (Rada)—and the president. The president is popularly elected and serves for a five-year term. Elections in the Rada follow a fifty-fifty allocation. Half the seats are allocated through proportional representation (5% threshold), and the other half are allocated through first-past-the-post elections in single member districts. It should be noted that Rada elections in 2006 and 2007 were held under a pure proportional representation system.

The president is the head of state, commander-in-chief of the armed forces, responsible for foreign policy, and also has control over the internal security services, and the Prosecutor General of Ukraine. The prime minister is nominated by the president. However the president must consult with the Rada on their appointment, and needs majority support in the Rada for any nomination. The prime minister selects members of the cabinet except those ministries which are reserved for the presidency (defense and foreign affairs). The Rada passes laws, but the president can veto them. The Rada can override the veto with a two-thirds vote. The president also has the ability to dissolve the Rada under certain circumstances and call early snap elections (as Zelensky did in 2019). Laws and official acts are subject to review by the 18 members of the Constitutional Court of Ukraine—six of whom are appointed by the president, six by the Rada, and six from the professional association of judges (Council of Judges). From 1996–2004, and then again from 2010–2014, the president enjoyed even stronger powers. These powers were rolled back during reforms following the Orange Revolution and Euromaidan which restricted the president's ability to appoint the prime minister and cabinet members.

A.2 Key Political Factions, Parties, and Personalities

Ukrainian politics during the period covered in this book (2001–2022) can be divided into the following different political blocs associated with major political factions and figures.

Far-Right and Ultra-Nationalist Bloc

Ideology: Far-right, ultranationalism, xenophobia, anti-LGBT, antisemitism, anti-Russian, Pro-Euromaidan.

Key parties: Svoboda, Right Sector, National Corps.

Key personalities: Dmytro Yarosh, Andriy Biletsky, Oleh Tyahnybok.

Years of strength: 2012 election watershed with 10%. Mostly a fringe part of the Rada. Post-Euromaidan capable of marshaling large street protests and violent actions.

Lyashko Bloc

Ideology: Populism, Ukrainian nationalism, anti-Russia, pro-agrarian, Pro-Euromaidan.

Key parties: Radical Party of Oleh Lyashko.

Key personalities: Oleh Lyashko, Ihor Mosiychuk, Rinat Akhmetov.

Years of strength: Third in 2014 presidential election, in coalition government (until 2015), opposition until 2019, then out of the Rada in 2019.

Center-Right Bloc

Ideology: Pro-Ukrainian, pro-European, pro-Orange Revolution, Pro-Euromaidan.

Key parties: Samopomich, Holos, People's Front, People's Movement, UDAR Ukrainian Democratic Alliance for Reform (UDAR) post-2019,[1] Ukrainian Association of Patriots (UKROP), Our Ukraine.[2]

Key personalities: Andriy Sadovyi, Vitali Klitschko (post-2019), Arseniy Yatsenyuk, Viktor Yushchenko, Arsen Avakov, Mikheil Saakashivili, Oleksandr Turchynov, Volodymyr Parasyuk.

[1] Note, UDAR was in alliance with Poroshenko's Bloc from 2015–2019, but since then has been independent.

[2] Note parties in the Center-Right Bloc range from more centrist-parties (UDAR) to more hard-line nationalist (UKROP).

Years of strength: From 2005–2010 held the presidency (Yushchenko), and 2014–2019 part of the majority coalition.

Poroshenko Bloc

Ideology: Pro-Ukrainian, pro-European, pro-Orange Revolution, Pro-Euromaidan.

Key parties: European Solidarity, UDAR (2015–2019).

Key personalities: Petro Poroshenko, Volodymyr Groysman, Yuriy Lutsenko, Vitali Klitschko (2015–2019).

Years of strength: From 2014–2019 held the presidency, finished second in the 2019 presidential election, and fourth in the 2019 Rada elections.

Tymoshenko Bloc

Ideology: Populism, Ukrainian nationalism, pro-European pro-agrarian, pro-Orange Revolution, Pro-Euromaidan.

Key parties: Fatherland.

Key personalities: Yulia Tymoshenko, Serhiy Sobolyev, Serhiy Taruta, Nadiya Savchenko (expelled 2016).

Years of strength: In 2005, and again 2007–2010, Tymoshenko was prime minister. Main opposition to pro-Russian and Yanukovych parties. Tymoshenko was imprisoned and banned from holding office 2011–2014. Finished third in the 2019 presidential first round, and third in the 2019 Rada elections.

Zelensky Bloc

Ideology: Populism, pro-European, anti-corruption.

Key parties: Servant of the People.

Key personalities: Volodymyr Zelensky, Dmytro Razumkov, Oleksandr Kornienko, Ihor Kolomoyskyi.

Years of strength: Formed ahead of the 2019 presidential election (won with President Zelensky) and the 2019 Rada election, where it controls a parliamentary majority since 2019.

Pro-Russian Bloc

Ideology: Eurosceptic, pro-Russian, pro-regionalism, anti-Orange Revolution, anti-Euromaidan.

Key parties: Party of Regions, Opposition Bloc, Opposition Platform For Life, Platform for Life and Peace.

Key personalities: Viktor Yanukovych. Leonid Kuchma, Rinat Akhmetov, Dmytro Firtash, Yuriy Boyko, Oleksandr Vilkul, Vadim Rabinovich, Viktor Medvedchuk.

Years of strength: Held the presidency from 2000–2005 (Kuchma), and 2010–2014 (Yanukovych). After Euromaidan the Party of Regions was banned. Finished in second place in the 2019 Rada elections (Opposition Platform For Life). Opposition Platform for Life was banned following the 2022 Russian invasion. Platform for Life and Peace was a parliamentary group formed in April 2022 that explicitly did not include Viktor Medvedchuk and Vadim Rabinovich.

Communists/Socialists

Ideology: Communism, left-wing, populist, pro-Soviet legacy, Eurosceptic, anti-Euromaidan.

Key parties: Communist Party of Ukraine, Socialist Party of Ukraine.

Key personalities: Petro Symonenko, Oleksandr Moroz, Ilya Kiva, Adam Martynyuk.

Years of strength: Much more prominent in the late 1990s, where it was the second largest party in Ukraine. Both parties spent time in coalition governments from 2000–2012, but neither party has been in the Rada since 2014. Communist Party of Ukraine has faced repeated attempts to ban it and has been charged with supporting pro-Russian separatists in the War in Donbas.

REFERENCES

112 Ukraine. 2019. "MP Boyko Stands for Retrenching of MPs in Parliament." 112 Ukraine. Accessed December 13, 2020. **URL:** https://112.international/politics/mp-boyko-stands-for-retrenching-of-mps-in-parliament-37689.html

ABC. 2019. "Donald Trump Tells US Congresswomen to Go Back to Where They Came From." Australian Broadcasting Corporation. Accessed September 8, 2020. **URL:** https://www.abc.net.au/news/2019-07-15/trump-tells-us-born-congresswomen-to-go-back-to-home-countries/11308368

Abou-Sabe, Kenzi, Tom Winter, and Max Tucker. 2017. "What Did Ex-Trump Aide Paul Manafort Really Do in Ukraine?" NBC News. **URL:** https://www.nbcnews.com/news/us-news/what-did-ex-trump-aide-paul-manafort-really-do-ukraine-n775431

Abramowitz, Alan I, and Steven Webster. 2016. "The Rise of Negative Partisanship and the Nationalization of US Elections in the 21st Century." *Electoral Studies* 41:12–22.

Abrams, Neil A. and M. Steven Fish. 2016. "Dethroning Ukraine's Oligarchs: A How-To Guide." Foreign Policy. Accessed October 27, 2020. **URL:** https://foreignpolicy.com/2016/06/13/dethroning-ukraines-oligarchs-a-how-to-guide/

Acocella, Joan. 2002. "On the Contrary: A New Look at the Work of H. L. Mencken." *The New Yorker*. **URL:** https://www.newyorker.com/magazine/2002/12/09/on-the-contrary

Adkins, Laura E. and Ben Sales. 2019. "The Kids Are all Right-Wing: How Israel's Younger Voters Have Grown More Conservative over Time." Jewish Telegraphic Agency. Accessed March 24, 2021. **URL:** https://www.jta.org/2019/04/10/israel/not-ready-younger-right-wing-voters

ADL. 2018. "Quantifying Hate: A Year of Anti-Semitism on Twitter." Anti-Defamation League. Accessed December 6, 2020. **URL:** https://www.adl.org/resources/reports/quantifying-hate-a-year-of-anti-semitism-on-twitterglobalist-as-code-word-for-jew

Agenda.ge. 2021. "PM Garibashvili: Saakashvili 'Staging a Show' with Hunger Strike, Eating Half a Kilo Honey." Agenda.ge. Accessed October 29, 2021. **URL:** https://agenda.ge/en/news/2021/3089

Akimenko, Valeriy. 2018. "Ukraine's Toughest Fight: The Challenge of Military Reform." Carnegie Endowment for International Peace. Accessed November 5, 2020. **URL:** https://carnegieendowment.org/2018/02/22/ukraine-s-toughest-fight-challenge-of-military-reform-pub-75609

Al-Hlou, Yousur, Masha Froliak, Evan Hill, Malachy Browne, and David Botti. 2022. "New Evidence Shows How Russian Soldiers Executed Men in Bucha." *New York Times*. **URL:** https://www.nytimes.com/2022/05/19/world/europe/russia-bucha-ukraine-executions.html

Al Jazeera. 2022. "Ukraine Accuses Former President Poroshenko of Treason." Al Jazeera. Accessed June 3, 2022. **URL:** https://www.aljazeera.com/news/2021/12/20/ukraine-accuses-former-president-poroshenko-of-treason

Albertson, Bethany and Shana Kushner Gadarian. 2015. *Anxious Politics: Democratic Citizenship in a Threatening World*. Cambridge University Press.

Alexa. 2021. "Top Sites in Israel." Amazon's Alexa. Accessed November 5, 2021. **URL:** https://www.alexa.com/topsites/countries/IL

All You Can Read. 2021. "Top 30 Ukrainian Newspapers Online." All You Can Read. Accessed December 5, 2020. **URL:** https://www.allyoucanread.com/ukrainian-newspapers/

AllSides. 2021. "AllSides Media Bias Chart." AllSides. Accessed December 5, 2020. **URL:** https://www.allsides.com/media-bias/media-bias-chart

Almond, Gabriel A. 1950. *The American People and Foreign Policy*. Harcourt, Brace.

Amnesty International. 2014. "Impunity Reigns for Abductions and Ill-Treatment by Pro-Kyiv Vigilantes in Eastern Ukraine." Amnesty International. Accessed September 29, 2020. **URL:** https://www.amnesty.org/en/latest/news/2014/08/impunity-reigns-for-abductions-ill-treatment-eastern-ukraine/

Anderson, Meg. 2021. "New Videos Underscore the Violence against Police at the Jan. 6 Capitol Riot." National Public Radio. Accessed August 10, 2021. **URL:** https://www.npr.org/2021/06/18/1008211655/new-videos-underscore-the-violence-against-police-at-the-jan-6-capitol-riot

Ansolabehere, Stephen and Shanto Iyengar. 1997. *Going Negative: How Political Advertisements Shrink and Polarize the Electorate*. The Free Press.

Antikor. 2019. "'I Will Take It by the Throat and Will Not Let It Go': Kiva Ran into Barna on the Air." Antikor. Accessed December 11, 2020. **URL:** https://antikor.com.ua/articles/302671-vozjmu_za_gorlo_i_ne_otpushchu_kiva_v_prjamom_efire_naletel_na_barnu

AP. 2016. "As Israel Remembers Rabin, Netanyahu Denies He Incited." Associated Press News. Accessed November 9, 2020. **URL:** https://apnews.com/article/ffae0646a86e49cda2c028d71fa107d2

Applebaum, Anne and Jeffrey Goldberg. 2022. "Liberation without Victory." *The Atlantic*. **URL:** https://www.theatlantic.com/international/archive/2022/04/zelensky-kyiv-russia-war-ukrainian-survival-interview/629570/

Arango, Tim and Ceylan Yeginsu. 2016. "Turks Can Agree on One Thing: U.S. Was behind Failed Coup." *New York Times*. **URL:** https://www.nytimes.com/2016/08/03/world/europe/turkey-coup-erdogan-fethullah-gulen-united-states.html

Arel, Dominique. 2018. "How Ukraine Has Become More Ukrainian." *Post-Soviet Affairs* 34(2–3):186–189.

Armus, Teo. 2021*a*. "Rep. Matt Gaetz and Other GOP Politicians Baselessly Suggest Antifa Is to Blame for Pro-Trump Mob Rioting into Capitol." *Washington Post*. **URL:** https://www.washingtonpost.com/nation/2021/01/07/antifa-capitol-gaetz-trump-riot/

Armus, Teo. 2021*b*. "A 'Stop the Steal' Organizer, Now Banned by Twitter, Said Three GOP Lawmakers Helped Plan His D.C. Rally." *Washington Post*. **URL:** https://www.washingtonpost.com/nation/2021/01/13/ali-alexander-capitol-biggs-gosar/

Associated Press. 2022. "Map: Russia's Invasion of Ukraine." Voice of America. Accessed August 13, 2022. **URL:** https://www.voanews.com/a/map-russia-s-invasion-of-ukraine/6463047.html

Atkinson, Mary Layton. 2017. *Combative Politics: The Media and Public Perceptions of Lawmaking*. University of Chicago Press.

Autor, David, David Dorn, Gordon Hanson, Kaveh Majlesi, et al. 2020. "Importing Political Polarization? The Electoral Consequences of Rising Trade Exposure." *American Economic Review* 110(10):3139–3183.

Axios. 2022. "100 Days That Rocked the Globe." Axios. Accessed August 13, 2022. **URL:** https://www.axios.com/2022/06/03/russia-ukraine-news-war-putin-zelensky-biden-timeline

Bade, Rachael and Isaac Stanley-Becker. 2020. "Trump, House Republicans Embrace Candidate Who Has Made Racist Statements, Drawing Attention to Party's Tolerance of Bigotry." *Washington Post*. **URL:** https://www.washingtonpost.com/politics/qanon-georgia-greene-trump/2020/08/12/150c3aa6-dcad-11ea-809e-b8be57ba616e_story.html

Baer, Daniel. 2022. "When Politics Returns to Kyiv." Foreign Affairs. Accessed August 15, 2022. **URL:** https://www.foreignaffairs.com/ukraine/when-politics-returns-kyiv

Baker, Mike and Zolan Kanno-Youngs. 2020. "Federal Agencies Agree to Withdraw from Portland, with Conditions." *New York Times*. **URL:** https://www.nytimes.com/2020/07/29/us/protests-portland-federal-withdrawal.html

Baker, Peter. 2019. "Trump Pressed Ukraine's President to Investigate Democrats as 'a Favor'." *New York Times*. **URL:** https://www.nytimes.com/2019/09/25/us/politics/donald-trump-impeachment-probe.html

Baker, Peter, Maggie Haberman, Katie Rogers, Zolan Kanno-Youngs, Katie Benner, Haley Willis, Christiaan Triebert, and David Botti. 2020. "How Trump's Idea for a Photo Op Led to Havoc in a Park." *New York Times*. **URL:** https://www.nytimes.com/2020/06/02/us/politics/trump-walk-lafayette-square.html

Bakker, Bert N., Yphtach Lelkes and Ariel Malka. 2021. "Reconsidering the link between self-reported personality traits and political preferences." *American Political Science Review* 115(4):1482–1498.

Ballard, Andrew O, Ryan DeTamble, Spencer Dorsey, Michael Heseltine, and Marcus Johnson. 2022. "Dynamics of Polarizing Rhetoric in Congressional Tweets." *Legislative Studies Quarterly*.

Balmaceda, Margarita Mercedes. 2013. *The Politics of Energy Dependency: Ukraine, Belarus, and Lithuania between Domestic Oligarchs and Russian Pressure*. Vol. 40, University of Toronto Press.

Balmforth, Richard and Natalia Zinets. 2015. "Ukraine's 'Pitchfork' Populist Could Be Wild Card in New Line-Up." Reuters. **URL:** https://www.reuters.com/article/uk-ukraine-crisis-idUKKCN0I80AP20141019

Barari, Soubhik, Christopher Lucas, and Kevin Munger. 2021. "Political Deepfake Videos Misinform the Public, But No More than Other Fake Media." OSF Preprints. January 13.

Barbaro, Michael. 2015. "Pithy, Mean and Powerful: How Donald Trump Mastered Twitter for 2016." *New York Times*. **URL:** https://www.nytimes.com/2015/10/06/us/politics/donald-trump-twitter-use-campaign-2016.html

Barberá, Pablo. 2015. "Birds of the Same Feather Tweet Together: Bayesian Ideal Point Estimation Using Twitter Data." *Political Analysis* 23(1):76–91.

Barberá, Pablo, Andreu Casas, Jonathan Nagler, Patrick J. Egan, Richard Bonneau, John T. Jost, and Joshua A. Tucker. 2019. "Who Leads? Who Follows? Measuring Issue Attention and Agenda Setting by Legislators and the Mass Public Using Social Media Data." *American Political Science Review* 113(4):883–901.

Barberá, Pablo, Joshua A. Tucker, Andrew Guess, Cristian Vaccari, Alexandra Siegel, Sergey Sanovich, Denis Stukal, and Brendan Nyhan. 2018. "Social Media, Political Polarization, and Political Disinformation: A Review of the Scientific Literature." Hewlett Foundation. **URL:** https://www.hewlett.org/wp-content/uploads/2018/03/Social-Media-Political-Polarization-and-Political-Disinformation-Literature-Review.pdf

Barberá, Pablo and Thomas Zeitzoff. 2018. "The New Public Address System: Why Do World Leaders Adopt Social Media?" *International Studies Quarterly* 62(1):121–130.

Barrett, Devlin. 2021. "Senate Report Gives New Details of Trump Efforts to Use Justice Dept. to Overturn Election." *Washington Post*. **URL:** https://www.washingtonpost.com/national-security/durbin-report-trump-pressure-justice/2021/10/07/b51712d4-2769-11ec-8d53-67cfb452aa60_story.html

Barry, Dan, Mike McIntire, and Matthew Rosenberg. 2021. " 'Our President Wants Us Here': The Mob That Stormed the Capitol." *New York Times*. **URL:** https://www.nytimes.com/2021/01/09/us/capitol-rioters.html

Barry, Ellen. 2011. "Former Ukraine Premier Is Jailed for 7 Years." *New York Times*. **URL:** https://www.nytimes.com/2011/10/12/world/europe/yulia-tymoshenko-sentenced-to-seven-years-in-prison.html

Barry, Ellen, Nicholas Bogel-Burroughs, and Dave Philipps. 2021. "Woman Killed in Capitol Embraced Trump and QAnon." *New York Times*. **URL:** https://www.nytimes.com/2021/01/08/us/who-was-ashli-babbitt.html

Bassan-Nygate, Lotem and Chagai M. Weiss. 2020. "Party Competition and Cooperation Shape Affective Polarization: Evidence from Natural and Survey Experiments in Israel." *Working Paper*.

Bateson, Ian. 2014. "Video of First Brawl in Verkhovna Rada Becomes a YouTube Hit." *Kyiv Post*. **URL:** https://www.kyivpost.com/article/content/kyiv-post-plus/video-of-first-brawl-in-verkhovna-rada-becomes-a-youtube-hit-374217.html

Bateson, Ian. 2019. "Volodymyr Zelensky Plays Himself." *The Atlantic*. **URL:** https://www.theatlantic.com/international/archive/2019/09/ukraine-volodymyr-zelensky-ubiquity-transparency/598774/

Batto, Nathan F. and Emily Beaulieu. 2020. "Partisan Conflict and Citizens' Democratic Attitudes: How Partisanship Shapes Reactions to Legislative Brawls." *Journal of Politics* 82(1):315–328.

Bauer, Nichole M., Nathan P. Kalmoe, and Erica B. Russell. 2021. "Candidate aggression and gendered voter evaluations." *Political Psychology*, 43(1): pp. 23–43.

Bayley, Edwin R. 1981. *Joe McCarthy and the Press*. University of Wisconsin Press.

BBC. 2016. "Ukraine MPs Throw Punches in Parliament." BBC News. Accessed September 28, 2020. **URL:** https://www.bbc.com/news/av/world-europe-37985071

BBC. 2019*a*. "Benjamin Netanyahu Becomes Israel's Longest-Serving Leader." BBC News. Accessed November 9, 2020. **URL:** https://www.bbc.com/news/world-middle-east-49043102

BBC. 2019*b*. "Georgiy Gongadze Murder Tied to Late Ukrainian Minister." BBC News. Accessed November 3, 2020. **URL:** https://www.bbc.com/news/world-europe-11297880

BBC. 2020*a*. "Antifa: Trump Says Group Will Be Designated 'Terrorist Organisation'." BBC News. Accessed December 3, 2020. **URL:** https://www.bbc.com/news/world-us-canada-52868295

BBC. 2020*b*. "More US States Begin Lifting Virus Lockdown Orders." BBC News. Accessed December 2, 2020. **URL:** https://www.bbc.com/news/world-us-canada-52435648

BBC. 2022. "Ukraine: Fugitive Putin Ally Medvedchuk Arrested - Security Service." BBC News. Accessed June 1, 2022. **URL:** https://www.bbc.com/news/world-europe-61089039

Beauchamp, Zack. 2021*a*. "The Big Lie Is the GOP's One and Only Truth." Vox. Accessed August 15, 2021. **URL:** https://www.vox.com/22420764/liz-cheney-trump-republicans-democracy-2024

Beauchamp, Zack. 2021*b*. "The Republican Revolt against Democracy, Explained in 13 Charts." Vox. Accessed August 15, 2021. **URL:** https://www.vox.com/policy-and-politics/22274429/republicans-anti-democracy-13-charts

Beaumont, Thomas and Jim Salter. 2021. "Republicans Recoil from Missouri Sen. Hawley after Siege." ABC News. **URL:** https://abcnews.go.com/Politics/wireStory/republicans-recoil-missouri-sen-hawley-siege-75134120

Beeri, Tamar and Yonah Jeremy Bob. 2020. "Miki Zohar Investigated for Alleged Extortion of A-G Mandelblit." *Jerusalem Post*. **URL:** https://www.jpost.com/breaking-news/miki-zohar-investigated-for-alleged-extortion-of-a-g-mandelblit-648114

Bellingcat. 2019*a*. "How to Mainstream Neo-Nazis: A Lesson from Ukraine's New Government." Bellingcat Anti-Equality Monitoring. Accessed November 5, 2020. **URL:** https://www.bellingcat.com/news/uk-and-europe/2019/10/21/how-to-mainstream-neo-nazis-a-lesson-from-ukraines-new-government/

Bellingcat. 2019*b*. "How to Mainstream Neo-Nazis: A Lesson from Ukraine's New Government." Bellingcat Anti-Equality Monitoring. Accessed December 13, 2020. **URL:** https://www.bellingcat.com/news/uk-and-europe/2019/10/21/how-to-mainstream-neo-nazis-a-lesson-from-ukraines-new-government/

Bellingcat. 2019*c*. "Ukraine's Ministry of Veterans Affairs Embraced the Far Right—With Consequences to the U.S." Bellingcat Anti-Equality Monitoring. Accessed November 5, 2020. **URL:** https://www.bellingcat.com/news/uk-and-europe/2019/11/11/ukraines-ministry-of-veterans-affairs-embraced-the-far-right-with-consequences-to-the-u-s/

Bennett, W. Lance. 2011. What's Wrong with Incivility? Civility as the New Censorship in American Politics. In *John Breaux Symposium, "In the Name of Democracy: Leadership, Civility, and Governing in a Polarized Media Environment."* Reilly Center for Media & Public Affairs, Manship School of Mass Communication, Louisiana State University, March. pp. 28–29.

Berger, Jonah. 2011. "Arousal Increases Social Transmission of Information." *Psychological Science* 22(7):891–893.

Berger, Miriam. 2018. "Israel's Hugely Controversial 'Nation-State' Law, Explained." Vox. Accessed November 9, 2020. **URL:** https://www.vox.com/world/2018/7/31/17623978/israel-jewish-nation-state-law-bill-explained-apartheid-netanyahu-democracy

Berman, Russell. 2020. "No, COVID–19 Is Not a Metaphor." *The Atlantic.* **URL:** https://www.theatlantic.com/politics/archive/2020/08/cuomo-new-york-coronavirus/615352/

Bernauer, Thomas and Tobias Böhmelt. 2020. "International Conflict and Cooperation over Freshwater Resources." *Nature Sustainability* 3(5):350–356.

Berry, Jeffrey M. and Sarah Sobieraj. 2013. *The utrage Industry: Political Opinion Media and the New Incivility*. Oxford University Press.

Bespalov, Denis. 2016. "Fight of Vilkul and Parasyuk: All the Details, the Reaction of Social Media." Segodnya. Accessed November 3, 2020. **URL:** https://politics.segodnya.ua/ua/politics/draka-vilkula-i-parasyuka-vse-podrobnosti-reakciya-socsetey-754221.html

Bikus, Zach. 2019. "World-Low 9% of Ukrainians Confident in Government." Gallup. Accessed March 23, 2021. **URL:** https://news.gallup.com/poll/247976/world-low-ukrainians-confident-government.aspx

Blair, Graeme, Alexander Coppock, and Margaret Moor. 2018. When to Worry about Sensitivity Bias: A social reference theory and Evidence from 30 Years of List Experiments." *American Political Science Review,* 114(4):1297–1315.

Blassnig, Sina, Sven Engesser, Nicole Ernst, and Frank Esser. 2019. "Hitting a Nerve: Populist News Articles Lead to More Frequent and More Populist Reader Comments." *Political Communication* 36(4):629–651.

Blum, Rachel M. 2020. *How the Tea Party Captured the GOP: Insurgent Factions in American Politics.* University of Chicago Press.

Bøggild, Troels, Lene Aarøe, and Michael Bang Petersen. 2021. "Citizens as Complicits: Distrust in Politicians and Biased Social Dissemination of Political Information." *American Political Science Review* 115(1):269–285.

Bonikowski, Bart. 2016. "Three Lessons of Contemporary Populism in Europe and the United States." *Brown Journal of World Affairs* 23:9.

Bonikowski, Bart. 2017. "Ethno-Nationalist Populism and the Mobilization of Collective Resentment." *British Journal of Sociology* 68:S181–S213.

Boxell, Levi, Matthew Gentzkow, and Jesse M. Shapiro. 2017. "Greater Internet Use Is Not Associated with Faster Growth in Political Polarization among US Demographic Groups." *Proceedings of the National Academy of Sciences* 114(40):10612–10617.

Brady, William J., Julian A. Wills, Dominic Burkart, John T. Jost, and Jay J. Van Bavel. 2019. "An Ideological Asymmetry in the Diffusion of Moralized Content on Social Media among Political Leaders." *Journal of Experimental Psychology: General* 148(10):1802.

Braley, Alia, Gabriel Lenz, Dhaval Adjodah, Hossein Rahnama, and Alex Pentland. 2021. "The Subversion Dilemma: Why Voters Who Cherish Democracy Vote It Away." Working Paper.

Brandt, Patrick T., John R., Freeman, and Philip A. Schrodt. 2011. "Real Time, Time Series Forecasting of Inter-and Intra-State Political Conflict." *Conflict Management and Peace Science* 28(1):41–64.

Brandt, Patrick T. and John T. Williams. 2006. *Multiple Time Series Models.* Sage Publications.

Brass, Paul R. 1997. *Theft of an Idol: Text and Context in the Representation of Collective Violence.* Princeton University Press.

Bratushcak, Alexey. 2018. "Lyashko Becomes Akhmetov's Mascot." Ukrainskaya Pravda. Accessed September 28, 2020. **URL:** https://blogs.pravda.com.ua/authors/bratushchak/5af3507e21111/

Brennan, Megan and Helen Stubbs. 2020. "News Media Viewed as Biased but Crucial to Democracy." Gallup. Accessed November 16, 2020. **URL:** https://news.gallup.com/poll/316574/news-media-viewed-biased-crucial-democracy.aspx

Brewer, Marilynn B. 1999. "The Psychology of Prejudice: Ingroup Love and Outgroup Hate?" *Journal of Social Issues* 55(3):429–444.

Broockman, David E. and Christopher Skovron. 2018. "Bias in Perceptions of Public Opinion among Political Elites." *American Political Science Review* 112(3):542–563.

Broockman, David E. and Joshua Kalla. 2020. "When and Why Are Campaigns' Persuasive Effects Small? Evidence from the 2020 US Presidential Election." *American Journal of Political Science* Forthcoming

Bryson Taylor, Derrick. 2021. "George Floyd Protests: A Timeline." *New York Times*. **URL:** https://www.nytimes.com/article/george-floyd-protests-timeline.html

Bueno de Mesquita, Ethan and Eric S. Dickson. 2007. "The Propaganda of the Deed: Terrorism, Counterterrorism, and Mobilization." *American Journal of Political Science* 51(2):364–381.

Bullock, John G. 2011. "Elite Influence on Public Opinion in an Informed Electorate." *American Political Science Review* 105(3):496–515.

Bullock, John G., Alan S. Gerber, Seth J. Hill, and Gregory A. Huber. 2015. "Partisan Bias in Factual Beliefs about Politics." *Quarterly Journal of Political Science* 10:519–578.

Burke, Garrett. 2020. "Bill Laimbeer Will Go Down as the Most Hated NBA Player Ever." Sportcasting. Accessed June 13, 2020. **URL:** https://www.sportscasting.com/bill-laimbeer-will-go-down-as-the-most-hated-nba-player-ever/

Bursztyn, Leonardo, Georgy Egorov, and Stefano Fiorin. 2020. "From Extreme to Mainstream: The Erosion of Social Norms." *American Economic Review* 110(11):3522–3548.

Buss, Arnold H. and Mark Perry. 1992. "The Aggression Questionnaire." *Journal of Personality and Social Psychology* 63(3):452.

Call, Charles T. 2021. "No, It's Not a Coup It's a Failed 'Self-Coup' That Will Undermine US Leadership and Democracy Worldwide." *Brookings*. Accessed September 1, 2021. **URL:** https://www.brookings.edu/blog/order-from-chaos/2021/01/08/no-its-not-a-coup-its-a-failed-self-coup-that-will-undermine-us-leadership-and-democracy-worldwide/

Campbell, Angus, Philip E. Converse, Warren E. Miller, and Donald E. Stokes. 1960. *The American Voter*. University of Chicago Press.

Carey, John M. 2021. "Perspective | Did Trump Prove That Governments with Presidents Just Don't Work?" *Washington Post*. Accessed February 5, 2021. **URL:** https://www.washingtonpost.com/outlook/did-trump-prove-that-governments-with-presidents-just-dont-work/2021/02/04/9e9c69f2-5f3f-11eb-9430-e7c77b5b0297_story.html

Carey, John M. and Matthew Soberg Shugart. 1995. "Incentives to Cultivate a Personal Vote: A Rank Ordering of Electoral Formulas." *Electoral Studies* 14(4):417–439.

Carless, Will. 2021. "Nation's Capital Braces for Violence as Extremist Groups Converge to Protest Trump's Election Loss." *USA Today*. **URL:** https://www.usatoday.com/story/news/nation/2021/01/04/january-6-dc-protests-against-election-certification-could-violent/4132441001/

Carpenter, Michael. 2019. "The Oligarchs Who Lost Ukraine and Won Washington." *Foreign Affairs*. **URL:** https://www.foreignaffairs.com/articles/russia-fsu/2019-11-26/oligarchs-who-lost-ukraine-and-won-washington

Carr Smyth, Julie. 2021. "Ohio GOP Censures 10 Republicans Who Voted to Impeach Trump." Associated Press. Accessed August 15, 2021. **URL:** https://apnews.com/article/donald-trump-ohio-censures-trump-impeachment-impeachments-578073278925ed09e4eb3bc6639e32a6

Carroll, Oliver. 2015. "Inside Ukraine's Violent, Messy Battle for Power." Politico Europe. Accessed December 11, 2020. **URL:** https://www.politico.eu/article/ukraine-saakashvili-poroshenko-crisis-donbas-sanctions/

Carroll, Oliver. 2018. "The Return of the Godfather: How Putin's Best Friend in Ukraine Is Staging an Improbable Comeback." Independent. Accessed November 3, 2020. **URL:** https://

www.independent.co.uk/news/world/europe/putin-russia-godfather-viktor-medvedchuk-us-sanctions-ukraine-politics-a8515456.html

Carroll, Oliver. 2019. "Ukrainian Parliament Approves Measures to Forcibly Castrate Paedophiles." Independent. Accessed December 13, 2020. **URL:** https://www.independent.co.uk/news/world/europe/ukraine-paedophiles-chemical-castration-sex-offenders-a9002791.html

Cassese, Erin C. 2019. "Partisan Dehumanization in American Politics." *Political Behavior* pp. 1–22.

Castronuovo, Celine. 2021. "Madison Cawthorn Doesn't Regret Participating in Jan. 6 'Stop the Steal' Rally." The Hill. Accessed February 10, 2021. **URL:** https://thehill.com/homenews/house/537440-madison-cawthorn-doesnt-regret-participating-in-jan-6-stop-the-steal-rally?rl=1

Censky, Abigail. 2020. "Heavily Armed Protesters Gather again at Michigan Capitol to Decry Stay-at-Home Order." National Public Radio. Accessed December 2, 2020. **URL:** https://www.npr.org/2020/05/14/855918852/heavily-armed-protesters-gather-again-at-michigans-capitol-denouncing-home-order%7D

Chapple, Amos. 2017. "Ukrainian Politics: The Greatest Hits." Radio Free Europe/Radio Liberty. Accessed December 11, 2020. **URL:** https://www.rferl.org/a/fighting-ukraine-politics-in-pictures/28771390.html

Charles, Ron. 2018. "Perspective: What Is Bigfoot Erotica? A Virginia Congressional Candidate Accused Her Opponent of Being Into It." *Washington Post.* **URL:** https://www.washingtonpost.com/entertainment/books/what-is-bigfoot-erotica-a-virginia-congressional-candidate-accused-her-opponent-of-being-into-it/2018/07/30/dc11b5fa-93e8-11e8-810c-5fa705927d54_story.html

Chaturvedi, Ashish. 2005. "Rigging Elections with Violence." *Public Choice* 125(1–2):189–202.

Chen, Shawna. 2021. "The Countries with the Most Politicians Named in the Pandora Papers." Axios. Accessed October 15, 2021. **URL:** https://www.axios.com/pandora-papers-politicians-countries-d8ca46fc-8422-4d39-b354-aa1de2a24a9f.html

Cheng, Amy. 2022. "How 50 Days of Russia's War in Ukraine Changed the World." *Washington Post.* **URL:** https://www.washingtonpost.com/world/2022/04/14/russia-ukraine-war-50-days-economy-sanctions-refugees/

Chenoweth, Erica and Jeremy Pressman. 2020. "This Summer's Black Lives Matter Protesters Were Overwhelmingly Peaceful, Our Research Finds." *Washington Post.* **URL:** https://www.washingtonpost.com/politics/2020/10/16/this-summers-black-lives-matter-protesters-were-overwhelming-peaceful-our-research-finds/

Chenoweth, Erica, Maria J. Stephan, and Maria J. Stephan. 2011. *Why Civil Resistance Works: The Strategic Logic of Nonviolent Conflict.* Columbia University Press.

Chivers, C. J. 2014. "A Kiev Question: What Became of the Missing?" *New York Times.* **URL:** https://www.nytimes.com/2014/03/10/world/europe/a-kiev-question-what-became-of-the-missing.html

Churanova, Elena. 2018. "Every Fifth News on the Internet Is 'In Question'. What Do We Read in Online Media?" Instytut Masovoyi Informatsiyi (Institute of Mass Media). Accessed December 5, 2020. **URL:** https://imi.org.ua/monitorings/kozhna-p-yata-novyna-v-interneti-pid-pytannyam-scho-chytajemo-v-onlajn-media-i28332

Cillizza, Chris. 2020. "Marco Rubio Goes Full Trump on Election Eve." Hungarian Spectrum. Accessed June 25, 2021. **URL:** https://edition.cnn.com/2020/11/02/politics/marco-rubio-donald-trump-election-2020/index.html

Clarke, Nick, Will Jennings, Jonathan Moss, and Gerry Stoker. 2018. *The Good Politician: Folk Theories, Political Interaction, and the Rise of Anti-politics.* Cambridge University Press.

Cleveland, Will. 2021. "Dominic Pezzola Held without Bail on Capitol Riot Charges, Says He Was Duped by Trump." *Rochester Democrat and Chronicle.* **URL:** https://www.democratandchronicle.com/story/news/2021/02/10/dominic-pezzola-rochester-ny-charged-in-capitol-riot-said-he-was-duped-by-trump/4361809001/

Cline Center. 2021. "It Was an Attempted Coup: The Cline Center's Coup D'etat Project Categorizes the January 6, 2021 Assault on the US Capitol." Cline Center for Advanced Social Research. Accessed February 2, 2021. **URL:** https://databank.illinois.edu/datasets/IDB-0433268

Cohen, Josh. 2015. "In the Battle between Ukraine and Russian Separatists, Shady Private Armies Take the Field." Reuters. Accessed November 5, 2020. **URL:** https://www.reuters.com/article/idIN60927080220150505

Cohen, Josh. 2018. "Not a Good Day for Ukraine." Atlantic Council. Accessed November 4, 2020. **URL:** https://www.atlanticcouncil.org/blogs/ukrainealert/not-a-good-day-for-ukraine/

Cohen, Joshua. 2017. "Opinion: Ukraine's Ultra-right Militias Are Challenging the Government to a Showdown." *Washington Post*. **URL:** https://www.washingtonpost.com/news/democracy-post/wp/2017/06/15/ukraines-ultra-right-militias-are-challenging-the-government-to-a-showdown/

Colborne, Michael. 2019. "Ukrainians Demand Answers Year after Murder of Kateryna Handziuk." Al Jazeera. Accessed December 11, 2020. **URL:** https://www.aljazeera.com/features/2019/11/7/ukrainians-demand-answers-year-after-murder-of-kateryna-handziuk

Cole, Devan. 2020. "Top House Judiciary Republican Makes Unfounded Claim That Democrats Are 'in Love with Terrorists.'" CNN Politics. Accessed November 4, 2020. **URL:** https://www.cnn.com/2020/01/09/politics/doug-collins-democrats-terrorists/index.html

Collier, Paul and Pedro C. Vicente. 2012. "Violence, Bribery, and Fraud: The Political Economy of Elections in Sub-Saharan Africa." *Public Choice* 153(1):117–147.

Collins, Randall. 2009. *Violence: A Micro-sociological Theory*. Princeton University Press.

Collinson, Stephen. 2022. "The Damning Case against Trump That the Jan. 6 Committee Has Uncovered—and What Comes Next." CNN. Accessed August 14, 2022. **URL:** https://www.cnn.com/2022/07/22/politics/trump-jan-6-hearings-damning-case/index.html

Concepcion, Jason. 2017. "Last of a Dying Breed." The Ringer. Accessed June 13, 2020. **URL:** https://www.theringer.com/2017/2/6/16047014/what-happened-to-the-nba-enforcer-2ea97992e534

Congressional Globe. 1858. "Congressional Globe, House of Representatives, 35th Congress, 1st Session (pg 603)." Library of Congress. Accessed November 3, 2020. **URL:** https://memory.loc.gov/cgi-bin/ampage?collId=llcg&fileName=045/llcg045.db&recNum=666

Cook, Jonathan. 2008. "The Acre Riots." Counterpunch. Accessed May 1, 2020. **URL:** https://www.counterpunch.org/2008/10/16/the-acre-riots/

Coppock, Alexander. 2017. "Did Shy Trump Supporters Bias the 2016 Polls? Evidence from a Nationally-Representative List Experiment." *Statistics, Politics and Policy* 8(1):29–40.

Costa, Mia. 2021. "Ideology, not affect: What Americans want from political representation." *American Journal of Political Science* 65(2):342–358.

Cox, Ana Marie. 2005. "How Howard Stern Became 'King of all Media.'" WIRED. Accessed November 5, 2020. **URL:** https://www.wired.com/2005/03/stern/

Coynash, Halya. 2014. "6 Year Sentences in Surreal Vasylkiv 'Terrorist Trial.'" Kharkiv Human Rights Protection Group. Accessed December 11, 2020. **URL:** https://khpg.org/en/1389380286

Crockett, Molly J. 2017. "Moral Outrage in the Digital Age." *Nature Human Behaviour* 1(11): 769–771.

Cummings, William. 2019. "Trump Tells Congresswomen to 'Go Back' to the 'Crime Infested Places from Which They Came.'" *USA Today*. **URL:** https://www.usatoday.com/story/news/politics/arizona/2019/07/14/president-donald-trump-tells-democratic-congresswomen-go-back/1728525001/

Curl, Joseph. 2020. "Joe Biden's Basement Strategy Really IS His Plan." *Washington Times*. **URL:** https://www.washingtontimes.com/news/2020/oct/27/joe-bidens-basement-strategy-really-is-his-plan/

Daly, Matthew and Michael Balsamo. 2021. "Deadly Siege Focuses Attention on Capitol Police." AP News. Accessed June 15, 2021. **URL:** https://apnews.com/article/capitol-police-death-brian-sicknick-46933a828d7b12de7e3d5620a8a04583

Danielson, Chris. 2013. *The Color of Politics: Racism in the American Political Arena Today*. ABC-CLIO.

D'Anieri, Paul. 2015. *Understanding Ukrainian Politics: Power, Politics, and Institutional Design: Power, Politics, and Institutional Design*. Routledge.

Darden, Keith. 2009. "Ukraine's Post-Maidan Struggles: II. Free Speech in a Time of War." *Politics, & Society* 36(1):35–59.

Davenport, Christian. 2009. *Media Bias, Perspective, and State Repression: The Black Panther Party*. Cambridge University Press.

Davidzon, Vladislav. 2015. "Spurned Ukrainian Oligarch Heads to America." *Tablet Magazin*. **URL:** https://www.tabletmag.com/sections/news/articles/spurned-ukrainian-oligarch-heads-to-america

Davis, William P. 2018. "'Enemy of the People': Trump Breaks Out This Phrase during Moments of Peak Criticism." *New York Times*. **URL:** https://www.nytimes.com/2018/07/19/business/media/trump-media-enemy-of-the-people.html

De Dreu, Carsten K.W. and Jörg Gross. 2019. "Revisiting the Form and Function of Conflict: Neurobiological, Psychological, and Cultural Mechanisms for Attack and Defense within and between Groups." *Behavioral and Brain Sciences* 42.

De Figueiredo, Rui, Barry Weingast, Barbara Walter, and Jack Snyder. 1998. "The politics of interpretation: Rationality, culture, and transition." *Politics & Society* 26(4):603–642.

De Mesquita, Bruce Bueno, Alastair Smith, Randolph M. Siverson, and James D. Morrow. 2005. *The Logic of Political Survival*. MIT Press.

Bueno de Mesquita, Ethan Bueno. 2010. "Regime Change and Revolutionary Entrepreneurs." *American Political Science Review* 104(3):446–466.

de Moraes, Lisa. 2018. "Donald Trump Campaigns in Houston for 'Beautiful Ted' Cruz." Deadline. Accessed December 6, 2020. **URL:** https://deadline.com/2018/10/donald-trump-ted-cruz-campaigns-houston-1202487537/

DellaVigna, Stefano and Ethan Kaplan. 2007. "The Fox News Effect: Media Bias and Voting." *Quarterly Journal of Economics* 122(3):1187–1234.

Democracy House. 2019. "Prospects of Oleg Lyashko in 2019: A Future Parliamentary Speaker or a Political Outcast?" Democracy House Ukraine. Accessed September 6, 2020. **URL:** http://www.democracyhouse.com.ua/en/2019/prospects-of-oleg-lyashko-in-2019-a-future-parliamentary-speaker-or-a-political-outcast/

Denham, Hannah. 2021. "These Are the Platforms That Have Banned Trump and His Allies." *Washington Post*. **URL:** https://www.washingtonpost.com/technology/2021/01/11/trump-banned-social-media/

DeWall, C. Nathan, Craig A. Anderson, and Brad J. Bushman. 2011. "The General Aggression Model: Theoretical Extensions to Violence." *Psychology of Violence* 1(3):245.

Dezenski, Lauren. 2020. "GOP House Incumbents Are Leaving at a Record Pace." CNN Politics. Accessed March 24, 2021. **URL:** https://edition.cnn.com/2020/07/01/politics/house-gop-losses-retirements-trump/index.html

Diamond, Jeremy. 2015*a*. "Trump on Protester: 'Maybe He Should Have Been Roughed Up.'" CNN Politics. Accessed November 4, 2020. **URL:** https://www.cnn.com/2015/11/22/politics/donald-trump-black-lives-matter-protester-confrontation/index.html

Diamond, Larry. 2015*b*. "Facing Up to the Democratic Recession." *Journal of Democracy* 26(1): 141–155.

Dniprovska Panorama. 2017. "'Kremlin Prostitutes Have No Place in Ukraine'—Dmitry Yarosh." Dniprovska Panorama. Accessed November 5, 2020. **URL:** https://dnpr.com.ua/post/kremlevskim-prostitutkam-ne-mesto-v-ukraine-dmitrij-jarosh

Dolan, David and Gulsen Solaker. 2016. "Turkey Rounds Up Plot Suspects after Thwarting Coup against Erdogan." Reuters. Accessed September 20, 2021. **URL:** https://www.reuters.com/article/us-turkey-security-primeminister-idUSKCN0ZV2HK

Douek, Daniel. 2016. "Lawmaker Backs Segregated Jewish, Arab Maternity Wards." *The Times of Israel*. **URL:** https://www.timesofisrael.com/lawmaker-backs-segregated-jewish-arab-maternity-wards/#gs.fpi2v7

Douglas, Karen M., Joseph E. Uscinski, Robbie M. Sutton, Aleksandra Cichocka, Turkay Nefes, Chee Siang Ang, and Farzin Deravi. 2019. "Understanding Conspiracy Theories." *Political Psychology* 40:3–35.

Dovere, Edward-Isaac. 2020. "How a Georgia Republican Hit His Breaking Point with Trump." *The Atlantic*. **URL:** https://www.theatlantic.com/politics/archive/2020/12/gabe-sterling-georgia-republican-trump/617295/

Dowling, Conor M. and Yanna Krupnikov. 2016. "The Effects of Negative advertising." In *Oxford Research Encyclopedia of Politics*. Oxford University Press.

Downs, George W. and David M. Rocke. 1994. "Conflict, Agency, and Gambling for Resurrection: The Principal-Agent Problem Goes to War." *American Journal of Political Science* pp. 362–380.

Draper, Robert. 2022. "The Arizona Republican Party's Anti-Democracy Experiment." *New York Times* Accessed August 17, 2022. **URL:** https://www.nytimes.com/2022/08/15/magazine/arizona-republicans-democracy.html

Dreyfus, Emmanuel. 2020. "Six Years after Crimea: The Outlook for a 'Russia-Friendly Political Establishment in Ukraine." Wilson Center: Focus Ukraine. Accessed October 22, 2021. **URL:** https://www.wilsoncenter.org/blog-post/six-years-after-crimea-outlook-russia-friendly-political-establishment-ukraine

Dunning, Thad. 2011. "Fighting and Voting: Violent Conflict and Electoral Politics." *Journal of Conflict Resolution* 55(3):327–339.

Edmondson, Catie and Luke Broadwater. 2021. "Before Capitol Riot, Republican Lawmakers Fanned the Flames." *New York Times*. **URL:** https://www.nytimes.com/2021/01/11/us/politics/republicans-capitol-riot.html

Edwards, Griffin Sims and Stephen Rushin. 2018. "The Effect of President Trump's Election on Hate Crimes." *Available at SSRN 3102652*.

Ehley, Brianna. 2016. "Franken Jokes Cruz is 'Lovechild of Joe McCarthy and Dracula.'" Politico. Accessed November 16, 2020. **URL:** https://www.politico.com/story/2016/04/al-franken-ted-cruz-jokes-222212

Emerson, Kirk, Alexandra P. Joosse, Frank Dukes, Wendy Willis, and Kim Hodge Cowgill. 2015. "Disrupting Deliberative Discourse: Strategic Political Incivility at the Local Level." *Conflict Resolution Quarterly* 32(3):299–324.

Engelhardt, Andrew M. 2021. "The content of their coverage: contrasting racially conservative and liberal elite rhetoric." *Politics, Groups, and Identities*, 9(5):935–954.

Engelhardt, Andrew M and Stephen M Utych. 2020. "Grand old (Tailgate) party? Partisan discrimination in apolitical settings." *Political Behavior* 42(3):769–789.

Engelhardt, Andrew M. et al. 2019. "Trumped by Race: Explanations for Race's Influence on Whites' Votes in 2016." *Quarterly Journal of Political Science* 14(3):313–328.

Enli, Gunn. 2017. "Twitter as Arena for the Authentic Outsider: Exploring the Social Media Campaigns of Trump and Clinton in the 2016 US Presidential Election." *European Journal of Communication* 32(1):50–61.

Enos, Ryan D., Aaron R. Kaufman, and Melissa L. Sands. 2019. "Can Violent Protest Change Local Policy Support? Evidence from the Aftermath of the 1992 Los Angeles Riot." *American Political Science Review* 113(4):1012–1028.

Estrin, Daniel. 2020. "What to Know as Israel's Netanyahu Goes on Trial for Corruption Charges." National Public Radio. Accessed December 14, 2020. **URL:** https://www.npr.org/2020/05/23/860166840/what-to-know-as-israels-netanyahu-goes-on-trial-for-corruption-charges

Evans, Heather K., Sean Smith, Alexis Gonzales, and Kayla Strouse. 2017. "Mudslinging on Twitter during the 2014 Election." *Social Media+ Society* 3(2):2056305117704408.

Faryna, Oksana. 2011. "Trouble Brews at Akhmetov's Segodnya Daily." *Kyiv Post*. **URL:** https://www.kyivpost.com/article/content/business/trouble-brews-at-akhmetovs-segodnya-daily-119059.html

Fearon, James D. and David D. Laitin. 1996. "Explaining Interethnic Cooperation." *American Political Science Review* pp. 715–735.

Fearon, James D. and David D. Laitin. 2000. "Violence and the Social Construction of Ethnic Identity." *International Organization* pp. 845–877.

Fearon, James D. and David D. Laitin. 2003. "Ethnicity, Insurgency, and Civil War." *American Political Science Review* pp. 75–90.

Fenno, Richard F. 1978. *Home Style: House Members in Their Districts*. Little Brown.

Fenster, Mark. 1999. *Conspiracy Theories: Secrecy and Power in American Culture*. University of Minnesota Press.

Ferling, John. 2004. *Adams vs. Jefferson: The Tumultuous Election of 1800*. Oxford University Press.

Finkel, Eli J., Christopher A. Bail, Mina Cikara, Peter H. Ditto, Shanto Iyengar, Samara Klar, Lilliana Mason, Mary C. McGrath, Brendan Nyhan, David G. Rand, et al. 2020. "Political Sectarianism in America." *Science* 370(6516):533–536.

Fischer, Jordan, Eric Flack, and Stephanie Wilson. 2021. "'Are You an American!?': New Video Shows New Jersey Man Punching Police during Capitol Riot." WUSA 9. Accessed August 10, 2021. **URL:** https://www.wusa9.com/article/news/national/capitol-riots/are-you-an-american-new-video-shows-new-jersey-man-scott-fairlamb-punching-police-during-capitol-riot-january-6-back-the-blue/65-8e604fd9-cda1-4ab6-9561-da5709215aaf

Flynn, D.J., Brendan Nyhan, and Jason Reifler. 2017. "The Nature and Origins of Misperceptions: Understanding False and Unsupported Beliefs about Politics." *Political Psychology* 38: 127–150.

Flynn, Meagan. 2021. "D.C. Jail Officials Turn Away GOP Members of Congress Who Showed Up to Check on Jan. 6 Suspects." *Washington Post*. **URL:** https://www.washingtonpost.com/local/dc-politics/dc-jail-gop/2021/07/29/8362d17e-f096-11eb-bf80-e3877d9c5f06_story.html

Foa, Roberto Stefan and Yascha Mounk. 2016. "The Danger of Deconsolidation: The Democratic Disconnect." *Journal of Democracy* 27(3):5–17.

Foner, Eric. 1995. *Free Soil, Free Labor, Free Men: The Ideology of the Republican Party Before the Civil War: With a New Introductory Essay*. Oxford University Press.

Forgey, Quint. 2022. "The Damning Case against Trump That the Jan. 6 Committee Has Uncovered—and What Comes Next." Politico. Accessed August 12, 2022. **URL:** https://www.politico.com/news/2022/01/28/ukrainian-president-downplays-imminent-invasion-00003219

Foxall, Andrew and Lincoln Pigman. 2017. "Ukraine's Stalled Revolution." *Foreign Affairs*.

France 24. 2010. "Former President Testifies in Tymoshenko Trial." France 24. **URL:** https://www.france24.com/en/20110817-europe-ukraine-justice-former-president-testify-tymoshenko-trial-russia-gas-deal-yushchenko-yanukovich

France 24. 2019. "Vakarchuk: The Rock Star Shaking Up Ukrainian Politics." France 24. Accessed March 24, 2021. **URL:** https://www.france24.com/en/20190721-vakarchuk-rock-star-shaking-ukrainian-politics

Francis, Diane. 2019. "Why Poroshenko Doesn't Deserve a Second Term." Atlantic Council. Accessed November 5, 2020. **URL:** https://www.atlanticcouncil.org/blogs/ukrainealert/why-poroshenko-doesn-t-deserve-a-second-term/

Freedland, Jonathan. 2020. "The Assassination of Yitzhak Rabin: 'He Never Knew It Was One of His People Who Shot Him in the Back.'" *The Guardian*. Accessed November 9, 2020. **URL:** https://www.theguardian.com/world/2020/oct/31/assassination-yitzhak-rabin-never-knew-his-people-shot-him-in-back

Freelon, Deen, Charlton D. McIlwain, and Meredith Clark. 2016. "Beyond the Hashtags:# Ferguson,# Blacklivesmatter, and the Online Struggle for Offline Justice." Center for Media & Social Impact, American University, Forthcoming.

Freeman, Joanne B. 1999. "The Election of 1800: A Study in the Logic of Political Change." *Yale Law Journal* 108(8):1959–1994.

Freeman, Joanne B. 2018. *The Field of Blood: Violence in Congress and the Road to Civil War*. Farrar, Straus and Giroux.

Freking, Kevin. 2021. "Trump Tweets Words 'He Won'; Says Vote Rigged, Not Conceding." Associated Press. Accessed August 10, 2021. **URL:** https://apnews.com/article/donald-trump-tweets-he-won-not-conceding-9ce22e9dc90577f7365d150c151a91c7

Fridkin, Kim and Patrick Kenney. 2019. *Taking Aim at Attack Advertising: Understanding the Impact of Negative Campaigning in US Senate Races*. Oxford University Press.

Fried, Richard M. 1991. *Nightmare in Red: The McCarthy Era in Perspective*. Oxford University Press.

Friedman, Matti. 2019. "The One Thing No Israeli Wants to Discuss." *New York Times*. **URL:** https://www.nytimes.com/2019/09/09/opinion/israel-election-netanyahu.html

Frimer, Jeremy A. and Linda J. Skitka. 2018. "The Montagu Principle: Incivility Decreases Politicians' Public Approval, Even with Their Political Base." *Journal of Personality and Social psychology*.

Frimer, Jeremy A. and Linda J. Skitka. 2020. "Americans Hold Their Political Leaders to a Higher Discursive Standard Than Rank-and-File Co-partisans." *Journal of Experimental Social Psychology* 86:103907.

Gagnon, Valère Philip. 2006. *The Myth of Ethnic War: Serbia and Croatia in the 1990s*. Cornell University Press.

Gall, Carlotta. 2019. "Ukrainian Orthodox Christians Formally Break from Russia." *New York Times*. **URL:** https://www.nytimes.com/2019/01/06/world/europe/orthodox-church-ukraine-russia.html

Gambino, Lauren. 2020. "Joe Biden Officially Clinches Democratic Presidential Nomination." *The Guardian*. **URL:** https://www.theguardian.com/us-news/2020/jun/05/joe-biden-clinches-democratic-presidential-nomination

Gandrud, Christopher. 2016. "Two Sword Lengths Apart: Credible Commitment Problems and Physical Violence in Democratic National Legislatures." *Journal of Peace Research* 53(1): 130–145.

Gangel, Jamie, Jeremy Herb, Marshall Cohen, Elizabeth Stuart, and Barbara Starr. 2021. "'They're Not Going to F**King Succeed': Top Generals Feared Trump Would Attempt a Coup after Election, According to New Book." CNN Politics. Accessed August 10, 2021. **URL:** https://www.cnn.com/2021/07/14/politics/donald-trump-election-coup-new-book-excerpt/index.html

Gedeon, Joseph. 2022. "10 House Republicans Voted to Impeach Trump. Cheney's Loss Means Only 2 Made It Past Their Primaries." Politico. Accessed August 17, 2022. **URL:** https://www.politico.com/news/2022/08/13/cheney-10-house-republicans-trump-impeachment-00050991

Geer, John G. 2008. *In Defense of Negativity: Attack ads in Presidential Campaigns*. University of Chicago Press.

Gerring, John. 2016. *Case Study Research: Principles and Practices*. Cambridge University Press.

Gerstlé, Jacques and Alessandro Nai. 2019. "Negativity, Emotionality and Populist Rhetoric in Election Campaigns Worldwide, and Their Effects on Media Attention and Electoral Success." *European Journal of Communication* 34(4):410–444.

Gervais, Bryan T. 2014. "Following the News? Reception of Uncivil Partisan Media and the Use of Incivility in Political Expression." *Political Communication* 31(4):564–583.

Gervais, Bryan T. 2015. "Incivility Online: Affective and Behavioral Reactions to Uncivil Political Posts in a Web-Based Experiment." *Journal of Information Technology & Politics* 12(2): 167–185.

Gervais, Bryan T. and Irwin L. Morris. 2018. *Reactionary Republicanism: How the Tea Party in the House Paved the Way for Trump's Victory*. Oxford University Press.

Gibson, James L. 1989. "Understandings of Justice: Institutional Legitimacy, Procedural Justice, and Political Tolerance." *Law and Society Review* 23(3):469–496.

Gillman, Todd J. 2013. "Q&A with Sen. Ted Cruz." *Dallas Morning News*. **URL:** https://www.dallasnews.com/news/politics/2013/03/24/qa-with-sen-ted-cruz/

Glaeser, Edward L. 2005. "The Political Economy of Hatred." *Quarterly Journal of Economics* 120(1):45–86.

Glavnoe. 2017. "The Maidan Brought to the Surface Many Destructive and Useless Idiots - Filatov." Glavnoe Dnipro. Accessed September 9, 2022 **URL:** http://glavnoe.dp.ua/articles/Majdan-vynes-na-poverhnost-mnogo-destruktivnyh-i-bespoleznyh-idiotov-Filatov/

Godfrey, Elaine. 2021. "It Was Supposed to Be So Much Worse." *The Atlantic*. **URL:** https://www.theatlantic.com/politics/archive/2021/01/trump-rioters-wanted-more-violence-worse/617614/

Gold, Hadas. 2016. "Survey: Donald Trump Supporters Most Aggressive Online." Politico. Accessed October 24, 2020. **URL:** https://www.politico.com/blogs/on-media/2016/05/survey-donald-trump-supporters-most-aggressive-online-222912

Goldberg, Jeffrey. 2020. "James Mattis Denounces President Trump, Describes Him as a Threat to the Constitution." *The Atlantic*. **URL:** https://www.theatlantic.com/politics/archive/2020/06/james-mattis-denounces-trump-protests-militarization/612640/

Goldenberg, Tia. 2020. "Arrests and Clashes Follow Anti-Netanyahu Protests in Israel." Associated Press. Accessed December 14, 2020. **URL:** https://apnews.com/article/virus-outbreak-israel-international-news-middle-east-benjamin-netanyahu-8830464bdd80827797dfa68687198316

Goldstein, Joshua S. 1992. "A Conflict-Cooperation Scale for WEIS Events Data." *Journal of Conflict Resolution* 36(2):369–385.

Goncharenko, Roman. 2014. "Titushki—the Ukrainian President'S Hired Strongmen." Deutsche Welle. Accessed November 4, 2020. **URL:** https://www.dw.com/en/titushki-the-ukrainian-presidents-hired-strongmen/a-17443078

Gongadze, Myroslava. 2020. "Ukraine Media Leaders Sound Alarm on Oligarchical Control at Virtual VOA Town Hall." VOA. Accessed June 10, 2020. **URL:** https://www.voanews.com/a/press

Goodman, Ryan, Mari Dugas, and Nicholas Tonckens. 2021. "Incitement Timeline: Year of Trump's Actions Leading to the Attack on the Capitol." Reiss Center on Law and Security at New York University School of Law: Just Security. Accessed February 10, 2021. **URL:** https://www.justsecurity.org/74138/incitement-timeline-year-of-trumps-actions-leading-to-the-attack-on-the-capitol/

Gordiienko, Olena. 2015. "Fresh Fighting in Ukraine's Parliament (VIDEO)." *Kyiv Post*. **URL:** https://www.kyivpost.com/article/content/ukraine-politics/fight-in-the-parliament-video-2-380475.html

Graham, David A. 2019. "Trump's White Identity Politics Appeals to Two Different Groups." *The Atlantic*. **URL:** https://www.theatlantic.com/ideas/archive/2019/08/who-does-trumps-white-identity-politics-reach/595189/

Graham, Matthew H. and Milan W. Svolik. 2020. "Democracy in America? Partisanship, Polarization, and the Robustness of Support for Democracy in the United States." *American Political Science Review* 114(2):392–409.

Gray, Ian. 2012. "DCCC Calls on Voters to 'Fire the Tea Party Congress'." Huffington Post. Accessed November 16 2020. **URL:** https://www.huffpost.com/entry/dccc-tea-party-congress_n_1913553

Grimmer, Justin. 2013. *Representational Style in Congress: What Legislators Say and Why It Matters*. Cambridge University Press.

Groeling, Tim. 2008. "Who's the Fairest of Them All? An Empirical Test for Partisan Bias on ABC, CBS, NBC, and Fox News." *Presidential Studies Quarterly* 38(4):631–657.

Groeling, Tim. 2010. *When Politicians Attack: Party Cohesion in the Media*. Cambridge University Press.

Grossman, Guy, Yotam Margalit, and Tamar Mitts. 2022. "How the ultra-rich use media ownership as a political investment." Forthcoming.

Grytsenko, Oksana. 2018. "Poll: Ukrainians Say Bribe Problem Worse Now than in 2015." *Kyiv Post*. **URL:** https://www.kyivpost.com/ukraine-politics/poll-ukrainians-say-bribe-problem-worse-now-than-in-2015.html

Grytsenko, Oksana. 2019. "Investigation Reveals More Links between Zelenskiy's Team and Oligarch Kolomoisky." *Kyiv Post*. **URL:** https://www.kyivpost.com/ukraine-politics/investigation-reveals-more-links-between-zelenskiys-team-and-oligarch-kolomoisky.html

Grytsenko, Oksana and Shaun Walker. 2014. "Ukraine's New Parliament Sits for First Time." *The Guardian*. **URL:** https://www.theguardian.com/world/2014/nov/27/ukraine-new-parliament–war-east-mps

Grzymala-Busse, Anna. 2019. "How Populists Rule: The Consequences for Democratic Governance." *Polity* 51(4):707–717.

GU Institute of Politics and Public Service. 2019*a*. "Georgetown Institute of Politics and Public Service Battleground Poll: October 2019." Georgetown Institute of Politics and Public Service. Accessed October 15, 2020. **URL:** https://politics.georgetown.edu/battleground-poll/october-2019/

GU Institute of Politics and Public Service. 2019*b*. "Georgetown Institute of Politics and Public Service Battleground Poll: October 2019." Georgetown Institute of Politics and Public Service. Accessed October 15, 2020. **URL:** https://politics.georgetown.edu/2019/04/24/new-survey-overwhelming-number-of-americans-frustrated-by-incivility-in-politics-but-conflicted-on-desire-for-compromise-and-common-ground/

Guiler, Kimberly. 2016. "Towards Erdogan and the East: Conspiracies and Public Perception in Post-coup Turkey." *Contemporary Turkish Politics*, POMEPS Studies 22:28.

Haaretz. 2016. "Ukraine Investigating Trump Campaign's Paul Manafort for Inciting Crimean Separatism." *Haaretz*. **URL:** https://www.haaretz.com/world-news/ukraine-investigating-trump-campaign-chair-for-inciting-crimean-separatism-1.5426422

Haaretz. 2020*a*. "Israel Election: Netanyahu Denied It, but Evidence Proves He Spoke to Rabbi Who Recorded Gantz Adviser Blasting Him." *Haaretz*. **URL:** https://www.haaretz.com/israel-news/elections/.premium-israel-election-netanyahu-spoke-to-rabbi-who-recorded-gantz-adviser-blasting-him-1.8614509

Haaretz. 2020*b*. "Israel Ranks Third in Highest Daily Infection Rate among European Countries, WHO Says." *Haaretz*. Accessed December 14, 2020. **URL:** https://www.haaretz.com/israel-news/coronavirus-israel-breaking-live-updates-july-1.8970693

Habermas, Jürgen. 1998. "Between facts and norms: An author's reflections." *Denver University Law Review* 76(4):937–942.

Hacker, Jacob S. and Paul Pierson. 2020. *Let Them Eat Tweets: How the Right Rules in an Age of Extreme Inequality*. Liveright Publishing.

Hafner-Burton, Emilie M., D. Alex Hughes, and David G. Victor. 2013. "The Cognitive Revolution and the Political Psychology of Elite Decision Making." *Perspectives on Politics* 11(2):368–386.

Hafner-Burton, Emilie M., Neil Narang, and Brian C. Rathbun. 2019. "Introduction: What Is Populist Nationalism and Why Does It Matter?" *Journal of Politics* 81(2):707–711.

Halbfinger, David M. 2019. "Israel's Netanyahu Indicted on Charges of Fraud, Bribery and Breach of Trust." *New York Times*. **URL:** https://www.nytimes.com/2019/11/21/world/middleeast/netanyahu-corruption-indicted.html

Halbfinger, David M. 2020*a*. "Deadlocked after 3 Elections, Israel Seeks Ways to Avert a 4th." *New York Times*. **URL:** https://www.nytimes.com/2020/03/04/world/middleeast/israel-election-netanyahu.html

Halbfinger, David M. 2020*b*. "A Would-Be Netanyahu Nemesis Snipes from the Sidelines." *New York Times*. **URL:** https://www.nytimes.com/2020/06/04/world/middleeast/israel-liberman-netanyahu-annexation-west-bank.html

Halbfinger, David M. and Photographs by Dan Balilty. 2020. "Israeli Slugfest: The Campaign in Pictures." *New York Times*. **URL:** https://www.nytimes.com/2020/03/01/world/middleeast/israeli-campaign-in-pictures.html

Hale, Henry E. 2010. "Ukraine: The Uses of Divided Power." *Journal of Democracy* 21(3):84–98.

Hall, Andrew B. 2019. *Who Wants to Run?: How the Devaluing of Political Office Drives Polarization*. University of Chicago Press.

Hall, Madison, Skye Gould, Rebecca Harrington, Jacob Shamsian, Azmi Haroun, Taylor Ardrey, and Erin Snodgrass. 2022. "At Least 846 People Have Been Charged in the Capitol

Insurrection So Far." Insider. Accessed June 3, 2022. **URL:** https://www.insider.com/all-the-us-capitol-pro-trump-riot-arrests-charges-names-2021-1

Haney-López, Ian. 2015. *Dog Whistle Politics: How Coded Racial Appeals Have Reinvented Racism and Wrecked the Middle Class*. Oxford University Press.

Hansen, Suzy. 2017. "Inside Turkey's Purge." *New York Times*. **URL:** https://www.nytimes.com/2017/04/13/magazine/inside-turkeys-purge.html

Harding, Luke. 2022. "Former Ukraine President Returns to Kyiv to Face Treason Charges." *The Guardian*. **URL:** https://www.theguardian.com/world/2022/jan/17/petro-poroshenko-former-ukraine-president-kyiv-treason-case

Haring, Melinda. 2020. "Mission Accomplished? Vakarchuk Quits but His Political Party Lives On." Atlantic Council. Accessed March 23, 2021. **URL:** https://www.atlanticcouncil.org/blogs/ukrainealert/mission-accomplished-vakarchuk-quits-but-his-political-party-lives-on/

Harish, S.P. and Andrew T. Little. 2017. "The Political Violence Cycle." *American Political Science Review* 111(2):237–255.

Harris, Shane, Karen DeYoung, Isabelle Khurshudyan, Ashley Parker, and Liz Sly. 2022. "Road to War: U.S. Struggled to Convince Allies, and Zelensky, of Risk of Invasion." *Washington Post*. **URL:** https://www.washingtonpost.com/national-security/interactive/2022/ukraine-road-to-war/

Hart, Roderick P. 2020. "Donald Trump and the Return of the Paranoid Style." *Presidential Studies Quarterly* 50(2):348–365.

Haslett, Malcom. 2005. "Yushchenko's Auschwitz Connection." BBC News. Accessed Novebmer 4, 2020. **URL:** http://news.bbc.co.uk/2/hi/europe/4215101.stm

Herbst, Susan. 2010. *Rude Democracy: Civility and Incivility in American Politics*. Temple University Press.

Hermann, Tamar, Or Anabi, William Cubbison, and Ella Heller. 2020. "IDI Releases 2019 Democracy Index." The Israel Demcocracy Institute. Accessed November 9, 2020. **URL:** https://en.idi.org.il/articles/29494

Herszenhorn, David M. 2012. "Ukraine's Ultranationalists Show Surprising Strength at Polls." *New York Times*. **URL:** https://www.nytimes.com/2012/11/09/world/europe/ukraines-ultranationalists-do-well-in-elections.html

Herszenhorn, David M. 2014. "With Stunts and Vigilante Escapades, a Populist Gains Ground in Ukraine." *New York Times*. **URL:** https://www.nytimes.com/2014/10/25/world/europe/with-stunts-and-vigilante-escapades-a-populist-gains-ground-in-ukraine.html

Herszenhorn, David M. 2019. "Poroshenko Warns against 'Revenge' of Oligarch Forces." Politico Europe. Accessed December 10, 2020. **URL:** https://www.politico.eu/article/petro-poroshenko-warns-ukraine-volodymyr-zelenskiy-against-revenge-of-oligarch-forces/

Hesli, Vicki L., William M. Reisinger, and Arthur H. Miller. 1998. "Political Party Development in Divided Societies: The Case of Ukraine." *Electoral Studies* 17(2):235–256.

Hetherington, Marc J. and Jonathan D. Weiler. 2009. *Authoritarianism and Polarization in American Politics*. Cambridge University Press.

Higgins, Andrew. 2018. "Ex-President of Georgia Is Seized at Restaurant in Ukraine, and Deported to Poland." *New York Times*. **URL:** https://www.nytimes.com/2018/02/12/world/europe/saakashvili-deported-ukraine-poland.html

Hill, Fiona. 2021. "Opinion: Yes, It Was a Coup Attempt. Here's Why." Politico. Accessed August 14, 2022. **URL:** https://www.politico.com/news/magazine/2021/01/11/capitol-riot-self-coup-trump-fiona-hill-457549

Hirschman, Albert O. 1970. *Exit, Voice, and Loyalty: Responses to Decline in Firms, Organizations, and States*. Vol. 25. Harvard University Press.

Hodson, Gordon and Kimberly Costello. 2007. "Interpersonal Disgust, Ideological Orientations, and Dehumanization as Predictors of Intergroup Attitudes." *Psychological Science* 18(8): 691–698.

Hoffman, Gil. 2019. "Former Minister Benny Begin: I'm Not Going to Vote for Likud." *Jerusalem Post*. **URL:** https://www.jpost.com/breaking-news/former-likud-minister-bennie-begin-im-not-going-to-vote-for-likud-601071

Holmes, Oliver. 2020. "Benny Gantz Elected Israeli Speaker, Signalling Deal with Netanyahu." *The Guardian*. **URL:** https://www.theguardian.com/world/2020/mar/26/benny-gantz-elected-israeli-speaker-signalling-deal-with-netanyahu

Horovitz, David. 2020. "Coronavirus or Democracy? Which Crisis Should Israelis Be More Worried About?" *The Times of Israel*. **URL:** https://www.timesofisrael.com/coronavirus-or-democracy-which-crisis-should-israelis-be-more-worried-about/#gs.fvva3e

Horowitz, Jason. 2014. "Exile in Brooklyn, with an Eye on Georgia." *New York Times*. **URL:** https://www.nytimes.com/2014/09/20/world/europe/mikheil-saakashvili-georgias-ex-president-plots-return-from-williamsburg-brooklyn.html

Hsiao, Yuan and Scott Radnitz. 2021. "Allies or Agitators? How Partisan Identity Shapes Public Opinion about Violent or Nonviolent Protests." *Political Communication* 38(4):479–497.

Hsu, Spencer S. 2021. "Tennessee Man with Zip Ties at Capitol Could Face Charges of Sedition, Other Felonies after Riot, Prosecutors Say." *Washington Post*. **URL:** https://www.washingtonpost.com/local/legal-issues/tennessee-man-with-zip-ties-at-capitol-could-face-charges-of-sedition-other-felonies-after-riot-prosecutors-say/2021/01/24/d9c3cc58-5e83-11eb-9430-e7c77b5b0297_story.html

Huff, Connor and Joshua D Kertzer. 2018. "How the Public Defines Terrorism." *American Journal of Political Science* 62(1):55–71.

Human Rights Watch. 2017. "Turkey: Alarming Deterioration of Rights." Human Rights Watch. Accessed September 20, 2021. **URL:** https://www.hrw.org/news/2017/01/12/turkey-alarming-deterioration-rights

Hume, Tim. 2019. "Far-Right Extremists Have Been Using Ukraine's War as a Training Ground. They're Returning Home." Vice. Accessed January 12, 2021. **URL:** https://www.vice.com/en/article/vb95ma/far-right-extremists-have-been-using-ukraines-civil-war-as-a-training-ground-theyre-returning-home

i24 News. 2018. "Vote on Controversial Israeli 'Loyalty in Culture' Law Postponed." i24 News. Accessed November 9, 2020. **URL:** https://www.i24news.tv/en/news/israel/politics/189571-181126-israel-vote-on-controversial-loyalty-in-culture-law-likely-to-be-postponed

i24 News. 2020. "Israel: Lapid Slams Former Partner Benny Gantz in TV Address, Vows to Fight Government." i24 News. Accessed December 15, 2020. **URL:** https://www.i24news.tv/en/news/israel/1587499832-israel-lapid-slams-former-partner-benny-gantz-in-tv-address-vows-to-fight-government

IFES. 2017. "IFES Public Opinion Surveys: (Interview with) Dr. Vladimir Paniotto, Kiev International Institute of Sociology (KIIS), Ukraine." International Foundation for Electoral Systems. Accessed December 10, 2020. **URL:** https://www.ifes.org/news/ifes-public-opinion-surveys

IFES. 2019. "IFES: Ukraine Election Guide." International Foundation for Electoral Systems. Accessed October 10, 2021. **URL:** https://www.electionguide.org/countries/id/223/

Ignazi, Piero. 2020. "The Four Knights of Intra-party Democracy: A Rescue for Party Delegitimation." *Party Politics* 26(1):9–20.

IHME and Christopher J. L. Murray. 2020. "Forecasting COVID-19 Impact on Hospital Bed-days, ICU-Days, ventilator-Days and Deaths by US State in the Next 4 Months." *MedRxiv* .

Illing, Sean. 2019. "Can American Nationalism Be Saved? A Debate with National Review Editor Rich Lowry." Vox. Accessed March 23, 2021. **URL:** https://www.vox.com/policy-and-politics/2019/11/22/20952353/trump-nationalism-america-first-rich-lowry

Illing, Sean. 2020. "'Flood the Zone with Shit': How Misinformation Overwhelmed Our Democracy." Vox. Accessed June 4, 2021. **URL:** https://www.vox.com/policy-and-politics/2020/1/16/20991816/impeachment-trial-trump-bannon-misinformation

Ingraham, Christopher. 2021. "Analysis | How Experts Define the Deadly Mob Attack at the U.S. Capitol." *Washington Post*. **URL:** https://www.washingtonpost.com/business/2021/01/13/autogolpe-self-coup-capitol/

Ingram, Mathew. 2017. "The 140-Character President." Columbia Journalism Review. Accessed December 5, 2020. **URL:** https://www.cjr.org/Special_Report/Trump-Twitter-Tweets-President.Php

Interfax Ukraine. 2019. "Avakov Dismisses Criticisms of Azov Battalion." *Kyiv Post*. **URL:** https://www.kyivpost.com/ukraine-politics/avakov-dismisses-criticisms-of-azov-battalion.html

International Republican Institute. 2019. "Public Opinion Survey of Residents of Ukraine: September 29-October 14, 2018." Center for Insights in Survey Research. Accessed December 13, 2020. **URL:** https://www.iri.org/sites/default/files/2018.12.4_ukraine_poll.pdf

Ioffe, Julia. 2011. "Taking Out Tymoshenko." *New Yorker*. **URL:** https://www.newyorker.com/news/news-desk/taking-out-tymoshenko

IRI. 2022. "IRI Ukraine Poll Shows Overwhelming Support for Zelensky, Confidence in Winning the War, Desire for EU Membership." International Republican Institute. Accessed August 13, 2022. **URL:** https://www.iri.org/news/iri-ukraine-poll-shows-overwhelming-support-for-zelensky-confidence-in-winning-the-war-desire-for-eu-membership/

Ishchenko, Volodymyr. 2016. "Far Right Participation in the Ukrainian Maidan Protests: An Attempt of Systematic Estimation." *European Politics and Society* 17(4):453–472.

Itkowitz, Colby. 2020. "Obama's Former Aides Angry, Hurt over Ronny Jackson's Embrace of Trump's Conspiracy Theories." *Washington Post*. **URL:** https://www.washingtonpost.com/politics/2020/05/14/obamas-former-aides-angry-hurt-over-ronny-jacksons-embrace-trumps-conspiracies/

Ivanova, Polina and Pavel Polityuk. 2019. "Ukrainian Presidential Candidates Trade Insults in Rowdy Stadium Debate." Reuters. Accessed December 16, 2020. **URL:** https://www.reuters.com/article/us-ukraine-election-debate/ukrainian-presidential-candidates-trade-insults-in-rowdy-stadium-debate-idUSKCN1RV16C

Iyengar, Shanto and Sean J. Westwood. 2015. "Fear and Loathing across Party Lines: New Evidence on Group Polarization." *American Journal of Political Science* 59(3):690–707.

Iyengar, Shanto, Yphtach Lelkes, Matthew Levendusky, Neil Malhotra, and Sean J. Westwood. 2019. "The Origins and Consequences of Affective Polarization in the United States." *Annual Review of Political Science* 22:129–146.

Jaffe, Alexandra. 2016. "Donald Trump Has 'Small Hands,' Marco Rubio Says." NBC News. Accessed June 10, 2020. **URL:** https://www.nbcnews.com/politics/2016-election/donald-trump-has-small-hands-marco-rubio-says-n527791

Jamieson, Kathleen Hall. 1993. *Dirty Politics: Deception, Distraction, and Democracy*. Oxford University Press.

Jardina, Ashley. 2019. *White Identity Politics*. Cambridge University Press.

John, Tara and Tim Lister. 2022. "A Far-Right Battalion Has a Key Role in Ukraine's Resistance. Its Neo-Nazi History Has Been Exploited by Putin." CNN. Accessed June 23, 2022. **URL:** https://www.cnn.com/2022/03/29/europe/ukraine-azov-movement-far-right-intl-cmd/index.html

Jones, Kerry, Kelsey Libert, and Kristin Tynski. 2016. "The Emotional Combinations That Make Stories Go Viral." Harvard Business Review. Accessed October 23, 2020. **URL:** https://hbr.org/2016/05/research-the-link-between-feeling-in-control-and-viral-content

Joo, Jungseock and Zachary C. Steinert-Threlkeld. 2018. "Image as Data: Automated Visual Content Analysis for Political Science." *arXiv preprint arXiv:1810.01544*.

Jordan, Jillian J., Moshe Hoffman, Paul Bloom, and David G. Rand. 2016. "Third-Party Punishment as a Costly Signal of Trustworthiness." *Nature* 530(7591):473–476.

Jost, John T. 2017. "Ideological Asymmetries and the Essence of Political Psychology." *Political Psychology* 38(2):167–208.

Jost, John T., Jack Glaser, Arie W. Kruglanski, and Frank J. Sulloway. 2003. "Political Conservatism as Motivated Social Cognition." *Psychological Bulletin* 129(3):339.

JTA. 2013. "Ultranationalist Ukrainian Political Party Leaders Banned from U.S." Jewish Telegraphic Agency. Accessed December 13, 2020. **URL:** https://www.jta.org/2013/06/27/global/ultranationalist-ukrainian-political-party-leaders-banned-from-u-s

Kahneman, Daniel and Jonathan Renshon. 2007. "Why Hawks Win." *Foreign Policy* 158:34–38.

Käihkö, Ilmari. 2018. "A Nation-in-the-Making, in Arms: Control of Force, Strategy and the Ukrainian Volunteer Battalions." *Defence Studies* 18(2):147–166.

Kakkar, Hemant and Niro Sivanathan. 2017. "When the Appeal of a Dominant Leader Is Greater than a Prestige Leader." *Proceedings of the National Academy of Sciences* 114(26):6734–6739.

Kalla, Joshua L. and David E. Broockman. 2018. "The Minimal Persuasive Effects of Campaign Contact in General Elections: Evidence from 49 Field Experiments." *American Political Science Review* 112(1):148–166.

Kalmoe, Nathan P. 2014. "Fueling the Fire: Violent Metaphors, Trait Aggression, and Support for Political Violence." *Political Communication* 31(4):545–563. **URL:** https://doi.org/10.1080/10584609.2013.852642

Kalmoe, Nathan P. 2017. "Mobilizing Voters with Aggressive Metaphors." *Political Science Research and Methods* 7(3):411–429

Kalmoe, Nathan P. 2020. *With Ballots & Bullets: Partisanship & Violence in the American Civil War*. Cambridge University Press.

Kalmoe, Nathan P., Joshua R. Gubler, and David A. Wood. 2018. "Toward Conflict or Compromise? How Violent Metaphors Polarize Partisan Issue Attitudes." *Political Communication* 35(3):333–352. **URL:** https://doi.org/10.1080/10584609.2017.1341965

Kalmoe, Nathan P. and Lilliana Mason. 2020. "Most Americans Reject Partisan Violence, but There Is Still Cause for Concern." Democracy Fund Voter Study Group. Accessed March 15, 2021. **URL:** https://www.voterstudygroup.org/blog/has-american-partisanship-gone-too-far

Kalmoe, Nathan P. and Lilliana Mason. 2022. *Radical American Partisanship: Mapping Violent Hostility, Its Causes, and the Consequences for Democracy*. University of Chicago Press.

Kanthak, Kristin and Jonathan Woon. 2015. "Women Don't Run? Election Aversion and Candidate Entry." *American Journal of Political Science* 59(3):595–612.

Katchanovski, Ivan. 2012. Democracy and Political Values in Ukraine. In *17th Annual World Convention of the Association for the Study of Nationalities, New York, April*. pp. 19–21.

Kaufman, Stuart J. 2001. *Modern Hatreds: The Symbolic Politics of Ethnic War*. Cornell University Press.

Keneally, Meghan. 2018. "What Happened When Republican Greg Gianforte Body-Slammed a Reporter." ABC News. Accessed December 6, 2020. **URL:** https://abcnews.go.com/Politics/happened-republican-greg-gianforte-body-slammed-reporter/story?id=58610691

Kershner, Isabel and Pam Belluck. 2020. "When Covid Subsided, Israel Reopened Its Schools. It Didn't Go Well." *New York Times*. **URL:** https://www.nytimes.com/2020/08/04/world/middleeast/coronavirus-israel-schools-reopen.html

Kertzer, Joshua D. 2020. "Re-assessing Elite-Public Gaps in Political Behavior." *American Journal of Political Science*.

Kharkiv Human Rights Protection Group. 2008. "Open Letter from KHPG Regarding the Organization 'Patriot of Ukraine.'" Kharkiv Human Rights Protection Group. Accessed September 22, 2020. **URL:** https://khpg.org//en/1220644493

Khokhlova, Veronica. 2004. "New Kids on the Bloc." *New York Times*. **URL:** https://www.nytimes.com/2004/11/26/opinion/new-kids-on-the-bloc.html

Kim, Caitlyn. 2021*a*. "Boebert Clashes with Capitol Police after Setting Off Metal Detectors." Colorado Public Radio. Accessed February 10, 2021. **URL:** https://www.cpr.org/2021/01/12/boebert-clashes-with-capitol-police-after-setting-off-metal-detectors/

Kim, Taegyoon. 2022. "Violent Political Rhetoric on Twitter." *Political Science Research and Methods Forthcoming.*

Kinder, Donald R. and Nathan P. Kalmoe. 2017. *Neither Liberal nor Conservative: Ideological Innocence in the American Public*. University of Chicago Press.

Kinglsey, Patrick. 2020. "Israel's Right Had a Good Election. So Did Israeli Arabs. That May Be No Coincidence." *New York Times*. https://www.nytimes.com/2020/03/04/world/middleeast/israel-election-arabs.html.

Kiousis, Spiro. 2004. "Explicating Media Salience: A Factor Analysis of New York Times Issue Coverage during the 2000 US Presidential Election." *Journal of Communication* 54(1): 71–87.

Kirvy, Paul. 2022. "Why Has Russia Invaded Ukraine and What Does Putin Want?" BBC. Accessed August 13, 2022. **URL:** https://www.bbc.com/news/world-europe-56720589

Kis, Oksana. 2007. "'Beauty Will Save the World': Feminine Strategies in Ukrainian Politics and the Case of Yulia Tymoshenko." *Spacesofidentity* 7(2):31–75.

Kleefeld, Eric. 2009. "Joe Wilson a Hit at Capitol Hill Tea Party." Talking Points Memo. Accessed November 15, 2020. **URL:** https://talkingpointsmemo.com/dc/joe-wilson-a-hit-at-capitol-hill-tea-party

Klein, Ezra. 2019. "The Post-Christian Culture Wars." Vox. Accessed September 15, 2020. **URL:** https://www.vox.com/policy-and-politics/2019/11/26/20978613/donald-trump-christians-william-barr-impeachment

Klein, Ezra. 2020. "Why the Media Is So Polarized—and How It Polarizes Us." Vox. Accessed October 22, 2020. **URL:** https://www.vox.com/2020/1/28/21077888/why-were-polarized-media-book-ezra-news

Knell, Yolande. 2020. "Netanyahu Focus of Israeli Protests against 'The King.'" BBC News. **URL:** https://www.bbc.com/news/world-middle-east-53724095

Knott, Eleanor. 2018. "Perpetually—"Partly Free": Lessons from Post-Soviet Hybrid Regimes on Backsliding in Central and Eastern Europe." *East European Politics* 34(3):355–376.

Korolenko, Ihor. 2018. "Studio Sleight of Hand: How Ukraine's Talk Shows Work." Ukrainian Week. Accessed December 11, 2020. **URL:** https://ukrainianweek.com/Society/209484

Korrespondent. 2011*a*. "Martynyuk Apologized for Attacking Lyashko." Korrespondent.net. Accessed November 2, 2020. **URL:** https://korrespondent.net/ukraine/politics/1218550-martynyuk-izvinilsya-za-to-chto-nabrosilsya-na-lyashko

Korrespondent. 2011*b*. "Tymoshenko Called Kireev a Parrot, a Dummy, an Executioner and an Idiot." Korrespondent.net. Accessed November 5, 2020. **URL:** https://korrespondent.net/ukraine/politics/1258411-timoshenko-obozvala-kireeva-popugaem-bolvanchikom-palachom-i-nedoumkom

Korrespondent. 2011*c*. "A Video of Martynyuk's Fight with Lyashko in the Rada's Presidium Appeared on the Internet." Korrespondent.net. Accessed November 2, 2020. **URL:** https://korrespondent.net/ukraine/politics/1218591-v-internete-poyavilos-video-draki-martynyuka-s-lyashko-v-prezidiume-rady

Korrespondent. 2012*a*. "Live Shuster Live a Fight between Deputies Kolesnichenko and Kirilenko." Korrespondent.net. Accessed November 4, 2020. **URL:** https://korrespondent.net/ukraine/politics/1353527-v-pryamom-efire-shuster-live-podralis-deputaty-kolesnichenko-i-kirilenko

Korrespondent. 2012*b*. "Live Shuster Live a Fight between Deputies Kolesnichenko and Kirilenko." Korrespondent.net. Accessed September 6, 2020. **URL:** https://korrespondent.net/ukraine/politics/1353527-v-pryamom-efire-shuster-live-podralis-deputaty-kolesnichenko-i-kirilenko

Kossov, Igor. 2019*a*. "Ex-lawmaker Lyashko Attacks Energy Committee Head over Russian Electricity (VIDEO)." *Kyiv Post*. **URL:** https://www.kyivpost.com/ukraine-politics/ex-lawmaker-lyashko-attacks-energy-committee-head-in-airport-over-russian-electricity.html

Kossov, Igor. 2019*b*. "Hladkovsky, a Top Poroshenko Ally, Is Arrested in Defense Corruption Scandal." *Kyiv Post*. **URL:** https://www.kyivpost.com/ukraine-politics/hladkovsky-a-top-poroshenko-ally-is-arrested-in-defense-corruption-scandal.html

Kovensky, Josh and Kostyantyn Chernichkin. 2018. "Filatov Plans to Make Dnipro Great Again (VIDEO)." *Kyiv Post*. **URL:** https://www.kyivpost.com/business/filatov-plans-to-make-dnipro-great-again.html

Kramer, Adam D. I., Jamie E. Guillory, and Jeffrey T. Hancock. 2014. "Experimental Evidence of Massive-Scale Emotional Contagion through Social Networks." *Proceedings of the National Academy of Sciences* 111(24):8788–8790.

Kramer, Andrew E. 2014. "Ukraine Sends Force to Stem Unrest in East." *New York Times.* **URL:** https://www.nytimes.com/2014/04/16/world/europe/ukraine-russia.html

Kramer, Andrew E. 2018. "Now Prohibited in Ukraine's Parliamentary Chamber: Weapons." *New York Times.* **URL:** https://www.nytimes.com/2018/03/22/world/europe/ukraine-guns-parliament-savchenko.html

Kramer, Andrew E. 2020. "Ukraine Is Threatening to Arrest Its Former President." *New York Times.* **URL:** https://www.nytimes.com/2020/02/28/world/europe/ukraine-petro-poroshenko.html

Kramer, Andrew E., Andrew Higgins, and Michael Schwirtz. 2019. "The Ukrainian Ex-Prosecutor behind the Impeachment Furor." *New York Times.* **URL:** https://www.nytimes.com/2019/10/05/world/europe/ukraine-prosecutor-trump.html

Krehbiel, Keith. 1998. *Pivotal Politics: A Theory of US Lawmaking.* University of Chicago Press.

Krymeniuk, Oleksii. 2019. "How MPs Moved between Factions: The Analysis of Party Switching in Ukrainian Parliaments | VoxUkraine." VoxUkraine. Accessed October 20, 2020. **URL:** https://voxukraine.org/en/how-mps-moved-between-factions-the-analysis-of-party-switching-in-ukrainian-parliaments

Kryvtsun, Dmytro. 2014. "The Liashko Phenomenon." The Day (Kyiv). Accessed September 29, 2020. **URL:** https://day.kyiv.ua/en/article/topic-day/liashko-phenomenon

Kteily, Nour, Emile Bruneau, Adam Waytz, and Sarah Cotterill. 2015. "The Ascent of Man: Theoretical and Empirical Evidence for Blatant Dehumanization." *Journal of Personality and Social Psychology* 109(5):901.

Kudelia, Sergiy. 2014. "Ukraine's 2014 Presidential Election Result Is Unlikely to Be Repeated." *Washington Post.* **URL:** https://www.washingtonpost.com/news/monkey-cage/wp/2014/06/02/ukraines-2014-presidential-election-result-is-unlikely-to-be-repeated/

Kudelia, Serhiy. 2013. "When External Leverage Fails: The Case of Yulia Tymoshenko's Trial." *Problems of Post-Communism* 60(1):29–42.

Kupatadze, Alexander. 2012. *Organized Crime, Political Transitions and State Formation in Post-Soviet Eurasia.* Springer.

Kupchinsky, Roman. 2006. "Ukraine: Mystery behind Yushchenko's Poisoning Continues." Radio Free Europe/Radio Liberty. Accessed November 4, 2020. **URL:** https://www.rferl.org/a/1071434.html

Kupfer, Matthew and Bermet Talant. 2020. "How to Salvage Ukraine's Failing COVID-19 response." *Kyiv Post.* **URL:** https://www.kyivpost.com/article/opinion/op-ed/matthew-kupfer-bermet-talant-how-to-salvage-ukraines-failing-covid-19-response.html

Kuzio, Taras. 2004. "Yushchenko Finally Gets Tough on Nationalists." *Eurasia Daily Monitor (Jamestown Foundation)* 1(66). **URL:** https://jamestown.org/program/yushchenko-finally-gets-tough-on-nationalists/

Kuzio, Taras. 2005. "From Kuchma to Yushchenko Ukraine's 2004 Presidential Elections and the Orange Revolution." *Problems of Post-Communism* 52(2):29–44.

Kuzio, Taras. 2008. "Democratic Breakthroughs and Revolutions in Five Postcommunist Countries: Comparative Perspectives on the Fourth Wave." *Demokratizatsiya* 16(1).

Kuzio, Taras. 2010. "State-Led Violence in Ukraine's 2004 Elections and Orange Revolution." *Communist and Post-Communist Studies* 43(4):383–395.

Kuzio, Taras. 2015. *Ukraine: Democratization, Corruption, and the New Russian Imperialism: Democratization, Corruption, and the New Russian Imperialism.* ABC-CLIO.

Kuzio, Taras. 2019. "Who Gains from Using the Far-Right in Ukraine's Elections?" Atlantic Council. **URL:** https://www.atlanticcouncil.org/blogs/ukrainealert/who-gains-from-using-the-far-right-in-ukraine-s-elections/

Kuzmenko, Oleksiy. 2019. 'Defend the White Race': American Extremists Being Co-Opted by Ukraine's Far-Right." Bellingcat Anti-Equality Monitoring. Accessed November 3, 2020. **URL:** https://www.bellingcat.com/news/uk-and-europe/2019/02/15/defend-the-white-race-american-extremists-being-co-opted-by-ukraines-far-right/

Kydd, Andrew H. and Barbara F. Walter. 2006. "The Strategies of Terrorism." *International Security* 31(1):49–80.

Kyiv Post. 2004. "Yushchenko Takes Symbolic Oath of Office; Mass Protests Continue." *Kyiv Post*. **URL:** https://www.kyivpost.com/article/content/business/yushchenko-takes-symbolic-oath-of-office-mass-prot-21853.html

Kyiv Post. 2010. "Yulia Tymoshenko Bloc Expels Two Deputies from Parliament Faction." *Kyiv Post*. **URL:** https://www.kyivpost.com/article/content/ukraine-politics/yulia-tymoshenko-bloc-expels-two-deputies-from-par-86768.html

Kyiv Post. 2012*a*. "Lyashko: No Sponsors, Tycoons or Deputies on Election List of Radical Party." *Kyiv Post*. **URL:** https://www.kyivpost.com/article/content/ukraine-politics/liashko-no-sponsors-tycoons-or-deputies-on-election-list-of-radical-party-311218.html

Kyiv Post. 2012*b*. "Yanukovych Accuses Tymoshenko in Lawmaker's Murder." *Kyiv Post*. **URL:** https://www.rferl.org/a/yanukovych-says-tymoshenko-was-involved-in-lawmakers-murder/24612763.html

Kyiv Post. 2017. "Associated Press: Blast in Ukraine Capital Wounds Lawmaker, Kills Bodyguard." *Kyiv Post*. **URL:** https://www.kyivpost.com/ukraine-politics/associated-press-blast-ukraine-capital-wounds-lawmaker-kills-bodyguard.html

Kyiv Post. 2019. "Poroshenko, Zelenskiy Hold Presidential Debate at Sports Arena in Kyiv." *Kyiv Post*. **URL:** https://www.kyivpost.com/ukraine-politics/poroshenko-zelenskiy-hold-presidential-debate-at-sports-arena-in-kyiv-live-updates.html

Lake, David A. and Donald Rothchild. 1996. "Containing Fear: The Origins and Management of Ethnic Conflict." *International Security* 21(2):41–75.

Lakoff, George and Mark Johnson. 2008. *Metaphors We Live By*. University of Chicago Press.

Lau, Richard R., Lee Sigelman, and Ivy Brown Rovner. 2007. "The Effects of Negative Political Campaigns: A Meta-Analytic Reassessment." *Journal of Politics* 69(4): 1176–1209.

Laustsen, Lasse and Alexander Bor. 2017. "The Relative Weight of Character Traits in Political Candidate Evaluations: Warmth Is More Important than Competence, Leadership and Integrity." *Electoral Studies* 49:96–107.

Laustsen, Lasse and Michael Bang Petersen. 2017. "Perceived Conflict and Leader Dominance: Individual and Contextual Factors behind Preferences for Dominant Leaders." *Political Psychology* 38(6):1083–1101.

League, Anti-Defemation. 2017. "The Jewish Defense League." Anti-Defamation League. Accessed March 20, 2020. **URL:** https://www.adl.org/education/resources/profiles/jewish-defense-league

Leatherby, Lauren, Arielle Ray, Anjali Singhvi, Christiaan Triebert, Derek Watkins, and Haley Willis. 2021. "How a Presidential Rally Turned into a Capitol Rampage." *New York Times*. **URL:** https://www.nytimes.com/interactive/2021/01/12/us/capitol-mob-timeline.html

Lerer, Lisa. 2019. "The 'On Politics' Mueller Report Cheat Sheet." *New York Times*. **URL:** https://www.nytimes.com/2019/04/18/us/politics/on-politics-mueller-report-summary.html

Lerer, Lisa and Astead W. Herndon. 2021. "Menace Enters the Republican Mainstream." *New York Times*. **URL:** https://www.nytimes.com/2021/11/12/us/politics/republican-violent-rhetoric.html?referringSource=articleShare

Levitsky, Steven and Daniel Ziblatt. 2018. *How Democracies Die*. Broadway Books.

Levitsky, Steven and Daniel Ziblatt. 2020. "The Crisis of American Democracy." *American Educator* 44(3):6.

Levitsky, Steven and Lucan A. Way. 2010. *Competitive Authoritarianism: Hybrid Regimes after the Cold War*. Cambridge University Press.

Levy, Clifford J. 2010. "For Kremlin, Ukraine Election Cuts Two Ways." *New York Times*. **URL:** https://www.nytimes.com/2010/02/09/world/europe/09ukraine.html

Levy, Clifford J. 2011. "'Hero of Ukraine' Prize to Wartime Partisan Leader Is Revoked." *New York Times*. **URL:** https://www.nytimes.com/2011/01/13/world/europe/13ukraine.html

Lewandowsky, Stephan, Michael Jetter, and Ullrich K. H. Ecker. 2020. "Using the President's Tweets to Understand Political Diversion in the Age of Social Media." *Nature Communications* 11(1):1–12.

Lewis, Jeffrey B., Keith Poole, Howard Rosenthal, Adam Boche, Aaron Rudkin, and Luke Sonnet. 2020. "Voteview: Congressional Roll-Call Votes Database." Accessed November 10, 2020. **URL:** https://voteview. com/

Lilleker, Darren G., Jens Tenscher, and Václav Štětka. 2015. "Towards Hypermedia Campaigning? Perceptions of New Media's Importance for Campaigning by Party Strategists in Comparative Perspective." *Information, Communication & Society* 18(7):747–765.

Lima, Cristiano. 2020. "Twitter Adds Warning Label to Gaetz Tweet on Antifa for Glorifying Violence." Politico. Accessed December 3, 2020. **URL:** https://www.politico.com/news/2020/06/01/twitter-gaetz-antifa-violence-295116

Lindsay, James M. 2011. "The Water's Edge Remembers: Joseph McCarthy's Wheeling Speech." Council on Foreign Relations. Accessed November 15, 2020. **URL:** https://www.cfr.org/blog/twe-remembers-joseph-mccarthys-wheeling-speech

Linz, Juan J. 1990. "The Perils of Presidentialism." *Journal of Democracy* 1(1):51–69.

Liptak, Kevin. 2020. "Former White House Physician Ronny Jackson Dives Headfirst into 'Obamagate' and Angers Former Colleagues." CNN Politics. Accessed October 22, 2020. **URL:** https://edition.cnn.com/2020/05/14/politics/ronny-jackson-obamsa-tweets/index.html

Liptak, Kevin, Paul LeBlanc, and Olanma Mang. 2019. "Whistleblower Timeline: Team Trump Contacts and Ukraine." CNN Politics. Accessed September 8, 2020. **URL:** https://www.cnn.com/2019/09/20/politics/whistleblower-timeline-ukraine-team-trump/index.html

Little, Andrew T, and Thomas Zeitzoff. 2017. "A Bargaining Theory of Conflict with Evolutionary Preferences." *International Organization* 71(3):523–557.

Londoño, Ernesto, Flávia Milhorance, and Jack Nicas. 2021. "Brazil's Far-Right Disinformation Pushers Find a Safe Space on Telegram." *New York Times*. **URL:** https://www.nytimes.com/2021/11/08/world/americas/brazil-telegram-disinformation.html

Lytvynenko, Jane and Molly Hensley-Clancy. 2021. "The Rioters Who Took Over the Capitol Have Been Planning Online in the Open for Weeks." Buzzfeed News. Accessed August 1, 2021 **URL:** https://www.buzzfeednews.com/article/janelytvynenko/trump-rioters-planned-online?scrolla=5eb6d68b7fedc32c19ef33b4%7D

MacDonald-Evoy, Jerod. 2020. "Far-Right Protesters Demand Ballots Be Counted, Spread Misinformation." Arizona Mirror. Accessed February 10, 2021. **URL:** https://www.azmirror.com/2020/11/05/far-right-protesters-demand-ballots-be-counted-spread-misinformation/

Macdonald, Maggie and Whitney Hua. 2020. "Mind the Gap? Negative Tweets & Partisanship in the House of Representatives." *Working Paper*.

MacWilliams, Matthew C. 2016. "Who Decides When the Party Doesn't? Authoritarian Voters and the Rise of Donald Trump." *PS: Political Science & Politics* 49(4):716–721.

Madestam, Andreas, Daniel Shoag, Stan Veuger, and David Yanagizawa-Drott. 2013. "Do Political Protests Matter? Evidence from the Tea Party Movement." *Quarterly Journal of Economics* 128(4):1633–1685.

Magnan, Dan and Hannah Miao. 2021. "Capitol Rioter Jeffrey Sabol Dragged Cop to Be Beaten with a Flagpole 'in a Fit of Rage,' Prosecutor Says." CNBC Accessed March 15, 2021. **URL:** https://www.cnbc.com/2021/01/22/capitol-riots-man-admits-dragging-cop-to-be-beaten-by-flag-pole.html

Maheshwari, Vijai. 2019. "The Comedian and the Oligarch." Politico EU. Accessed September 22, 2020. **URL:** https://www.politico.eu/article/volodomyr-zelenskiy-ihor-kolomoisky-the-comedian-and-the-oligarch-ukraine-presidential-election/

Makor Rishon. 2012. "The New Star of the Right Wants to Cleanse Tel Aviv of Infiltrators." Makor Rishon. Accessed March 23, 2021. **URL:** https://www.makorrishon.co.il/nrg/online/54/ART2/419/030.html

Maor, Moshe, Raanan Sulitzeanu-Kenan, and David Chinitz. 2020. "When COVID-19, Constitutional Crisis, and Political Deadlock Meet: The Israeli Case from a Disproportionate Policy Perspective." *Policy and Society* 39(3):442–457.

Marchenko, Yuriy. 2015. "From all the Forks: Where Did Oleh Lyashko Come From and What Will He Do." Ukrainskaya Pravda. Accessed September 5, 2020. **URL:** https://www.pravda.com.ua/articles/2015/09/18/7081809/

Margalit, Ruth. 2016. "Miri Regev's Culture War." *New York Times*. **URL:** https://www.nytimes.com/2016/10/23/magazine/miri-regevs-culture-war.html

Mark, David. 2020. "Even if Trump Loses the Election, the Next Congress Will Be Even Trumpier." NBC News. Accessed March 24, 2021. **URL:** https://www.nbcnews.com/think/opinion/even-if-trump-loses-election-next-congress-will-be-even-ncna1246629

Marson, James and Richard Boudreaux. 2010. "Brawl Marks Kiev's Approval of Fleet." *Wall Street Journal*. **URL:** https://www.wsj.com/articles/SB10001424052748704471204575209572380473814

Marten, Kimberly and Olga Oliker. 2017. "Ukraine's Volunteer Militias May Have Saved the Country, but Now They Threaten It." War on the Rocks. Accessed November 5, 2020. **URL:** https://warontherocks.com/2017/09/ukraines-volunteer-militias-may-have-saved-the-country-but-now-they-threaten-it/

Martin, Jonathan. 2018. "Democrats Confront Democrats Over How to Confront Trump." *New York Times*. **URL:** https://www.nytimes.com/2018/06/25/us/politics/trump-liberal-activists-shaming.html

Martosko, David, Hannah Parry, and Francesca Chambers. 2017. "Trump: 'I Wasn't Aware AT ALL' That Jeff Sessions Had Met Russia's Ambassador Twice - but President Still Says He Has 'Total Confidence' in Attorney General as Calls Mount for Him to Quit over Lies." Daily Mail. Accessed December 6, 2020. **URL:** https://www.dailymail.co.uk/news/article-4273676/Jeff-Sessions-spoke-twice-year-Russians.html

Mason, Liliana, Julie Wronski, and John V. Kane. 2021. "Activating Animus: The Uniquely Social Roots of Trump Support." *American Political Science Review* 115(4):1508–1516.

Mason, Lilliana. 2018. *Uncivil Agreement: How Politics Became Our Identity*. University of Chicago Press.

Matuszak, Sławomir et al. 2012. *The Oligarchic Democracy. The Influence of Business Groups on Ukrainian Politics*. Ośrodek Studiów Wschodnich im. Marka Karpia.

Matveyev, Vladimir. 2009. "Ukrainian Party Picks Xenophobic Candidate." Jewish Telegraphic Agency. Accessed March 23, 2021. **URL:** https://www.jta.org/2009/05/25/global/ukrainian-party-picks-xenophobic-candidate

Matviyishyn, Iryna. 2019. "Memocracy: How Social Networks Affect Politics in Ukraine." Ukraine World. Accessed October 23, 2020. **URL:** https://ukraineworld.org/articles/infowars/memocracy-how-social-networks-affect-politics-ukraine

Maurer, Paul J. 1999. "Media Feeding Frenzies: Press Behavior during Two Clinton Scandals." *Presidential Studies Quarterly* 29(1):65–79.

Maza, Cristina. 2018. "A Ukraine Coup? War Hero Politician Nadiya Savchenko Arrested for Plotting to Overthrow Government Using Grenades and Automatic Weapons." *Newsweek*. **URL:** https://www.newsweek.com/ukraine-coup-war-hero-politician-nadiya-savchenko-arrested-plotting-overthrow-857675

Mazur, Mieszko, Man Dang, and Miguel Vega. 2020. "COVID-19 and the March 2020 Stock Market Crash. Evidence from S&P1500." *Finance Research Letters* p. 101690.

Mazurenko, Alyona. 2021. "'Voice' Expelled 7 People's Deputies from the Party." Ukrainskaya Pravda. Accessed August 15. 2021. **URL:** https://www.pravda.com.ua/news/2021/07/29/7302126/

McAdam, Doug. 1983. "Tactical Innovation and the Pace of Insurgency." *American Sociological Review* 735–754.

McAdam, Doug. 2010. *Political Process and the Development of Black Insurgency, 1930–1970*. University of Chicago Press.

McAdam, Doug, Charles Tarrow, Sidney Tarrow, Charles Tilly, et al. 2001. *Dynamics of Contention*. Cambridge University Press.

McCammond, Alexi. 2021. "Alexandria Ocasio-Cortez Tutors Dems on Mastering Social Media." Axios. Accessed June 15, 2021. **URL:** https://www.axios.com/aoc-instagram-social-media-b1caf529-601a-4820-97ab-5be73bc50185.html

McCarty, Nolan, Keith T. Poole, and Howard Rosenthal. 2016. *Polarized America: The Dance of Ideology and Unequal Riches*. MIT Press.

McConnell, Christopher, Yotam Margalit, Neil Malhotra, and Matthew Levendusky. 2018. "The Economic Consequences of Partisanship in a Polarized Era." *American Journal of Political Science* 62(1):5–18.

McDermott, Rose. 2010. "Emotional Manipulation of Political Identity". In *Manipulating Democracy*. Routledge, pp. 131–152.

McFaul, Michael. 2007. "Ukraine Imports Democracy: External Influences on the Orange Revolution." *International Security* 32(2):45–83.

McLaughlin, Daniel. 2019. "Departing Poroshenko Warns Ukraine of Russian Threat to Pro-Western Path." *Irish Times*. **URL:** https://www.irishtimes.com/news/world/europe/departing-poroshenko-warns-ukraine-of-russian-threat-to-pro-western-path-1.3897480

McPhedran, Charles. 2014. "Thug Politics, Kiev." Foreign Policy. Accessed September 28, 2020. **URL:** https://foreignpolicy.com/2014/10/09/thug-politics-kiev/

Melkozerova, Veronika. 2016. "War Reshapes Ukraine's Hardcore Soccer Fans." *Kyiv Post*. **URL:** https://www.kyivpost.com/lifestyle/war-reshapes-ukraines-hardcore-soccer-fans-414739.html

Melkozerova, Veronika. 2017. "Ukrainian Interior Minister Adviser 'Comes Out' as a Sexist." *Kyiv Post*. **URL:** https://www.kyivpost.com/ukraine-politics/ukrainian-interior-minister-adviser-comes-sexist.html

Mendelberg, Tali. 2001. *The Race Card: Campaign Strategy, Implicit messages, and the Norm of Equality*. Princeton University Press.

Mercieca, Jennifer. 2020. *Demagogue for President: The Rhetorical Genius of Donald Trump*. Texas A&M University Press.

Mernyk, Joseph S., Sophia L. Pink, James N. Druckman, and Robb Willer. 2022. "Correcting Inaccurate Metaperceptions Reduces Americans' Support for Partisan Violence." *Proceedings of the National Academy of Sciences* 119(16):e2116851119.

Merolla, Jennifer L. and Elizabeth J. Zechmeister. 2009. "Terrorist Threat, Leadership, and the Vote: Evidence from Three Experiments." *Political Behavior* 31(4):575.

Metzger, Megan MacDuffee and Joshua A. Tucker. 2017. "Social Media and EuroMaidan: A Review Essay." *Slavic Review* 76(1):169–191.

Michaels, Samantha. 2020. "Alexandria Ocasio-Cortez Speaks to Supporters about the Minneapolis Protests." Mother Jones. Accessed December 3, 2020. **URL:** https://www.motherjones.com/politics/2020/05/alexandria-ocasio-cortez-minneapolis-protests-george-floyd/

Michelitch, Kristin. 2015. "Does Electoral Competition Exacerbate Interethnic or Interpartisan Economic Discrimination? Evidence from a Field Experiment in Market Price Bargaining." *American Political Science Review* 109(1):43–61.

Mickey, Robert. 2015. *Paths Out of Dixie: The Democratization of Authoritarian Enclaves in America's Deep South, 1944–1972*. Vol. 147. Princeton University Press.

Milanova, Yana. 2019. "National Corps: By Order of Poroshenko, Kononenko Is Going to Eliminate Nationalists." *Ukrainskaya Pravda*. **URL:** http://www.pravda.com.ua/rus/news/2019/03/11/7208871/

Miller, Christopher. 2018*a*. "Azov, Ukraine's Most Prominent Ultranationalist Group, Sets Its Sights on U.S., Europe." *Radio Free Europe/Radio Liberty*. **URL:** https://www.rferl.org/a/azov-ukraine-s-most-prominent-ultranationalist-group-sets-its-sights-on-u-s-europe/29600564.html

Miller, Christopher. 2018*b*. "Azov, Ukraine's Most Prominent Ultranationalist Group, Sets Its Sights on U.S., Europe." Radio Free Europe/Radio Liberty. Accessed January 12, 2021.

URL: https://www.rferl.org/a/azov-ukraine-s-most-prominent-ultranationalist-group-sets-its-sights-on-u-s-europe/29600564.html

Miller, Christopher. 2018*c*. "With Axes and Hammers, Far-Right Vigilantes Destroy Another Romany Camp in Kyiv." Radio Free Europe/Radio Liberty. Accessed November 3, 2020. **URL:** https://www.rferl.org/a/ukraine-far-right-vigilantes-destroy-another-romany-camp-in-kyiv/29280336.html

Miller, Christopher. 2019*a*. "Crowdsourcer in Chief: Ukrainian Funnyman Takes Unorthodox Path to Top of Presidential Pack." Radio Free Europe/Radio Liberty. Accessed December 10, 2020. **URL:** https://www.rferl.org/a/crowdsourcer-in-chief-ukrainian-funnyman-takes-unorthodox-path-to-top-of-presidential-pack/29796662.html

Miller, Christopher. 2019*b*. "Deputized as Election Monitors, Ukrainian Ultranationalists 'Ready to Punch' Violators." Radio Free Europe/Radio Liberty. Accessed August 22, 2022. **URL:** https://www.rferl.org/a/deputized-as-election-monitors-ukrainian-ultranationalists-ready-to-punch-violators/29809207.html

Miller, Christopher. 2019*c*. "Hundreds Gather at Far-Right Rally in Kyiv amid Military Corruption Scandal." Radio Free Europe/Radio Liberty. Accessed December 10, 2020. **URL:** https://www.rferl.org/a/hundreds-gather-at-far-right-rally-in-kyiv-amid-military-corruption-scandal/29825013.html

Miller, Christopher J. and Isaac Webb. 2014. "Militia Backed by Presidential Candidate Lyashko Takes Credit for Assassination of Russian-Backed Separatist (VIDEO)." *Kyiv Post*. **URL:** https://www.kyivpost.com/article/content/war-against-ukraine/militia-backed-by-presidential-candidate-lyashko-takes-credit-for-murder-of-russian-backed-separatists-349093.html

Miller, Joanne M. and Jon A. Krosnick. 2004. "Threat as a Motivator of Political Activism: A Field Experiment." *Political Psychology* 25(4):507–523.

Mills, Robert. 2020. "James Carville Scorches Earth of Political Landscape." *Boston Herald*. **URL:** https://www.bostonherald.com/2020/02/08/james-carville-scorches-earth-of-political-landscape/

Minakov, Mykhailo. 2021. "Just Like All the Others: The End of the Zelensky Alternative?" The Wilson Center. Accessed August 14, 2022. **URL:** https://www.wilsoncenter.org/blog-post/just-all-others-end-zelensky-alternative

Mitchell, Tia and Sarah Kallis. 2020. "GOP Congressional Candidate's Comments Divide Georgia's 14th District." *Atlanta Journal and Constitution*. **URL:** https://www.ajc.com/news/state–regional-govt–politics/gop-congressional-candidate-comments-divide-georgia-14th-district/5v5kC1yf0zoD20rtUlDOEJ/

Moffitt, Benjamin. 2013. "The Good, the Bad and the Ugly: Hugo Chávez and the International Left." The Conversation. Accessed September 20, 2021. **URL:** https://theconversation.com/the-good-the-bad-and-the-ugly-hugo-chavez-and-the-international-left-12651

Montanaro, Domenico. 2018. "Poll: Nearly 4 In 5 Voters Concerned Incivility Will Lead to Violence." NPR. **URL:** https://www.npr.org/2018/11/01/662730647/poll-nearly-4-in-5-voters-concerned-incivility-will-lead-to-violence

Moser, Michael. 2013. *Language Policy and Discourse on Languages in Ukraine under President Viktor Yanukovych*. Vol. 122. Columbia University Press.

Mualem, Mazal. 2018. "Netanyahu Backs Main Likud Rival into Corner." Al-Monitor. Accessed November 9, 2020. **URL:** https://www.al-monitor.com/originals/2018/10/israel-benjamin-netanyahu-reuven-rivlin-elections-knesset.html

Mualem, Mazal. 2020. "Naftali Bennett, Propelled by Coronavirus Crisis, Challenges Netanyahu—Al-Monitor: The Pulse of the Middle East." Al Monitor. Accessed June 20, 2021. **URL:** https://www.al-monitor.com/originals/2020/10/israel-benjamin-netanyahu-naftali-bennett-avigdor-liberman.html

Mueller, John. 2000. "The Banality of "Ethnic war"." *International Security* 25(1):42–70.

Munger, Kevin. 2020. "All the News That's Fit to Click: The Economics of Clickbait Media." *Political Communication* 37(3):376–397.

Munger, Kevin. 2022. "We Lived in a Society: Conviviality Is a Commons." Substack: Never Met a Science. Accessed August 17, 2022. **URL:** https://kevinmunger.substack.com/p/we-lived-in-a-society

Muñoz, Jordi and Eva Anduiza. 2019. "'If a Fight Starts, Watch the Crowd': The Effect of Violence on Popular Support for Social Movements." *Journal of Peace Research* 56(4):485–498.

Muraoka, Taishi, Jacob Montgomery, Christopher Lucas, and Margit Tavits. 2021. "Love and Anger in Global Party Politics: Facebook Reactions to Political Party Posts in 79 Democracies." *Journal of Quantitative Description: Digital Media* 1.

Murphy, Tim. 2021. "Donald Trump's Parting Gift to Washington Was a Party of Shitposters." Mother Jones. Accessed August 17, 2021. **URL:** https://www.motherjones.com/politics/2021/06/donald-trumps-parting-gift-to-washington-was-a-party-of-shitposters/

Mutz, Diana C. 2016. *In-Your-Face Politics: The Consequences of Uncivil Media.* Princeton University Press.

Mutz, Diana C. 2018. "Status Threat, Not Economic Hardship, Explains the 2016 Presidential Vote." *Proceedings of the National Academy of Sciences* 115(19):E4330–E4339.

Mutz, Diana C. and Byron Reeves. 2005. "The New Videomalaise: Effects of Televised Incivility on Political Trust." *American Political Science Review* 99(1):1–15.

Myroniuk, Anna. 2020. "Infamous Populist Lyashko Loses Special Election to Reenter Parliament." *Kyiv Post.* **URL:** https://www.kyivpost.com/ukraine-politics/infamous-populist-lyashko-loses-special-election-to-reenter-parliament.html

Nacos, Brigitte L., Robert Y. Shapiro, and Yaeli Bloch-Elkon. 2020. "Donald Trump: Aggressive Rhetoric and Political Violence." *Perspectives on Terrorism* 14(5):2–25.

Nai, Alessandro and Jürgen Maier. 2021. "Is Negative Campaigning a Matter of Taste? Political Attacks, Incivility, and the Moderating Role of Individual Differences." *American Politics Research* 49(3):269–281.

Naylor, Brian. 2021. "Read Trump's Jan. 6 Speech, a Key Part of Impeachment Trial." NPR. Accessed March 14, 2021. **URL:** https://www.npr.org/2021/02/10/966396848/read-trumps-jan-6-speech-a-key-part-of-impeachment-trial

Neavling, Steve. 2019. "Rep. Tlaib's Re-election Campaign is Selling 'Impeach the MF' T-shirts." *Detroit Metro Times.* Accessed January 9, 2021. **URL:** https://www.metrotimes.com/news-hits/archives/2019/09/26/rep-tlaibs-re-election-campaign-is-selling-impeach-the-mf-t-shirts

Nelson, Candice J. and James A. Thurber. 2018. *Campaigns and Elections American Style: The Changing Landscape of Political Campaigns.* Routledge.

Nelson, Louis. 2015. "Good News for Rubio in GOP Poll." Politico. Accessed June 11, 2020. **URL:** https://www.politico.com/story/2015/03/good-news-for-marco-rubio-in-gop-poll-116081

New Inform. 2017. "Lyashko Harshly Besieged Saakashvili and Called Him a 'Bum'." New Inform. Accessed December 11, 2020. **URL:** https://newinform.com/22927-lyashko-zhestko-osadil-saakashvili-i-nazval-ego-bomzhom

Newman, Dina. 2014. "Ukraine Conflict: 'White Power' Warrior from Sweden." BBC News. Accessed November 5, 2020. **URL:** https://www.bbc.com/news/world-europe-28329329

Newman, Lindsay Shorr. 2013. "Do Terrorist Attacks Increase Closer to Elections?" *Terrorism and Political Violence* 25(1):8–28.

Nichols, Tom. 2021. "Worse Than Treason." *The Atlantic.* **URL:** https://www.theatlantic.com/ideas/archive/2021/01/what-republicans-are-doing-worse-treason/617538/

Nielsen, Richard A. 2017. *Deadly Clerics: Blocked Ambition and the Paths to Jihad.* Cambridge University Press.

Norris, Pippa and Ronald Inglehart. 2019. *Cultural Backlash: Trump, Brexit, and Authoritarian Populism.* Cambridge University Press.

NSDC. 2015. "Olexandr Turchynov: The Situation in Travel Corridors in the Anti-Terrorist Operation Zone Can Be Monitored in Real Time Mode." National Security and Defense Council of Ukraine. Accessed November 4, 2020. **URL:** https://www.rnbo.gov.ua/en/Diialnist/2091.html

Nyhan, Brendan. 2020. "Facts and myths about misperceptions." *Journal of Economic Perspectives* 34(3):220–236.

Obozrevatel. 2015. "Kaplin Threatened Not to Leave Yatsenyuk a 'Wet Spot'." Obozrevatel News. Accessed December 10, 2020. **URL:** https://news.obozrevatel.com/ukr/politics/65837-kaplin-prigroziv-ne-zalishiti-vid-yatsenyuka-mokrogo-mistsya.htm

O'Grady, Siobhán. 2016. "Israeli Politician: My Wife Should Not Have to Give Birth Next to an Arab." Foreign Policy. Accessed December 15, 2020. **URL:** https://foreignpolicy.com/2016/04/05/israeli-politician-my-wife-should-not-have-to-give-birth-next-to-an-arab/

Oksana, Grytsenko. 2014. "Lyashko's Party Set to Win Seats with Radical Populism." *Kyiv Post.* **URL:** https://www.kyivpost.com/kyiv-post-plus/lyashkos-party-set-to-win-seats-with-radical-populism-366002.html

Oliphant, James and Chris Kahn. 2021. "Half of Republicans Believe False Accounts of Deadly U.S. Capitol Riot-Reuters/Ipsos Poll." Reuters. Accessed August 15, 2021. **URL:** https://www.reuters.com/article/us-usa-politics-disinformation-idUSKBN2BS0RZ

Oliver, J. Eric and Thomas J. Wood. 2014. "Conspiracy Theories and the Paranoid Style (s) of Mass Opinion." *American Journal of Political Science* 58(4):952–966.

Onuch, Olga. 2015. "EuroMaidan Protests in Ukraine: Social Media versus Social Networks." *Problems of Post-Communism* 62(4):217–235.

Onuch, Olga, Emma Mateo, and Julian G. Waller. 2021. "Mobilization, Mass Perceptions, and (Dis) information: 'New' and 'Old' Media Consumption Patterns and Protest." *Social Media+ Society* 7(2):2056305121999656.

Onuch, Olga and Henry E. Hale. 2018. "Capturing Ethnicity: The Case of Ukraine." *Post-Soviet Affairs* 34(2–3):84–106.

Osnos, Evan. 2020. "Why Democracy Is on the Decline in the United States." *New Yorker.* **URL:** https://www.newyorker.com/news/daily-comment/why-democracy-is-on-the-decline-in-the-united-states

Oster, Marcy. 2020. "Yair Lapid Once Allied with Benny Gantz. Now He Wants to Keep Him from Becoming Prime Minister." Jewish Journal. Accessed December 14, 2020. **URL:** https://jewishjournal.com/israel/314748/yair-lapid-once-allied-with-benny-gantz-now-he-wants-to-keep-him-from-becoming-prime-minister/

Ostrovsky, Simon. 2014. "Russian Roulette (Dispatch 56)." Vice News. Accessed September 25, 2020. **URL:** https://www.vice.com/en/article/xw3j8z/russian-roulette-dispatch-56

Packer, George. 2019. "The Mafia Style in American Politics." *The Atlantic.* **URL:** https://www.theatlantic.com/ideas/archive/2019/10/roy-cohn-mafia-politics/599320/

Paniotto, Vladimir. 2014. "Euromaidan: Profile of a Rebellion." *ISA Global Dialogue* 4(2). **URL:** https://globaldialogue.isa-sociology.org/euromaidan-profile-of-a-rebellion/

Parker, Christopher S. and Matt A. Barreto. 2014. *Change They Can't Believe In: The Tea Party and Reactionary Politics in America—Updated Edition.* Princeton University Press.

Paz, Christian. 2020. "All the President's Lies about the Coronavirus." *The Atlantic.* **URL:** https://www.theatlantic.com/politics/archive/2020/11/trumps-lies-about-coronavirus/608647/

Pedahzur, Ami. 2012. *The Triumph of Israel's Radical Right.* Oxford University Press.

Petersen, Michael Bang. 2020. "The Evolutionary Psychology of Mass Mobilization: How Disinformation and Demagogues Coordinate Rather than Manipulate." *Current Opinion in Psychology* 35:71–75.

Petersen, Michael Bang and Lasse Laustsen. 2020. "Dominant Leaders and the Political Psychology of Followership." *Current Opinion in Psychology* 33:136–141.

Petersen, Roger D. 2002. *Understanding Ethnic Violence: Fear, Hatred, and Resentment in Twentieth-Century Eastern Europe.* Cambridge University Press.

Pew Research Center. 2016. "Partisanship and Political Animosity in 2016." Technical report. Accessed October 20, 2020. **URL:** https://www.pewresearch.org/politics/2016/06/22/partisanship-and-political-animosity-in-2016/

Phillips, Amber. 2017. "'They're Rapists.' President Trump's Campaign Launch Speech Two Years Later, Annotated." *Washington Post.* **URL:** https://www.washingtonpost.com/news/the-fix/wp/2017/06/16/theyre-rapists-presidents-trump-campaign-launch-speech-two-years-later-annotated/

Picheta, Rob and Katie Polglase. 2019. "Ukraine President Takes Drug Test before Debating Comedian in 70,000-Seater Stadium." CNN. Accessed December 11, 2020. **URL:** https://www.cnn.com/2019/04/06/europe/ukraine-elections-drug-test-intl/index.html

Pifer, Steven. 2015. "Putin and Ukraine's East/West Divide." Brookings Institution. Accessed November 2, 2020. **URL:** https://www.brookings.edu/blog/order-from-chaos/2015/05/14/putin-and-ukraines-eastwest-divide/

Pilkington, Ed. 2018. "Feel the Love, Feel the Hate–My Week in the Cauldron of Trump's Wild Rallies." *The Guardian*. **URL:** https://www.theguardian.com/us-news/2018/nov/01/trump-rallies-america-midterms-white-house

Pilkington, Ed. 2022. "US Intelligence Believes Russia Has Ordered Ukraine Invasion—Reports." *The Guardian*. **URL:** https://www.theguardian.com/us-news/2022/feb/20/russia-invasion-ukraine-biden-blinken-us-national-security-council

Pleasance, Chris. 2022. "Pro-Russian Former Ukrainian MP Urges Putin to Carry Out 'Pre-emptive Strike' with 'Weapons of Mass Destruction' against his Home Country after Zelensky Warned Russia Could Resort to Using Nukes." Daily Mail. Accessed June 23, 2022. **URL:** https://www.dailymail.co.uk/news/article-10731057/Ukraine-war-Ex-MP-urges-Putin-use-weapons-mass-destruction-Ukraine.html

Pleines, Heiko. 2016. "Oligarchs and Politics in Ukraine." *Demokratizatsiya: The Journal of Post-Soviet Democratization* 24(1):105–127.

Plokhy, Serhii. 2015. *The Gates of Europe: A History of Ukraine*. Basic Books.

Politi, James, Max Seddon, and Roman Olearchyk. 2022. "US Shares Fresh Claims of Moscow Coup Plot for Ukraine." *Financial Times*. Accessed August 19, 2022. **URL:** https://www.ft.com/content/57792de1-664f-4d8e-a706-c8cea30015f0

Polityuk, Pavel and Natalia Zinets. 2017. "Supporters Free Ex-Georgian Leader Saakashvili from Ukrainian Police amid Chaotic Scenes." Reuters. Accessed October 22, 2020. **URL:** https://www.reuters.com/article/us-ukraine-saakashvili/supporters-free-ex-georgian-leader-saakashvili-from-ukrainian-police-amid-chaotic-scenes-idUSKBN1DZ0VU

Poole, Keith T. 2007. "Changing Minds? Not in Congress!" *Public Choice* 131(3–4):435–451.

Pop-Eleches, Grigore and Joshua A. Tucker. 2014. "Communist Socialization and Post-Communist Economic and Political Attitudes." *Electoral Studies* 33:77–89.

Posen, Barry R. 1993. "The Security Dilemma and Ethnic Conflict." *Survival* 35(1):27–47.

Pratto, Felicia, Jim Sidanius, Lisa M. Stallworth, and Bertram F. Malle. 1994. "Social Dominance Orientation: A Personality Variable Predicting Social and Political Attitudes." *Journal of Personality and Social Psychology* 67(4):741.

Preece, Jessica and Olga Stoddard. 2015. "Why Women Don't Run: Experimental Evidence on Gender Differences in Political Competition Aversion." *Journal of Economic Behavior & Organization* 117:296–308.

Prior, Markus. 2007. *Post-broadcast Democracy: How Media Choice Increases Inequality in Political Involvement and Polarizes Elections*. Cambridge University Press.

Protess, David L. 1992. *The Journalism of Outrage: Investigative Reporting and Agenda Building in America*. Guilford Press.

Przeworski, Adam. 1991. *Democracy and the Market: Political and Economic Reforms in Eastern Europe and Latin America*. Cambridge University Press.

Psaropoulos, John. 2022. "Timeline: The First 100 Days of Russia's War in Ukraine." Al Jazeera. Accessed June 7, 2022. **URL:** https://www.aljazeera.com/features/2022/6/3/timeline-the-first-100-days-of-russias-war-in-ukraine

Qiu, Linda and Mikayla Bouchard. 2020. "Tracking Trump's Claims on the Threat from Coronavirus." *New York Times*. **URL:** https://www.nytimes.com/2020/03/05/us/politics/trump-coronavirus-fact-check.html

Quinn, Allison. 2015. "Third Servicemen Dies from Rada Grenade Attack." *Kyiv Post*. **URL:** https://www.kyivpost.com/article/content/kyiv-post-plus/third-servicemen-dies-from-rada-grenade-attack-396940.html

Quinn, Chris. 2021. "When Candidates Make Reckless Statements Just to Get Attention, Should They Get Attention?" *Plain Dealer*. **URL:** https://www.cleveland.com/news/2021/03/when-candidates-make-reckless-statements-just-to-get-attention-should-they-get-attention-letter-from-the-editor.html

Radnitz, Scott. 2016. "Paranoia with a Purpose: Conspiracy Theory and Political Coalitions in Kyrgyzstan." *Post-Soviet Affairs* 32(5):474–489.

Radnitz, Scott. 2021. *Revealing Schemes: The Politics of Conspiracy in Russia and the Post-Soviet Region*. Oxford University Press.

Ragusa, Jordan M. 2016. "Partisan Cohorts, Polarization, and the Gingrich Senators." *American Politics Research* 44(2):296–325.

Ratzlav-Katz, Nissan. 2008. "Riots in Akko on Yom Kippur." *Israel National News*. Accessed May 1, 2020. **URL:** https://www.israelnationalnews.com/News/News.aspx/127921

Rauschenbach, Mascha and Katrin Paula. 2019. "Intimidating Voters with Violence and Mobilizing Them with Clientelism." *Journal of Peace Research* 56(5):682–696.

Reed, John, Guy Chazan, and Roman Olearchyk. 2022. "The Damning Case against Trump that the Jan. 6 Committee has Uncovered—and What Comes Next." *Financial Times*. Accessed August 12, 2022. **URL:** https://www.ft.com/content/9ab50dee-67f5-4e1b-8456-d8f11814ef18

Reeves, Jay, Lisa Mascaro, and Calvin Woodward. 2021. "Capitol Assault a More Sinister Attack than First Appeared." ABC News. Accessed March 16, 2021. **URL:** https://abcnews.go.com/Politics/wireStory/capitol-assault-sinister-attack-appeared-75171068

Republicans, E & C. 2020. "Governor Cuomo Can't Pass the Buck on His Deadly Mistakes." The Republican Energy and Commerce Subcommittees. Accessed Demcember 2, 2020. **URL:** https://republicans-energycommerce.house.gov/news/governor-cuomo-cant-pass-the-buck-on-his-deadly-mistakes/

Resende, Erica. 2018. *Crisis and Change in Post-Cold War Global Politics*. Springer.

Rettig Gur, Haviv. 2020. "Naftali Bennett Wants to Be the Right's Anti-Netanyahu and It's Working." *The Times of Israel*. **URL:** https://www.timesofisrael.com/naftali-bennett-wants-to-be-the-rights-anti-netanyahu-and-its-working/#gs.fpdt37

Reuters. 2009. "FACTBOX: Israel's Lieberman and Controversial Comments." Reuters. Accessed December 15, 2020. **URL:** https://www.reuters.com/article/us-israel-lieberman-quotes-sb/factbox-israels-lieberman-and-controversial-comments-idUSTRE52U3FU20090401

Reuters. 2015. "Ukraine Lawmaker Manhandles PM Yatseniuk in Rowdy Parliament Scenes." Reuters. Accessed December 11, 2020. **URL:** https://www.reuters.com/article/us-ukraine-crisis-parliament/ukraine-lawmaker-manhandles-pm-yatseniuk-in-rowdy-parliament-scenes-idUSKBN0TU1C920151211

Reuters. 2016. "Ukrainian MPs Throw Punches over Accusations of Kremlin Links." Reuters. Accessed December 15, 2020. **URL:** Ukrainian MPs throw punches over accusations of Kremlin links

Reuters. 2021. "Ukrainian President's Party Removes Speaker in Dispute over Anti-oligarch Bill." Reuters. Accessed August 14, 2022. **URL:** https://www.reuters.com/world/europe/ukrainian-presidents-party-removes-speaker-dispute-over-anti-oligarch-bill-2021-10-05/

Reuters. 2022*a*. "Timeline: The Events Leading Up to Russia's Invasion of Ukraine." Reuters. Accessed June 1, 2022. **URL:** https://www.reuters.com/world/europe/events-leading-up-russias-invasion-ukraine-2022-02-28/

Reuters. 2022*b*. "Ukraine's Former President Poroshenko Blocked from Leaving the Country." Reuters. Accessed August 17, 2022. **URL:** https://www.reuters.com/world/europe/ukraines-former-president-blocked-leaving-country-2022-05-28/

Reynolds, Nick and Jack Watling. 2021. "Ukraine through Russia's Eyes." The Royal United Services Institute for Defence and Security Studies (RUSI). Accessed August 14, 2022. **URL:** https://rusi.org/explore-our-research/publications/commentary/ukraine-through-russias-eyes

RFE/RL. 2012. "Ukrainian Lawmakers Reject Call to Dissolve Parliament after Fistfight." Radio Free Europe/Radio Liberty. Accessed November 3, 2020. **URL:** https://www.rferl.org/a/ukraine-parliament-reject-call-to-dissolve-fistfight/24592852.html

RFE/RL. 2017. "Smoke Bomb in Ukrainian Parliament." Radio Free Europe/Radio Liberty. Accessed December 11, 2020. **URL:** https://www.rferl.org/a/ukraine-parliament-smokebomb/28778074.html

RFE/RL. 2019*a*. "Amnesty International: Five Years after Euromaidan, Justice for the Victims 'Still Not Even in Sight.'" Radio Free Europe/Radio Liberty. Accessed November 5, 2020. **URL:** https://www.rferl.org/a/ukraine-maidan-justice-victims-amnesty-fifth-anniversary/29779358.html

RFE/RL. 2019*b*. "Tymoshenko Accuses Parliament's Leadership of Blocking Presidential Impeachment." Radio Free Europe/Radio Liberty. **URL:** https://www.rferl.org/a/tymoshenko-accuses-parliament-s-leadership-of-blocking-presidential-impeachment/29796009.html

RFE/RL. 2020*a*. "Ukrainian President Names Saakashvili to Head Reform Council." Radio Free Europe/Radio Liberty. Accessed October 22, 2020. **URL:** https://www.rferl.org/a/ukraine-president-names-saakashvili-to-head-reform-council/30599789.html

RFE/RL. 2020*b*. "Ukrainian Singer Vakarchuk Steps Down as Head of Holos Political Party." Radio Free Europe/Radio Liberty. Accessed March 24, 2021. **URL:** https://www.rferl.org/a/ukrainian-singer-vakarchuk-steps-down-as-head-of-holos-political-party/30482463.html

RFE/RL. 2021*a*. "Ukraine Says Russia Blocking Most of Sea of Azov As Tensions Mount between Kyiv and Moscow." Radio Free Europe/Radio Liberty. Accessed December 25, 2021. **URL:** https://www.rferl.org/a/ukraine-azov-sea-russia-tensions/31604367.html

RFE/RL. 2021*b*. "Ukraine's Powerful Interior Minister Tenders Resignation." Radio Free Europe/Radio Liberty. Accessed August 15, 2021. **URL:** https://www.rferl.org/a/ukraine-avakov-minister-resigns/31356810.html

RFE/RL. 2021*c*. "Ukrainian Police Clash with Far-Right Group at Odesa Pride March." Radio Free Europe/Radio Liberty. Accessed October 2, 2021. **URL:** https://www.rferl.org/a/ukraine-pride-lgbt-odesa-/31432989.html

Ricci, Andrew. 2016. "The Dirty Secret about Negative Campaign Ads—They Work." *The Hill*. Accessed December 20, 2020. **URL:** https://thehill.com/blogs/pundits-blog/presidential-campaign/304141-the-dirty-secret-about-negative-campaign-ads-they

Rizzo, Salvador. 2018. "Analysis: The Kooky Tale of 'Cocaine Mitch.'" *Washington Post*. **URL:** https://www.washingtonpost.com/news/fact-checker/wp/2018/05/04/the-kooky-tale-of-cocaine-mitch/

Roberts, Margaret E. 2018. *Censored*. Princeton University Press.

Roberts, Roxanne and Amy Argetsinger. 2010. "Who Says Washington Is 'Hollywood for Ugly People'?: We Trace a Cliche Back to Its Origin." *Washington Post*. **URL:** http://voices.washingtonpost.com/reliable-source/2010/12/who_says_washington_is_hollywo.html

Rogin, Michael Paul. 1967. *The Intellectuals and McCarthy: The Radical Specter*. MIT Press.

Romaliiska, Irina. 2022. "'Putin Only Understands Force,' Says Ukrainian Ex-President in Call for United Response against Russia." Radio Free Europe/Radio Liberty. Accessed May 30, 2022. **URL:** https://www.rferl.org/a/ukraine-poroshenko-unity-no-compromise/31861410.html

Romero, Simon. 2020. "After Trump's Loss in Arizona, State Republicans Hurl Insults at One Another." *New York Times*. **URL:** https://www.nytimes.com/2020/12/08/us/arizona-ducey-republicans.html

Ronen, Gil. 2015. "Media Poll War: 'Bibiton' Lashes Out at 'Bujiton.'" *Israel National News*. Accessed October 22, 2020. **URL:** https://www.israelnationalnews.com/News/News.aspx/190490

Rosenfeld, Sam. 2022. "Democracy Is on the Brink of Disaster. For Voters, It's Politics as Usual." *Washington Post*. Accessed August 17, 2022. **URL:** https://www.washingtonpost.com/outlook/2022/01/07/democracy-threat-voters-politics/

Rosenzweig, Steven C. 2017. "Voter Backlash, Elite Misperception, and the Logic of Violence in Electoral Competition" PhD thesis Yale University.

Rosner, Shmuel. 2019. "Why Israel Still Loves Netanyahu." *New York Times*. **URL:** https://www.nytimes.com/2019/04/10/opinion/netanyahu-israel-election.html

Roth, Andrew and J. David Goodman. 2012. "Push Comes to Shove, and Punch, in Ukraine Parliament." *New York Times*. **URL:** https://www.nytimes.com/2012/05/26/world/europe/ukraine-parliament-debate-over-language-escalates-into-a-brawl.html

Rothschild, Neal. 2019. "Trump's Tweets Are Losing their Potency." Axios. Accessed September 8, 2020. **URL:** https://www.axios.com/president-trump-tweets-engagement-4c6067a8-734d-4184-984a-d5c9151aa339.html

Rubin, Shira. 2021. "Israeli Security Chief Issues Rare Warning over Potential for Jan. 6-Style Mob Violence ahead of Netanyahu Departure." *Washington Post*. **URL:** https://www.washingtonpost.com/world/middle_east/netanyahu-trump-capitol-mob-siege/2021/06/06/40a1d10e-c68a-11eb-89a4-b7ae22aa193e_story.html

Rubryka. 2018. "Avakov Called Muraev 'Trash.'" Rubryka. Accessed August 10, 2021. **URL:** https://rubryka.com/2018/06/08/avakov-obizvav-murayeva-pokydkom/

Rudenko, Olga. 2021. "Pro-Kremlin Politicians Medvedchuk, Kozak Charged with Treason (UPDATED)." *Kyiv Post*. **URL:** https://www.kyivpost.com/ukraine-politics/pro-russian-politicians-medvedchuk-kozak-charged-with-treason.html

Rudnitzky, Arik. 2021. "Survey among Arab Voters in Israel Ahead of the 24th Knesset Elections." Moshe Dayan Center for Middle Eastern and African Studies. Accessed November 2, 2021. **URL:** https://dayan.org/content/survey-among-arab-voters-israel-ahead-24th-knesset-elections

Rumer, Eugene and Andrew S. Weiss. 2021. "Ukraine: Putin's Unfinished Business." Carnegie Endowment for International Peace. Accessed June 1, 2022. **URL:** https://carnegieendowment.org/2021/11/12/ukraine-putin-s-unfinished-business-pub-85771

Rupar, Aaron. 2020. "Trump's Latest Tweet about Coronavirus Testing Is Like a Greatest Hits of His Favorite Lies." Vox. Accessed August 9 2021. **URL:** https://www.vox.com/2020/5/18/21262183/trump-coronavirus-testing-tweet-false-claims

Russell, Annelise. 2018. "US Senators on Twitter: Asymmetric Party Rhetoric in 140 Characters." *American Politics Research* 46(4):695–723.

Russonello, Giovanni. 2019. "Four Problems with 2016 Trump Polling That Could Play Out Again in 2020." *New York Times*. **URL:** https://www.nytimes.com/2019/11/23/us/politics/2020-trump-presidential-polls.html

Russonello, Giovanni. 2020. "Who Can Beat Trump? Who Knows?" *New York Times*. **URL:** https://www.nytimes.com/2020/02/20/us/politics/democrats-ask-who-can-beat-trump.html

Ryabinska, Natalya. 2022. "Politics as a Joke: The Case of Volodymyr Zelensky's Comedy Show in Ukraine." *Problems of Post-Communism* 69(2):179–191.

Ryan, Timothy J. 2012. "What Makes Us Click? Demonstrating Incentives for Angry Discourse with Digital-Age Field Experiments." *Journal of Politics* 74(4):1138–1152.

Sachs, Natan and Kevin Huggard. 2020. "Order from Chaos: In Israel, Benny Gantz Decides to Join with Rival Netanyahu." Brookings Institution. Accessed December 14, 2020. **URL:** https://www.brookings.edu/blog/order-from-chaos/2020/03/27/in-israel-benny-gantz-decides-to-join-with-rival-netanyahu/

Samuels, Alex and Patrick Svitek. 2021. "After Riot at the U.S. Capitol, Ted Cruz Gets Fierce Blowback for His Role in Sowing Doubts about Joe Biden's Victory." *Texas Tribune*. Accessed September 3, 2022. **URL:** https://www.texastribune.org/2021/01/07/ted-cruz-riot-capitol/

Sasse, Gwendolyn. 2019. "What Does Zelenskiy's Victory Say about Ukraine?" Carnegie Europe. Accessed November 5, 2020. **URL:** https://carnegieeurope.eu/strategiceurope/78965

Sauer, Pjotr. 2022. "Ukraine Suspends 11 Political Parties with Links to Russia." *The Guardian*. **URL:** https://www.theguardian.com/world/2022/mar/20/ukraine-suspends-11-political-parties-with-links-to-russia

Schmidt, Michael S. and Luke Broadwater. 2021. "Officers' Injuries, Including Concussions, Show Scope of Violence at Capitol Riot." *New York Times.* **URL:** https://www.nytimes.com/2021/02/11/us/politics/capitol-riot-police-officer-injuries.html

Schmidt, Michael S. and Maggie Haberman. 2019. "Macabre Video of Fake Trump Shooting Media and Critics Is Shown at His Resort." *New York Times.* **URL:** https://www.nytimes.com/2019/10/13/us/politics/trump-video.html

Schmidt, Michael S. and Maggie Haberman. 2021. "The Lawyer behind the Memo on How Trump Could Stay in Office." *New York Times.* **URL:** https://www.nytimes.com/2021/10/02/us/politics/john-eastman-trump-memo.html

Schmidt, Samantha. 2017. "Rep. Farenthold of Texas Says He Would Challenge Female GOP Senators to a Duel–if They Were South Texas Men." *Washington Post.* **URL:** https://www.washingtonpost.com/news/morning-mix/wp/2017/07/25/texas-rep-farenthold-says-he-would-challenge-female-gop-senators-to-a-duel-if-they-were-south-texas-men/

Schofield, Norman and Itai Sened. 2005. "Multiparty Competition in Israel, 1988–96." *British Journal of Political Science* 35(4):635–663.

Schrecker, Ellen. 1999. *Many Are the Crimes: McCarthyism in America.* Princeton University Press.

Schrodt, Philip A., Shannon G. Davis and Judith L. Weddle. 1994. "Political Science: KEDS—a Program for the Machine Coding of Event Data." *Social Science Computer Review* 12(4):561–587.

Schulz, Anne, Werner Wirth, and Philipp Müller. 2020. "We Are the People and You Are Fake News: A Social Identity Approach to Populist Citizens' False Consensus and Hostile Media Perceptions." *Communication Research* 47(2):201–226.

Schwartz, Matthew S. 2022. "Who Is Yevheniy Murayev, the Man the U.K. Says Russia Wants to Install in Ukraine?" National Public Radio. Accessed August 14, 2022. **URL:** https://www.npr.org/2022/01/23/1075199404/yevheniy-murayev-russia-ukraine-british-foreign-office

Seawright, Jason and John Gerring. 2008. "Case Selection Techniques in Case Study Research: A Menu of Qualitative and Quantitative Options." *Political Research Quarterly* 61(2):294–308.

Sebastian Parker, Christopher and Rachel M. Blum. 2021. "Why the GOP Can't Quit Trump." *Washington Post.* **URL:** https://www.washingtonpost.com/politics/2021/03/02/why-gop-cant-quit-trump/

Segodnya. 2018. "Mosiychuk Had a Fight with Shakhov on Live TV: Video." Segodnya. Accessed December 5, 2020. **URL:** https://politics.segodnya.ua/politics/mosiychuk-podralsya-s-shahovym-v-pryamom-efire-tv-video-1163488.html

Shaheen, Kareem. 2017. "Erdoğan Clinches Victory in Turkish Constitutional Referendum." *The Guardian.* **URL:** https://www.theguardian.com/world/2017/apr/16/erdogan-claims-victory-in-turkish-constitutional-referendum

Shalev, Chemi. 2018. "Railroad Row Highlights Netanyahu's Never-Ending Purge of Political Rivals." *Haaretz.* **URL:** https://www.haaretz.com/israel-news/.premium-railroad-row-highlights-pms-endless-purge-of-rivals-1.5436369

Shamota, Mariia. 2013. "SBU Admits Some Foreigners Banned from Ukraine, but Refuses to Confirm, Deny Names." *Kyiv Post.* **URL:** https://www.kyivpost.com/article/content/euromaidan/sbu-admits-some-foreigners-banned-from-ukraine-but-refuses-to-confirm-deny-names-334243.html

Sharon, Jeremy. 2020. "Is Netanyahu's Historic Right-Wing Pact at an End?" *Jerusalem Post.* **URL:** https://www.jpost.com/israel-news/politics-and-diplomacy/is-netanyahus-historic-right-wing-pact-at-an-end-638570

Shear, Michael D. and Lola Fadulu. 2019. "Trump Says Mueller Was 'Horrible' and Republicans 'Had a Good Day.'" *New York Times.* **URL:** https://www.nytimes.com/2019/07/24/us/politics/trump-mueller.html

Sheerin, Jude. 2022. "January 6 Hearing: Trump Accused of Attempted Coup." BBC. Accessed June 28, 2022. **URL:** https://www.bbc.com/news/world-us-canada-61753870

Shekhovtsov, Anton. 2011. "The Creeping Resurgence of the Ukrainian Radical Right? The Case of the Freedom Party." *Europe-Asia Studies* 63(2):203–228.

Sherman, Amy. 2021. "A Timeline of What Trump Said before Jan. 6 Capitol Riot." PolitiFact. Accessed August 11, 2021. **URL:** https://www.politifact.com/article/2021/jan/11/timeline-what-trump-said-jan-6-capitol-riot/

Sherman, Mark and Jessica Gresko. 2021. "With Counting Winding Down, Trump Team Pushes Legal Fights." AP News. Accessed March 2, 2021. **URL:** https://apnews.com/article/donald-trump-sues-3-states-election-c93acbc3e1f31baf3e9023b9b61696f7

Shevchuk, Maria. 2022. "Collaborator Yevhen Murayev Fled to Moscow, the Kremlin Wanted to Appoint Him as the President of Ukraine—Sources." The Royal United Services Institute for Defence and Security Studies (RUSI). Accessed August 14, 2022. **URL:** https://news.obozrevatel.com/ukr/society/kolaborant-evgen-muraev-vtik-do-moskvi-kreml-hotiv-priznachiti-jogo-prezidentom-ukraini-vertikal.htm

Shevel, Oxana. 2015. "The Parliamentary Elections in Ukraine, October 2014." *Electoral Studies* 39(September):153–177.

Shezaf, Hagar. 2020. "Refugees from the Zionist Left: How the Jewish Vote for Arab Party Spiked in Israel's Election—Israel Election 2021—Haaretz.com." *Haaretz*. **URL:** https://www.haaretz.com/israel-news/elections/.premium-how-the-jewish-vote-for-arab-party-spiked-in-israeli-election-1.8633435

Shindler, Colin. 2015. *The Rise of the Israeli Right: From Odessa to Hebron*. Cambridge University Press.

Shinkman, Paul D. 2014. "Defiant Yanukovych Fights for Control in Ukraine." *U.S. News & World Report*. **URL:** https://www.usnews.com/news/articles/2014/02/28/viktor-yanukovych-vows-to-fight-for-ukraine-in-russian-press-conference

Shore, Marci. 2018. *The Ukrainian Night: An Intimate History of Revolution*. Yale University Press.

Shuster, Simon. 2014. "Putin's Man in Crimea Is Ukraine's Worst Nightmare." *Time Magazine*. **URL:** https://time.com/19097/putin-crimea-russia-ukraine-aksyonov/

Siddiqui, Sabrina. 2016. "Rubio: Trump Is 'an Embarrassment' and Republicans Will Pay Big in November." *The Guardian*. **URL:** https://www.theguardian.com/us-news/2016/mar/15/marco-rubio-trump-already-embarrassment-for-republican-party

Sides, John. 2016. "It's Time to Stop the Endless Hype of the 'Willie Horton' Ad." *Washington Post*. **URL:** https://www.washingtonpost.com/news/monkey-cage/wp/2016/01/06/its-time-to-stop-the-endless-hype-of-the-willie-horton-ad/

Sides, John, Michael Tesler, and Lynn Vavreck. 2019. *Identity Crisis: The 2016 Presidential Campaign and the Battle for the Meaning of America*. Princeton University Press.

Sigelman, Lee and Mark Kugler. 2003. "Why Is Research on the Effects of Negative Campaigning So Inconclusive? Understanding Citizens' Perceptions of Negativity." *The Journal of Politics* 65(1):142–160.

Simpson, Brent, Robb Willer, and Matthew Feinberg. 2018. "Does Violent Protest Backfire? Testing a Theory of Public Reactions to Activist Violence." *Socius* 4:2378023118803189.

Sims, Christopher A. and Tao Zha. 1999. "Error Bands for impulse responses." *Econometrica* 67(5):1113–1155.

Singh, Naunihal. 2021. "Analysis: Was the U.S. Capitol Riot Really a Coup? Here's Why Definitions Matter." *Washington Post*. **URL:** https://www.washingtonpost.com/politics/2021/01/09/was-us-capitol-riot-really-coup-heres-why-definitions-matter/

Skorkin, Konstantin. 2020. "Last Man Standing: How Avakov Survived in Ukraine." Carnegie Moscow Center. **URL:** https://carnegiemoscow.org/commentary/81054

Skytte, Rasmus. 2020. "Dimensions of Elite Partisan Polarization: Disentangling the Effects of Incivility and Issue Polarization." *British Journal of Political Science* 1–19.

Smale, Alison and Steven Erlanger. 2014. "Ukraine Mobilizes Reserve Troops, Threatening War." *New York Times*. **URL:** https://www.nytimes.com/2014/03/02/world/europe/ukraine.html

Smith, Alastair. 1996. "Diversionary Foreign Policy in Democratic Systems." *International Studies Quarterly* 40(1):133–153.

Smith, Allan. 2021. "Anti-Trump Republicans Are Facing Punishment Back Home. But Don't Call It a Civil War." NBC News. Accessed August 15, 2021. **URL:** https://www.nbcnews.com/politics/donald-trump/anti-trump-republicans-are-facing-punishment-back-home-don-t-n1256292

Smith, David. 2022. "Democrats Confront Democrats over How to Confront Trump." *The Guardian*. **URL:** https://www.theguardian.com/us-news/2022/jul/12/january-6-hearing-trump-analysis

Smith, David Livingstone. 2011. *Less than Human: Why We Demean, Enslave, and Exterminate Others*. St. Martin's Press.

Snyder, Timothy. 2002. *The Reconstruction of Nations: Poland, Ukraine, Lithuania, Belarus, 1569–1999*. Yale University Press.

Snyder, Timothy. 2021. "The American Abyss." *New York Times*. **URL:** https://www.nytimes.com/2021/01/09/magazine/trump-coup.html

Sobieraj, Sarah and Jeffrey M. Berry. 2011. "From Incivility to Outrage: Political Discourse in Blogs, Talk Radio, and Cable News." *Political Communication* 28(1):19–41.

Soltys, Dennis and Alexander J. Motyl. 2019. "Ukraine' Democracy Is (Almost) All Grown Up." Foreign Policy. Accessed November 11, 2020. **URL:** https://foreignpolicy.com/2019/08/28/ukraines-democracy-is-almost-all-grown-up/

Sommer, Will. 2021. "'Stop the Steal' Organizer in Hiding after Denying Blame for Riot." Daily Beast. Accessed September 20, 2021. **URL:** https://www.thedailybeast.com/stop-the-steal-organizer-in-hiding-after-denying-blame-for-riot

Sorokin, Oleksiy. 2019. "22 Officers Injured after Clashes with Protesters in Cherkasy as Poroshenko Speaks." *Kyiv Post*. **URL:** https://www.kyivpost.com/ukraine-politics/22-police-officers-injured-after-clashes-with-far-right-protesters-in-cherkasy-as-poroshenko-delivered-a-speech.html

Spary, Carole. 2013. "Legislative Protest as Disruptive Democratic Practice." *Democratization* 20(3):392–416.

Spring, Victoria L., C. Daryl Cameron, and Mina Cikara. 2018. "The Upside of Outrage." *Trends in Cognitive Sciences* 22(12):1067–1069.

Steinel, Wolfgang, Carsten K. W. De Dreu, Elsje Ouwehand, and Jimena Y. Ramírez-Marín. 2009. "When Constituencies Speak in Multiple Tongues: The Relative Persuasiveness of Hawkish Minorities in Representative Negotiation." *Organizational Behavior and Human Decision Processes* 109(1):67–78.

Stenner, Karen. 2005. *The Authoritarian Dynamic*. Cambridge University Press.

Stephens-Dougan, LaFleur. 2020. *Race to the Bottom: How Racial Appeals Work in American Politics*. University of Chicago Press.

Stern, David. 2010. "Parliamentary Chaos as Ukraine Ratifies Fleet Deal." BBC News. Accessed October 28, 2020. **URL:** http://news.bbc.co.uk/2/hi/europe/8645847.stm

Stern, David. 2012. "Svoboda: The Rise of Ukraine's Ultra-nationalists." BBC News. Accessed March 23, 2021. **URL:** https://www.bbc.com/news/magazine-20824693

Stern, David L. 2021. "Ukraine's Zelensky Alleges Russia Plotting Coup against Him for Next Week." *Washington Post*. **URL:** https://www.washingtonpost.com/world/europe/ukraine-zelensky-russia-coup/2021/11/26/16e51c80-4e0d-11ec-a7b8-9ed28bf23929_story.html

Stiers, Dieter, Jac Larner, John Kenny, Sofia Breitenstein, Florence Vallee-Dubois, and Michael Lewis-Beck. 2019. "Candidate Authenticity: 'To Thine Own Self Be True.'" *Political Behavior* pp. 1–24.

Stracqualursi, Veronica. 2019. "New House Democrat Rashida Tlaib: 'We're Gonna Impeach the Motherf****r.'" CNN News. Accessed January 10, 2021. **URL:** https://www.cnn.com/2019/01/04/politics/rashida-tlaib-trump-impeachment-comments/index.html

Stracqualursi, Veronica. 2020. "Marjorie Taylor Greene Posts Image of Herself with Gun Alongside 'Squad' Congresswomen, Encourages Going on the 'Offense against These Socialists'." CNN Politics. Accessed March 24, 2021. **URL:** https://edition.cnn.com/2020/09/04/politics/marjorie-taylor-greene-gun-post-squad/index.html

Straus, Scott. 2007. "What Is the Relationship between Hate Radio and Violence? Rethinking Rwanda's "Radio Machete"." *Politics & Society* 35(4):609–637.

Stryker, Robin, Bethany Anne Conway, and J. Taylor Danielson. 2016. "What Is Political Incivility?" *Communication Monographs* 83(4):535–556.

Sullivan, John L., James Piereson, and George E. Marcus. 1993. *Political Tolerance and American Democracy*. University of Chicago Press.

Sullivan, Katie. 2019. "Here Are the 4 Congresswomen Known as 'The Squad' Targeted by Trump's Racist Tweets." CNN Politics. Accessed September 8, 2020. **URL:** https://www.cnn.com/2019/07/15/politics/who-are-the-squad/index.html

Swire-Thompson, Briony, Ullrich K. H. Ecker, Stephan Lewandowsky, and Adam J. Berinsky. 2020. "They Might Be a Liar but They're My Liar: Source Evaluation and the Prevalence of Misinformation." *Political Psychology* 41(1):21–34.

Sydnor, Emily. 2019. *Disrespectful Democracy: The Psychology of Political Incivility*. Columbia University Press.

Talant, Bermet. 2019. "Vakarchuk's Voice Seeks to Challenge Old Rules of Game." *Kyiv Post*. **URL:** https://www.kyivpost.com/ukraine-politics/vakarchuks-voice-seeks-to-challenge-old-rules-of-game.html

Taub, Amanda. 2015. "We Just Got a Glimpse of How Oligarch-Funded Militias Could Bring Chaos to Ukraine." Vox. Accessed November 5, 2020. **URL:** https://www.vox.com/2015/3/23/8279397/kolomoisky-oligarch-ukraine-militia

Taylor, Derrick Bryson. 2019. "Kamala Harris Apologizes for Her Reaction to 'Mentally Retarded' Remark about Trump." *New York Times*. **URL:** https://www.nytimes.com/2019/09/08/us/kamala-harris-trump-apologizes.html

Tessler, Mark. 2009. *A History of the Israeli-Palestinian Conflict*. Indiana University Press.

Tharoor, Ishaan. 2015. "Israeli Foreign Minister Says Disloyal Arabs Should Be Beheaded." *Washington Post*. **URL:** https://www.washingtonpost.com/news/worldviews/wp/2015/03/10/israeli-foreign-minister-says-disloyal-arabs-should-be-beheaded/

Tharoor, Ishaan. 2017. "Turkey's Erdogan Turned a Failed Coup into his Path to Greater Power." *Washington Post*. **URL:** https://www.washingtonpost.com/news/worldviews/wp/2017/07/17/turkeys-erdogan-turned-a-failed-coup-into-his-path-to-greater-power/

The Daily Beast. 2020. "Trump Isn't Playing 3-D Chess. He's Eating the Checker." *Daily Beast*. Accessed October 30, 2020. **URL:** https://www.thedailybeast.com/trump-isnt-playing-3-d-chess-hes-eating-the-checker

The Economist. 2012. "Ukraine's Language Law: Hate Speech, or Merely Dislike It?" *The Economist*. **URL:** https://www.economist.com/eastern-approaches/2012/07/05/hate-speech-or-merely-dislike-it

The Guardian. 2010. "Fighting Breaks Out in Ukraine's Parliament." *The Guardian*. **URL:** https://www.theguardian.com/world/gallery/2010/apr/27/ukraine

Theise, Eugen. 2019. "Investigative Journalism Is a Dangerous Job in Ukraine." Deutsche Welle. Accessed January 9, 2021. **URL:** https://www.dw.com/en/investigative-journalism-is-a-dangerous-job-in-ukraine/a-48670080

Theocharis, Yannis, Pablo Barberá, Zoltán Fazekas, and Sebastian Adrian Popa. 2020. "The Dynamics of Political Incivility on Twitter." *Sage Open* 10(2):2158244020919447.

Theocharis, Yannis, Pablo Barberá, Zoltán Fazekas, Sebastian Adrian Popa, and Olivier Parnet. 2016. "A Bad Workman Blames His Tweets: The Consequences Of Citizens' uncivil Twitter Use When Interacting with Party Candidates." *Journal of Communication* 66(6):1007–1031.

Thomas, Emma F., Craig McGarty, and Kenneth I. Mavor. 2009. "Transforming "Apathy into Movement": The Role of Prosocial Emotions In Motivating Action for Social Change." *Personality and Social Psychology Review* 13(4):310–333.

Tilly, Charles. 2002. "Event Catalogs as Theories." *Sociological Theory* 20(2):248–254.

Tilly, Charles. 2008. *Contentious Performances*. Cambridge University Press.

Times, New York. 2008. "On Rose Revolution Anniversary, Mixed Feelings in Georgia." *New York Times*. **URL:** https://www.nytimes.com/2008/11/23/world/europe/23iht-georgia.4.18076404.html

Times of Israel. 2019. "Netanyahu: Gantz Planning Government with Backing of 'Dangerous' Arab Parties." *The Times of Israel.* **URL:** https://www.timesofisrael.com/netanyahu-gantz-planning-government-with-backing-of-dangerous-arab-parties/

Times of Israel. 2020*a*. "Annual Poll: Most Israelis Distrust Leadership, Say Democracy 'in Grave Danger.'" *The Times of Israel.* **URL:** https://www.timesofisrael.com/annual-poll-most-israelis-distrust-leadership-say-democracy-in-grave-danger/

Times of Israel. 2020*b*. "Far-Right MK: Bedouin Birthrate Like a 'Bomb' That Must Be Defused." *The Times of Israel.* **URL:** https://www.timesofisrael.com/far-right-mk-bedouin-birthrate-like-a-bomb-that-must-be-defused/

Times of Israel. 2021*a*. "Full Text: Netanyahu's Furious Final Speech After 12 Years as Prime Minister." *The Times of Israel.* **URL:** https://www.timesofisrael.com/full-text-netanyahus-furious-final-speech-after-12-years-as-prime-minister/

Times of Israel. 2021*b*. "Netanyahu: Bennett Committed the 'Greatest Fraud,' the Public Won't Forget It." *The Times of Israel.* **URL:** https://www.timesofisrael.com/liveblog_entry/netanyahu-bennett-committed-the-greatest-fraud-the-public-wont-forget-it/

Times of Israel. 2021*c*. "With His paPty's Support, Bennett Says He's Heading into Government with Lapid." *The Times of Israel.* **URL:** https://www.timesofisrael.com/with-his-partys-support-bennett-says-hes-heading-into-government-with-lapid/

Tolan, Casey, Curt Devine, Drew Griffin, and Scott Bronstein. 2021. "GOP Lawmakers' Fiery Language under More Scrutiny After Deadly Capitol Riot." CNN Politics. Accessed September 20, 2022 **URL:** https://edition.cnn.com/2021/01/12/politics/gop-lawmakers-fiery-language-under-scrutiny-invs/index.html

Traynor, Ian. 2009. "Georgian President Mikheil Saakashvili Blamed for Starting Russian War." *The Guardian.* **URL:** https://www.theguardian.com/world/2009/sep/30/georgia-attacks-unjustifiable-eu

Traynor, Ian. 1999. "A Talent for Playing with Fire." *The Guardian.* **URL:** https://www.theguardian.com/world/1999/mar/27/balkans9

Trenin, Dmitri. 2009. "Russia's Spheres of Interest, Not Influence." *Washington Quarterly* 32(4): 3–22.

Tress, Luke. 2019. "Smotrich Israel Should Follow Torah Law, Drawing Ire of Liberman." *The Times of Israel.* **URL:** https://www.timesofisrael.com/smotrich-says-israel-should-follow-torah-law-again-drawing-ire-of-liberman/#gs.fpeuws

Troianovski, Anton. 2019. "A Ukrainian Billionaire Fought Russia. Now He's Ready to Embrace It." *New York Times.* **URL:** https://www.nytimes.com/2019/11/13/world/europe/ukraine-ihor-kolomoisky-russia.html

TSN UA. 2018. "The Scandalous Deputy Barna Had a Fight with a 'Svoboda' Member on the Air of the Parliamentary TV Channel." TSN UA. Accessed October 15, 2020. **URL:** https://tsn.ua/ru/politika/skandalnyy-deputat-barna-podralsya-so-svobodovcem-v-pryamom-efire-parlamentskogo-telekanala-1261683.html

Tuchynska, Svitlana. 2010. "Fearing Scandal for being Different, Politicians Keep Themselves, Nation in Closet." *Kyiv Post.* **URL:** https://www.kyivpost.com/article/opinion/op-ed/fearing-scandal-for-being-different-politicians-ke-86373.html

Tucker, Joshua A., Andrew Guess, Pablo Barberá, Cristian Vaccari, Alexandra Siegel, Sergey Sanovich, Denis Stukal, and Brendan Nyhan. 2018. "Social Media, Political Polarization, and Political Disinformation: A Review of the Scientific Literature." (March 19, 2018).

Tucker, Joshua A., Yannis Theocharis, Margaret E. Roberts, and Pablo Barberá. 2017. "From Liberation to Turmoil: Social Media and Democracy." *Journal of Democracy* 28(4):46–59.

Tweetbinder. 2021. "Donald Trump and Twitter—2009/2021 Analysis." Tweet Binder Blog. Accessed November 6, 2021. **URL:** https://www.tweetbinder.com/blog/trump-twitter/

Twitter Inc. 2021. "Permanent Suspension of @realDonaldTrump." Twitter Blog. Accessed February 10, 2021. **URL:** https://blog.twitter.com/en_us/topics/company/2020/suspension

UAWire. 2019. "Zelensky Challenges Ukrainian President Poroshenko to Debate in Olimpiyskiy Stadium." UAWire. Accessed December 11, 2020. **URL:** https://www.uawire.org/zelensky-challenges-poroshenko-to-debate-in-olimpiyskiy-stadium

Ukrainskaya Pravda. 2017*a*. "43 Deputies Almost Never Voted in the Rada—KIU." *Ukrainskaya Pravda*. **URL:** http://www.pravda.com.ua/rus/news/2017/11/14/7162071/

Ukrainskaya Pravda. 2017*b*. "A Case Was Opened against Parasyuk for Beating Up Police Officers." Ukrainskaya Pravda. Accessed October 24, 2020. **URL:** https://www.pravda.com.ua/rus/news/2017/12/5/7164336/

UNHCR. 2022. "UNHCR: Ukraine Refugee Situation." United Nations High Commission for Refugees. Accessed June 1, 2022. **URL:** https://data.unhcr.org/en/situations/ukraine

UNIAN. 2011. "Lyashko Fought with Martynyuk in VRU (video)." Ukrainian Independent Information Agency of News. Accessed November 2, 2020. **URL:** https://www.unian.info/politics/496379-lyashko-fought-with-martynyuk-in-vru-video.html

UNIAN. 2016. "New Cabinet Formed in Ukraine." Ukrainian Independent Information Agency. Accessed December 11, 2020. **URL:** https://www.unian.info/politics/1319232-new-cabinet-formed-in-ukraine.html

UNIAN. 2018. "Ukrainian Chief Prosecutor Lutsenko Decides to Resign." Ukrainian Independent Information Agency. Accessed December 11, 2020. **URL:** https://www.unian.info/politics/10326951-ukrainian-chief-prosecutor-lutsenko-decides-to-resign.html

UNIAN. 2019. "Ukraine's Political Parties Already Spend over US$22 Mln on Election Campaigns: 'NGO CHESNO'." Ukrainian Independent Information Agency. Accessed June 10, 2021. **URL:** https://www.unian.info/politics/10616952-ukraine-s-political-parties-already-spend-over-us-22-mln-on-election-campaigns-ngo-chesno.html

UNIAN. 2020*a*. "Batkivshchyna Party Leader Tymoshenko to Back Liashko of Radical Party in Rada By-Elections." Ukrainian Independent Information Agency of News. Accessed September 28, 2020. **URL:** https://www.unian.info/politics/rada-by-election-tymoshenko-to-back-radical-party-leader-liashko-11036663.html

UNIAN. 2020*b*. "Ukrainian MP Valeriy Davydenko Found Dead in Own Office's Restroom." Ukrainian Independent Information Agency of News. Accessed September 28, 2020. **URL:** https://www.unian.info/society/ukrainian-mp-valeriy-davydenko-found-dead-in-own-office-s-restroom-11008841.html

Uscinski, Joseph E. and Joseph M. Parent. 2014. *American Conspiracy Theories*. Oxford University Press.

Ustinov, Alexandra. 2018. "Kholodnytsky's 'Dear Friends': Who Defended the Anti-Corruption Prosecutor." Ukrainskaya Pravda. Accessed November 1 2020. **URL:** https://www.pravda.com.ua/columns/2018/07/20/7186906/

Vaccari, Cristian and Andrew Chadwick. 2020. "Deepfakes and Disinformation: Exploring the Impact of Synthetic Political Video on Deception, Uncertainty, and Trust in News." *Social Media+ Society* 6(1):2056305120903408.

Vaccari, Cristian and Rasmus Kleis Nielsen. 2013. "What Drives Politicians' Online Popularity? An Analysis of the 2010 US Midterm Elections." *Journal of Information Technology & Politics* 10(2):208–222.

Vaishnav, Milan. 2017. *When Crime Pays: Money and Muscle in Indian Politics*. Yale University Press.

Valenti, Jessica. 2018. "Trump Officials Don't Get to Eat Dinner in Peace–Not While Kids Are in Cages." *The Guardian*. **URL:** https://www.theguardian.com/commentisfree/2018/jun/25/trump-sarah-huckabee-sanders-civility?fbclid=IwAR2zh5Zq-zzpaP_dTfyds0mHtKzehW_FvrVFaKaX44bq_qw90ZGeA_Wg9p

Valentino, Nicholas A., Vincent L. Hutchings, and Ismail K. White. 2002. "Cues That Matter: How Political Ads Prime Racial Attitudes during Campaigns." *American Political Science Review* 96(1):75–90.

Vasilogambros, Matt. 2020. "Oregon's Recent Walkout Reflects a Growing Trend." National Conference of State Legislatures. **URL:** https://www.ncsl.org/bookstore/state-legislatures-magazine/why-lawmakers-flee.aspx

Veidlinger, Jeffrey. 2022. "Analysis: Putin's Claim that War on Ukraine Is to Target Nazis Is Absurd. Here's Why." PBS Newshour. Accessed August 13, 2022. **URL:** https://www.pbs.org/newshour/world/analysis-putins-claim-that-war-on-ukraine-is-to-target-nazis-is-absurd-heres-why

Verlanov, Serhiy. 2020. "Taming Ukraine's Oligarchs." Atlantic Council. Accessed March 20, 2021. **URL:** https://www.atlanticcouncil.org/blogs/ukrainealert/taming-ukraines-oligarchs/

Verstyuk, Ivan. 2013. "Ukraine's Deep-Rooted Media Problem." Columbia Journalism Review. Accessed October 20, 2021. **URL:** https://www.cjr.org/behind_the_news/ukraines_deep-rooted_media_pro.php

Vogt, Manuel, Kristian Skrede Gleditsch, and Lars-Erik Cederman. 2021. "From Claims to Violence: Signaling, Outbidding, and Escalation in Ethnic Conflict." *Journal of Conflict Resolution* 65(7–8):1278–1307

Vox. 2020. "QAnon: The Conspiracy Theory Embraced by Trump, Several Politicians, and some American Moms." Vox. Accessed March 24, 2021. **URL:** https://www.vox.com/2020/10/9/21504910/qanon-conspiracy-theory-facebook-ban-trump

VoxUkraine. 2019. "How Viktor Medvedchuk Uses His Pocket Media. The Case of Informational Attack on VoxCheck." VoxUkraine. Accessed October 22, 2020. **URL:** https://voxukraine.org/en/how-viktor-medvedchuk-uses-his-pocket-media-the-case-of-informational-attack-on-voxcheck/

Wagner, John. 2020. "Trump Calls Romney a 'LOSER' Following Sharp Criticism for Firing Inspectors General." *Washington Post.* **URL:** https://www.washingtonpost.com/politics/trump-calls-romney-a-loser-following-sharp-criticism-for-firing-inspectors-general/2020/05/18/8c0a0be2-9919-11ea-ac72-3841fcc9b35f_story.html

Wagner, Kurt. 2022. "Facebook Parent Says Users Can't Post Calls to Assassinate Putin." Bloomberg. Accessed August 21, 2022. **URL:** https://www.bloomberg.com/news/articles/2022-03-14/facebook-parent-says-users-can-t-post-calls-to-assassinate-putin

Wagner, Michael W. and Mike Gruszczynski. 2018. "Who Gets Covered? Ideological Extremity and News Coverage of Members of the US Congress, 1993 to 2013." *Journalism & Mass Communication Quarterly* 95(3):670–690.

Walker, James. 2020. "Donald Trump Calls Adam Schiff 'Little Pencil Neck' Again, Mocks Idea of Calling Him about Soleimani Strike." *Newsweek.* **URL:** https://www.newsweek.com/donald-trump-adam-schiff-little-pencil-neck-soleimani-strike-1481460

Walter, Nathan and Sheila T. Murphy. 2018. "How to Unring the Bell: A Meta-analytic Approach to Correction of Misinformation." *Communication Monographs* 85(3):423–441.

Ward, Michael D., Andreas Beger, Josh Cutler, Matthew Dickenson, Cassy Dorff, and Ben Radford. 2013. "Comparing GDELT and ICEWS Event Data." *Analysis* 21(1):267–297.

Washington Post. 2020. "Opinion: Israel Was a Covid-19 Success. Then Netanyahu Showed How Not to Manage the Disease." *Washington Post.* **URL:** https://www.washingtonpost.com/opinions/global-opinions/israel-was-a-covid-19-success-then-netanyahu-showed-how-not-to-manage-the-disease/2020/07/31/0eb62914-d0e6-11ea-8d32-1ebf4e9d8e0d_story.html

Wasow, Omar. 2020. "Agenda Seeding: How 1960s Black Protests Moved Elites, Public Opinion and Voting." *American Political Science Review* 114(3):638–659.

Way, Lucan Ahmad. 2019. "Ukraine's Post-Maidan Struggles: II. Free Speech in a Time of War." *Journal of Democracy* 30(3):48–60.

Waytz, Adam, Liane L. Young, and Jeremy Ginges. 2014. "Motive Attribution Asymmetry for Love vs. Hate Drives Intractable Conflict." *Proceedings of the National Academy of Sciences* 111(44):15687–15692.

Webster, Steven W. 2020. *American Rage.* Cambridge University Press.

Webster, Steven W., Adam N. Glynn, and Matthew P. Motta. 2021. "Partisan Schadenfreude and the Demand for Candidate Cruelty."

Wedeen, Lisa. 2015. *Ambiguities of Domination.* University of Chicago Press.

Weigel, David. 2022. "Democrats Confront Democrats over How to Confront Trump." *Washington Post.* **URL:** https://www.washingtonpost.com/politics/2022/07/24/republicans-civil-war-midterms/

Weir, Fred. 2019. "Militaristic and Anti-democratic, Ukraine's Far-Right Bides Its Time." *The Christian Science Monitor.* **URL:** https://www.csmonitor.com/World/Europe/2019/0415/Militaristic-and-anti-democratic-Ukraine-s-far-right-bides-its-time

Weiss, Mark. 2020. "Third Election Leaves an Ominous Impasse." *Jerusalem Post*. **URL:** https://www.jpost.com/jerusalem-report/third-election-leaves-an-ominous-impasse-620675

Wells, Chris, Dhavan V. Shah, Jon C. Pevehouse, JungHwan Yang, Ayellet Pelled, Frederick Boehm, Josephine Lukito, Shreenita Ghosh, and Jessica L. Schmidt. 2016. "How Trump Drove Coverage to the Nomination: Hybrid Media Campaigning." *Political Communication* 33(4):669–676.

Westwood, Sean J., Justin Grimmer, Matthew Tyler, and Clayton Nall. 2022. "Current Research Overstates American Support for Political Violence." *Proceedings of the National Academy of Sciences* 119(12):e2116870119.

Whitmore, Sarah. 2019. "Disrupted Democracy in Ukraine? Protest, Performance and Contention in the Verkhovna Rada." *Europe-Asia Studies* 71(9):1474–1507.

Whitmore, Sarah. 2020. "Performing Protest and Representation? Exploring Citizens' Perceptions of Parliament in Ukraine." *East European Politics* 36(1):86–106.

Whittaker, Francis. 2014. "Ukrainian Politician Is Nearly Knocked Out After Calling Rival a 'Pot-Bellied Fatty.'" Buzzfeed News. Accessed October 30, 2020. **URL:** https://www.buzzfeednews.com/article/franciswhittaker/ukrainian-politician-is-nearly-knocked-out-after-calling-riv

Wilkinson, Steven I. 2006. *Votes and Violence: Electoral Competition and Ethnic Riots in India*. Cambridge University Press.

Williams, Matthias and Pavel Polityuk. 2019. "Ukraine's Tymoshenko: 'Gas Princess', Prisoner, and Next President?" Reuters. Accessed December 10, 2020. **URL:** https://www.reuters.com/article/us-ukraine-election-tymoshenko/ukraines-tymoshenko-gas-princess-prisoner-and-next-president-idUSKCN1QL0LT

Wilson, Andrew et al. 2005. *Virtual Politics: Faking Democracy in the Post-Soviet world*. Yale University Press.

Wilson, Richard Ashby. 2017. *Incitement on Trial: Prosecuting International Speech Crimes*. Cambridge University Press.

Wilson, Woodrow. 1901. *A History of the American People*. Vol. 10, Harper & Brothers.

Winer, Stuart. 2018. "Israeli Lawmaker Proclaims Supremacy of 'Jewish Race.'" *The Times of Israel*. **URL:** https://www.timesofisrael.com/israeli-lawmaker-lauds-supremacy-of-jewish-race/

Winer, Stuart and Toi Staff. 2018. "Justice Minister Exults: High Court No Longer a Branch of Left-Wing Meretz Party." *The Times of Israel*. **URL:** https://www.timesofisrael.com/justice-minister-high-court-no-longer-a-branch-of-left-wing-meretz-party/

Wirz, Dominique. 2018. "Persuasion through Emotion? An Experimental Test of the Emotion-Eliciting Nature of Populist Communication." *International Journal of Communication* 12: 1114–1138.

Woodward, Calvin. 2021. "AP FACT CHECK: Trump's Team Glosses over His Jan. 6 Tirade." Associated Press. Accessed August 11, 2021. **URL:** https://apnews.com/article/ap-fact-check-donald-trump-capitol-siege-violence-elections-507f4febbadecb84e1637e55999ac0ea

Wootliff, Raoul. 2020. "Israel Calls 4th Election in 2 Years as Netanyahu-Gantz Coalition Collapses." *The Times of Israel*. **URL:** https://www.timesofisrael.com/israel-calls-4th-election-in-2-years-as-netanyahu-gantz-coalition-collapses/

Wu, Tim. 2017. *The Attention Merchants: The Epic Scramble to Get Inside Our Heads*. Vintage.

Yablokov, Ilya. 2018. *Fortress Russia: Conspiracy Theories in the Post-Soviet World*. John Wiley & Sons.

Yanagizawa-Drott, David. 2014. "Propaganda and Conflict: Evidence from the Rwandan Genocide." *Quarterly Journal of Economics* 129(4):1947–1994.

Yen, Hope, Ali Swenson, and Amanda Seitz. 2020. "AP FACT CHECK: Trump's Claims of Vote Rigging Are All Wrong." Associated Press. Accessed August 10, 2021. **URL:** https://apnews.com/article/election-2020-ap-fact-check-joe-biden-donald-trump-technology-49a24edd6d10888dbad61689c24b05a5

Yen, Hope and Colleen Long. 2018. "AP Fact Check: President Trump's Rhetoric and the Truth about Migrant Caravans." Associated Press. Accessed December 10, 2020. **URL:** https://

www.pbs.org/newshour/politics/ap-fact-check-president-trumps-rhetoric-and-the-truth-about-migrant-caravans

Yermolenko, Volodymyr. 2018. "Ukraine's New Populists: Who They Are and Why They're Dangerous." Atlantic Council. Accessed September 28, 2020. **URL:** https://www.atlanticcouncil.org/blogs/ukrainealert/ukraine-s-new-populists-who-they-are-and-why-they-re-dangerous/

Yong, Ed. 2020. "How the Pandemic Defeated America." *The Atlantic.* **URL:** https://www.theatlantic.com/magazine/archive/2020/09/coronavirus-american-failure/614191/

Young, Dannagal Goldthwaite. 2019. *Irony and Outrage: The Polarized Landscape of Rage, Fear, and Laughter in the United States.* Oxford University Press.

Yourish, Karen, Dan Keating, Nathaniel V. Kelso, and Laura Stanton. 2010. "An Up-Close Look at the Tea Party and Its Role in the Midterm Elections." *Washington Post.* **URL:** https://www.washingtonpost.com/wp-srv/special/politics/tea-party-canvass/

Zaller, John R. 1992. *The Nature and Origins of Mass Opinion.* Cambridge University Press.

Zanona, Melanie. 2020. "House Ethics Panel Admonishes Gaetz over Michael Cohen Tweet." Politico. Accessed December 3, 2020. **URL:** https://www.politico.com/news/2020/08/21/matt-gaetz-cohen-tweet-ethics-panel-400043

Zanona, Melanie, Burgess Everett, and Marianne Levine. 2019. "Republicans Quit Trying to Rein In Trump after 'Lynching' Tweet." Politico. Accessed March 24, 2021. **URL:** https://www.politico.com/news/2019/10/22/congress-reaction-trump-lynching-tweet-054387

Zavoyra, Inna. 2016. "Emotional Lawmaking: Top 7 Brawls in Ukrainian Parliament." 112 Ukraine. Accessed December 11, 2020. **URL:** https://112.international/article/emotional-intensity-top-7-brawls-in-ukrainian-parliament-6286.html

Zeitz, Joshua. 2018. "How Trump Is Making Us Rethink American Exceptionalism." Politico. Accessed September 25, 2021. **URL:** http://politi.co/2ACdQ1K

Zeitzoff, Thomas. 2011. "Using Social Media to Measure Conflict Dynamics: An Application to the 2008–2009 Gaza Conflict." *Journal of Conflict Resolution* 55(6):938–969.

Zeitzoff, Thomas. 2014. "Anger, Exposure to Violence, and Intragroup Conflict: A 'Lab in the Field' Experiment in Southern Israel." *Political Psychology* 35(3):309–335.

Zeitzoff, Thomas. 2017. "How Social Media is Changing Conflict." *Journal of Conflict Resolution* 61(9):1970–1991.

Zeitzoff, Thomas. 2018. "Anger, Legacies of Violence, and Group Conflict: An Experiment in Post-Riot Acre, Israel." *Conflict Management and Peace Science* 35(4):402–423.

Zeitzoff, Thomas. 2019. "More Than Just Hurdles: How Fieldwork Difficulties Provide Insights into Conflict." *PS: Political Science & Politics* 52(3):507–512.

Zelensky, Volodymyr. 2021. "President Zelenskyy: Deoligarchization Is the Key to Ukraine's Future Success." Atlantic Council. Accessed September 20, 2021. **URL:** https://www.atlanticcouncil.org/blogs/ukrainealert/president-zelenskyy-deoligarchization-is-the-key-to-ukraines-future-success/

Zeveloff, Naomi. 2019. "Why the Film 'Incitement' Is Hitting a Political Nerve in Israel." National Public Radio. **URL:** https://www.npr.org/2019/12/25/791351652/why-the-film-incitement-is-hitting-a-political-nerve-in-israel

Zhukov, Yuri M. 2016. "Trading Hard Hats for Combat Helmets: The Economics of Rebellion in Eastern Ukraine." *Journal of Comparative Economics* 44(1):1–15.

Zhurzhenko, Tatiana. 2010. *Borderlands into Bordered Lands: Geopolitics of Identity in Post-Soviet Ukraine.* Vol. 98. Columbia University Press.

Zonszein, Mairav. 2015. "Binyamin Netanyahu: 'Arab Voters Are Heading to the Polling Stations in Droves.'" *The Guardian.* **URL:** https://www.theguardian.com/world/2015/mar/17/binyamin-netanyahu-israel-arab-election

INDEX

Note: Page numbers followed by "*t*" indicate table; an "*f*" indicates figure.